AFRICA IN WORLD POLITICS

SIXTH EDITION

AFRICA
IN WORLD POLITICS

CONSTRUCTING POLITICAL
AND ECONOMIC ORDER

EDITED BY

JOHN W. HARBESON AND
DONALD ROTHCHILD

WESTVIEW
PRESS

Westview Press was founded in 1975 in Boulder, Colorado, by notable publisher and intellectual Fred Praeger. Westview Press continues to publish scholarly titles and high-quality undergraduate- and graduate-level textbooks in core social science disciplines. With books developed, written, and edited with the needs of serious nonfiction readers, professors, and students in mind, Westview Press honors its long history of publishing books that matter.

Westview Press books are available at special discounts for bulk purchases in the United States by corporations, institutions, and other organizations. For more information, please contact the Special Markets Department at Perseus Books, 2300 Chestnut Street, Suite 200, Philadelphia, PA 19103, or call (800) 810-4145, ext. 5000, or e-mail special.markets@perseusbooks.com.

Designed by Jack Lenzo

Library of Congress Cataloging-in-Publication Data
Names: Harbeson, John W. (John Willis), 1938– editor. | Rothchild, Donald S., editor.
Title: Africa in world politics: constructing political and economic order / edited by John W. Harbeson and Donald Rothchild.
Description: Sixth edition. | Boulder, CO: Westview Press, 2016. | Includes bibliographical references and index.
Identifiers: LCCN 2016046556 | ISBN 9780813350288 (pbk.)
Subjects: LCSH: Africa—Politics and government—1960– | World politics—1989–
Classification: LCC DT30.5 .A3544 2016 | DDC 960.33—dc23 LC record available at https://lccn.loc.gov/2016046556

10 9 8 7 6 5 4 3 2 1

Contents

Tables and Figures

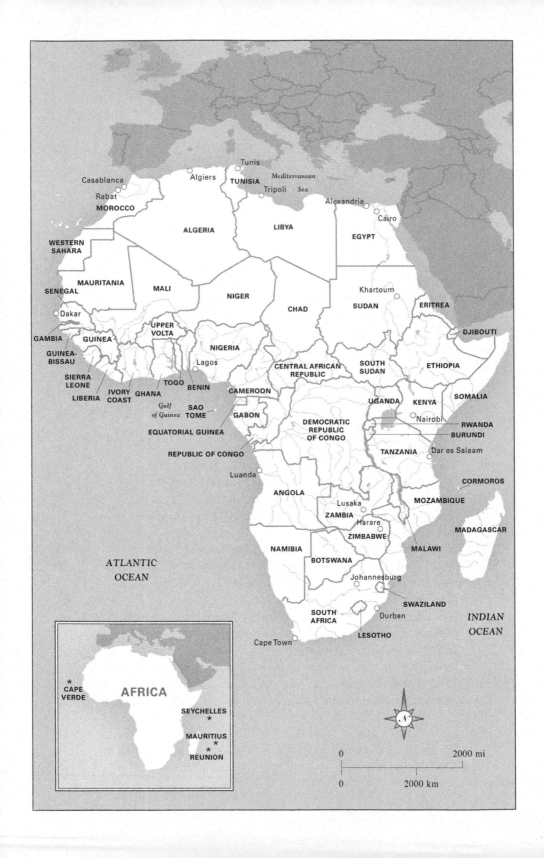

Acronyms

ACP	African, Caribbean, and Pacific States group
ADB	African Development Bank
ADFL	Alliances of Democratic Forces for the Liberation of the Congo
AEF	French Equatorial Africa
AfDB	African Development Bank
AFRICOM	US Africa Command
AGOA	African Growth and Opportunity Act (US)
AIAI	Al Itihaad al Islaami
AIPPA	Access to Information and Protection of Privacy Act (Zimbabwe)
AMIS	Africa Union Mission
AMU	Arab Mahgreb Union
ANC	African National Congress (South Africa)
AOF	French West Africa
APF	Africa Union Peace Fund
APRM	African Peer Review Mechanism
AU	African Union
AUHLIP	African Union High Level Implementation Panel
BRICS	Brazil, Russia, India, China, and South Africa
BRVM	Bourse Régionale des Valeurs Mobilières
CDR	Coalition for the Defense of the Republic (Rwanda)
CEAO	West African Economic Community
CEEAC	Economic Union of the States of Central Africa
CfA	Commission for Africa (Blair Commission)
CFA	Communauté Financière Africaine
CFSP	Common Foreign and Security Policy (Europe)
CJTF-HOA	Combined Joint Task Force–Horn of Africa
COMESA	Common Market of East and Southern Africa
CPA	Comprehensive Peace Agreement
CSSDCA	Conference on Security, Stability, Development, and Cooperation in Africa
DANIDA	Danish International Development Authority
DATA	Debt, AIDS, Trade, Africa report

DFID	British Department of International Development
DRC	Democratic Republic of the Congo (Kinshasa)
EACU	East African Customs Union
ECA	Economic Commission for Africa
ECA	Excess Crude Account (Nigeria)
ECOMOG	West African Military Observer Group
ECOWAS	Economic Commission of West African States
EPAs	Economic Partnership Agreements
EPLF	Eritrean People's Liberation Front
EPRDF	Ethiopian People's Revolutionary Democratic Front
ESCE	Economic Security and Cooperation in Europe
ESDI	Europe's Common Security and Defense Identity
EU	European Union
EUCOM	US European Command
EUFOR	European Force
FDC	Forum for Democratic Change (Uganda)
FDI	foreign direct investment
FNLA	National Front for the Liberation of Angola
FOMWAN	Federation of Muslim Women's Associations of Nigeria
FRELIMO	Mozambique Liberation Front
FTAs	free trade areas
G8	Group of eight leading industrial economies
GDA	Global Development Alliance
GEPF	Government Employees Pension Fund
GFATM	Global Fund to Fight AIDS, Tuberculosis, and Malaria
GLPF	Great Lakes Policy Forum
GNP	gross national product
GPRA	Provisional Government of the Republic of Algeria
GSPC	Salafist Group for Preaching and Combat
HIPC	Highly Indebted Poor Countries (initiative)
IBRD	International Bank for Reconstruction and Development (World Bank)
ICG	International Crisis Group
IFIs	international financial institutions
IGAD	Inter-Governmental Agency for Development
IGADD	Inter-Governmental Agency on Drought and Development
IGEPE	Institute for the Management of State Holdings (Portugese)
IMF	International Monetary Fund
LIFG	Libyan Islamic Fighting Group
MDGs	UN Millennium Development Goals
MDRI	Multilateral Debt Relief Initiative
MOI	Mo Ibrahim Index
MOSOP	Movement for the Survival of the Ogoni People

MSF	Medicin Sans Frontieres (Doctors Without Borders)
NANGO	National Association of Non-Governmental Organizations (Zimbabwe)
NANGOF	Namibian Nongovernmental Organization Federation
NATO	North Atlantic Treaty Organization
NCP	National Congress Party (Sudan)
NEPAD	New Partnership for African Development
NIF	National Islamic Front (Sudan)
NSIA	Nigerian Sovereign Investment Authority
NSSF	National Social Security Fund
OAU	Organization of African Unity (predecessor of AU)
ODA	Official Development Assistance
OECD	Organization for Economic Cooperation and Development
OIC	Organization of the Islamic Conference
ONLF	Ogaden National Liberation Front
OOTW	Operations Other Than War
OSCE	Organization for Security and Cooperation in Europe
PAGAD	People Against Gangsterism and Drugs (South Africa)
PEPFAR	Presidential Emergency Program for AIDS Relief
PIC	Public Investment Corporation
PMLA	Popular Movement for the Liberation of Angola
POSA	Public Order and Security Act (Zimbabwe)
PRSP	Poverty Reduction Strategy Paper
PSFU	Private Sector Foundation of Uganda
PSI	Policy Support Instrument
PTA	Preferential Trade Area
RBA	Revenue Benefits Authority
RBAs	Rights Based Approaches
RENAMO	Mozambique National Resistance Organization
RUF	Revolutionary United Front (Sierra Leone)
SACU	Southern African Customs Union
SADC	Southern African Development Council
SADR	Sahrawi Democratic Republic
SIDA	Swedish International Development Authority
SNA	Somali National Alliance
SOEs	state-owned enterprises
SPLM/A	Sudan People's Liberation Movement Army
SRSG	Special Representative of the Secretary General
SSA	Sub-Saharan Africa
SSLM	Southern Sudan Liberation Movement
SST	states sponsoring terrorism
SWFs	sovereign wealth funds
TCSTI	Trans-Saharan Counter Terrorism Initiative

TFG	Transitional Federal Government (Somalia)
TRIPS	Trade-Related Aspects of International Property Rights
UDEAC	Customs Union of the Central African States
UEAC	Economic Union of Central Africa
UEMOA	West African Monetary and Economic Union
UIC	Union of Islamic Courts (Somalia)
UNAIDS	Joint UN Program on HIV/AIDS
UNCTAD	UN Conference on Trade and Development
UNDP	United Nations Development Program
UNDRD	United Nations Declaration on the Right to Development
UNESCO	United Nations Educational, Scientific, and Cultural Organization
UNFPA	United Nations Population Fund
UNICEF	United Nations Children's Fund
UNITA	Union for the Total Independence of Angola
UNITAF	United Nations Task Force (Somalia)
UNODC	UN Office on Drugs and Crime
UNOSOM	United Nations Operations in Somalia
USAID	United States Agency for International Development
WHO	World Health Organization
WILDAF	Women in Law and Development in Africa
WTO	World Trade Organization
ZCCM-IH	Zambia Consolidated Copper Mines-International Holdings, Ltd.

Preface

The dramatic changes in the contours of African politics in the past few years led to the decision to launch this sixth edition of *Africa in World Politics* more closely following the previous edition than might otherwise have been the case. Among the most prominent of these developments have been the rapid expansion of China's economic engagement, African governments' new state-led economic development strategies, markedly improved rates of economic growth for many countries paralleling Africa's emergence from marginalization to greater economic prominence on the world stage, and the transformation of the global economic and political order itself heralded by the growing power of many G-20 countries.

Strikingly, however, a political renaissance to accompany the continent's economic advances has remained elusive for many if not most African countries. Armed insurgencies threaten many states, both cause and consequence of their continued weakness. Democratization has stalled or ebbed across much of the continent for a decade, typified domestically by elected leaders testing constitutional limits on their powers and imposing restrictions on civil society. Externally, meanwhile, the African Union has signaled an intention to disavow the International Criminal Court, which its member countries had helped to establish, and, thereby, the Court's efforts to uphold governments' responsibility to protect the fundamental human rights of their citizens.

A central concern of this volume is, therefore, this fundamental question: To what extent will Africa's growing prominence on the world stage translate into greater and more sustainable well-being for the continent in political, socioeconomic, environmental, and cultural terms? It is not yet clear to what degree continuing rapid economic growth, to the extent it proves sustainable, will reach all countries on the continent, occur in ways so as to enduringly diminish African economic dependency, substantially diminish poverty and inequality, support sustainable democracy, and broadly improve the quality of life for most of the continent's peoples.

The essays in this volume also attest to the profound elusiveness of the goal of building stronger and reformed states, given their deeply rooted weakness and ineffectiveness that arises from decades of postcolonial authoritarian, corrupt, and clientelistic stewardship. Continuing manifestations are present most dramatically in the fragile, still-tentative easing of the Great Lakes crisis, the precarious viability of newly independent South Sudan, and violent insurgencies, especially by Boko Haram in West Africa and Al Shabaab in the east.

Notwithstanding all these profound challenges, this edition of *Africa in World Politics*, like its predecessors, is born of resilient optimism, which I believe all the authors share, that the seeds of genuine and sustainable political, economic, and cultural well-being may yet grow in African soils and continue to offer fresh and encouraging hints of an attainable bountiful harvest.

Our late, wonderful colleague and friend, Don Rothchild, remains a model and an inspiration for all of us, and in that sense he has continued with us in spirit in planning this volume and preparing the chapters that follow.

The publication of this sixth edition is an appropriate time to recognize and express once again my great appreciation to each and every one of the scholars and friends who have written chapters for one or more of these editions. In addition to the authors of chapters in this sixth edition, the other members of the *Africa in World Politics* family have included Thomas Callaghy, Naomi Chazan, Herman Cohen, Larry Diamond, Kenneth Grundy, Jeffrey Herbst, Gilbert Khadiagala, Carol Lancaster, Rene Lemarchand, Victor LeVine, Guy Martin, the late Ali Mazrui, Rob Mortimer, Marina Ottaway, Anokhi Parikh, John Ravenhill, Donald Rothchild, Denis Tull, Nicolas van de Walle, Vitaley Vasikov, and Alan Whiteside.

I have greatly appreciated the encouragement, assistance, and friendship of the editors at Westview with whom we have had the pleasure of working. I want especially to thank my Westview editor for this edition, Katharine Moore, for all her support, encouragement, and, especially, flexibility in working with me on the challenges we have encountered in launching this edition. Finally, I greatly appreciate the feedback we have received from our readers and those who have adopted editions of this book in their courses. My thanks to Westview and to everyone who responded to the readers' survey conducted in preparation for this edition for the recommendations it produced, several of which I have attempted to incorporate.

My colleagues and I offer this sixth edition of *Africa in World Politics* in hopes that in some small way it will broaden and deepen understanding of the human condition in sub-Saharan Africa and, thereby, help lead to a brighter future for the continent's people and their countries.

JOHN W. HARBESON
Bethesda, Maryland

THE CONTEMPORARY CONTEXT
IN HISTORICAL PERSPECTIVE

Constructing Political and Economic Order

JOHN W. HARBESON

The countries of sub-Saharan Africa in the second decade of the twenty-first century, as much or more than in any previous period in their more than half-century of independence, have continued to be deeply engaged in constructing and reconstructing viable political and economic orders in partnerships with each other and other nations of the international community. What has distinguished their situations in the first decades of the twenty-first century has been the degree to which they have engaged with an array of emerging economic powers, and with these and other powers in countering non-state-based terrorism. They have done this while continuing to wrestle with significant weaknesses in their own political economies.

To sharply varying degrees, African countries have pursued agendas of political and economic reform generated by external as well as domestic pressures during the first decade following the end of the Cold War, when the West enjoyed a relatively high degree of ideological hegemony and shared policy focus vis-à-vis African and other developing countries. More than anything else, however, the international political and economic order in the new century has been transformed by strong emerging economies led by the BRICS, especially China; the syndrome of state- and non-state-based terrorism and counter-terrorism initiatives; and the revolution in information technology. To these transformative developments must be added more recent surges of hundreds of thousands of refugees from repression, civil war, and accompanying destitution in the Middle East and parts of Africa. Nationalist resistance to these tides of refugees has threatened to weaken long-standing and emergent regional economic cooperation, especially in the European Union.

These twenty-first-century realities have counterbalanced and diminished the collective global pursuit of post–Cold War liberal political and economic agendas. To a degree unmatched since they gained independence, sub-Saharan African countries in the twenty-first century have been less subject to coordinated, bilaterally, and multilaterally imposed political and economic agendas. To a greater extent they have been left to negotiate on their own terms their political, security, and economic cooperation arrangements with major enduring and emergent powers in the global arena.

This edition of *Africa in World Politics* reflects on the resulting complexities of the political and economic development trajectories of sub-Saharan African countries in these challenging early-twenty-first-century circumstances. On the one hand, a number of these countries have registered at least modest to strong rates of gross domestic product growth since the beginning of the century that have been unprecedented in the first half-century of their independence. At the same time, although pronounced state weakness has remained endemic, most sub-Saharan African countries have overcome the rash of civil conflict that befell a number of countries in the late 1990s as authoritarian rulers fell, having lost the backing of the major powers, who were no longer concerned with maintaining global Cold War alliances.

More or less simultaneously and against the background of a preceding decade of bilateral and international financial institution pressure on African countries to liberalize their economies, democracy's Third Wave reached Africa's shores.[1] From the early 1990s to well into the first decade of the twenty-first century, African countries made significant if sharply variable progress in upholding political liberties and civil rights and in constitutionalizing multiparty elections and other democratic institutions.

On the other hand, dramatically transformed twenty-first-century international realities have, at best, complicated incipient trajectories that had pointed toward a once-envisaged sub-Saharan region of sustainable democratic states, initiatives borne of the preceding decade. Pervasive state weakness throughout most of sub-Saharan Africa became increasingly evident and explicit with the demise of a number of authoritarian rulers. For more than two decades their harsh and ineffective rule through corrupt, patronage-based networks had papered over the reality that perpetuated: colonially fashioned authoritarian governance structures were insufficient bases for both effective economic development and modern postindependence states in a post–Cold War democratic era.

At the same time, however, progress in upholding and advancing civil and political liberties and democratic structures and practices began to crest in Africa midway into the new century's first decade. Since then, democratic momentum has noticeably ebbed, and gradual democratic retreat has occurred in some countries. Stalled democratic momentum has constituted an ongoing challenge and test of the consistent findings of Afrobarometer surveys that sizeable majorities of Africans throughout the continent have retained their belief in and preference for democracy over all of the nondemocratic alternatives they have experienced. At this writing, the most recent Afrobarometer surveys indicate that only a bare majority of African citizens believe their countries are democratic with no or only minor problems.[2]

Indeed, at this writing the respected Freedom House has chronicled a full decade of democratic retreat in sub-Saharan Africa, explaining most if not all of the declines that its surveys have found worldwide. Despite the evident popular appeal of presidential term limits throughout the continent, elected leaders have found ways to extend their tenure in several cases. They have also acted to curb the advocacy of civil society organizations that had provided much of the early domestic impetus for democratization. These developments have adversely affected further rights-based advocacy, which had yielded significant gains in gender equality.

Paralleling these democratization trajectories, African countries have been the recipients of significant trade and investment participation by the BRICS and other emergent midlevel economic powers. The BRICS and others have, to some extent, stepped in where Western private investors have chosen to engage to a lesser degree. Nonetheless, as the century's third decade approaches, the economic outlook for sub-Saharan African countries is generally mixed. Not every country has engaged these emergent sources of capital and trade to the same extent, creating the prospect of some countries being left behind as others advance.

Moreover, high levels of investment by the BRICS countries, led by China, is not necessarily a long-term given. China in particular and other emergent midlevel economies have shown signs of looking inward to a greater extent in order to address imbalances in their own economies. Also debatable is the extent to which African countries' economic engagement with these emergent economies has tended to either entrench or liberate them from patterns of dependency characterized by their long-standing lack of sufficient economic diversification, dating back well into colonial times. Whether a recent trend of African governments activating sovereign wealth funds, especially to exploit their own natural resources and real estate markets, will prove to be a positive development in this regard will depend in no small measure on how transparently and sagaciously the funds are managed.

Ultimately, a crucial measure of the effectiveness of African governments' economic engagement with their own private sectors as well as with China and other emergent economic powers is how these emergent contours impact the lives of Africa's millions of citizens at the grassroots. The UN-sponsored Millennium Development Goals project, aimed at radically diminishing poverty throughout the global South as well as within sub-Saharan Africa between 2000 and 2015, has yielded important but still incomplete progress toward this goal. Following extensive inquiry into the factors underlying these shortcomings, a substantially expanded follow-on project, Sustainable Development Goals, has begun. Meanwhile, evidence of substantial if not growing economic inequality within many countries has remained deeply troubling, and the Oxford Poverty and Human Development Initiative has documented continued, albeit varied, levels of often intensive poverty throughout the continent.[3]

Moreover, substantial evidence of illicit international financial flows—parking wealth in external tax havens instead of in productive in-country investment—has acted as an ongoing brake on development benefits for the home countries and especially for those at the grassroots. Refugees fleeing domestic conflict and internal displacement from land alienations to external actors, compounding already existent land tenure insecurities in many countries, have been among the factors that have sharply qualified the significance of the positive macro-level growth numbers. These healthy gross domestic product numbers have led some observers to identify emerging middle classes in terms of consumer spending patterns. However, remembering the contributions of middle classes to the building of the planet's stronger economies, it is one thing to identify a middle class in terms of income levels and consumer practices; it is quite another for a middle class to be self-conscious and assertive of its independence vis-à-vis the state and for democratization. To date, such middle classes have yet to emerge.

This edition includes three case studies of very difficult-to-ameliorate violence in three different regions of the continent. These studies elucidate dramatically the profound dimensions of state failure that have seemed to lurk just below the surface throughout much of the continent, even if in most countries it is somewhat better checked (albeit still in evidence). One case centers on Boko Haram, which operates principally in Nigeria. Boko Haram is a viciously violent non-state-based insurgency bent on extinguishing Western influence in a state whose very legitimacy it denies. Another centers on the Great Lakes region where, principally, Rwanda, Burundi, Uganda, and the Democratic Republic of the Congo deal with quasi-Hobbesian violent conflicts of all against all. These conflicts have been exacerbated by the region's prodigious potential wealth, and the task of demarcating a community of sustainable states has been an unmet responsibility of all involved, local and external powers alike. Lastly, the final case details the collapse of the Comprehensive Peace Agreement that successfully facilitated South Sudan's independence from Sudan; however, the latter remains a pariah state and the former teeters on the brink of unsustainability.

Perversely, as Will Reno has observed in his chapter in this edition, in many cases the advent of political and economic liberalism has tended to shred the threadbare fabric of patronage-based ruling regimes rather more than it has facilitated the reweaving and strengthening of that fabric as a basis for viable democratic states. The inherited imperfections of colonially fashioned political orders, pervasive impunity, and the profitability of warfare intermixed with long-standing ethnic rivalries and the self-interest of threatened ruling and rival elites clinging to remnants of patronage networks have remained the residual, irreducible obstacles thwarting the realization of ever-elusive quests for viable, legitimate postcolonial states.

African countries acting collectively through the African Union and the continent's regional economic communities have put in place a rich, even dense array of resources for defusing conflicts and attacking gross regime abuses of basic human rights, including those causing and accompanying humanitarian disasters. These resources have complemented those evolved by the wider international community. Collectively these developments have confirmed that the principle of unfettered national sovereignty, on which the state system has been built since 1648 and on which the United Nations itself has been founded, is no longer a sufficient foundation for a peaceful and humane international order. States' responsibility to protect their citizens' fundamental welfare and rights has increasingly infused contemporary understandings of the definition of sovereignty. There has emerged widespread—if perhaps not universal—international agreement that the international community must intervene when states deny their citizens the most basic human rights or they are unable or unwilling to shield their citizens from humanitarian catastrophes or the violence they engender.

The essays in the final section of this book make clear that these resources, in and of themselves, although invaluable, to date have been insufficient in the face of the complexity of the tasks at hand. Competitive conflict resolution venues can become aspects of the conflicts they have been put in place to quell. Although most are signatories to the Rome Statute, African states have become disillusioned with its key creation, the International Criminal Court, which many African regimes believe has disproportionately singled them out for indictment and prosecution. The African Union's own extensive conflict mediation mechanisms remain works in progress that still benefit from the singular resources and networks possessed by bilateral actors. A benchmark of notable achievement, however, has been the 2016 conviction and imprisonment of former Chad president Hissène Habré for crimes against humanity, torture, and sex crimes.

Key to strengthened and continued development by sub-Saharan African states, as they navigate the shoals of a transformed twenty-first-century international political and economic order, will be their ability to effect positive, reinforcing linkages among processes of state strengthening and reform, democratization, and sustainable economic development. Received theory, heavily influenced by distilled European and North American experience, has appeared to be of limited utility in its holding that economic development, state-building, and democratization predictably are to occur sequentially, more or less in that order.

A quarter-century of post–Cold War experience has yielded empirical challenges to these venerable predicted trajectories in sub-Saharan Africa. Since the end of the Cold War, in sub-Saharan Africa crises of state formation and reformation, democratization initiatives, and continuing economic liberalization initiatives have occurred more or less simultaneously with each other rather than sequentially, as received theory would have it. An important corollary has been that each would appear necessarily to have important significance for the meanings and forms that the others may take, thereby further complicating policy formation and rendering policy outcomes correspondingly more uncertain and unpredictable. Going forward, therefore, what is most needed is systematic inquiry and exploration along with empirically based research, policy formation, and theory that is sharply focused on how best to advance simultaneously formation of viable, legitimate states, democracy, and economic development in a rapidly changing international environment in ways that are mutually reinforcing. This edition of *Africa in World Politics* undertakes to advance that objective.

NOTES

1. The term *Third Wave* has been associated with the late Samuel Huntington, *The Third Wave: Democratization in the Late Twentieth Century* (Norman: University of Oklahoma Press, 1991). Huntington observed that the late– and post–Cold War surge of democratization had been preceded by similar waves following the two world wars.

2. Afrobarometer, www.Afrobarometer.org.

3. OPHI, Oxford Poverty and Human Development Initiative, www.ophi.org.uk.

The Heritage of Colonialism

CRAWFORD YOUNG

Africa, in the rhetorical metaphor of imperial jingoism, was a ripe melon awaiting carving in the late nineteenth century. Those who scrambled fastest won the largest slices and the right to consume at their leisure the sweet, succulent flesh. Stragglers snatched only small servings or tasteless portions; Italians, for example, found only arid deserts on their plate. In this mad moment of imperial atavism—in Schumpeterian terms, the objectless disposition to limitless frontier expansion—no one imagined that a system of states was being created. Colonial rule, assumed by its initiators to be perpetual, later proved to be a mere interlude in the broader sweep of African history; however, the steel grid of territorial partition that colonialism imposed appears permanent. Although the patterns of disorder and state collapse that emerged in the 1990s led some to call for a reconsideration of the existing territorial system, the stubborn resilience of the largely artificial boundaries bequeathed by the colonial partition remains astonishing.[1]

Colonial heritage is the necessary point of departure for analysis of African international relations. The state system—which is, transnational vectors notwithstanding, the fundamental structural basis of the international realm—inherits the colonial partition. A few African states have a meaningful precolonial identity (Morocco, Tunisia, Egypt, Ethiopia, Burundi, Rwanda, Madagascar, Swaziland, Lesotho, and Botswana), but most are products of the competitive subordination of Africa—mostly between 1875 and 1900—by seven European powers (Great Britain, France, Germany, Belgium, Portugal, Italy, and Spain).

AFRICAN COLONIAL HERITAGE COMPARED

The colonial system totally transformed historical political geography Africa in a few years' time, and the depth and intensity of alien penetration of subordinated societies continues to cast its shadow.[2] The comprehensive linkages with the metropolitan economies in many instances were long difficult to disentangle. In the majority of cases in which decolonization was negotiated, the colonizer retained some capacity to shape the choice of postcolonial successors and often—especially in the French case—enjoyed extensive networks of access and influence long after independence was attained. The cultural and linguistic impact was pervasive, especially in sub-Saharan Africa, where the language of the colonizer continues to enjoy official status. Embedded in the institutions of the new states was the deep imprint of mentalities and routines of their colonial predecessors. Overall, colonial legacy cast its shadow over the emergent African state system to a degree unique among the major world regions.

In Latin America, although colonial administrative subdivisions shaped the state system, Spain and Portugal swiftly ceased to be major regional players after Creole elites won independence in the nineteenth century. Great Britain and, later, the United States were the major external forces impinging upon the region. In Asia, the first target and long the crown jewel of the colonial enterprise, imperial conquest tended to follow the contours of an older state system; not all Asian states have a historical pedigree (the Philippines, Pakistan, Indonesia), but a majority do. The circumstances surrounding Asian independence, the discontinuities imposed by the Japanese wartime occupation of Southeast Asia, the larger scale of most Asian states, and the greater autonomy of their economies all meant that the demise of the colonial order there was far more sharp and definitive than was the case in Africa.

Perhaps the closest parallel to Africa in terms of durable and troubled colonial impact on regional international relations is found in the Middle East. The partition of the Ottoman domains in the Levant between Great Britain and France and the imperial calculus employed in territorial definitions and structures of domination left in their wake a series of cancerous conflicts: the duplicity of incompatible World War I promises to Arabs and Zionists bore the seeds of inextricable conflict over whether the Palestine mandate awarded to Great Britain by the League of Nations would develop as a Jewish homeland or an Arab state; Great Britain invented Jordan as a territory for its wartime ally Prince Abdullah; Lebanese borders were drawn so as to maximize the zone of dominance for Maronite Christians; Sunni Arab nationalism in Syria was countered by heavy recruitment of minority Alawites for the colonial militia; and Kurdish state demands were denied so that oil-rich zones could be attached to the British-Iraqi mandate.[3] The unending turbulence in this region provides daily confirmation of the colonial roots of many intractable contemporary conflicts. But even here, colonial penetration of Middle Eastern Arab societies and economies was much less than was the case in Africa, and the erstwhile colonial connections weigh less heavily.

In the African instance, the shadow of the colonial past falls upon the contemporary state system in several critical features. The sheer number of sovereign units and the weakness and vulnerability of many due to their small scale are the most obvious. At the same time, the struggle for territorial independence always had an associated pan-African vision, which became a permanent vector in African international relations. The continuing importance of former economic and political colonial linkages—most of all for the twenty states formerly under French rule—significantly shapes regional politics, both as an active channel of influence and as a negative point of reference. Finally and perhaps most important, the bureaucratic authoritarianism that was the institutional essence of the colonial state quickly resurfaced in the guise of single-party or military regimes whose failure led to a widespread state crisis by the 1980s.[4] In this chapter I will consider these components of the colonial heritage in turn.

FRAGMENTATION OF AFRICA

The African continent in 2016 (and its offshore islands) contained no fewer than fifty-four sovereign units (using UN membership as the criterion)—nearly one-third of the world total.[5] Although this large number has some advantages in guaranteeing a voice in international forums where the doctrine of sovereign equality ensures equal voting rights for states large and small, this is little compensation for the disabilities of being tiny. Sheer economic weakness is one disadvantage. Most African states had a GNP less than the Harvard University endowment or the profits of a major multinational corporation. The limits of choice imposed by a narrow national market and circumscribed agricultural and mineral resource bases rendered most states highly vulnerable to the vagaries of commodity markets and the workings of the global economic system. Although some minuscule mercantile states elsewhere have achieved prosperity (Singapore is an obvious example) and tiny sovereignties perched on vast oil pools may accumulate enormous wealth (Kuwait, Bahrain, and Qatar are illustrations, now joined by Equatorial Guinea in Africa), of the microstates among Africa's fifty-four polities, only Mauritius, Equatorial Guinea, Cape Verde, and Seychelles have prospered.

The full scope of the fragmentation of independent Africa was not apparent until the virtual eve of independence. Most of the vast sub-Saharan domains under French domination were joined in two large administrative federations: Afrique Occidentale Française (AOF) and Afrique Equatoriale Française (AEF). Political life, however, germinated first at the territorial level; the crucial 1956 *Loi-cadre* (framework law) located the vital institutions of African political autonomy at this echelon. Although some nationalist leaders dreamed of achieving independence within the broader unit, especially in the AOF, the wealthier territories, Ivory Coast and Gabon, were strongly opposed. In the final compressed surge to independence, the interaction of divisions among nationalist leaders and movements, combined with French interests, resulted in twelve states of modest size rather than two large ones.[6] In the 1950s Great Britain did promote federations of its colonial possessions as a formula for self-government in the West Indies, the United Arab Emirates, and Malaysia as well as in east and central Africa, but with indifferent success. In east and central Africa the fatal flaw was linking the project of broader political units to the entrenchment of special privilege for the European settler communities. Thus contaminated, the federation idea was bound to fail as a framework for independence, although the dream of an East African Federation was revived in the 1960s and again at the turn of the twenty-first century.[7] In instances in which large territories had been governed as single entities—Nigeria, Sudan, and Congo-Kinshasa—independence as one polity was possible, although all three countries have at times been beset by separatist pressures and in 2011 Sudan broke in two.

Since sovereignty gave life to colonial territories as independent nations, the African state system has proven to be singularly refractory to broader movements of unification. The 1964 amalgamation of Tanganyika and Zanzibar to form Tanzania and the 1960 unification of British Somaliland and Italian-administered Somalia at the moment of independence remain the sole such cases. At times the Tanzania union with Zanzibar has been questioned, and in the wake of the collapse of a Somali state in 1991 Somaliland reemerged, although unrecognized by the international community, as a separate and functioning unit, in contrast to the prolonged anarchy in the rest of Somalia.

DREAM OF AFRICAN UNITY

The dream of a broader African unity persists, first nurtured by intellectuals of the diaspora and expressed through a series of pan-African conferences beginning in 1900, then embraced by the radical wing of African nationalism in the 1950s by, above all, Kwame Nkrumah of Ghana. The Organization of African Unity (OAU) was created in 1963 to embody this dream, but even its charter demonstrated its contradictions. The OAU was structured as a cartel of states whose territorial integrity was a foundational principle. Rather than transcending the state system, the OAU consolidated it. Although the vocation of African unity was reaffirmed with the 2002 official launch of the African Union to replace an OAU that was deemed moribund, the ascendancy of states remains.

The urgency of regional and ultimately continental unification is nonetheless repeatedly endorsed in solemn documents. Innumerable regional integration schemes have been launched, of which the most important are the (moribund) Union du Maghreb Arabe, the Economic Community of West African States, the Southern African Development Community, the various customs and monetary unions of the francophonic West African states, and renewed efforts to build an East African Federation. But the goal of effective integration remains elusive; the impact of the colonial partition remains an enduring obstacle.

The colonial origins of most African states weighed heavily upon the consciousness of postindependence rulers. Initially the fundamental illegitimacy of the boundaries was a central tenet of pan-African nationalism; the 1945 Manchester Pan-African Congress excoriated "the artificial divisions and territorial boundaries created by the Imperialist Powers." As late as 1958 the Accra All-African Peoples' Conference denounced "artificial frontiers drawn by the imperialist Powers to divide the peoples of Africa" and called for "the abolition or adjustment of such frontiers at an early date."[8] But once African normative doctrine was enunciated by the states rather than by nationalist movements, the tone changed, and the sanctity of colonial partition frontiers was asserted. The consensus of the first assembly of African independent states—also in Accra in 1958—was expressed by Nkrumah, the leading apostle of African unification: "Our conference came to the conclusion that in the interests of that Peace which is so essential, we should respect the independence, sovereignty and territorial integrity of one another."[9]

The OAU charter referred to territorial integrity no fewer than three times, and at the Cairo OAU summit in 1964 the assembled heads of state made the commitment even more emphatic with a solemn pledge to actively uphold existing borders, a level of responsibility that goes significantly further than the mere passive recognition of the inviolability of frontiers.[10] Although a certain number of boundary disputes have arisen in independent Africa, the principle of the sanctity of colonial partition boundaries—the juridical concept of *uti possidetis*—remains a cornerstone of a solidifying African regional international law.[11] Most of the disputes have been resolved through negotiation by applying the colonial treaties as the point of juridical reference.[12] The enduring fear of the fragility of the African state system paradoxically endows the artificial, colonially imposed boundaries with astonishing durability. The one apparent exception, the independence of Eritrea from Ethiopia in 1993, can be said to prove the point. Eritrean nationalists grounded their claim to self-determination in the argument that Eritrea, as a former Italian colonial territory, should have had the opportunity for independence like all other former colonies rather than being forcibly joined (in the Eritrean view) to Ethiopia by the international community. The same argument is advanced by the Western Saharan independence movement to contest Moroccan annexation being justified by precolonial historic claims.

The colonial system profoundly reordered economic as well as political space. During their seventy-five years of uncurbed sovereignty, colonial powers viewed their African domains as veritable *chasses gardées* (private preserves). Metropolitan capital enjoyed privileged access; to varying degrees, other foreign investment was viewed with reserve or even hostility (especially by the Portuguese until the final colonial years). The security logic of the colonial state joined the metropolitan conviction that the occupant was entitled to exclusive economic benefits in return for the "sacrifice" of supplying governance services to foster trade and investment linkages, which tied African territories to metropolitan economies as subordinated appendages. Territorial infrastructure, particularly the communications systems, was shaped by the vision of imperial integration; road networks ran from the centers of production to the ports and colonial capitals. Although over time a shrinkage of the once-exclusive economic ties with the erstwhile colonizers has occurred, these bonds were so pervasive that they have been difficult to disentangle. It is no accident that regional economic integration schemes joining states once under different colonial jurisdictions have had only limited success; the most resilient mechanism of regional economic cooperation has been the Communauté Financière Africaine (CFA) franc zone, a product of the economic space defined by the former French empire in sub-Saharan Africa.

INFLUENCE OF FORMER COLONIZERS

The colonial occupation of Africa, which occurred relatively late in the global history of imperial expansion, was comparatively dense and thorough. The multiplex apparatus of domination was constructed to ensure the "effective occupation" stipulated by the 1884–1885 Berlin Conference as a condition for the security of the proprietary title and to extract from the impoverished subjects the labor service and fiscal tribute to make alien hegemony self-financing. As metropolitan finance ministries required, this apparatus was unlikely to dissolve instantly once the occupying country's flag was lowered on independence day. Over time the many linkages, both manifest and submerged, binding the decolonized state to the former metropole have slowly eroded. They were a central dimension in the international relations of new states, especially in the early years of independence. Even five decades later, especially in the case of France, colonial connections still play a role.

Several factors influence the importance of ties with former colonizers. In those cases in which independence was won through armed liberation struggles rather than bargaining, the power transfer brought initial rupture (Algeria, Guinea-Bissau, Mozambique, Angola). In some other cases (Guinea, Congo-Kinshasa) the circumstances of independence brought immediate crisis and discontinuity in relationships; even though relations were ultimately restored, the degree of intimacy between the two countries could never be the same. Generally the smaller erstwhile colonial powers played a less visible role than did the two major imperial occupants, Great Britain and France.

Italy was largely eliminated by being on the losing side in World War II. Although it regained a ten-year trust territory mission in Somalia in 1950, Rome was never permitted to return to Libya and Eritrea and quickly ceased to be a factor in either territory. Spain was the last country to enter the colonial scramble, and it had only a superficial hold on its territories in northwest Africa (former Spanish Morocco, Ifni, Western Sahara) and Equatorial Guinea. Its minor interests were swallowed up in postcolonial turmoil in its erstwhile domains (the Moroccan annexation of Western Sahara, the Macías Nguema capricious tyranny in Equatorial Guinea from its independence in 1968 until 1979). Emblematic of Spain's elimination from Africa was the affiliation of Equatorial Guinea with the French-tied CFA franc zone after Macías Nguema was overthrown in 1979.[13]

Belgium retained a role in its small former colonies of Rwanda and Burundi, but its economic interests in these states were not large. In Congo-Kinshasa, where the financial stake was considerable, relationships were punctuated with repeated crises.[14] The sudden and aborted power transfer left inextricably contentious disputes over the succession to the extensive colonial state holdings in a wide array of colonial corporations. These disputes were seemingly resolved several times, only to reemerge in new forms of contention.[15]

In the Portuguese case an imperial mythology of the global Lusotropical multiracial community was a keystone of the corporatist authoritarianism of the Salazar-Caetano *Estado Novo*. However, the utter discrediting of this regime by its ruinous and unending colonial wars in Africa from 1961 to 1974 repudiated this mythology.[16] More broadly, in the postcolonial era a common element for the minor participants in the African partition was an abandonment of earlier notions that overseas proprietary domains validated national claims to standing and respect in the international arena.

Particularly intriguing has been the relative effacement over time of Great Britain on the African scene. Great Britain has long seen itself as a great power, although the resources to support such a claim silently ebbed away because of imperial overreach, according to one influential analysis.[17] In the 1950s, as the era of decolonization opened for Africa, conventional wisdom held that Great Britain was the most likely of the colonizers to maintain a permanent role in its vast colonial estates because of the flexible framework for evolution supplied by the British Commonwealth. This illusion proved to be based upon false inferences deduced from the older constellation of self-governing dominions, which had remained closely bound in imperial security relationships with London. Many thought the Commonwealth could preserve a British-ordered global ensemble beyond the formal grant of sovereignty in Asia and Africa. The illusion of permanence in which British imperialism had so long basked dissipated slowly.[18] The doctrine enunciated at the 1926 Imperial Conference still dominated official thinking as the African hour of self-government approached. This document perceived the future as incorporating "autonomous communities within the British Empire, equal in status, in no way subordinate one to another in any aspect of their domestic or external affairs, though united by a common allegiance to the Crown and freely associated as members of the British Commonwealth of Nations."[19] As one of its commentators then wrote, "The British Empire is a strange complex. It is a heterogeneous collection of separate entities, and yet it is a political unit. It is wholly unprecedented; it has no written constitution; it is of quite recent growth; and its development has been amazingly rapid."[20] Membership is even open to countries never under British rule, such as Mozambique and Rwanda, which joined after 1995.

These lyrical notions of a global commonwealth operating in a loose way as a political unit in world affairs so that Great Britain's claim to major power status might survive the decolonization of the empire eroded gradually. India's independence in 1947 was a crucial turning point; with the country as the true jewel in the imperial crown, its metamorphosis from the pivot of empire security to a self-assertive "neutralist" Asian power should have ended the illusion that an enlarged commonwealth could remain in any sense a "political unit." Yet when African members of the Commonwealth began joining with Ghanaian independence in 1957, it was apparent that some of the old mystique still persisted.

For most former British territories, joining the Commonwealth formed part of the *rite de passage* of independence; only Egypt and Sudan declined to enter its ranks.[21] Paradoxically, as Commonwealth membership became numerically dominated by Asian, African, and Caribbean states, it ceased to serve as a loose-knit, worldwide, British-inspired combine, and its meetings became occasions for heated attacks on British policy in Rhodesia and South Africa. Instead of the ingenious instrument for the subtle nurture of British global influence its designers imagined, the Commonwealth thus seemed by the 1970s a funnel for unwelcome pressures upon British diplomacy. Even imperial nostalgia could not stave off recognition of these facts, and waning British interest removed the Commonwealth's energizing center. In the words of one influential study, "The Commonwealth has survived only in [a] very attenuated form. . . . [It is] still a useful argumentative forum for its governments, offering a place for small states to be heard, extending benefits (albeit on a modest scale) to its members, and providing opportunities for discussion of problems of common interest."[22] This adjustment in the British images of the Commonwealth goes hand in hand with the gradual reduction of London's self-perception from global hegemon to middle-size European power.

The diminishing mystique of the Commonwealth as the vessel for a global British role helps to explain the relative effacement of Great Britain on the African scene. In the first years of African independence the British disposition for intervention was still visible. In the army mutinies that swept Uganda, Kenya, and Tanganyika in 1964, British troops intervened to check the mutineers, at the request of the embattled regimes. In Nigeria, Great Britain initially had a defense agreement; however, this was annulled in 1962 due to Nigerian nationalist pressure. In a number of cases national armies remained under British command for a few years after independence; in 1964 the British commander of the Nigerian army refused the solicitation of some Nigerian leaders to intervene after scandal-ridden national elections brought the country to the brink of disintegration. Security assistance and economic aid in modest quantities continue, and in a few cases—most notably Kenya—influence remains significant. But since 1970 the relatively subdued role of Britain, if set against the expectations of 1960, is what stands out. One striking exception was the energetic British military intervention under a UN cover in 1999–2000 in Sierra Leone, which put a final end to the macabre atrocities of the rebel Revolutionary United Front of Foday Sankoh.

THE FRENCH CONNECTION

The case of France, which has played a pervasive role in the seventeen sub-Saharan states formerly under its rule, is completely different from that of Great

Britain. The political, cultural, economic, and military connection Paris has maintained with the erstwhile *bloc africain de l'empire* has been frequently tutelary, often intrusive, and sometimes overtly interventionist. The intimacy and durability of these linkages are as surprising as the eclipse of the United Kingdom. When African independence loomed on the horizon, France still suffered from its World War II humiliation and bitter internal divisions. The country was weakened by the chronic instability of the Fourth Republic, with one-third of its electorate aligned with the antiregime Stalinist French Communist Party and its army locked in unending and unwinnable colonial wars—first in Indochina, then in Algeria. *France Against Itself* was the title of the most influential portrait of the epoch.[23] Few anticipated the recapture of its European status and sub-Saharan role as regional hegemon under the Fifth Republic.

In grasping the pervasive African role of the resurrected postcolonial France, one first must draw a sharp distinction between the Maghreb and sub-Saharan Africa, which is sometimes overlooked in the fascination with the French connection. In reality, French influence was shattered in what had been the most important parts of the former empire: North Africa and Indochina. In terms of the size of the economic stake, AOF (French West Africa federation) and especially AEF (French Equatorial Africa federation) were far behind the core regions of the imperial era. Psychologically the heart of overseas France was Algeria, whose northern portions were considered to be full French departments. The savagery of the eight-year war for Algerian independence, especially the self-destructive fury of its final phases, compelled the exodus of most of the one million French settlers and the abandonment of much of their stranglehold on the Algerian economy.[24] The independent Algerian state pursued a consistently radical anti-imperial foreign policy until the 1990s, rendered financially possible by its relatively ample oil and natural gas revenues. Although Tunisia and Morocco were less assertive in international politics and leaned toward Western positions in their nonalignment, neither accepted the degree of French tutelage that was common in sub-Saharan Africa.

Several factors explain the comprehensive nature of the French relationship with sub-Saharan states formerly under its domination.[25] The terminal colonial effort in this zone to construct an elusive "federalism" as permanent institutional bonding, although failing in its manifest goal of defining political status short of independence, had important consequences. The representation accorded emergent African leaders in the Fourth and (briefly) Fifth Republics in French institutions, especially the Parliament but also the cabinet of ministers, drew much of the sub-Saharan independence generation into the heart of French political processes. In the Algerian instance, Paris representation was dominated by settler interests and a small number of collaborating Algerians; Tunisia and Morocco, which had a different international legal status, were not given parliamentary seats.

Sub-Saharan Africans elected to French Parliament were far more representative of emergent political forces than the few Algerians who served in the Paris Legislative Assembly. As early as the 1946 constitutional deliberations Leopold Senghor of Senegal played an influential role. By the late Fourth Republic

African leaders held ministerial positions as well (for example, future presidents Félix Houphouët-Boigny of Ivory Coast, Modibo Keita of Mali). Until literally the eve of independence the "federal" formula the Fifth Republic Constitution sought to institutionalize had the assent of most of the current francophone African political class, with the exception of the more radical intelligentsia, especially the students. The referendum approving the Fifth Republic Constitution in 1958, which proposed keeping the French-ruled sub-Saharan territories within a French sovereign framework, drew large, usually overwhelming majorities in all territories except Guinea, reflecting the strong wishes of the African leadership for its approval. Jarring as his words now sound, Houphouët-Boigny spoke for a political generation in his often-quoted 1956 statement: "To the mystique of independence we oppose the reality of fraternity." The degree of incorporation of the sub-Saharan African political elite into the French political world in the 1940s and 1950s has no parallel, and it left a lasting imprint on the texture of postcolonial relationships.[26] Successive French presidents, from Charles de Gaulle to Jacques Chirac, brought to office long-standing intimate ties with many sub-Saharan political leaders, linkages notably absent with former President Nicolas Sarkozy.

The original Fifth Republic concept of sub-Saharan territorial autonomy with an array of core sovereign functions (defense, money, and justice, for example) vested in the France-centered French community swiftly vanished.[27] In its place emerged an array of devices giving institutional expression to intimacy. Some form of defense accord was negotiated with fourteen sub-Saharan former colonies[28]; French troops were permanently garrisoned in Djibouti, the Central African Republic, Gabon, the Ivory Coast, and Senegal; and a reserve intervention force earmarked for swift African deployment was held in readiness in France. Except for Guinea, Mali, Mauritania, and Madagascar, all these ex-colonies remained within a French currency zone (and Guinea and Mali eventually sought reentry).

By the 1970s Franco-African summit conferences became a regular and lavish part of the diplomatic landscape; often these attracted more heads of state than the OAU or AU summits. *Francophonie* as a cultural instrument finds expression in the French educational systems and linguistic policies; the nurture of the French language enjoys a priority in French diplomacy that is unique among former colonizers. In the Maghreb *francophonie* competes with the active policies of affirmation of the Arab language and culture; in sub-Saharan Africa (excepting Madagascar and Mauritania) retention of French as the primary state vehicle has been internalized as a political value by most of the state class.[29] Even a populist socialist leader such as Alphonse Massemba-Débat of Congo-Brazzaville exclaimed in the late 1960s that the Congolese and the French were "Siamese twins," separable only by surgery.[30] Senghor, who was the most intellectually brilliant member of the independence political generation, summed up the pervasive relationship as *francité* (Frenchness, Francehood).[31] His induction into the Académie Française was, in his own eyes, a crowning achievement in a splendid career. A neologism such as *francité* has plausible resonance in the Franco-African case, but its analogues would be preposterous in characterizing any other postcolonial ties.

A singular form of tutelary, or dependent, linkages results from this broad set of connections, not all of which are well captured in the visible aspect of politics or in the asymmetrical core-periphery economic flows to which "dependency theory" draws attention. The francophonic African community counts upon the senior French partner to defend its interests within the European Union and among the international financial institutions, both public and private. Priority access to French aid is assumed, including periodic budgetary bailouts for the more impoverished states.[32] French willingness to occasionally intervene militarily to protect clients is of crucial importance; between 1960 and 2003 Victor Le Vine tallied fifteen major instances of such intervention.[33] As then-president Valéry Giscard d'Estaing stated, "We have intervened in Africa whenever an unacceptable situation had to be remedied."[34] Perhaps even more critical to the nurture of tutelary standing are French security services of a more clandestine nature. French intelligence services provide invaluable protection to rulers by their capacity to monitor and penetrate opposition groups and to foil potential conspiracies by providing early warning to incumbents. These security operations have always enjoyed high-level attention in Paris through such presidential advisers as the late éminence grise Jacques Foccart, master manipulator of the shadowy *réseaux* (networks) that provided the sinews of *Françafrique* from 1960 until his death in 1987. The absence of a full replacement is one measure of the slow decline of *Françafrique* itself.

By the final years of the twentieth century there were signs that the silken threads binding francophonic Africa to France were fraying. France made no move to prevent the overthrow of Hissène Habré by armed insurgents enjoying Libyan support in Chad at the end of 1990, although French troops in Chad could have easily prevented the takeover, and French air power did block an effort by armed insurgents to oust his successor, Idriss Déby Itno. Nor did France lift a finger to avert the overthrow of Ivory Coast ruler Henri Bédié in December 1999 when he was forced out by a military coup; French contingents did serve under a UN mandate to separate the parties to a 2002–2003 civil war and also in the final action on behalf of the AU and UN to oust usurper Laurent Gbagbo in 2011 and install the elected president, Allasane Ouattara.[35]

Supporting the CFA franc zone is more expensive and less profitable than it once was, and France engineered a large devaluation in 1994 in the face of heated opposition by a number of African clients. Protection of friendly incumbents appears to have lost some of its attraction, as in early 1990 when France softened its long-held view that single-party rule, with its corollary of life presidency, was the most "realistic" political formula for Africa. But the closely woven fabric of the French connection is too sturdy to quickly unravel, and France was more ambivalent toward democratization than the other former colonial powers.

STRUGGLE TO ELIMINATE COLONIAL INFLUENCE

The importance of the colonial past in shaping contemporary African international relations is thus beyond dispute. At the same time, the colonial system serves, paradoxically, as a negative point of reference for the African concert of nations. The legitimacy of the first generation of African regimes was rooted in the regimes' achievement—by conquest or negotiation—of independence. The two transcendent unifying principles of the pan-African movement from its inception have been opposition to both colonialism and racism, evils that were joined on the African continent. The independent states that assembled to create the OAU in 1963 were divided on many questions of ideology and interpretation of non-alignment; all could rally behind the combat to complete the liberation of Africa from colonial occupation and regimes of white racial domination. The elemental notion of African solidarity arose out of the shared experience of racial oppression, a point made explicit by W. E. B. DuBois many years ago: "There is slowly arising not only a curiously strong brotherhood of Negro blood throughout the world, but the common cause of the darker races against the intolerable assumption and insults of Europeans has already found expression. Most of humanity are people of color. A belief in humanity means a belief in [people of color]. The future world will in all reasonable possibility be what colored men make of it."[36] Nearly five decades later Julius Nyerere translated these thoughts into African nationalist language: "Africans all over the continent, without a word being spoken, either from one individual to another, or from one African country to another, looked at the European, looked at one another, and knew that in relation to the European they were one."[37]

Indeed, at the moment of the OAU's creation many of the most arduous independence struggles still lay ahead, such as those in the Portuguese territories, Zimbabwe, and Namibia as well as the mortal combat with apartheid in South Africa. The OAU had a mediocre record in coping with conflicts within Africa (Somalia, Liberia, Eritrea, Western Sahara, the Nigerian civil war, the Congo rebellions, and Chad-Libya, for example). However, its anticolonial role was important in providing a continental focus for African liberation diplomacy.

Within their own territorial domain independent states faced a compulsion to demarcate themselves from their colonial past, to render visible the new status. The superficial symbolic accoutrements of independence—flags and postage stamps—might serve for a time. Africanization of the state apparatus might help as well, although over time the perception could arise that the real benefits of this change accrued above all to state personnel.

The imperative of demarcation eventually spread to the economic realm. In the 1970s a wave of seizures of foreign assets with potent colonial connotations swept through Africa: Idi Amin's "economic war" against the Asian community in 1972, Mobutu Sese Seko's "Zairianization" (Congolization) and "radicalization" campaigns of 1973 and 1974, Tanzania's socialization measures after the 1967 Arusha Declaration, the 1972 and 1976 Nigerian "indigenization decrees," the copper-mine nationalizations in Zambia and Congo-Kinshasa, and parallel measures in many other countries. Measures of expropriation of foreign assets almost exclusively affected holdings associated with the colonial past. This partly reflected a distinction often made between postindependence investments, which involved contractual commitments (presumably) freely made by the African state, and those made under alien sovereignty, which lacked moral standing (and doubtless had been well amortized). More important, moves to indigenize the economy reflected pressures to move beyond purely political independence, which would be denatured if all the structures of economic subordination remained intact. By the 1980s this surge of economic demarcation had run its course; the deepening economic crisis and heightened vulnerability to external pressures made such measures unfeasible. In addition, the measures were frequently discredited by the chaotic improvisation of their implementation and consequent dislocations (Congo-Kinshasa, Uganda) or by the perception that only narrow politico-mercantile classes had benefited (Nigeria).[38]

The compulsion for demarcation from the colonial past was driven by psychological as well as political and economic factors. Particularly in sub-Saharan Africa the colonial era brought a broad-front assault upon African culture that was far more comprehensive than similar experiences in the Middle East and Asia. The "colonial situation," to borrow Georges Balandier's evocative concept,[39] was saturated with racism. African culture was, for the most part, regarded as having little value, and its religious aspect, outside the zones in which Islam was well implanted, was subject to uprooting through intensive Christian evangelical efforts, which were often state supported. European languages supplanted indigenous ones for most state purposes; for the colonial subject, social mobility required mastering the idiom of the colonizer. In innumerable ways colonial subjugation in Africa brought not only political oppression and economic exploitation but also profound psychological humiliation. In the nationalist response to colonialism, psychological themes are prevalent to a degree unique in Third World anti-imperialist thought. Frantz Fanon, the Martinique psychiatrist who supplied so powerful a voice to the Algerian revolution, was only the most eloquent such spokesman.[40] Such doctrines as *négritude* and "African personality" were central components in nationalist thought, asserting the authenticity and value of African culture. This dimension of African nationalism gave a special emotional edge to the postcolonial quest for demarcation as well as to the fervor of African state reaction to racism and colonialism.

Colonial heritage as a negative point of reference also influenced the contours of Cold War intrusion into Africa. The United States and the Soviet Union both represented themselves as alternatives to exclusive reliance of African nations upon the erstwhile colonizers for succor and support, as has China more recently. Particularly in the early phases of independence, visible Soviet linkages served as a badge of demarcation. The extravagant fears of all colonizers—and of the West generally—regarding "Communist penetration" of Africa enhanced the value of Soviet relations, even if Soviet economic assistance was minimal. For those states that wanted—or felt compelled to undertake—a more comprehensive break with the Western colonial system, for a short period in the early 1960s and again in the

1970s the Soviet bloc appeared to offer an alternative. The bargain proved to be rather fruitless, however, as the Soviet Union began to disengage from Africa in the early 1980s.[41]

AUTHORITARIAN LEGACY OF THE COLONIAL STATE

Finally, the defining attribute of the colonial state in Africa until its final years was the monopoly of central authority enjoyed by its almost entirely European top administration. The structures of a postindependence polity were grafted onto the robust trunk of colonial autocracy, which proved a much more enduring legacy than the hastily created and weakly rooted democratic institutions normally assembled at the final hour before independence. The command habits and authoritarian routines of the colonial state were in most countries soon reproduced in single-party or military-political monopolies.

In the final colonial years after World War II the superstructure of imperial rule had become well professionalized, its European cadres trained in specialized institutes, and its chiefly African intermediaries now requiring literacy and competence as well as customary qualifications. The imperial administration enjoyed exceptional insulation from an emergent African civil society denied organizational scope until the eve of independence by repressive colonial legislation. The African colonial state was a pure model of bureaucratic authoritarianism.

Swelling postwar colonial revenues fueled by the global commodity boom and, for the first time, significant metropolitan public investment yielded rapid expansion of state services and social infrastructure in the final colonial decade. Though some authors, notably Jeffrey Herbst, argue that the colonial state was weak,[42] in my reading, in the form bequeathed to the African independence elite generation, the late colonial state was a robust and effective hegemonic apparatus habituated to a command relationship with its subject population. The African state weakness stressed in the introductory chapter is rather a product of political itineraries since 1960 than an immediate consequence of colonial legacy.[43]

Postcolonial rulers, inspired by a vision of high modernity to be swiftly realized, sought a rapid expansion in the mission and scope of the state.[44] African independence coincided with a moment of peak confidence in state-led development; the example of the apparent centrally planned transformation of the Soviet Union and China stood as a potent model. To release the developmental state from the constraints of democratic process, the fragile representative institutions belatedly created by the withdrawing colonizer for the transition to independence were set aside in favor of single parties or, when these lost public favor, military regimes restoring the colonial legacy of authoritarian rule.

However, effective centralization and monopolization of power and political space did not suffice to ensure the unhindered hegemony of the postcolonial state, which could never match the autonomy from society enjoyed by the imperial bureaucracy. The command state could not operate on the basis of impersonal authority and coercive force alone; indispensable were supplementary mechanisms translating state rule into personalized linkages with key intermediaries and their ramifying networks of clientele. By subtle metamorphosis the bureaucratic authoritarianism of the colonial state legacy became the patrimonial autocracy almost everywhere ascendant by the 1970s. As numerous works attest,[45] this pathway led to the economic and political bankruptcy afflicting most states by the calamitous 1980s, and the battered, delegitimated—and weak—state that faced the democracy moment of 1990, a tale beyond the scope of this chapter.

Thus, in various ways the colonial heritage intrudes into postindependence African international relations. Perhaps more than five decades after the great surge to independence in 1960 the colonial shadow begins to fade, overwritten by the turbulent history of the postindependence years. Important new trends that may tug colonial legacy further into the background will have a critical impact as the new century unfolds.[46] The end of the Cold War has had a profound influence. There is a widening consensus that regional integration that bridges the old colonial divisions is indispensable to overcoming them, which may lead to innovations in the state system that will begin to transcend the colonial partition. For the first half century of African independence, however, colonial heritage has powerfully shaped the African international system.

NOTES

1. Jeffrey Herbst, *States and Social Power in Africa: Comparative Lessons in Authority and Control* (Princeton, NJ: Princeton University Press, 1994).

2. For a more extended argument on the pathology of the African colonial state, see Crawford Young, *The African Colonial State in Comparative Perspective* (New Haven, CT: Yale University Press, 1994).

3. In the extensive literature on these themes I have found especially useful Charles Issawi, *An Economic History of the Middle East and North Africa* (New York: Columbia University Press, 1972); Peter Sluglett, *Britain in Iraq, 1914–1932* (London: Ithaca Press, 1976); William Roger Louis, *The British Empire in the Middle East, 1945–1951: Arab Nationalism, the United States, and Postwar Imperialism* (Oxford: Clarendon Press, 1984); George Antonius, *The Arab Awakening* (New York: Capricorn Books, 1965); and Mary C. Wilson, *King Abdullah, Britain and the Making of Jordan* (Cambridge: Cambridge University Press, 1987).

4. This argument is advanced in detail in Young, *The African Colonial State.*

5. This total does not include Western Sahara, which is recognized as a member state by the Organization of African Unity but not by the United Nations. Eritrea and South Africa were added in the 1990s.

6. The most careful political history of this process of fragmentation is Joseph-Roger de Benoist, *La Balkanisation de l'Afrique Occidentale Française* (Dakar, Senegal: Nouvelles Editions Africaines, 1979). His study clearly demonstrates that the balkanization was less a product of Machiavellian French design than the outcome of a complicated interplay of African political competition and French improvised response. Resentment of the distant bureaucratic despotism of the AOF French administrative headquarters was common in the outlying territories. Those nationalist leaders who at various times fought to preserve the unit—Léopold Senghor, Sékou Touré, Modibo Keita—were constrained both by their

own rivalries and by the absence of a strong popular attachment to the AOF as a geographical entity.

7. Among the works on this subject see Arthur Hazlewood, ed., *African Integration and Disintegration: Case Studies in Economic and Political Union* (London: Oxford University Press, 1967); Joseph S. Nye, *Pan-Africanism and East African Integration* (Cambridge: Cambridge University Press, 1965); Patrick Keatley, *The Politics of Partnership* (Harmondsworth, UK: Penguin Books, 1964); Philip Mason, *Year of Decision: Rhodesia and Nyasaland in 1960* (London: Oxford University Press, 1960); and Donald S. Rothchild, *Toward Unity in Africa: A Study of Federalism in British Africa* (Washington, DC: Public Affairs, 1960).

8. Saadia Touval, *The Boundary Politics of Independent Africa* (Cambridge, MA: Harvard University Press, 1972), pp. 22–23, 56–57.

9. Ibid., p. 54.

10. Onyeonoro S. Kamanu, "Secession and the Right of Self-Determination: An O.A.U. Dilemma," *Journal of Modern African Studies* 12, no. 3 (1974), pp. 371–373.

11. *Uti possidetis* is derived from a Roman private law concept that holds that, pending litigation, the existing state of possession of immovable property is retained. Translated into international law, the phrase means that irrespective of the legitimacy of the original acquisition of territory, the existing disposition of the territory remains in effect until altered by a freely negotiated treaty. For a passionate attack on this doctrine by a Moroccan jurist, see Abdelhamid El Ouali, "L'uti possidetis ou le non-sens du principe de base de l'OUA pour le règlement des différends territoriaux," *Le mois en Afrique* 227–228 (December 1984–January 1985), pp. 3–19.

12. For major studies on African boundary issues see, in addition to the previously cited Touval work, Ricardo René Larémont, *Borders, Nationalisms, and the African State* (Boulder, CO: Lynne Rienner Publishers, 2005); Carl Gosta Widstrand, ed., *African Boundary Problems* (Uppsala, Sweden: Scandinavian Institute of African Studies, 1969); A. I. Asiwaju, *Partitioned Africans: Ethnic Relations Across Africa's International Boundaries, 1884–1984* (London: C. Hurst, 1984); Ian Brownlie, *African Boundaries: A Legal and Diplomatic Encyclopedia* (Berkeley: University of California Press, 1979); and Markus Kornprobst, "Border Disputes in African Regional Sub-Systems," *Journal of Modern African Studies* 40, no. 2 (2002), pp. 360–394.

13. On the limited nature of Spanish rule see Ibrahim Sundiata, *Equatorial Guinea: Colonialism, State Terror, and the Search for Stability* (Boulder, CO: Westview Press, 1989); and Tony Hodges, *Western Sahara: The Roots of a Desert War* (Westport, CT: Lawrence Hill, 1983).

14. For thorough detail see Gauthier de Villers, "Belgique-Zaire: Le grand affrontement," *Cahiers du CEDAF* 1–2 (1990).

15. For detail on the *contentieux* see Crawford Young and Thomas Turner, *The Rise and Decline of the Zairian State* (Madison: University of Wisconsin Press, 1985), pp. 276–325. By the turn of the twenty-first century the large corporations that had dominated the colonial economy had entirely redeployed their capital and no longer had a Congo presence.

16. Patrick Chabal with David Birmingham, Joshua Forrest, Malyn Newitt, Gerhard Seibert, and Elisa Silva Andrade, *A History of Postcolonial Lusophone Africa* (Bloomington: Indiana University Press, 2002). In the revolutionary moment in Portugal following the coup in 1974 and 1975 some radical Portuguese leaders dreamed of a Marxist federation linking Portugal in an ideological federation to its former colonies; this vision was short-lived.

17. Paul Kennedy, *The Rise and Fall of the Great Powers: Economic Change and Military Conflict from 1500 to 2000* (New York: Vintage Books, 1987).

18. The phrase is drawn from the intriguing study by Francis G. Hutchins, *The Illusion of Permanence: British Imperialism in India* (Princeton, NJ: Princeton University Press, 1967).

19. Cited in Cecil J. B. Hurst et al., *Great Britain and the Dominions: Lectures on the Harris Foundation 1927* (Chicago: University of Chicago Press, 1928), p. 9.

20. Ibid., p. 3.

21. South Africa, which had been a member since its accession to "dominion" status in 1910, quit in 1961 in the face of increasing attacks from the swelling ranks of African members but rejoined after the fall of the apartheid regime.

22. Dennis Austin, *The Commonwealth and Britain* (London: Routledge & Kegan Paul, 1988), pp. 62, 64.

23. Herbert Luthy, *France Against Itself* (New York: Meridian Books, 1959).

24. For a graphic account of the holocaust during the final year of the Algerian war, with a mutinous army and a murderous settler force, the Organization de l'Armée Secrète, see Paul Henissart, *Wolves in the City: The Death of French Algeria* (New York: Simon & Schuster, 1970).

25. Useful studies on this topic include Stephen Smith, *Voyage en postcolonie: Le nouveau monde franco-africain* (Paris: Bernard Grasset, 2010); Edward Corbett, *The French Presence in Black Africa* (Washington, DC: Black Orpheus Press, 1972); Guy Martin, "Bases of France's African Policy," *Journal of Modern African Studies* 23, no. 2 (1985), pp. 189–208; George Chaffard, *Les carnets secrets de la décolonisation* (Paris: Calmass-Levy, 1965); Pierre Pean, *Affaires africaines* (Paris: Fayard, 1983); and Charles-Robert Ageron, *Les chemins de la décolonisation de l'empire français, 1936–1956* (Paris: Editions du CNRS, 1986).

26. Victor T. Le Vine, *Politics in Francophone Africa* (Boulder, CO: Lynne Rienner Publishers, 2004), pp. 61–102.

27. For a painstaking account by a highly informed French observer, see Joseph-Roger de Benoist, *Afrique Occidentale Française de 1944 à 1960* (Dakar, Senegal: Nouvelles Editions Africaines, 1982).

28. Martin, "Bases of France's African Policy," p. 204.

29. One encounters some exceptions among the intelligentsia; one example was the late Cheikh Anta Diop of Senegal, a cultural nationalist of great influence who strongly urged promotion of the most widely spoken Senegalese language, Wolof. But overall the commitment to French as the cultural medium is far more entrenched in the former French sub-Saharan territories than anywhere else in Africa.

30. Corbett, *The French Presence*, p. 66.

31. Léopold Sédar Senghor, *Ce que je crois: Négritude, francité et civilisation de l'universel* (Paris: B. Crasset, 1988).

32. In theory, financial injections to meet budgetary crises—most commonly, payments to civil servants—have long ceased; in practice, they continue to occur. For fascinating details on the process and its political importance see Raymond Webb, "State Politics in the Central African Republic" (PhD diss., University of Wisconsin–Madison, 1990).

33. Le Vine, *Politics in Francophone Africa*, pp. 380–381.

34. Martin, "Bases of France's African Policy," p. 194.

35. Thomas J. Bassett and Scott Straus, "Defending Democracy in Côte d'Ivoire," *Foreign Affairs* 90, no. 4 (2011), pp. 130–140.

36. Quoted in Victor Bakpetu Thompson, Africa and Unity: The Evolution of Pan-Africanism (London: Longman, 1969), p. 36.

37. Lecture by Julius Nyerere at Wellesley College, Wellesley, MA, April 1961; from my notes attending the lecture.

38. For details see Crawford Young, *Ideology and Development in Africa* (New Haven, CT: Yale University Press, 1982).

39. Georges Balandier, "The Colonial Situation," in *Africa: Social Problems of Change and Conflict*, ed. Pierre van den Berghe (San Francisco: Chandler Publishing, 1965), pp. 36–57.

40. See, for example, Frantz Fanon, *Black Skin, White Masks* (New York: Grove Press, 1967). On this theme see also O. Mannoni, *Prospero and Caliban: The Psychology of Colonization* (London: Methuen, 1956); and A. Memmi, *Portrait du colonisé, précédé du portrait du colonisateur* (Paris: Buchet-Chastel, 1957).

41. Arnold Hughes, ed., *Marxism's Retreat from Africa* (London: Frank Cass, 1992).

42. Herbst, *States and Social Power*.

43. For a more extended argument, see Young, *The African Colonial State*.

44. James C. Scott, *Seeing Like a State: How Certain Schemes to Improve the Human Condition Have Failed* (New Haven, CT: Yale University Press, 1998).

45. Among other sources see Achille Mbembe, *On the Postcolony* (Berkeley: University of California Press, 2001); Mark R. Beissinger and Crawford Young, eds., *Beyond State Crisis? Postcolonial Africa and Post-Soviet Eurasia in Comparative Perspective* (Washington, DC: Woodrow Wilson Center Press, 2002); Patrick Chabal and Jean-Pascal Daloz, *Africa Works: Disorder as Political Instrument* (Oxford: James Currey, 1999); and Jean-François Bayart, *The State in Africa: The Politics of the Belly* (New York: Longman, 1993).

46. For analysis of some such trends see Thomas Callaghy, Ronald Kassimir, and Robert Latham, eds., *Intervention and Transnationalism in Africa: Global-Local Networks of Power* (Cambridge: Cambridge University Press, 2001).

BUILDING VIABLE
POLITICAL ECONOMIES

Africa's post–Cold War quarter-century of political reform and unprecedented economic growth has reached a crossroads as the third decade of the twenty-first century approaches. By all measures the continent has experienced clear and demonstrable overall improvement in the observance of basic human rights and has made important strides in institutionalizing democratic structures and practices. Perhaps a dozen of the region's fifty-four countries have appeared on the road to sustainability, even if they fall well short of the perfection that eludes all democracies worldwide. At the same time, not only have most African countries made either no progress or, at best, only partial democratic progress, but since about 2005 there has been a notable, continuing plateauing and slippage of democratic progress across the region.

Some elected leaders have demonstrated perverse ingenuity in finding ways to bend constitutional democratic guarantees so as to remain in power beyond ordained term limits and to restrict and sharply limit the activities of civil society organizations that have been instrumental in the continent's democratic progress. As Aili Mari Tripp points out, civil society organizations have nonetheless staked out frontiers of human rights in the areas of climate change, gender, and other areas even as there has been considerable ferment within these movements over what the meaning of those rights should be, and rights movements have on occasion worked at cross-purposes to one another.

The twenty-first century has witnessed unparalleled significant and sustained economic growth rates in many African countries, many of which managed to escape the global economic downturn of 2008 from which the world has struggled gradually to recover. Important contributions to these growth rates have been significant new investments and trade relationships by the BRICS and other emergent economies, led by China. Progress in reducing some of the worst aspects of grinding, endemic poverty through the UN-sponsored Millennium Development Goals project from 2000 to 2015 has been significant if incomplete as the follow-on Sustainable Development Goals project gets under way. Evidence of emergent African middle classes is important even if the political and economic meaning of that development has yet to be fully explored.

At the same time, the long-term meaning and significance of Africa's contemporary economic progress is debatable, and incipient divisions between the leading African countries and the laggards in this regard are likely to deepen. Todd Moss observes that some African leaders have found ways to engage with public and private international actors to invest in their countries' respective economic futures, while others have not and face ongoing economic stagnation. Ian Taylor's essay reminds us that growth rates do not equate to economic development, that the BRICS have their own issues and are not necessarily "external heroes" for Africa, and that these relationships to date have not been sufficiently based on requisite African manufacturing, industrialization, and economic diversification. Anne Pitcher notes that a number of African governments have aligned their development strategies more closely than ever with the private sector by turning to the use of sovereign wealth funds, pension funds, parastatals, and political party companies to generate returns from natural resource extraction and property development. But she cautions that these initiatives expose governments to potential global economic downturns like the one they avoided in 2008 and afterward. She observes that adopting principles, structures, and practices of corporate governance to regulate these initiatives will require sustained, collective efforts by citizen groups through civil society and democratic governance institutions if they are to be effective, given the continent's continuing poor record of transparency and corruption avoidance.

Reflections on Africa's Rocky Love-Hate Relationship with International Capital

Todd Moss

Sub-Saharan Africa's rocky and volatile relationship with international capital markets has moved into a new phase. Over the past decade private capital flows have rocketed upward just at a time when public-sector aid flows have been leveling off and will likely soon start declining. Africa should soon expect to make a transition, as happened in Asia and Latin America, where private capital becomes much more important than public aid. (If the data were better, we would know for sure if this threshold has in fact already been crossed.) This trend not only represents a major financial watershed for the continent but will also signify an important historical and political shift. This chapter outlines some of the key trends driving international public and private investment in sub-Saharan Africa and highlights a few of the key policy agendas—and constraints—that remain.

LOST DECADES OF GROWTH

The starting point for any discussion of Africa's relationship with the global economy is the continent's dismal economic performance over the latter half of the twentieth century. At the time of independence Africa's economic prospects were believed to be very bright. Both private and public investment flowed into the continent to support ambitious plans for rapid industrialization on the widely held assumption that in the wake of investment flows, economic growth and, indeed, modernization would naturally follow. Most newly independent countries, supported by external donors, believed that the economic foundations in mining and farming could be quickly transformed via robust government action and capital investment into broad economic gains. Instead, most African economies faltered miserably. Several decades of postindependence investment and aggressive policy intervention were almost universally a dismal failure.[1] The subsequent period of adjustment and reflection has been equally long, and still today, the results are largely ambiguous. Few countries followed the reform prescriptions, and those that did had highly uneven implementation. Even among those economies that have recovered the most ground and made the most improvements, few have successfully transitioned beyond the skeleton of the inherited colonial economy. Copper, for instance, still accounts for more than three-quarters of Zambia's exports.

Africa's headline economic growth rates, as measured by changes in real gross national income (GNI), in the immediate postindependence period were fairly positive, with income per capita rising about 2.6 percent per year during the 1960s. But this slowed to just 0.9 percent per year in the 1970s and then turned sharply negative. The 1980s, often called the "lost decade" for Africa, saw average incomes decline by 1 percent per year. The 1990s were still a time of moving backward, albeit at only half the pace, with income per capita losing only 0.4 percent per year. Underneath these broad macroeconomic trends for the continent as a whole there is of course great variance for individual countries. But for the thirty-three countries for which reasonable data are available, sixteen of them were poorer in 2000 than they were in 1970. The growth failure led to several outcomes: plunging incomes, mounting external debt burdens, and severe capital flight. This put Africa on a course for substantial financial dependence on a cartel of Western donors,[2] which is only today being (selectively) broken.

THE RISE OF PUBLIC-SECTOR AID DEPENDENCY

By the early 1980s many countries had hit bottom and had little choice but to continue to turn to the international financial institutions (IFIs) and Western donors for assistance. The donors almost always agreed to provide new capital, but only if the African governments promised to fix what donors viewed as the policy shortcomings that caused the trouble in the first place. Although there was a diversity of economic problems across countries, there was a general agreement that many of the aggressive policies pursued by African governments were failing and that the state was not facilitating economic growth but rather strangling it.

A crucial aspect of the donor strategy was the recipients' promise to make policy changes in exchange for aid—what came to be called "conditionality." A prerequisite for receiving new loans was agreeing with the lender on what they would do differently. The centerpiece of this approach is the "letter of intent" written by a finance minister to the International Monetary Fund (IMF) outlining reform plans. At the time such promises seemed reasonable given the poor economic performance and the long list of identifiable problems. The basket of macroeconomic reforms, based on changes adopted by Latin American countries facing their own not-too-dissimilar debt problems, came to be known as the "Washington Consensus" (see Box 3.1). For the receiving governments, making a long series of promises seemed a fair price to pay for low-interest money to fill their budget gaps and enable them to service their debt obligations. In practice, of course, conditionality was itself a near-total failure. Even if the policies asked for by the donors seemed reasonable on paper, governments had little reason to actually implement policy changes and plenty of latitude to manipulate the system. In hindsight it was also obvious that the dynamics of aid and bureaucratic inertia also provided donors with few reasons to ever enforce their previous demands.[3]

The end result was nonetheless clear: steadily rising dependence of most African economies on publicly funded capital and on the advice from the providers

---

Box 3.1 The "Washington Consensus"

In 1990 economist John Williamson coined the phrase the "Washington Consensus" to describe (not necessarily advocate!) a list of the policies most commonly given as advice to Latin American countries in the late 1980s. The list is:

1. *Fiscal discipline.* Shrink large budget deficits that may create balance-of-payments crises and drive inflation.
2. *Reorder public expenditure priorities.* Switch spending away from the unproductive (e.g., subsidies, overbloated civil services) to the productive (e.g., health, education, infrastructure).
3. *Tax reform.* Build a fair and effective tax system.
4. *Liberalize interest rates.* Encourage savings by lifting state control of interest rates.
5. *Liberalize the exchange rate.* End currency manipulation (which tended to favor imports at the expense of export competitiveness).
6. *Liberalize trade.* Reduce barriers to exchange of goods.
7. *Liberalize inward investment.* Reduce barriers to foreign investors.
8. *Privatization.* Sell state-owned industries, starting with those draining the treasury.
9. *Deregulation.* Reduce legal barriers to private business operations.
10. *Property rights.* Enforce contracts and encourage land ownership.

Source: John Williamson, *Progress of Policy Reform in Latin America*, Policy Analyses in International Economics, Issue 28. (Washington DC: Institute for International Economics, 1990).

of that very same aid. Despite a downturn in the immediate aftermath of the end of the Cold War, aid flows into Africa have been strong. Indeed, contemporary sub-Saharan Africa is by far the most aid-dependent region of the globe at any time in history. By the late 2000s at least twenty different countries received total aid in excess of 10 percent of GDP. (By comparison, the US Marshall Plan to reconstruct postwar Europe never rose above 3 percent of any recipient European economy.) The ideological peak of the global aid movement was likely the 2005 Summit of the Group of Eight at Gleneagles when then British prime minister Tony Blair extracted aggressive new commitments from all members, including pledges to double aid to Africa. Total (self-reported) net aid to sub-Saharan Africa from all traditional donors has roughly held steady at about $45 billion per year for 2011–2014, more than double the levels in real terms from 2000.

While the traditional donors have generally held aid levels high, new actors have arrived. China's rapid and dramatic push into Africa has shaken much of the aid community.[4] China has long been involved in Africa—for example, building most of the stadiums and railroads constructed there after independence. Yet in recent years China's engagement on the continent has accelerated spectacularly. The anecdotes are compelling: Chinese companies and workers are building major infrastructure projects in almost every African country, and China has announced some enormous financing package deals for new projects, such as $9 billion in the Democratic Republic of the Congo and $13 billion in Ghana. The 2015–2016 economic slowdown in China along with the related decline in commodity prices is likely to affect Chinese involvement in the continent, but no such changes are yet reflected in the newspapers or in the data.

The true extent of Chinese investment, however, is largely unknown for several reasons. First, China does not have an "aid" program like other countries. Various agencies within the Chinese government and many state-owned companies engage in activities that appear very aid-like, but they also often have commercial purposes. (If a Chinese company builds a road from a Chinese mine to the port using subsidized credit from a Chinese bank, is that "aid"?) Second, China is not part of the "aid club" within the Organization for Economic Cooperation and Development (OECD) and does not report its aid spending in any manner that allows comparison. The World Bank guesses Chinese aid is about $2 to 4 billion per year. The Chinese government occasionally announces an official figure for its aid; the most recent such statement declared total aid to Africa to be $14 billion for the 2010–2012 period. Third, China is still very secretive with a lot of its activities, so it is difficult from the outside to know the terms of an announced deal (is the loan soft or hard?) or whether it is even true (as for all donors, announcements don't always lead to actual projects). Lastly, there is much speculation that many of the aid packages are part of larger deals, such as cheap loans in exchange for mining or oil concessions for Chinese companies.

These characteristics have sometimes put China and occasionally other new entrants like India or the Gulf states in apparent conflict with the other donors, who may be trying to promote transparency of aid and natural resource contracts or denying aid to rogue regimes, such as those in Khartoum or Harare. However, most of the mainstream donors have concentrated resources in health and education with only a small—but in some cases growing—portion funding roads, ports, and bridges. (The major exception to the aversion to infrastructure is a new push on energy, with many donors getting heavily involved in electrification expansion.) Thus the Chinese reasonably argue that they are responding to demand from Africa for large infrastructure investments and are often seen on the continent as filling that need rather than displacing traditional donors.

THE BEGINNING—AND END—OF THE DEBT CRISIS

The buildup of the aid business over the decades—combined with repeated investments in projects that rarely led to the increased exports that are required in order to generate hard currency to repay foreign loans—eventually contributed to the debt crisis. Africa's debt became a significant problem in the 1980s when the total debt started to mount up at the same time that countries encountered problems paying back older loans. The total amount owed by the continent grew from just $6 billion in 1970 (or about $22 billion in today's dollars after adjusting for inflation) to nearly $200 billion by the mid-1990s. This debt represented less than 15 percent of the continent's total GDP in 1970 but jumped to over 100 percent by the 1990s. More important, it was clear that for many African countries these debts were unpayable and that the rising level of debt itself was becoming a barrier to progress on other fronts.

As early as the 1970s bilateral creditors began writing off debts to some low-income countries or at least agreeing to easier repayment plans.[5] For some creditors it was merely another way to transfer resources to countries, either as another form of aid or to help a strategic ally. But it was also part of a growing realization that much of the old lending was lost. The past projects financed by old loans were probably not going to generate returns sufficient to enable repayment. The major bilateral official creditors organized into the Paris Club to provide a framework for renegotiating old debts. Even though various forms of debt relief were available in the 1980s and early 1990s, advocates began to call for more widespread and systematic debt relief. Campaigns, such as the Jubilee Movement, began to urge the rich-country creditors to not just reduce but to completely erase the debts owed by poor countries.

One problem was that the World Bank and IMF were not legally allowed to provide debt relief. As bilateral and other credit was dealt with, this left the multilateral financial institutions as the major sticking point. So in 1996, at the behest of their major shareholders, the IMF and World Bank created the Heavily Indebted Poor Countries (HIPC) initiative that for the first time tackled multilateral credit. The HIPC process calls for countries to first seek a Paris Club deal; then, assuming their debt numbers are still too high, they can apply for HIPC, which determines eligibility based on debt sustainability and some record of good performance. In 1999 the initiative was enhanced and the terms were softened further, including 90 percent bilateral relief on Cologne terms and further multilateral debt reductions through HIPC. In 2005 the major economic powers agreed to even further cuts among the HIPC-qualified countries, with up to 100 percent debt reduction for the qualified countries. The so-called Multilateral Debt Relief Initiative (MDRI) expanded the HIPC program to completely erase the remaining debt owed to the World Bank, IMF, and the regional African Development Bank. Thirty-six countries, of which thirty-one were African, eventually reached a successful "completion point" in MDRI and started with a nearly clean debt slate.

SEEDS OF A NEW DEBT CRISIS?

These efforts effectively made debt a passé problem (with the exception of a handful of countries, such as Myanmar or Zimbabwe, who were deliberately left out of the process for a variety of reasons). However, countries that go through HIPC and have their books cleaned usually want to borrow again. Such countries have frequently asked the IMF for more "flexibility" in deciding when they should be allowed to borrow again and how much new debt they can assume responsibly. The IMF, under growing pressure from borrowers, tweaked the formulas they use to determine debt sustainability. In effect HIPC has—as some critics of the program charged it would—not erased the debt problem but merely cleared the decks for countries to start borrowing again. Although MDRI was supposed to be the final answer, some have asked the question whether we might just be back with the same problem in a few years.

In fact, there are already some worrying signs. First, many of the same financial institutions (the World Bank, IMF, and African Development Bank) have been relending to the very same countries. Surprisingly, the lending has been at a similar rate: in the years immediately before MDRI, lending to all HIPC countries was about $4 billion per year; in the years after MDRI the lending volume was roughly the same.[6] During the financial crisis of 2008–2009 new lending volumes even went higher as part of a fiscal stimulus aimed at preventing recession. Although most bilateral donors have shifted to giving grants instead of loans to these low-income countries, a few bilaterals (France, Spain, Japan) still mostly lend.

Second, borrowing from new creditors, such as China, Iran, India, Saudi Arabia, and elsewhere, has grown just as the HIPCs are finally getting out from under their debts. For example, within a few years of Ghana receiving nearly $4 billion in debt relief under HIPC/MDRI, the country agreed to a $13 billion credit line with two Chinese banks. Some countries didn't even wait for the ink to dry: the Democratic Republic of Congo finalized a $9 billion line of credit agreement with China at the same time it was reaching the HIPC completion point. Although some of these new loans are for construction projects that may very well turn out to be good investments, thus justifying the new borrowing, these new lenders typically do not reveal the terms of their loans, and the deals are often shrouded in secrecy, which raises all kinds of new worries.

Finally, several HIPC countries have started borrowing from commercial markets again as well. Less than a year after receiving debt relief for its old close-to-zero-interest loans, Ghana successfully issued a $750 million Eurobond. Other countries, such as Senegal, Uganda, and Tanzania, have either also floated commercial bonds or plan to do so soon (see Table 3.1). One interpretation of this trend is a new market confidence that these countries will be better placed to grow and repay these debts. However, if these new loans aren't much more productive than the old loans were, these same countries could find themselves once again in debt distress. An especially worrying trend is the rising premium that African countries must pay in order to raise new capital on global markets. Ghana, for instance, offered an interest rate of 8.5 percent in 2007 but had to raise this to 10.75 percent in 2015.

Table 3.1   Eurobond Issuance

Country	Year issued	Amount offered (mil USD)	Priced yield (%)	Long-term credit rating
Rwanda	2013	$400	6.88	B
Ghana	2007	$750	8.50	B+
	2013	$750	8.00	B
	2014	$1,000	8.13	B
	2015	$1,000	10.75	B
Senegal	2009	$200	9.25	B
	2011	$500	9.13	B1
	2014	$500	6.25	B2
Nigeria	2011	$500	7.00	BB
	2013	$500	5.375	BB-
		$500	6.63	
Côte d'Ivoire	2010	$2,300	10.18	—
	2014	$750	5.63	B
	2015	$1,000	6.63	B
Kenya	2014	$500	5.875	B+
		$1,500	6.88	
Zambia	2012	$750	5.63	B+
	2015	$1,250	9.38	B
Gabon	2007	$1,000	8.20	BB-
	2013	$1,500	6.38	BB-
	2015	$500	6.95	B+

Source: Reuters; IMF Article IV (Ghana, Senegal, Nigeria, Gabon); Fitch; Moody's; Deutsche Bank, "African Eurobonds," 2015.

THE RETURN OF PRIVATE CAPITAL

The vast majority of development policy debates remain stuck in the public sector, the role of the African state in promoting (or hindering) development, and what rich-world governments can do to help (or hurt). But the history of capitalism and the transition from poverty to wealth in other regions of the globe has mostly been about private actors. Progress in wealth and humankind has generally come not from politicians at home or abroad but from the activities of farmers, investors, small businesses, and big corporations. The development community has increasingly, if a bit belatedly, recognized that the private sector and private capital can each play a vital role in promoting economic progress in Africa as well. African governments have taken some steps to try to attract foreign investment, while many of the donors have created programs to try to boost Africa's indigenous entrepreneurs and to help catalyze private-capital flows to the continent. Although recent signs have been encouraging, the private sector often remains a marginal player in many countries. This is a shame because if Africa is going to grow out of

Figure 3.1   Private Flows and Official Development Assistance to Sub-Saharan Africa, 1980–2013

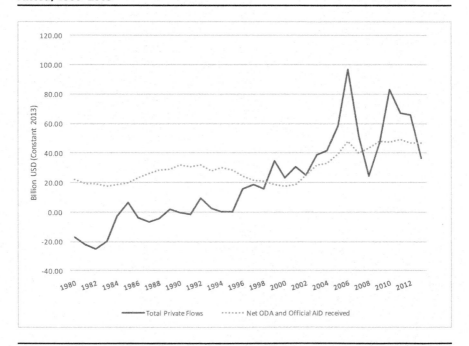

Source: ODA figures from World Bank, World Development Indicators (Washington, DC, 2016). Total Private Flows is an aggregate of net FDI inflows (WDI 2016), net portfolio equity inflows (WDI 2016), and other private investments (IMF WEO 2015)

poverty and create a more prosperous future, it is unavoidable that these economies will need more and bigger businesses.

Several broad trends are currently defining the private investment landscape.
First, private-capital flows to Africa, using the best available estimates, have been
rising (see Figure 3.1). Foreign direct investment (FDI) in particular has been
growing from around $1 billion per year in the 1970s and 1980s to $4 billion per
year in the 1990s, and an average of more than $20 billion per year for the 2000s.
In recent years this has spiked to roughly $40 billion per year. Portfolio flows (in-
vestments via publicly traded stocks or bonds or minority private equity stakes)
have also grown from close to zero in the 1970s to several billion dollars per
year in recent years. Despite the big gains in attracting new investment, however,
the continent has largely missed out on a global investment boom that has seen
flows to other regions accelerate even faster. As a result, Africa's relative share of
global FDI, which averaged around 5 percent in the early 1970s, fell to just 1 to 2
percent by the early 1980s and has only recovered to around 3 percent in recent
years.

Second, the continent-wide aggregates mask major and strong heterogeneity
among countries; indeed, private investment to Africa has clustered very strongly
in a handful of countries and sectors. Over the period 2010–2014 the top ten countries received 69 percent, leaving just 11 percent of the total for the bottom twenty-
four countries (see Table 3.2). At the same time, there has been a long-standing

Table 3.2   Top FDI Recipients, 2010–2014

Rank	Country	FDI net inflows (mil $)	% of SSA total	Cumulative %
1	Nigeria	32,444	14.5	14.5
2	South Africa	26,450	11.8	26.3
3	Mozambique	21,283	9.5	35.8
4	Ghana	15,642	7.0	42.8
5	Congo	13,676	6.1	48.9
6	DR Congo	12,100	5.4	54.3
7	Equatorial Guinea	10,571	4.7	59.1
8	Tanzania	9,115	4.1	63.1
9	Zambia	8,471	3.8	66.9
10	Sudan	5,277	2.4	69.3
		Top 10 total = 69		

23	Kenya	2,266	1.0	89
24–48	Bottom 24 countries	23,736	11.0	100

Source: World Bank, *World Development Indicators* (Washington, DC, 2016).

concentration in the extractive sectors, particularly petroleum and mining. All of the top ten destinations have very strong enclave mining or offshore oil sectors.

Another significant trend—although one that is not always apparent in much of the available data—is that FDI and other private-capital inflows are now coming from a range of new sources. Major investors from other emerging regions, especially Asia, are now joining the traditional sources of FDI, large corporations in upper-income Western countries. Chinese investment in particular, both by private Chinese companies and by projects financed through quasi-public Chinese banks, is now among the largest sources of new capital flowing into Africa.[7] One of the main channels for Chinese investment in Africa is through the China Export-Import Bank (China Ex-Im). This is a state agency that directs capital to support trade and investments by Chinese companies. China Ex-Im is similar to the export credit agencies in the United States or in Europe, but the scale is very different: China Ex-Im is today larger than all of the export credit agencies of all the OECD countries combined. Recent commitments from China Ex-Im to African projects are estimated at some $6 to 7 billion per year. Through Ex-Im and other quasi-official banks significant Chinese investments have been made in infrastructure (especially roads, telecommunications, and power), manufacturing, mining, fisheries, and agribusiness.

A lack of regular reporting about deals, however, complicates the full picture of Chinese investments in Africa. The Chinese government tends not to share information about such matters. If this is true for aid, it is even more so for investment flows where commercial propriety may be valuable. Of course, much of what is called "private" investment is actually by state-owned banks or companies that may be partly directed by government policy or, at a minimum, have some kind of relationship to state entities. The mechanisms often used to avoid taxation or hide the true ownership further this confusion. Much of the truly private investment, such as that by small or medium-sized companies, is done through intermediaries in tax havens that intentionally obscure the origin of the capital. Finally, local press reports often declare major investments by Chinese firms, but project implementation is another matter. For example, the local Nigerian press once announced with great fanfare that a massive Chinese-financed and -operated project would soon connect all thirty-six state capitals by railway, and a newspaper in Hong Kong reported on a Chinese government pledge to provide $1 trillion in finance to Africa by 2025. These types of declarations are neither unusual nor close to the truth.

THE RISE OF AFRICAN STOCK MARKETS
AND DOMESTIC CAPITAL MOBILIZATION

Africa has also attempted to attract private capital via stock exchanges. The subcontinent now has sixteen stock markets with nearly a thousand publicly listed companies. Most of these markets only opened in the 1990s, part of the wave of reform that coincided with an emerging markets boom cycle (see Table 3.3). South Africa dominates the market, accounting for nearly 80 percent of the total capitalization (i.e., the value of all the companies listed on the market). But even without South Africa there are more than five hundred African companies that are publicly listed and whose shares are traded. Given their relatively small size, relative to both global markets and their own economies, there has long been talk of merging into larger regional exchanges. In 1998 the stock exchange in Abidjan became Bourse Régionale des Valeurs Mobilières (BRVM), the first official regional market, but the grand plans have largely fizzled. More important many of the markets have begun to cross-list companies from other exchanges, such as the listing of Kenya Airways and East African Breweries on all three East African exchanges (Kenya, Tanzania, and Uganda). Several South African companies are also listed on exchanges in Namibia, Botswana, Zimbabwe, Malawi, and Zambia.

Despite their relatively small size, African stock markets were established with the strong support of governments and remain fairly popular. There are clearly political and national pride factors behind some of the minor markets, but there are also real economic benefits. Most immediately, the stock markets have been useful vehicles for spreading ownership during privatization. In Tanzania, for example, almost all of the listings are former state-owned companies, and listing

Table 3.3   Sub-Saharan Africa's Stock Markets

	Year opened	Market capitalization (end-2014, US $ bn)
Botswana	1989	4.40
Cameroon	2001	0.30
Cape Verde	2005	0.08
Côte d'Ivoire*	1998	11.70
Ghana	1989	20.11
Kenya	1954	25.57
Malawi	1996	15.74
Mauritius	1989	8.66
Namibia	1992	148.48
Nigeria	1961	61.72
Rwanda	2008	1.93
South Africa	1887	1150.50
Sudan	1994	2.10
Tanzania	1996	12.80
Uganda	1997	9.50
Zimbabwe	1946	4.33

Source: African Securities Exchanges Association, *2014 Annual Report and Statistics Report*, 2015.
*BRVM (Benin, Burkina Faso, Cote d'Ivoire, Guinee-Bissau, Mali, Niger, Senegal, and Togo).

these firms on the Dar es Salaam exchange has allowed trading by smallholders and encouraged wider shareholding. Kenya has been highly successful in attracting its own middle-class investors to buy local shares.

In the long term it is hoped that more domestic firms will use the markets to mobilize capital for expansion, a trend that seems to be emerging already in countries like Botswana and Kenya; however, many of the markets remain dominated by local subsidiaries of foreign multinationals, which are able to access capital more easily and more cheaply by turning to the parent company. Over time, as firms become more comfortable with the idea of public ownership and a greater number make the leap in size, more companies may turn to the local market. Similarly, the markets have not yet become a major destination for either local or global investors, but as the markets continue to grow, this should also change.

Remittances, the private money sent home by Africans living abroad, are another important source of private capital for Africa that is often forgotten. For a long time there was little hard data on this important financial flow, in part because most of these transactions take place outside formal banking channels and deliberately out of sight of tax collectors. But more recently the World Bank has invested in better understanding the scale and characteristics of remittances. Their latest estimate is that 23 million overseas sub-Saharan migrants sent $35 billion home in 2015.[8] Regardless of their exact size, remittances are very substantial for countries with large populations living abroad, such as Somalia, Cape Verde, Ghana, Nigeria, Ethiopia, and Zimbabwe. Remittances are likely to be particularly vital in poverty reduction because they are cash sent directly to families. Because much higher wages can be found in the rich world, even for the very same job, there is a strong incentive for both temporary and permanent emigration, an option taken by millions of Africans, and many of these migrants continue to support family members in their country of origin. For the recipient families, remittances can be a crucial source of income for everyday household spending and investments in schooling, housing, or a business. For the countries involved, it is a source of foreign exchange, and the migrants, if they return, often bring back capital, ideas, and new skills. Some development agencies are trying to find ways to channel remittances for an even greater impact on poverty—for example, linking them to more formal financial services.

A LINGERING SKEPTICISM?

These trends in investment flows are relevant to development because such flows are believed to bring major benefits. At the macroeconomic level FDI by definition is new investment capital, contributing to the balance of payments, adding to the country's capital stock, and (assuming the money is used at least moderately productively) contributing toward future economic growth. There is some evidence that foreign investment can contribute to raising exports for a country and can help the economy integrate into global economic networks. At the microeconomic level there is also a range of possible benefits, especially higher productivity through new investment in physical and human capital (machines and training), increased job creation, better management, and bringing new technology into the country. Foreign investment also is thought to have important follow-on effects on local companies, or spillovers, through supply and distribution chains, trading, and outsourcing.[9]

FDI is sometimes considered more development-friendly than portfolio flows because it is more stable and can often be visibly linked to things such as jobs, buildings, and tax payments. But portfolio flows are also potentially beneficial because they still represent money flowing into a country. To the extent that this raises stock prices or lowers the yield on bonds, it makes money cheaper for companies to use to expand. There are also indirect gains from having portfolio investor interest, such as the impact on corporate governance and helping to link economies into the global financial network, giving access to money for local businesses, and lowering the overall cost of capital.

Despite the growing competition for private investment and Africa's ability to attract only modest amounts outside of the extractive industries, the continent still has a strong historical skepticism toward foreign capital.[10] Much of the prevailing attitude toward foreign investment is rooted in history, ideology, and the politics of the postindependence period. Africa's early experiences with foreign companies continue to affect official and public perceptions of FDI. The arrival of European capitalism in West Africa, first with the Portuguese in the fifteenth century and later the Dutch, French, and British, is indelibly connected with the slave trade and seen as a precursor for colonialism. The use of European companies as proxies for sovereign powers has helped to link in the public's mind international business with imperial expansion. In 1652 Jan van Riebeeck arrived in the Cape on behalf of the Dutch East India Company. In the late nineteenth century Cecil Rhodes claimed swathes of southern Africa on behalf of the British South Africa Company. Through the company Rhodes secured mining concessions in gold, copper, and diamonds, playing the dual roles of entrepreneur and representative of the British crown. Harsh conditions and treatment of laborers added to the linking of foreign companies and exploitation, such as in the mines (e.g., under the Witwatersrand Native Labor Association) or plantations.[11] As with the United Fruit Company in Latin America, foreign companies in Africa are sometimes thought of as agents of imperialism and exploitation, a perception that politicians can conveniently exploit.

Second and perhaps just as importantly, most of Africa's anticolonial movements were heavily supported by the Soviet Union, China, Cuba, and other states that brought a very particular ideology and economic model. This encouraged the spread of socialism—or, rather, African variants on socialism—and a general bias against Western capital. This was closely complemented by dependency theory, which argued that capitalism in general and foreign companies in particular were agents of underdevelopment and merely continuing colonialism in another guise.[12] Although dependency theory has been widely discredited, it continues to flourish among certain academic circles, many NGOs, and in some political circles today and contributes to a lingering climate of distrust of foreign investors. Although there has been substantial turnover of political leadership in Africa over the past decade, many of the current decision makers, including those frequently hailed as reformers, have held political positions for decades and were originally trained on the socialist model steeped in antiforeign investment ideology. Even as most of Africa's finance ministers have become increasingly convinced that economic openness can be beneficial for their countries and fluent in the language of international capitalism, many of their cabinet colleagues remain unreconstructed economic nationalists.

Third, ideas of economic nationalism and a desire to use state institutions for rapid industrialization have affected sentiment toward foreign investment, and they continue to influence policy today. Kenneth Kaunda's statement "political independence is meaningless without economic independence" shaped not only Zambian investment policy but also those of his entire generation of leaders.[13] In this spirit, leaders frequently sought a symbolic break with foreign players that were closely identified with colonialism or external control. On a more practical level, political elites also did not want to be constrained by foreigners who might control key strategic sectors of the economy or their access to foreign exchange. Although FDI may be considered more stable than other types of capital flows, the flip side is that foreign investors with a greater stake in the long term might be more inclined to get involved in influencing policy or, in the extreme, supporting opposition political groups. In practice this has sometimes created a dilemma for politicians who want to be seen attracting foreign investors and creating jobs but not being taken advantage of or allowing outsiders to push local entrepreneurs aside.

THE NEW "BUSINESS ENVIRONMENT" AGENDA

The phrases "business environment" or "investment climate" refer to a broad range of microeconomic conditions that affect entrepreneurs.[14] One thing that has become increasingly apparent is that these conditions are particularly unfriendly to business in much of Africa. These include legal restrictions (such as requiring multiple licenses), lack of property protection (the state can seize assets), excessive regulations of all kinds, and colossal amounts of red tape and other headaches. The World Bank has undertaken several efforts to try to document such barriers (e.g., the average number of days to start a business or time spent with officials), not to embarrass governments so much as to give them the information to better make policy as they try to revive the private sector and attract more investment. The results have been enlightening, with many of the worst offenders taking clear steps to fix such problems. The Bank's "Doing Business" surveys have in the past found massive administrative barriers, but more recently many African countries have improved, coming closer to or even beating OECD averages (see Table 3.4 for a sample of indicators and countries).

Table 3.4   Doing Business in Africa

Number of days to:	Nigeria	Chad	Uganda	SSA average	OECD average
Start a business	31	60	63	27	9
Get construction permit	106	66	154	156	150
Register property	12	44	43	57	24
Export	23	70	28	31	11
Import	34	90	31	38	10
Enforce a contract	510	743	490	650	539

Source: Doing Business Annual Report 2015; Doing Business Regional Reports 2015.

Although much attention has been focused on foreign investment, it is also clear that local businesses, especially budding entrepreneurs, face considerable barriers. (Anyone who doubts that Africa has entrepreneurial potential should visit the huge open-air markets of Merkato in Addis Ababa or Bakara in Mogadishu where, even during periods of conflict, almost anything can be found.) Although large foreign companies seeking to expand business may get access to high officials who may help facilitate their entry, the average small businessperson in Africa has no such luxury and often is vulnerable to extortion by local officials. Perhaps just as important, most domestic businesses in Africa have little access to credit, fewer resources to buy their way out of problems (such as buying a generator to get around electricity blackouts), and generally lower skills and less management experience.

CONCLUDING COMMENT ON DIVERGENCE

Africa's interaction with international capital has been volatile and complex, often infused not just with the changing norms of economic policymaking but also with the emotional and political implications of economic change and power. The broad trends have been driven by a combination of external conditions and internal reforms that today leave Africa in perhaps the strongest position since independence to take advantage of international capital to promote its own development. It appears clear that some African leaders have recognized this and are actively seeking ways to engage with international actors—both public sector and private—to invest in their countries' futures. Other leaders do not yet seem to have adjusted to the emerging world, and their countries are destined to lag. As such, the dominant macroeconomic and macropolitical trend is one of intraregional divergence. Whatever the rocky relationship holds, international capital will help to drive that wedge between the next generation of emerging markets and those that will remain left behind.

NOTES

1. William Easterly and Ross Levine, "Africa's Growth Tragedy: Policies and Ethnic Divisions," *Quarterly Journal of Economics* 112 (November 1997), pp. 1203–1250; Paul Collier and Jan Willem Gunning, "Why Has Africa Grown Slowly?" *The Journal of Economic Perspectives* 13, no. 3. (Summer 1999), pp. 3–22; Nicolas van de Walle, *African Economies and the Politics of Permanent Crisis, 1979–1999* (New York: Cambridge United Press, 2001); William Easterly, *The Elusive Quest for Growth: Economists Adventures and Misadventures in the Tropics* (Cambridge, MA: MIT Press, 2001).

2. Thomas Callaghy and John Ravenhill, eds., *Hemmed In: Responses to Africa's Economic Decline* (New York: Columbia University Press, 1993).

3. Paul Mosley, "How to Confront the World Bank and Get Away with It: A Case Study of Kenya," in *Policy Adjustment in Africa*, ed. Chris Milner and A. J. Rayner (London: MacMillan, 1992); Paul Collier, "The Failure of Conditionality," in *Perspectives on Aid and Development*, ed. C. Gwyn and J. Nelson (Washington, DC: ODC, 1997).

4. Deborah Brautigam, *The Dragon's Gift: The Real Story of China in Africa* (Oxford: Oxford University Press, 2010).

5. William Easterly, "How Did Heavily Indebted Poor Countries Become Heavily Indebted? Reviewing Two Decades of Debt Relief," *World Development* 30, no. 10 (2002), pp. 1677–1696.

6. Benjamin Leo, "Will World Bank and IMF Lending Lead to HIPC IV? Debt Déjà-Vu All Over Again," *CGD Working Paper 193* (Washington, DC: Center for Global Development, 2009).

7. Brautigam, *The Dragon's Gift.*

8. World Bank, *Migration and Remittances Factbook 2016* (Washington DC: World Bank, 2015).

9. Theodore Moran, Edward Graham, and Magnus Blomström, eds., *Does Foreign Direct Investment Promote Development?* (Washington, DC: Institute for International Economics, 2005).

10. Todd Moss, Vijaya Ramachandran, and Manju Shah, "Is Africa's Skepticism of Foreign Capital Justified? Preliminary Evidence from Firm Survey Data in East Africa," in *Does Foreign Direct Investment Promote Development?*, ed. T. Moran, E. Graham, and M. Blomstrom (Washington, DC: Institute for International Economics, 2005).

11. For conditions on rubber plantations in the Belgian Congo see, for example, Adam Hochschild, *King Leopold's Ghost: A Story of Greed, Terror and Heroism in Colonial Africa* (Boston: Houghton Mifflin Company, 1999).

12. Colin Leys, *Underdevelopment in Kenya: The Political Economy of Neo-Colonialism* (Nairobi: General Printers Ltd., 1975); Walter Rodney, *How Europe Underdeveloped Africa* (Washington, DC: Howard University Press, 1981).

13. Roger Tangri, *The Politics of Patronage in Africa: Parastatals, Privatization, and Private Enterprise in Africa* (Oxford: James Currey Ltd., 1999).

14. Vijaya Ramachandran, Alan Gelb, and Manju Kedia Shah, *Africa's Private Sector: What's Wrong with the Business Environment and What to Do About It* (Washington DC: Brookings Press/Center for Global Development, 2009).

Entrepreneurial Governance and the Expansion of Public Investment Funds in Africa

M. ANNE PITCHER

From Nigeria to Mozambique, governments across the African continent have created new public investment vehicles to participate alongside private capital in consumer goods investments, property development, and even city-building projects. In a process that might appropriately be called "entrepreneurial governance," many national and municipal governments are relying on sovereign wealth funds, public pension funds, and even state enterprises to realize financial returns on their investments. This chapter describes new forms of public-funding mechanisms, explains why governments are deploying them, and highlights the opportunities and the pitfalls of governments' new roles as money managers. It argues that four factors—the role of donors, the growth of private equity funds, the scale of investment, and the changed interests of governments—explain policy convergence around public-funding mechanisms. The chapter concludes by discussing the risks and gains brought by these African "investor states."

INTRODUCTION

As Todd Moss has shown in the previous chapter, the widespread liberalization and privatization of African economies over the past two decades have promoted greater integration with the global economy, increased the number of foreign investments from more traditional partners such as the United Kingdom and France, and led to the emergence of new actors across the continent from China, India, and Brazil. The skills, technology, and capital brought by foreign partners have been critical to expanding new investments in coal, natural gas, aluminum, telecommunications, housing, and consumer services across Africa. Just as important, domestic capital has seen significant growth over the last twenty years.

This expansion of the private sector and foreign investment raises questions regarding the extent to which governments retain a role in their economies and for what purpose. In spite of the spread of democracy and market economies, even the most casual observer recognizes that patron-client networks—in which government officials direct access to lucrative economic opportunities to potential supporters—persist. Moreover, government officials continue to use state power to enrich themselves. Of the 168 countries included in Transparency International's corruption index, African countries make up nearly half of the top third most corrupt countries in the world. Most of these twenty-six countries continue to be labeled as authoritarian, but democracies such as Kenya, Uganda, Malawi, and Mozambique are also listed.[1]

Besides the persistence of corruption and clientelism, several scholars have observed that following the global financial crisis of 2008–2009 African governments revived their use of developmental rhetoric and adopted recognizably developmental policies. To paraphrase Chalmers Johnson, who popularized the concept of the "developmental state" in his classic study of Japan's miraculous growth after World War II, such states prioritize development through active intervention in the economy. Although market principles still prevail, they are harnessed by well-trained state bureaucrats, often housed in specialized agencies within the government, to promote the social welfare and pursue growth.[2] Not all of the features that Johnson delineated in the Japanese case are present in Africa, but the use of developmental rhetoric is manifest in South Africa, where government officials assert that it is a "democratic developmental" or "developmental" state and where policies such as the expanded public works program provide jobs and skills training to the historically disadvantaged.[3] The government of Botswana also displays many of the characteristics typical of a developmental state. It has used its mineral wealth to invest in education, industry, and infrastructure and to harness the informal sector in pursuit of economic development.[4] Even more authoritarian regimes such as Angola, Ethiopia, and Rwanda have promoted investments in agriculture, industry, and tourism or embarked on grand public works projects, prompting scholars to label such regimes as cases of "developmental patrimonialism" or "developmental authoritarianism."[5]

Although there is little doubt that developmental approaches have enjoyed a revival across the continent *and* that government officials still find ways to enrich themselves, I argue that both of these characteristics are compatible with the rise across Africa of what I term *entrepreneurial governance*—that is, government agencies, state-owned entities, or public investment funds are, either singularly or in partnership with private-sector actors, seizing investment opportunities in order to make a profit. Although such an approach facilitates the expansion of markets, it is also meant to bring financial returns to the state.[6] In the urban geography and sociology literatures from which it originates, two dynamics are understood in the use of the term *entrepreneurial governance*. First, the term calls attention to the fact that with the adoption of neoliberal policies from the late 1980s many state functions have shifted to the private sector and are now subject to market mechanisms.[7] Second, it recognizes that governments themselves are increasingly assessing risks, calculating potential profits, and pursuing strategies that bring returns on their investments.[8]

What are the drivers of the entrepreneurial governance in Africa, what is its likely impact, and who will benefit? This chapter focuses particularly on the means by which African governments have become involved in activities that complement those of the private sector and that realize profits for the state. Investment opportunities have been pursued through the creation of sovereign wealth funds, the reconfiguration of pension funds, restructured public companies, or political party companies that partner with private capital to invest in telecommunications, consumer goods, finance, real estate, and even city-building projects. The chapter first describes the diverse public investment vehicles that African governments are relying on to participate in projects that potentially generate returns. It then highlights the structural and historical features that condition governments' preferences for different funding mechanisms. It explains policy convergence by recognizing the continuing influence of international financial institutions and donors, the increasing power of private equity firms across the continent, the scale of investment, and the changing interests of governments. Drawing on comparative research from other regions, it concludes by exploring the political and economic implications of the growth of entrepreneurial governance in Africa.

PUBLIC INVESTMENT VEHICLES

In contrast to the objectives that motivated state intervention in African economies just after independence, entrepreneurial governance is driven neither by an ideological imperative to control the "commanding heights" in order to build the nation nor by an economic rationale that states are central to the production process. Rather, I argue that entrepreneurial governance in Africa relies on the use of state assets or state companies to realize a return on an investment either alone or together with private capital. It entails policy approaches and modes of administration that aim to support private-sector development—hence, its complementarity with developmental policy goals *and* market-based models now favored by African governments.

At least three types of public investment exemplify entrepreneurial governance: all can be grouped under the umbrella of sovereign wealth instruments and include sovereign wealth funds (SWFs), public pension or social security funds, and investment-driven parastatals or state-owned enterprises (SOEs). Along with SOEs, we will discuss "partystatals," or political party companies, which are found in some countries. This fourth type is a hybrid investment category, part public and part private, that is often located in regimes such as Rwanda, Ethiopia, and Angola, where the ruling party has been in power for a long time. Countries show preferences for particular instruments depending on their history, the level of capital market development, and their access to mineral resources.

Sovereign Wealth Funds

SWFs are state-owned investment funds consisting of assets such as revenues from sales of natural resources, other commodities, or privatization; foreign currency reserves; or an existing surplus in the balance of payments. Legislation creating an SWF is not always explicit about the fund's purpose: Governments may invest these funds in new projects, existing state-owned enterprises, or the stock market in order to realize returns from investments. Alternatively, fund returns may serve as protection against macroeconomic shocks when a resource such as oil undergoes a price "bust."[9] Other governments may rely on the return from SWF investments to fund social programs. For example, since the 1980s many state governments in the United States have relied on the returns from SWF investments to fund education.[10]

SWFs are typically associated with countries such as Norway that have a significant income from the sale of extractive resources such as oil and gas. With US$825 billion, Norway's Government Pension Fund-Global is the world's largest SWF, and its remarkable success has encouraged other governments in the Middle East and Africa to emulate its institutional design.[11] SWFs are relatively recent in Africa, but as Table 4.1 indicates, ten out of fifty-five countries on the continent have set up one or more funds to manage revenues.[12] Botswana and Algeria have had SWFs in place for over a decade to control their returns from diamonds and minerals (Botswana) and oil and gas (Algeria). Recently Nigeria and Angola created SWFs to handle proceeds from the sale of oil. Governments in Cameroon, Mauritius, South Sudan, Tanzania, Kenya, and Zimbabwe have indicated they intend to create SWFs to deal with expected income from natural gas, financial services, state-owned enterprises, or minerals.

Space does not permit an exhaustive description of African SWFs nor is information complete on their operation.[13] Instead, I highlight two funds in different institutional environments. One of the oldest funds in Africa, Botswana's Pula Fund (currently worth US$5.7 billion) was established in 1994 to manage foreign exchange reserves accumulated from diamond exports. The fund engages in long-term investments in developed, industrialized markets and follows a model typically relied upon by mutual fund investors in the United States or the United Kingdom.[14] It maintains a diversified portfolio with investments in about eight asset classes, ranging from fixed income to equity, with varying levels of risk and

Table 4.1   Sovereign Wealth Funds in Selected African Countries, 2016

Country	Name	Created	Assets (US$bn)	Transparency index
Algeria	Revenue Regulation Fund	2000	77.2	1
Angola	Sovereign Fund of Angola	2012	5.0	8
Botswana	Pula Fund	1994	5.7	6
Equatorial Guinea	Fund for Future Generations	2002	0.08	n/a
Gabon	Gabon Sovereign Wealth Funds (renamed 2010)	1998	0.4	n/a
Ghana	Ghana Petroleum Funds	2011	0.45	n/a
Libya	Libyan Investment Authority	2006	66.0	4
Mauritania	National Fund for Hydrocarbon Reserves	2006	0.3	1
Nigeria	Nigeria Sovereign Investment Authority	2011	1.4	9
Senegal	Fonds Souverain D'investissements Strategiques (Fonsis)	2012	1.0	n/a

Notes: The Linaburg-Maduell Transparency Index uses a 10-point system to gauge the degree of transparency of a fund with regard to its history, management, ethical and allocation guidelines, auditing practices, and address and contact information. Ten is the best or highest score; 8 is the recommended benchmark score; and 1 is the minimum score a fund can receive. We return to the Index later in the chapter.

Sources: Sovereign Wealth Fund Institute, "Sovereign Wealth Fund Rankings," 2016, www.swfinstitute.org/sovereign-wealth-fund-rankings; and "Linaburg-Maduell Transparency Index," 2016, www.swfinstitute.org/statistics-research/linaburg-maduell-transparency-index.

expected return. Details of the fund's performance are readily available in the Bank of Botswana's Annual Report.[15] Governance of the fund is transparent but complex. The Bank of Botswana is responsible for the fund's overall performance, but investment managers in fixed income and equity markets in the United States, Japan, and Europe manage 50 percent of the fund.[16]

According to the IMF, the act that created the fund did not explicitly state the fund's objectives nor address payments into and out of the fund, but the fund's operations over the past twenty years suggest a two-pronged use. First, the government relies on the fund to stabilize revenue owing to drops in the terms of trade or severe external shocks such as the 2008–2009 financial crisis. Second, the government depends on the fund for public investments in infrastructure, health, education, training, and large capital projects. In the last two decades the government has consistently invested about 25 percent of GDP in the fund.[17] As diamond reserves decline, however, the fund will need to depend on revenue from other sources in order to sustain growth.[18]

Other resource-dependent countries such as Nigeria and Angola have also created SWFs but in more unstable institutional environments than that of Botswana. In 2011 the Nigerian federal government established the Nigerian Sovereign

Investment Authority (NSIA) to manage a portion of the revenue from oil sales. The NSIA consists of three separate sovereign wealth funds, each of which receives a percentage of the US$1.4 billion in funds earmarked for investment: a stabilization fund (20 percent of funds), which anticipates price volatility in the oil markets; a fund for infrastructure development (40 percent); and the "future generations" fund (40 percent).[19] The NSIA was expected to replace the Excess Crude Account (ECA, created in 2004) owing to the unclear legal status of the ECA. As of 2015, however, the ECA still existed and had a balance of US$2.2 billion following allegations of unaccounted-for withdrawals.[20] Moreover, state governors in Nigeria have contested federal control over the revenues of the NSIA, claiming that oil wealth should be shared between federal and state governments. The continued existence of the ECA and intragovernmental conflict over revenue allocation have hampered efforts to increase the capital of the NSIA, leading analysts to wonder whether it will ever realize the objectives for which it was created.[21] Later we explore how a country's institutional environment affects fund management and transparency.

Public Pension Funds and Social Security

Related to SWFs but sourced from different assets are revenues from social security or state employees' pension funds. Government agencies either directly manage the funds or rely on financial intermediaries to manage the assets on the government's behalf. Unlike SWFs, social security programs and pension plans have a long history in many African countries. Yet until recently management of the funds has been poor, coverage of the population inadequate, and the payout of benefits insufficient. In addition to their poor performance, the coverage and design of programs display numerous cross-national differences, complicating analysis of the causes of their poor results. In Francophone Africa public pension funds have not covered all public employees; instead, some civil servants have paid into private pension schemes. In Anglophone countries social security has been limited to retirement and has not included benefits for injuries at work, maternity, sickness, or family members.[22] Employee contributions to social security programs also have ranged from 35 percent of earnings in Senegal to less than 10 percent in Rwanda, Liberia, Mauritius, and South Africa. The median contribution is approximately 20 percent of earnings.[23]

Gaps in coverage, inadequate payments to beneficiaries, and the adoption of neoliberal policies by African governments have provided the impetus to overhaul both contributions and payouts.[24] Between 2000 and 2012 forty-four governments implemented 217 reforms to pension and social security schemes.[25] These included a shift from a defined benefit to a prefinanced, defined contribution pension plan or the extension of social security coverage to include disability. Four countries—Zimbabwe, Kenya, South Africa, and Ghana—account for one-third of the reforms adopted, but partly this is a function of their more piecemeal reform processes. By contrast, Cote d'Ivoire adopted a comprehensive new social insurance code in 1999 and has amended it only once.[26]

Moreover, governments have also started to take seriously the investment potential of pension funds in the last decade. The United States set the precedent for the use of social security or pension funds as investment vehicles in 1978 when legislation allowed fund administrators to invest the pension funds of private-sector employees with the expectation of returns on investment.[27] Because pensions need to be available when part of the workforce retires, governments and private firms ideally seek to make investments that provide a long-term return with limited risk and to have diverse portfolios that spread risk across several asset classes. Just as African countries differ regarding contribution approaches, they also vary with respect to their investment strategies, as South Africa and Kenya illustrate.

Public pension fund assets of sixteen African countries equaled about US$340 billion in 2013–2015.[28] Accounting for 76 percent of total known assets, the largest public-asset manager in sub-Saharan Africa is the Public Investment Corporation (PIC), owned by the South African government. PIC does not manage South Africa's social security funds because payouts are funded by tax revenues to the government's budget rather than by investments; rather, PIC manages public pension funds totaling over 1.6 trillion rands (US$120 billion at 2015 exchange rates) on behalf of over thirty-five public-sector clients, the largest of which is the Government Employees Pension Fund (GEPF); GEPF accounts for 90 percent of the fund contributions.[29] PIC aims to make low-risk, long-term investments, giving market-based returns in six different asset classes, as Table 4.2 demonstrates.

Four asset classes—equities, property, the Isibaya Fund, and the Africa and Overseas Funds—comprise 60 percent of the total assets managed by PIC.[30] They range from investments in equities, including publicly listed firms on the Johannesburg Stock Exchange to unlisted, privately held equities. PIC has shares in major South African banks such as Standard Bank, Absa, and Nedbank; mining and technology firms; shopping malls (including malls in underserviced areas);

Table 4.2   PIC: Classes of Investment and Percentage of Total Funds Invested

Investment class	Percent
Fixed income assets (money and bond markets)	40
Local equity	49
Properties	4
Isibaya Fund	1
Offshore investments (rest of Africa and Overseas)	6
Total	100

Source: PIC, "Celebrating 20 Years of Democracy: Integrated Annual Report, 2014," 2014.

office complexes; and developmental projects. PIC directors work with fund managers from private equity firms on these investments rather than working alone.[31]

Whereas South Africa funds the payment of social security and other grants to citizens out of tax revenues contributed to the state budget, Tanzania and Kenya increasingly rely on investment returns generated from contributions to social security funds to finance benefits. With twenty-one reforms to its pensions and social security plans since 2000, Kenya has implemented perhaps the most comprehensive overhaul of its system.[32] There are five social security or pension schemes in Kenya, four for the formal sector and a recent fund established for the informal sector. Except for civil servants, who have their own fund, the majority of employees in Kenya's formal sector (15 percent of the total workforce) contribute to the National Social Security Fund (NSSF), whose assets of around US$1.3 billion are managed by the Kenyan government.[33] The NSSF is financed in a manner similar to that of social security in the United States. All registered firms with over five employees must pay social security taxes, which then go to the payment of benefits upon retirement. The NSSF is governed by a committee composed of the Minister for Labor and Human Resources (chair); permanent secretaries from Labor, the Office of the President, and Finance; and two representatives of workers and employers, respectively.[34]

In the past the NSSF had a reputation for corruption, rent seeking, and mismanagement. With the change of the party in power in 2002, government officials brought NSSF into compliance with the guidelines of the Retirement Benefits Act and subjected it to the regulatory oversight of the Revenue Benefits Authority (RBA). The RBA was established by the Retirement Benefits Act of 1997 and then was formally created in 2000 to regulate government and private-sector management of retirement benefits.[35] In 2003 the RBA underscored the lack of diversification in the NSSF portfolio, a lack of due diligence regarding particular investments, mismanagement, and noncompliance with the terms of the Retirement Benefits Act. The RBA noted that 75 percent of the NSSF's portfolio was largely invested in real estate—more than double the 30 percent rate statutorily recommended by the Act. Overexposure to the property market resulted in poor returns, with benefits outstripping contributions by 1997/1998.[36] After a series of reforms the portfolio was more diverse by 2013: real estate investments had dropped to 30 percent, and assets had been shifted to equities and government treasury bills and bonds.[37] These changes suggest that with proper oversight and institutional reform, improvements are possible (we return to this issue below). Other countries, including Ghana, Senegal, Mauritius, Zambia, and Rwanda, have introduced or are proposing reforms to the fiscal management of pension and social security schemes.[38]

Parastatals and "Partystatals" as Investors

Following independence, most governments in Africa nationalized former colonial companies in economic sectors as diverse as utilities, agriculture, shipping, and manufacturing. With the adoption of structural adjustment policies in the

1980s and 1990s, governments sold a majority of their state assets to the private sector, but many retained majority and minority interests in strategic sectors such as electricity, water, telecommunications, and extractive resources such as diamonds, copper, oil, gas, and coal.[39] Most of these parastatals have been restructured and corporatized so they run like private enterprises. Governments now rely on them either to generate profits or to make investments in other profitable sectors or companies. Some governments, particularly those with a history of state intervention, such as Tanzania or Mozambique, retain shares in a broad array of companies just to diversify the state's portfolio.

Using parastatals in this manner follows one of two approaches. In the first approach countries establish government agencies that manage the state's equity in parastatals and private companies. In the second approach individual parastatals may, in consultation with the Ministry under whose authority they fall, make targeted investments in other companies. The Institute for the Management of State Holdings (the Portuguese acronym is IGEPE) in Mozambique offers an example of the first approach. IGEPE is an independent government agency created in 2001 following the government's privatization of 1,200 state-owned enterprises. Its purpose is to liquidate or sell additional SOEs; allocate the state's remaining shares to the management, staff, and workers of companies; or to manage the state's remaining equity.[40] Since IGEPE's founding it has liquidated, privatized, or shifted to employees about 165 companies in its initial portfolio of 279 companies. Of the remaining 114 companies, IGEPE expects eventually to manage the state's minority or majority shares in about 100 firms.[41]

Mozambique is not primarily retaining state enterprises due to a nostalgic yearning for the era of the command economy or to sustain clientelistic relations with underperforming, overpaid workers; rather, the principles governing IGEPE treat state-owned enterprises as if they were private firms whose goal is to maximize profit. About half of the companies are designated as "strategic" companies, either because they produce something that is especially valuable, such as the energy provided by the Cahora Bassa Dam, or because they are symbols of national sovereignty, such as LAM, the Mozambican airline. Others include profitable companies in telecommunications, banking, and entertainment.[42]

These companies now constitute part of the state's investment portfolio, and like investments by private-sector interests, they are expected to generate revenue for the treasury and for investment in additional enterprises. Annual reports issued by IGEPE read like company reports from large private companies. They stress the principles of corporate governance and analyze in detail the return on investments. In 2013 about 87 percent of IGEPE's revenue came from dividends created by these companies.[43] Although countries such as Brazil and China have similar models, Mozambique's approach is rather rare on the African continent— only recently have other countries such as Zimbabwe considered this approach.[44]

A more common practice in Africa is the second approach, which consists of restructuring state-owned enterprises to act as holding companies or to take on private companies as strategic partners. They invest in other SOEs as well as private companies to retain state participation in a strategic sector, realize returns, and diversify government portfolios. We can identify two subtypes of restructured SOEs. The first is a public company that invests across diverse, even unrelated sectors of the economy, similar to diversified business groups in Latin America. The second subtype concentrates investments in upstream and downstream activities linked to its core business activity, be it telecommunications or mining.

Sonangol, the state oil company of Angola, illustrates the first subtype. After independence in 1975, it formed joint ventures with private oil companies to engage in oil drilling, refining, and distribution. Now it has branched out into related businesses such as insurance, pipeline production, and packaging, servicing, and storage of crude oil.[45] Sonangol is also involved in noncore businesses, including partnerships with Chinese state-owned companies in banking, construction, and forestry.[46] Further, it has invested in airlines, hotels, upscale housing, commercial real estate, metalworking, plastics, glass, and mattress production.[47]

Sonangol may be one of the few African parastatals with such diverse investments, but many others in South Africa, Tanzania, Namibia, Botswana, and Nigeria have certainly restructured since the 1990s. These parastatals more often correspond to the second subtype, exemplified by Zambia Consolidated Copper Mines-International Holdings, Ltd. (ZCCM-IH), and Debswana in Botswana. ZCCM-IH is heir to the former copper parastatal in Zambia, which was responsible for mining and exporting Zambia's most important asset. Following the widespread privatization of most of Zambia's parastatals, the government restructured its remaining interests in copper into a holding company with 87.6 percent government participation. The remaining 12.4 percent of shares are publicly listed on the small Zambian stock market and currently are held by around twenty-four hundred private investors. ZCCM-IH is now a major investment company in Zambia, particularly in the mining and power sectors, and holds shares of 10 to 100 percent in thirteen companies.[48] It invests in upstream and downstream activities related to its core business. Similarly, Debswana, the joint venture between the government of Botswana and DeBeers, has investments in upstream and downstream activities related to its core diamond business. It has developed this investment strategy over the past forty years. Finally, the Nigerian National Petroleum Corporation (NNPC) and MTC, a wholly government-owned telecommunications company in Namibia, follow a similar practice of investing along with the private sector in ventures related to their core businesses.[49]

Finally, political party companies, or partystatals, occupy a hybrid category that blurs the line between public and private enterprise. They are owned by political parties or party elites and often legally registered as such; they often include prominent party members on their boards along with individuals with business expertise.[50] Their purposes are mixed depending on the country. In the case of Crystal Ventures Limited or Prime Holdings in Rwanda, for example, their practices and objectives appear to reinforce the state's market-based, developmental agenda. They have partnered with foreign capital to kick-start or expand sectors in Rwanda such as telecommunications, real estate, consumer goods, and food and beverage distribution, and in doing so, they contribute to state stability.[51] In other cases such as GEFI, a holding company of the ruling MPLA party in Angola, or SPI Gestão e Investimento, S.A.R.L., a company composed of Frelimo party notables in Mozambique, the goal is to realize revenue for the party and its members through diverse investments in hotels, breweries, casinos, banking, and media.[52] In most instances, however, party companies rely on special linkages and personal ties with different branches of the state administration to pursue their investments.

EXPLAINING ENTREPRENEURIAL STATE OBJECTIVES

The development and uses of different investment vehicles and revenue-enhancing policies is still taking place, thus explanations of their causes must necessarily be provisional rather than definitive. There are at least four reasons for the entrepreneurial practices of governments: the influence of donors, investment partners, and international financial institutions; the growth of private equity firms on the continent; the increased scale of investment; and changes in government priorities. Together they show how different interests have aligned around a common set of objectives. These features may explain why different regimes are demonstrating convergence with respect to policy choices and common investment tool kits while at the same time they exhibit mixed records regarding levels of investment expertise, accountability to stakeholders, and public transparency.

Donors, Investment Partners, and International Financial Institutions

In response to global changes and an increase in the presence of institutional investors, international financial institutions and donors have encouraged African governments to become more entrepreneurial through the mobilization of state assets for investment. For supporters of economic reforms, the formation of SWFs or the use of social security funds to finance investments is the logical next step in the prescription for creating or expanding markets. Complementing this effort, international and regional financial institutions such as the African Development Bank have investment arms that, along with private and public capital, help to finance large infrastructure projects or sectors such as health and agriculture. For example, the International Finance Corporation (IFC), a member of the World Bank Group, established an asset management company several years ago to strengthen local financial markets, especially in frontier and emerging markets.[53]

Moreover, developed, industrialized countries commonly rely on development finance institutions to seek returns on investments in developing countries. Most donors, including the United States, the United Kingdom, and France but also Brazil, China, and Saudi Arabia, have recently created or reorganized development finance institutions with mandates to pursue investments in emerging markets such as those in Africa. They contribute to private sector–driven retail development, office blocks, telecommunications infrastructure, cement factories, and Coca-Cola bottling plants. For example, the Overseas Private Investment Corporation (OPIC), the development finance arm of the US government established more than forty years ago, provides financing to American companies interested in investing in Africa and other regions of the world. It also supports projects that expand electrical services or provide loans for small businesses.[54] Similarly the Chinese government has created numerous holding and investment companies, banks, and other funding mechanisms to spearhead its investments abroad, notably in Angola but also in Tanzania, Congo, and Mozambique.[55]

The Growth of Private Equity Funds

Whereas donors often finance large infrastructural projects such as hydroelectric dams and major road corridors or provide budget support to cash-strapped African governments for education and health care, private investment has surpassed overseas development assistance (ODA) in importance. Historically, private investors have been both cautious and unwelcome in Africa, but owing to the exhaustion of markets and the effects of the global financial crisis in the United States and Europe, they have expanded into other markets.[56] As Moss shows, private inflows (FDI and portfolio investment) into Africa began to outstrip official overseas development assistance in the 2000s. Although FDI has been relatively stable, portfolio investment has replicated the volatility witnessed in global markets with the economic downturn. Nevertheless, it has recovered after a sharp drop in 2008.

Private equity (PE) groups are particularly noticeable for their rapid expansion as intermediaries in the investment process. PE groups typically rely on the capital of institutional investors, insurance companies, and wealthy individuals, or the pension funds of national and local governments to engage in high-risk, high-return investments. In exchange for capital, they research investment opportunities, provide information to clients, and evaluate risk. Recently PE groups have recognized opportunities in pension funds, SWFs, and other assets held by African governments.[57] There are approximately 172 global fund managers based in the United States, the United Kingdom, France, Saudi Arabia, China, and elsewhere that include African countries in their portfolios. In the last ten years private equity has raised nearly US$20 billion for projects on the continent. Intra-African investment is growing, too, with approximately US$4 billion in investments in 2013 and 120 PE firms registered across Africa. Multilateral or bilateral donors partially finance these funds, but public and private institutional investors and individuals of high net worth also contribute.[58]

Investments by PE firms include venture capital for new projects in consumer goods, health care, agribusiness, corporate and city branding campaigns, and ecotourism.[59] PE firms also engage in leveraged buyouts of existing, usually highly indebted firms in a variety of sectors, from an oil marketing firm in Nigeria to a media company in South Africa. Alternatively, PE firms rely on so called mezzanine capital, which is a hybrid funding tool that combines debt and equity financing to acquire whole or partial stakes in existing firms. The use of mezzanine capital has mostly been confined to South Africa, but it is expanding to other countries such as Botswana, Namibia, and Nigeria.[60]

The Scale of Investment

The characteristics of investments offer another explanation for the rise of entrepreneurial governance. The scale of projects, from mining to commercial agriculture, requires government capital. Banks' high interest rates and reluctance to loan money without substantial guarantees have prompted governments to finance large projects. Until recently, high prices and growing demand for commodities from Brazil, India, and China drove the creation or expansion of oil production by private and public investors in Ghana, Angola, Nigeria, Chad, South Sudan, and Algeria. The mining of copper in Zambia and the DRC; gold in Zimbabwe, Mali, South Africa, and Ghana; iron ore and bauxite in Guinea; and coal in Mozambique have seen rapid growth in the past five years, and nearly all of these investments include public participation. In connection with the African Union's promotion of the resource-based industrialization and development strategy (RAIDS), efforts by governments to foster local procurement, spatial-development initiatives, export-processing zones, and trade corridors are expected to lure additional investors to the continent and, hence, will require large outlays of capital.

Alongside investments in minerals, agricultural goods, and development corridors, financial services, consumer goods, and the provision of urban residential housing for Africa's rising urban middle class present attractive investment opportunities. Investors and governments recognized the value of African consumers when sales of cell phones expanded across the continent over a decade ago. Around 4 million Africans had access to cell phones in 1998; by 2011 there were nearly 500 million subscribers. Two South African cellular telecommunications companies, MTN and Vodacom, both around twenty years old, dominate the telecommunications market in countries such as Ghana, Tanzania, Democratic Republic of Congo, Nigeria, and Uganda.[61] Both companies are publicly listed on the JSE; PIC also holds about 18 percent of the shares in MTN. Given the consistent profitability of the telecommunications sector, such an investment brings a reliable return to PIC.[62]

The growth of the telecommunications sector supports claims by investment analysts and policymakers that urbanization and an African middle class are increasing. According to UN Habitat, about 40 percent of the continent's population lived in urban areas in 2009; the percentage is likely to be around 50 percent by 2035.[63] Alongside urbanization, a middle class is emerging, although estimates of its size vary depending on the criteria used to determine it. In a recent study

Thurlow, Resnick, and Ubogu define members of the middle class as those who have completed secondary school, have access to piped water and electricity (from any source), and are employed in skilled, nonfarm labor.[64] By this measure South Africa in the mid-2000s had the largest middle class as a percentage of its total population in Africa, whereas Nigeria had the smallest.[65] Although the middle class is fragile and varies considerably across the continent, its access to discretionary spending explains the growing demand for consumer goods. Panel data from Dar es Salaam shows that the share of the household budget going to nonfood goods such as cell phones, personal products, and food eaten outside the home rose between 2007–2009, while the share of the budget spent on charcoal declined.[66]

The prospect of making profits by tapping into the pent-up demand of mostly urban consumers drives a host of initiatives, many of which receive investments from government pension funds and SOEs. Some are eminently practical and long overdue, such as housing, retail banking services, processed food, ready-to-wear clothing, and cosmetics. Others are grandiose, such as the many city-building projects that are underway or completed in Zambia, Democratic Republic of Congo, Kenya, Ghana, Equatorial Guinea, Sudan, Tunisia, Angola, and South Africa.[67]

Government Interests

Most governments in Africa have identifiable political and economic reasons for pursuing investment opportunities in a particular way. As indicated above, countries with natural resources, such as Nigeria, Algeria, Botswana, and Ghana, hope to secure a revenue stream through SWFs. Equally, the institutional legacy of extensive state intervention in Tanzania, Angola, Ethiopia, and Mozambique partially explains why parastatals and party companies continue to operate in these countries. Governments not only want to retain assets they consider strategic but also they recognize the possibility of reaping profits from expanded investment opportunities in mining or biofuels. Except for South Africa, these countries have a low tax base and rely on revenue from restructured parastatals. Paulo Zucula, the minister for Transport and Communications in Mozambique, explained why the government retained ownership of the cellular telecommunications company: "the dividends from the company feed public revenue."[68]

Moreover, as life expectancy and, consequently, the number of retirees increases, governments face pressure from existing and former civil servants and parastatal employees to provide decent benefits. Equally, the effects of HIV/AIDS drive citizens' demands for greater social protection. In order to sustain such payouts, governments are looking for returns. The promise of a decent return on pension funds explains PIC's investment in office parks and malls in South Africa and on the continent.[69] Other countries' investments of public pension funds into residential and commercial projects follow a similar logic. In Ghana, for example, the Social Security and National Insurance Trust (SSNIT) seeks to provide "a safe investment portfolio for workers' pensions."[70] SSNIT invests about 10 percent of its portfolio in real estate and has financed and sold high-cost housing.[71]

Political and ideological considerations complement government efforts to seek a return on investments. Governments in Mozambique, Uganda, South Africa, Angola, and Kenya have made commitments to support the growth of indigenous entrepreneurs and a black middle class. Where investments include domestic capital, state involvement is a form of protection against undue risk taking by the private sector, but it is also linked to favors to party loyalists in exchange for support, especially in authoritarian countries.[72] In more democratic contexts such as Ghana, Botswana, and South Africa, political parties partially rely on urban middle-class managers, property owners, and formal-sector workers for votes. The distribution of goods, from housing to roads, is a means for ruling parties to receive a political return on their investment. Even where the votes of a particular group are not critical to a ruling party's electoral success, governments seek stability. To satisfy their constituents, national and provincial governments are partnering with international financial institutions and the private sector to invest in housing, shopping malls, and office blocks; to enhance the variety of financing mechanisms; and to offer consumer goods.

THE IMPLICATIONS OF THE INVESTOR STATE

Although the embrace of entrepreneurial governance is too recent to assess its impact systematically, it is possible to highlight its potential gains and risks. First, if governments can distribute public and merit goods while also receiving a return on their investments, then entrepreneurial ambitions can complement rather than conflict with developmental inclinations. Furthermore, if the provision of housing, electricity, and roads addresses rural and urban shortages, these gains could enhance the legitimacy of governments across Africa. This appears to be part of the motivation behind the creation of PIC's Isibaya Fund in South Africa. The fund invests in projects that support the government's Broad-Based Black Economic Empowerment (B-BBEE) policy. As stated in the revised legislation of 2003 and the accompanying B-BBEE Codes of good practice issued in 2007, the policy aims to provide opportunities to historically disadvantaged groups in South Africa and to create a workforce that is representative of the demographic makeup of the country.[73]

Consistent with the criteria expressed in the B-BBEE guidelines, the Isibaya Fund finances fund managers to start and sustain their own investment portfolios or to restructure companies that will create jobs for the historically disadvantaged. It invests in affordable housing projects, toll roads, health care provision, and small and medium-sized enterprises, especially those benefiting black youth and women.[74] Thus, some of PIC's investment objectives overlap with the broader social goals of the ANC government. In more democratic contexts such as South

Africa, these developments may satisfy voters and signal a more programmatic approach to policies than previous governments have had.

Second, as mortality rates drop and populations age in Africa, governments are facing pressures to fund more entitlements, not only for the poorest segments of the population but also for the disabled, the diseased, and the elderly.[75] In Kenya, for example, the number of elderly people in the population is expected to triple by 2050. Because customary forms of social support are declining owing to urbanization and migration, the government in association with other stakeholders expects to offer greater support to this segment of the population.[76] Pressures from civil servants and formal-sector workers—a small but politically powerful segment of the population—may be driving pension reform among the more democratic governments, as appears to be the case in Ghana.[77] But all across Africa pension and social security reforms, both prefunding and financing contributions, are common elements of social policy. By seeking returns on their investments and adopting diversified portfolios, governments appear to be more conscious than in the past of the need to assure adequate funding for future provisions. Although it may take a long time to cover the informal sector, which is the largest segment of most African economies, many governments are now proactively addressing pension and social security provisions and returns for this group.

Third, new financial tools such as SWFs, pensions, and social security funds to finance projects such as housing and infrastructure compensate for Africa's "shallow financial sectors," which remain weak in most countries.[78] State investments in mining, biofuels, and construction bring much needed capital to nascent or expanding projects in these areas and help build support for governments from foreign and indigenous businesses. Moreover, because these funds can be mobilized more quickly than financing from government budgets, their use may quicken the pace of project completion.[79]

Yet the risks of entrepreneurial approaches are considerable. First, whether returns are positive or negative, states' participation in revenue-generating activities politically and economically aligns them with the interests of finance capital and the goals of profit making.[80] In effect, governments become "money managers" for financial interests: They enable these interests to dominate by reducing regulatory oversight, and they facilitate the adoption of policies that stifle demands by labor or consumer groups.[81] Catering to the demands of a minority tends to concentrate power and resources in that group and reduces governmental responsiveness to ordinary citizens. Over time the penchant of states to act as investors could generate political and economic instability.

Second, one of the justifications for SWFs is that they offer a hedge against the price volatility of the resource that often comprises the basis of the funds. But this argument presumes that global markets are stable, that the economic climate is good, and that states make investments in their own best interests. Most African governments lack experience with investments. If history is any indication, too often governments in Africa rely on revenue to finance extravagant lifestyles or to buy voter support. Alternatively, overexposure to commodities and commercial and residential real estate markets could put many SWFs and social security funds at risk of heavy losses should market volatility occur.[82]

A third, related point is that SWFs give states the opportunity to be "autonomy-maximizing institutions"[83]—that is, they can become vehicles through which governments protect themselves against domestic or foreign competition by using their access to large amounts of capital to make strategic investments. These investments may be in economically valuable sectors, or they may buy political capital for political elites by ameliorating potential opponents. Where rules are more opaque and mechanisms of accountability function poorly, however, SWFs may simply serve the interests of a privileged elite.[84] Used in this way, SWFs may not enhance the general social welfare, nor can the public hold them accountable. These uses of SWFs are compatible with the notion of entrepreneurial governance, but they suggest that the public is less likely to enjoy the benefits of returns on investments.

Owing to their recent emergence, we do not know whether SWFs in Africa will have these characteristics, but the signs are discouraging. The SWF Institute's Transparency Index gauges the extent to which an SWF provides information about a fund's management, the value and structure of its portfolio, and its returns on investments. The index also determines whether the fund issues audited yearly reports and publicizes its ethical standards. It rates funds from 1 to 10 and recommends that an SWF achieves at least an 8 in order to meet the threshold for transparency.[85] As Table 4.1 above indicates, only two of the SWF funds, Angola and Nigeria, currently meet the minimum transparency rating of 8, and even these rankings are questionable. In Angola the head of the sovereign wealth fund is the son of the president, which suggests that "arm's length" criteria were not strictly applied to his appointment. Furthermore, the relationship between the Nigerian SWF and the excess crude account, which has been subject to much controversy over unauthorized withdrawals and was supposed to have been phased out, is unclear, and the NSIA is mired in squabbles over who has control over financing.[86]

Fourth, investments in real estate are problematic because these markets are underdeveloped, and assessing the value of property is in its infancy everywhere except in South Africa. Unfortunately, restricted options for investment across the continent have contributed to the concentration of state assets in real estate projects, especially in smaller markets such as Tanzania and Kenya or less diversified economies such as Angola. Although housing shortages are common in many urban areas and therefore demand is high, the explosive rise in housing and commercial real estate prices is, unfortunately, replicating some of the speculative patterns that characterize real estate markets in developed countries. In Kenya, for example, property values tripled between 2000 and 2012, and the average price for a one- to three-bedroom home in Nairobi was 11 million shillings, or nearly US$131,000.[87] At this price only wealthy residents and those with cash in hand are able to afford homes and apartments because mortgages are available to just a small percentage of the population.[88]

In Angola's capital of Luanda the surfeit of high- and upper-middle-income housing that has been built, often with government financing, suggests that there is a real danger of following the Minskyan boom-bust cycle of financial collapse, where investors and developers create housing bubbles based on unrealistic expectations about what the market can bear.[89] To the extent that states are engaging in such activities to support a rising middle class, they are also exposing that class to the risks inherent in speculative real estate booms. A collapse would therefore doubly affect a percentage of formal-sector workers: first because civil servants, the police, and bureaucrats in countries such as Tanzania and Kenya have relied on loans from their pension funds to purchase homes, and second because a portion of pension funds in countries such as South Africa, Ghana, Kenya, Rwanda, and Tanzania are often invested in real estate development.

Lastly, regulatory complications abound with these new financial tools. To an even greater extent than in the United States and Europe, there is limited oversight of institutional and private-investor practices and, thus, few means for ordinary citizens to hold investors accountable. A lack of constraints on the type of investment and on what constitutes an acceptable level of debt can lead to risky practices and negative results. Although most publicly financed funds claim to adhere to principles of corporate governance and corporate social responsibility, these claims are difficult to verify without effective regulatory oversight. Even PIC, which is one of the best managed funds on the African continent, had some financial inconsistencies in a recent audit, despite detailed regulations issued in the Public Finance Management Act (PFMA) of 2000. According to the auditor general, "irregular expenditures," procurement practices that failed to conform to the guidelines in the PFMA, and fraudulent behavior by an employee were noted in the annual audit of 2011.[90]

In South Africa the King Reports (1994, revised 2002 and 2009) articulate the principles of corporate governance that public entities should follow, and subsequent regulations such as the PFMA stipulate the procedures that enforce those principles.[91] Principles adopted in Kenya and Mauritius are closely modeled on those of South Africa,[92] but more oversight is required. A recent study in Mauritius noted that only 30 percent of companies surveyed complied with the government's code of corporate governance.[93] In the rest of Africa, where both markets and democracy are still fragile, principles of corporate governance are not widely known or practiced, despite commitments expressed in the New Partnership for African Development (NEPAD) and embodied in its Africa Peer Review Mechanism (APRM). NEPAD's Peer Review of Ghana noted, for example, that "there is little awareness about corporate governance in Ghana."[94]

Corporate governance also applies to the private sector, and here the actions of private equity firms raise a red flag. As they have done in other parts of the world, private equity firms have influenced governments in Africa's markets to underwrite risky and/or long-term investments and to contribute the assets of pension funds or resource revenues to these investments. Yet the identities of investors in private equity funds are often unknown, and their business dealings can be obscure. By definition, private equity is interested in high-risk, high-return investments. PE funds pose moral hazards in that fund managers have an incentive to accentuate the high expected returns on investment over the potential pitfalls, thereby exposing investors to losses if they do not carefully research fund managers' track records.[95] A lack of experience in investing and information asymmetries could leave SWFs or public pension funds vulnerable to abuse by such firms. Given the past records of African governments with respect to corruption, it cannot be expected that they will exercise the appropriate oversight.

CONCLUSION

To be certain, the rhetoric of the developmental state has resurfaced across Africa, and there have also been a number of high-profile projects, from South Africa to Ethiopia, that suggest that development is back on the agenda. Along with development finance institutions from other countries or international financial institutions, African governments are investing in infrastructure and banking. Together with domestic and foreign private equity firms, they are financing shopping malls and office complexes. Yet the different public-funding vehicles and their uses discussed in this chapter suggest that African states are also occupying new roles as investors or money managers[96] whose interests are more closely aligned with those of the private sector than ever before. Governments are seeking steady to high returns on investments in natural resources, energy, telecommunications, and housing. Moreover, states as economic actors serve different interest groups from those they served in the 1960s and 1970s. In the current economy states aid and protect foreign and domestic investors, civil servants, and the upper classes. In league with foreign companies, they are seeking returns from biofuels, coal, copper, and oil.

African countries managed to avoid the negative effects of the global financial crisis in 2008–2009 mostly because their level of exposure was not as great as that of more developed countries. This chapter demonstrates that investment forms taking shape in Africa are beginning to mimic those that have been adopted in the West and that great caution should be exercised to avoid the outcomes recently experienced by developed countries. Africa's exposure to the boom and bust of finance is increasing, and African governments will be heavily implicated in the misery that follows should a downturn occur. Because governments are using sovereign wealth funds, pension funds, parastatals, and party companies to generate returns from natural resource extraction and property development, the negative consequences of such a downturn may ripple through societies, affecting the highest as well as the lowest income groups.

The appearance of new sources and types of public investment across the continent thus places common demands on diverse governments to improve their regulatory and institutional environments. In response many countries have adopted principles of corporate governance, appointed auditor generals and other regulatory authorities, adhered to the APRM, and pledged to be more transparent. But if the past is any guide, enforcing principles of corporate governance and empowering regulatory authorities in this new political and economic climate will require sustained and collective efforts by citizens to hold entrepreneurial governments accountable.

NOTES

1. Transparency International, "Corruption Perceptions Index 2015" (2015), pp. 6–7, www.transparency.org/whatwedo/publication/cpi_2015. The findings are based on surveys of citizens' perceptions of corruption in those countries included in the index.

2. Chalmers Johnson, "The Developmental State: Odyssey of a Concept," in *The Developmental State*, ed. Meredith Woo-Cumings (Ithaca: Cornell University Press, 1999), pp. 32–60.

3. Trevor Manuel, "Address by the Minister in the Presidency: National Planning Commission, Trevor Manuel, at the Wits Graduate School of Public Development Management" (October 26, 2009); President Jacob Zuma, "Closing Address by President Jacob Zuma to the ANC National Policy Conference, Gallagher Estates, Johannesburg" (June 29, 2012), www.anc.org.za/show.php?id=9727.

4. Peter Meyns, and Charity Musamba, eds., "The Developmental State in Africa: Problems and Prospects," INEF-Report 101/2010 Institute for Development and Peace, University of Duisberg-Essen (2010), p. 52.

5. Hilary Matfess, "Developmental Authoritarianism in Rwanda and Ethiopia," *African Studies Review* 58, no. 2 (2015), 181–204; Centro de Estudos e Investigação Cientíca, *Relatório Económico de Angola 2010* (Luanda: Universidade Católica de Angola, June 2011), pp. 72–75, 141; Sylvia Croese, "1 Million Houses? Angola's National Reconstruction and Chinese and Brazilian Engagement," in *Strengthening the Civil Society Perspective Series II: China and Other Emerging Powers in Africa* (Cape Town: Fahamu, nd), 7–29; David Booth and Frederick Golooba-Mutebi, "Developmental Patrimonialism? The Case of Rwanda," *African Affairs* 111, no. 444 (2012), pp. 379–403.

6. Tuna Taşan-Kok, "Entrepreneurial Governance: Challenges of Property-Led Urban Regeneration Projects," *Tijdschrift voor Economische en Sociale Geografie* 2 (2010),126–149; Wendy Brown, *Undoing the Demos: Neoliberalism's Stealth Revolution* (Cambridge, MA: MIT Press, 2015).

7. David Harvey, "From Managerialism to Entrepreneurialism: The Transformation of Urban Governance in Late Capitalism," *Geografiska Annaler: Series B, Human Geography* 71, no. 1 (1989), pp. 3–17.

8. Jamie Peck, "Entrepreneurial Urbanism: Between Uncommon Sense and Dull Compulsion," *Geografiska Annaler: Series B, Human Geography* 96, no. 4 (2014), 396–401; Brown, *Undoing the Demos*.

9. Adam D. Dixon and Ashby H. B. Monk, "What Role for Sovereign Wealth Funds in Africa's Development?" Oil-to-Cash Initiative Background Paper, Center for Global Development (October 2011).

10. Ibid.

11. Gordon L. Clark, Adam D. Dixon, and Ashby H. B. Monk, *Sovereign Wealth Funds: Legitimacy, Governance, and Global Power* (Princeton, NJ: Princeton University Press,

2013), 124; Sovereign Wealth Fund Institute, "Sovereign Wealth Fund Rankings" (2016), www.swfinstitute.org/sovereign-wealth-fund-rankings.

12. Triki and Faye list fifteen SWFs in Africa, but operations or assets in Chad, Congo, Namibia, São Tomé and Principe, and Sudan could not be verified; see Thouraya Triki and Issa Faye, "Africa's Quest for Development: Can Sovereign Wealth Funds Help?" African Development Bank, Working Paper Series no. 142 (December 2011).

13. Triki and Faye, "Africa's Quest."

14. Sovereign Wealth Fund Institute, "Pula Fund" (2012), www.swfinstitute.org/swfs/pula-fund.

15. Bank of Botswana, "Annual Report 2014" (2014).

16. Linah K. Mohohlo, "Management of Commodity Revenues-Botswana's Case," IMF Institute and Central Bank of Algeria, High Level Seminar on Natural Resources, Finance and Development: Confronting Old and New Challenges, Algiers, Algeria (November 4–5, 2010), www.imf.org/external/np/seminars/eng/2010/afrfin/pdf/Mohohlo1.pdf.

17. International Monetary Fund, "Macroeconomic Policy Frameworks for Resource-Rich Developing Countries," Background Paper 1, suppl. 1 (August 24, 2012), pp. 33–38.

18. International Monetary Fund "Regional Outlook: Sub-Saharan Africa, Recovery and New Risks," World Economic and Financial Surveys (April 2011).

19. Ndubuisi Francis, "FG Injects $550m into Sovereign Wealth Fund," ThisDayLive (February 11, 2014), www.thisdaylive.com/articles/fg-injects-550m-into-sovereign-wealth-fund/171116.

20. Joshua Olufemi and Richard Akinwumi, "Investigation: At Least N11.56 Trillion Excess Crude Fund Unaccounted for in 8 Years," *Premium Times* (July 16, 2015), www.premiumtimesng.com/news/headlines/186/80-Investigation-at-least-N11–56-trillion-excess-crude-fund-unaccounted-for-in-8-years.html; George Taiwo, "FG to 'Empty' Excess Crude Account," *The Cable* (November 9, 2015), www.thecable.ng/fg-to-empty-excess-crude-account.

21. Editorial, "Controversial Sovereign Wealth Fund," *Punch* (September 11, 2012), www.punchng.com/editorial/controversial-sovereign-wealth-fund; Javier Blas, "Protecting Nigeria Oil SWF Is No Easy Task," Reports, FT.Com (October 10, 2013), www.ft.com/intl/cms/s/0/69325c28-2440-11e3-a8f7-00144feab7de.html#axzz2zpJjRW1s; Chris Kay and Gavin Serkin, "Nigeria Plans to Boost Capital of Sovereign Wealth Fund," *Bloomberg News* (January 20 2014), www.bloomberg.com/news/2014-01-20/nigeria-plans-to-boost-capital-of-sovereign-wealth-fund.html.

22. Luca Barbone and Luis-Alvaro Sanchez B., "Pensions and Social Security in Sub-Saharan Africa: Issue and Options," Paper presented at the XIII International Social Security Association African Regional Conference, Accra, Ghana (July 6–9, 1999).

23. Ibid.

24. Fiona Stewart and Juan Yermo, "Pensions in Africa," OECD Working Papers on Insurance and Private Pensions no. 30 (OECD publishing, January 2009).

25. International Social Security Association, "Social Security Country Profiles" (2014), www.issa.int.

26. Ibid.

27. Patrick Purcell and Jennifer Staman, "Summary of the Employee Retirement Security Act (ERISA)," Congressional Research Service, 7-5700, RL 34443 (May 19, 2009), http://aging.senate.gov/crs/pension7.pdf.

28. RisCura, "Bright Africa 2015: The Drivers, Enablers and Managers of Investment on the Continent" (2015), https://gallery.mailchimp.com/683490cbd9fe65e25cab9411d/files/Bright_Africa_2015_02.pdf.

29. PIC, "Celebrating 20 Years of Democracy: Integrated Annual Report, 2014" (2014).

30. Ibid.

31. Ibid. and Yondela Silimela, Asset Manager, PIC, Johannesburg, interview (July 14, 2011).

32. Kenya, Retirement Benefits Authority (2012), www.rba.go.ke.

33. Ibid. Private-sector employees may also contribute to pension funds at their place of work if their employer provides one.

34. Ibid.

35. Kenya, "Retirement Benefits Act" no. 3 (1997); Edward Odundo, "Supervision of a Public Pension Fund: Experience and Challenges in Kenya," Powerpoint presentation, Second Public Pension Fund Management Conference, World Bank, Washington, DC (May 5–7, 2003).

36. Odundo, "Supervision of a Public Pension."

37. Kenya, "NSSF Annual Report and Financial Statements 2013" (2013), p. 14.

38. World Bank, "Pensions," African Social Policy Protection Briefs (December 2012), http://siteresources.worldbank.org/INTAFRICA/Resources/social-protection-policy-brief-pensions-EN-2012.pdf; Eugene Kwibuka, "Pensioners Criticise New Pension Bill," New Times (February 25, 2015), www.newtimes.co.rw/section/article/2015–02–25/186332; Mauricio Soto, Vimal Thakoor, and Martin Petri, "Pension Reforms in Mauritius: Fair and Fast-Balancing Social Protection and Fiscal Sustainability," IMF Working Paper (June 2015), www.imf.org/external/pubs/ft/wp/2015/wp15126.pdf; Rebecca Mushota, "Pension Reforms On," Times of Zambia (April 8, 2015), www.times.co.zm/?p=55410.

39. M. Anne Pitcher, Party Politics and Economic Reform in Africa's Democracies (Cambridge: Cambridge University Press, 2012).

40. Hipolito Halema, president, Council of Administration, IGEPE, Maputo, interview (June 30, 2011).

41. IGEPE, "Relatorio e Contas" (2013), www.igepe.org.mz/images/stories/Relatorio_e_Contas_2013.pdf.

42. Ibid.

43. Ibid.

44. Tawanda Musarurwa, "Zimbabwe: Gov't to Draw Parastatal Lessons from BRICS," The Herald (July 6, 2012).

45. Ricardo Soares de Oliveira, Magnificent and Beggar Land: Angola Since the Civil War (London: Hurst and Company, 2015), pp. 35–40.

46. Lee Levkowitz, Marta McLellan Ross, and J. R. Warner, "The 88 Queensway Group: A Case Study in Chinese Investors' Operations in Angola and Beyond," US-China Economic Security Review Commission (July 10, 2009).

47. Aylton Melo, "Sonangol consolida investimento de 128 milhões USD na ZEE," Expansão (May 25, 2012); Soares de Oliveira, Magnificent and Beggar Land, 35–40, 63–66.

48. ZCCM-IH, "ZCCM-Investment Holdings PLC" (2014), www.zccm-ih.com.zm.

49. Nigerian National Petroleum Corporation (2012), www.nnpcgroup.com; MTC, "Annual Report" (2011), www.mtc.com.na/annual_reports/2011/annual_report_2011.pdf; State Mining Corporation (Stamico), "Stamico: State Mining Corporation" (2012), http://stamico.co.tz.

50. Pritish Behuria, "Between Party Capitalism and Market Reforms—Understanding Sector Differences in Rwanda," Journal of Modern African Studies 53, no. 3 (2015), 415–450.

51. Ibid.; Booth and Golooba-Mutebi, "Developmental Patrimonialism?"

52. Rafael Marques de Morais, "MPLA, Sociedade Anónima," Pambazuka News (February 8, 2010); Soares de Oliveira, Magnificent and Beggar Land, 98; M. Anne Pitcher, Transforming Mozambique: The Politics of Privatization, 1975–2000 (Cambridge: Cambridge

University Press, 2002), 158–162; SPI Gestão e Investimento, S.A.R.L., "Financial Shareholdings" (2016), www.spi.co.mz.

53. World Bank, "International Finance Corporation: What We Do" (2012), www1.ifc
.org/wps/wcm/connect/CORP_EXT_Content/IFC_External_Corporate_Site/What+We
+Do/Investment+Services.

54. Jim McTague, "Friendly Big Brother," *Barron's* 74, no. 28 (July 11, 1994), 32; Overseas Private Investment Corporation (2012), www.opic.gov.

55. Levkowitz, Ross, and Warner, "The 88 Queensway Group," p. 2.

56. Banker, Major South African Bank, Johannesburg, interview (July 14, 2011); Principal, Private Equity Firm, Nairobi, interview (August 15, 2012).

57. Principal, interview; David Ashiagbor, Nadiya Satyamurthy, Mike Casey, and Joevas Asare, eds., *Pension Funds and Private Equity: Unlocking Africa's Potential* (London: Commonwealth Secretariat, 2014).

58. Luke Goldsmith, "Africa-Based Private Equity Fund Managers," Prequin (March 6, 2013), www.prequin.com/blog/101/6321/africa-pe-gps; Private Equity Africa, "Africa Deals Hit $4bn in 2013" (June 2, 2014), cited on Prequin website, www.prequin.com/item
/africa-deals-hit-4bn-in-2013/102/8330.

59. Principal, interview.

60. Thomas Schwartz, "Mezzanine Financing Is the New Kid on the Block," *Business Report* (September 19, 2006); Vantage Capital (2012), www.vantagecapital.co.za; Patricia Kuo, "Vantage Capital Raises $223 Million for Second Mezzanine Fund," *Bloomberg Business Week* (June 4, 2012), www.businessweek.com/news/2012–06–04/vantage-capital
-raises-223-million-for-second-mezzanine-fund.

61. MTN, *MTN Group Limited Integrated Report* (December 31, 2013), 2–3; Vodacom, *Vodacom: Integrated Report* (March 31, 2013), pp. 20–21.

62. PIC, "Celebrating 20 Years of Democracy."

63. UN Habitat, *The State of African Cities 2014: Re-Imagining Sustainable Urban Transitions* (Nairobi: UN Habitat, 2014), p. 25.

64. James Thurlow, Danielle Resnick, and Dumebi Ubogu, "Matching Concepts with Measurement: Who Belongs to Africa's Middle Class?" *Journal of International Development*, 27 (2015), pp. 588–608, see especially Table 3. Alternative approaches rely on income to define the middle class, but see also the critique of income-based approaches by Thurlow, Resnick, and Ubogu, "Matching Concepts."

65. Ibid., Table 3.

66. Tanzania, "Tanzania National Panel Survey Report. Round 1, 2008–2009," National Bureau of Statistics (2009), 85.

67. Information based on site visits in Ghana, Zambia, Kenya, South Africa, and Angola as well as information from private equity investors and bankers.

68. allAfrica.com, "Mozambique: Government No Longer Want to Privatise Mcel" (December 12, 2011), www.allafrica.com.

69. Silimela, interview.

70. UN Habitat, *Ghana Housing Profile* (Nairobi: UN Human Settlements Program, 2011), p. 35.

71. Ghana, "SSNIT Annual Report," Social Security and National Insurance Trust (2010), www.ssnit.com; UN Habitat, *Ghana Housing Profile*.

72. Soares de Oliveira, *Magnificent and Beggar Land*; Matfess, "Developmental Authoritarianism."

73. South Africa, "Broad-Based Black Economic Empowerment Act," Department of Trade and Industry (2003); Organization for Economic Cooperation and Development

and African Development Bank, "South Africa," *African Economic Outlook* (Paris: OECD Publishing, 2007), p. 497.

74. Silimela, interview.

75. Stewart and Yermo, "Pensions in Africa."

76. Sundeep K. Raichura, "Analytical Review of the Pension System in Kenya," Working paper (September 2008), pp. 24–26.

77. Stewart and Yermo, "Pensions in Africa."

78. International Monetary Fund, "Regional Outlook: Sub-Saharan Africa, Recovery and New Risks," World Economic and Financial Surveys (April 2011), p. 64.

79. Elias E. M. Baruti, "The Role of Pension Funds as Institutional Investors in Tanzania: Challenges and Opportunities," The International Policy and Research Conference on Social Security, Luxembourg (September 29–October 1, 2010), 8; Principal, interview.

80. Eric Swyngedouw, "Governance Innovation and the Citizen: The Janus Face of Governance-Beyond-the-State," *Urban Studies* 42, no. 11 (October 2005), 1991–2006.

81. L. Randall Wray, "The Rise and Fall of Money Manager Capitalism: A Minskian Approach," *Cambridge Journal of Economics* 33 (2009), pp. 807–828.

82. UNCTAD, "Price Formation in Financialized Commodity Markets: The Role of Information" (June 2011).

83. Kyle Hatton and Katharina Pistor, "Maximizing Autonomy in the Shadow of Great Powers: The Political Economy of Sovereign Wealth Funds" (unpublished article, Columbia University, 2010), p. 1.

84. Ibid.; Clark, Dixon, and Monk, *Sovereign Wealth Funds*, pp. 38–39.

85. Sovereign Wealth Fund Institute, "Linaburg-Maduell Transparency Index" (2016), www.swfinstitute.org/statistics-research/linaburg-maduell-transparency-index.

86. Chris Kay, "Nigeria S&P Upgrade Hindered by Fund Tensions with States," *Bloomberg News* (October 19, 2012), www.bloomberg.com/news/2012–10–18/nigeria-s-p-upgrade-hindered-by-wealth-fund-tension-with-states.html.

87. Peter Ondabu, "Property Value More Than Tripled Since 2000," *Metropolitan Property* (July–August 2012), p. 12.

88. Representative, Housing Finance Institution, Nairobi, interview (August 10, 2012).

89. Roberto Frenkel and Martin Rapetti, "A Developing Country View of the Current Global Crisis: What Should Not Be Forgotten and What Should Be Done," *Cambridge Journal of Economics* 33 (2009), pp. 685–702.

90. PIC, "Celebrating 20 Years of Democracy," pp. 68–70.

91. G. J. Rossouw, "Business Ethics and Corporate Governance in Africa," *Business and Society* 44 (2005), 94–106; South African Institute of Chartered Accountants (SAICA), "King Report on Corporate Governance," SAICA (2014), www.saica.co.za/Technical/LegalandGovernance/King/tabid/2938/language/en-ZA/Default.aspx.

92. Raichura, "Analytical Review."

93. Mauritius, "Survey on the State of Compliance with the Code of Corporate Governance in Mauritius," Report, National Committee on Corporate Governance, DCDM Marketing Research (October 1, 2009).

94. Namibia Economic Policy Review Unit, "Findings of APRM Assessment in Ghana," NEPAD Briefing no. 17 (December 2006).

95. Stephen D. Prowse, "The Economics of the Private Equity Market," *Economic Review*, Federal Reserve Bank of Dallas (3rd quarter, 1998).

96. Wray, "The Rise and Fall of Money Manager Capitalism."

The Sad Story of "Africa Rising" and the Continent's Romance with the BRICS

Ian Taylor

In the last fifteen years or so, Africa was said to be rising, turning a definitive page in its history. Numerous reports rapidly constructed a narrative of an inextricable upward trajectory. Though all evidence suggested that an upsurge in economic growth had been built on the back of a commodity super-cycle, the Africa Rising discourse preferred to insist that improved governance and qualitative endogenous dynamics had been responsible. Equally, emerging economies, emblematized by the BRICS (Brazil, Russia, India, China, and South Africa) were placed centrally as playing an important role in diversifying Africa's international relations and, thus, granting Africa new and exciting possibilities. A great deal of excitement was generated in the media and in some academic quarters to suggest that not only was Africa on the up but that this was taking place within a global order that was on the cusp of radical change, one that would be favorable to the underdeveloping world. Such analyses cast the BRICS in leading roles in such processes.

However, now that commodity prices have collapsed and the BRICS themselves have entered into various stages of political and economic crises, the nature and implications of Africa's "rise" and the role that the BRICS played in it require attention. It is a fact that Africa still has yet to go through any structural transformation and that there is strong evidence to suggest that deindustrialization and

Table 5.1   Commodity Prices: May 2016 Compared with May 2015 (%)

Natural gas	-27.2	Rubber	-3.8	Aluminium	5.4
Gold	4.3	Cocoa	-2.4	Tin	-18.9
Silver	-1.7	Coffee	-33.6	Zinc	-18.1
Platinum	-23.1	Oats	-11.1	Coal	-21.1
Palladium	-7.0	Iron ore	-12.8	Cobalt	-23.1
Cotton	-11.0	Lead	-37.5		
Wheat	-22.8	Nickel	-15.6		

Source: Financial Times, May 13, 2016.

jobless growth accompanied the upsurge of interest in the continent. Far from bringing about a milieu where Africa was turning the corner in its developmental trajectory, the continent has been pushed further into the resource corner, with all the well-known attendant pathologies associated with such a situation in terms of price shocks (see Table 5.1).

At the same time, hope that the BRICS might offer up an alternative for Africa were misplaced. The ruling classes of the BRICS have an integral stake in maintaining the current unequal global system within which Africa is so disadvantaged. The postcolonial project of fashioning an independent path remains. Relying on the BRICS—or any other external actors—simply reproduces Africa's state of underdevelopment.

THE BRICS

The BRICS term was a neologism that for a brief period symbolized a putative changing world order. Originally coined in 2001 by Jim O'Neill, chief economist for Goldman Sachs, the term's normative element advanced the argument that a select group of emerging economies were likely to surpass the traditional economic powerhouses of the global economy by 2040.[1] According to the report prepared by Goldman Sachs, "in less than 40 years" the states dubbed the BRICs were expected to surpass the G-6, making up the world's main "engine of new demand growth and spending power" and thereby "offset[ting] the impact of greying populations and slower growth in the advanced economies."[2] The Goldman Sachs report saw the four initial BRIC states as prospective "engines of growth," arguing that stable and cumulative growth in Brazil and India alongside the sheer size of China and Russia's economies would fundamentally change the global economy and, by implication, the global balance of power away from the dominant West. Methodologically the concept had severe flaws. Its projections were based on trends in demography and a fairly simple model of capital accumulation and productivity, with an extrapolation of current growth trajectories on a straight line—always upward. As Sharma notes, "These forecasts typically took the developing world's high growth rates from the middle of the last decade and extended them straight into the future, juxtaposing them against predicted sluggish growth in the United States and other advanced industrial countries."[3] Furthermore, "The Goldman Sachs concept merely 'projected' (rather than recommended or proposed) on the basis of demographic trends and a largely unrealistic model of growth what could be expected to (rather than made to) happen in case of two resource-rich and two human resource–rich economies."[4]

The concept was based on superficial research ("when O'Neill coined the term BRIC in 2001, he had never properly visited three of the four countries").[5] Yet precisely because it reified the global thrusts of neoliberal policy prescriptions, the concept caught on rapidly among global elites and entered the global lexicon: "Embodying neo-liberalism and reworking prior categories, the designation of emerging markets began with a section of the World Bank and was soon embraced by fund managers, traders, and the financial media in the early 1990s."[6] Extremely low interest rates in the US, liquidity injections, and similarly low interest rates in most OECD economies stimulated a flood of speculative capital toward the so-called emerging markets.[7] Recognizing both the economic and political capital to be made from Goldman Sachs's anointing (and advertisement) of their growing economies, policymakers and academics within the BRICS states enthusiastically embraced the concept.

What is interesting—and revealing—about the BRICS concept is that it is but the latest incarnation of efforts by the capitalist core to define and incorporate centers of accumulation as well as locate and identify new spaces for capitalist investment. Up until the 1980s the term *less economically developed countries* (LEDCs) was used to denote markets that were deemed less "developed" than the West. According to Antoine van Agtmael, the World Bank economist in the International Finance Corporation (IFC) widely credited with inventing the term "emerging markets," by the 1980s the Bank was "identifying the opportunity to rebrand these countries, which, despite their enormous economic potential, were still lumped together with the world's perennial basket cases as 'underdeveloped countries' stuck in the 'Third World.' At the time, Third World stock markets were simply off the radar screen of most international investors. . . . But until the IFC built its Emerging Markets Database and index in 1981, there was no way to measure stock performance for a representative group of these markets, a disabling disadvantage when stacked against other international indices, which were skewed in favor of developed countries."[8] As van Agtmael made clear, this branding was done with the aim that it "provided investors with the confidence to launch diversified emerging-market funds."[9]

Asset managers, bankers, and speculators swiftly and enthusiastically embraced the concept of emerging markets. Given that the concept emerged from the IFC, an institution mandated to offer advice on investment and asset management, it was unsurprising that the very purpose of the emerging markets idea was to promote the integration of the world's key stock markets with markets in peripheral and semiperipheral states for the purposes of portfolio investment. This process reflected the geographical "Imagineering" that went into constructing and maintaining "emerging markets" as a category and the roles played by fund managers, brokers, and analysts.[10]

As economies outside of the capitalist core began to develop, policymakers and academics both began to focus increased attention on these upstarts, with discussion about the roots behind the "rise of the rest."[11] The implications of such developments for dominant power relations in the global political economy were often the implicit subtext behind such analysis: Alice Amsden's book's subtitle was, in fact, "Challenges to the West from Late-Industrialising Economies." High levels of economic growth and future projections were invariably tied to geopolitical considerations. This became quite explicit in the concept of the "pivotal states" of the late 1990s, which was primarily focused on security matters and the implications for American *military* status.[12] In such futurology these pivotal states—Algeria, Brazil, Egypt, India, Indonesia, Mexico, Pakistan, South Africa, and Turkey—were identified as those where there was a threat of internal instability but that exert significant influence in their respective regions and, possibly, at the international level.

Alternatively, Jeffrey Garten, as another formulation of The Future, had postulated the concept of the "Big Ten" emerging markets.[13] The total Big Ten— Argentina, Brazil, China, India, Indonesia, Mexico, Poland, South Africa, South Korea, and Turkey—was proposed as fundamentally changing international relations. This futurology industry became ridiculous, however, with further neologisms and acronyms put forward, such as BRICSAM (BRICS plus Mexico), the BRIICKS (the BRICS plus Indonesia and South Korea), the Next-11 (Bangladesh, Egypt, Indonesia, Iran, Mexico, Nigeria, Pakistan, Philippines, Turkey, South Korea, and Vietnam), CIVETS (Colombia, Indonesia, Vietnam, Egypt, Turkey, and South Africa), TIMBIs (Turkey, India, Mexico, Brazil, and Indonesia), and others ad nauseam. Interestingly, these collective tropes—that late industrializers would necessarily either threaten the West's domination or require a robust response—can trace their origins to the ideas of Oswald Spengler and his pessimistic predictions about the inevitable decline of the West, which has a long pedigree. Existentialist angst about Western supremacy and its longevity was, once again, acute post-2008. Thus, we were told that the West ruled, but only *for now.*[14] Alternatively, the West had already reached the end of the road.[15]

Of course, there can be little doubt that some of the BRICS had indeed grown spectacularly in terms of GDP. If the purchasing power parity (PPP) measure of GDP is used, Beijing's economy is already three-quarters the size of that of the United States, whereas Brazil, Russia, and India have economies of similar size to Japan, Germany, Britain, France, and Italy. Yet what the BRICS term really captured were both anxieties and expectations regarding how these states challenged the core. When it came to Africa, apprehension about how such countries—specifically China—were "taking over" the continent and displacing Western influence was acute, momentarily elevating the continent's importance in Western strategic thinking.

The increasing role of emerging economies in Africa was and will continue to be of importance to the continent. What has been most interesting about such developments is the apparent sudden realization that Africa is not marginal to the world. Sub-Saharan Africa is in fact very well integrated into the global system and has been for decades. It is the pundits as well as diverse speculators and opportunists who have abruptly discovered that Africa's foreign trade represents 45 percent of its gross national product (compared to 30 percent for Asia and Latin America and 15 percent for the core countries). Quantitatively, the continent is more—not less—globally integrated. The role of emerging economies, exemplified by the BRICS, in Africa's putative "rise" generated a great deal of excitement in this regard. However, the problem is the terms of Africa's integration and how this then relates to the political economy of its external relations, the BRICS included.

THE AFRICAN CONTEXT

Although the situation obviously depends on national context, "As a result of their colonial legacy, the present-day economies of the African countries are characterized by a lop-sided dependence on the export of raw materials, and the import of manufactured goods."[16] This assessment was written nearly forty years ago, and there has not been any radical departure from such a milieu for most countries, reflecting the tragedy of much of Africa's postcolonial trajectory. Set in motion by colonialism and the insertion of Africa into the global political economy, the status quo has been ably assisted by the African elite political class, which has assumed state power since independence.

Any analysis of Africa's relations with the BRICS (or any other external actors) needs to be grounded in the above understanding of the dialectical relationships engendered. This necessarily recognizes that "government serves as the foreman to keep civil society producing a surplus to be accumulated by foreign finance capital and parasitic native social classes that enjoy almost absolutist power."[17] Despite the celebration of "democratization" across the continent and the attempts to link this to Africa's recent growth spurt, there has been little evidence that overall the quality of Africa's democracies is improving or that governance is dramatically improving across the continent. In fact, it is a distinct possibility that the elites have just become better at managing the game and satisfying various internal and external patrons and clients.

The sort of political culture that has matured postindependence has had important consequences for Africa, further adding to the problem of underdevelopment. Here, a brief definition of what we mean is required. The orthodox criterion is the per capita measurement of national income, used in a rather formalized comparative fashion. This chapter follows Tamás Szentes's objection to such quantitative indices, asserting that underdevelopment is a much too multifaceted phenomenon, irreducible to mere quantitative portrayals; instead, "there are two aspects, two sides of underdevelopment: the basically external, international aspect, which, from the historical point of view of the emergence of the present state, is the primary aspect; and the internal aspect, which from the point of view of future development, is increasingly important."[18] In short, "poverty [is] not the result of some historical game of chance in which [Africa] happened to be the losers; it [is] the result of a set of economic relationships, rooted in the colonial era, that [has] served to enrich a minority by impoverishing the majority."[19]

Underdevelopment is a dynamic—not static—condition: a relationship. It "expresses a particular relationship of *exploitation*: namely, the exploitation of one country by another. All of the countries named as 'underdeveloped' in the world are exploited by others; and the underdevelopment with which the world is now pre-occupied is a product of capitalist, imperialist and colonialist exploitation."[20] The export of the surplus generated, denying these societies of the fruits of their natural resources and labor, is a fundamental component of underdevelopment. Such processes necessarily affect the economic base that then configures the superstructure.

In general, the modes of governance in Africa have encouraged despotism and unpredictability. Neopatrimonialism rules and, in many countries, the separation of the public from the private is minimal. As a result, for most of the postcolonial period much of Africa has been trapped in cycles of crises, which have stimulated societal conflict. In the absence of hegemony Africa's leaders have relied on effected control and patronage. Although Africa's elites undoubtedly command the state apparatus with varying levels of intensity, their own practices often undermine and subvert the state's institutions and the effectiveness of its bureaucracy on a daily basis. Because most African elites exercise power in circumstances that lack hegemony, the relative autonomy of the state is absent and their rule is intrinsically unstable. This means that there is very little political space to allow reform and that autocracy is relied on as a means of control.

Such a milieu necessarily breeds a deep reluctance to give up state power. Instead of a stable hegemonic project that binds different levels of society together, what exist in much of Africa are intrinsically unstable personalized systems of domination. Corruption, not hegemonic rule, is the cement that binds the system together and links the patron and their predatory ruling class together. Consequently, capturing the state is usually a precondition for acquisition, and questions of national development are deemed abstract and unimportant unless they either directly threaten the incumbents' positions or can be utilized to garner increased resource flows. If political elites do ever articulate a vision for the country, "their notion of emerging out of economic backwardness amounts essentially to Westernisation," where "the general trend is to try and stimulate economic growth within the context of the existing neo-colonial economic structure."[21] This is indeed an accurate appraisal of the contemporary "development strategies" that characterize much of Africa, only now with the BRICS included as part of the broader international economic structure.

The external domination of Africa's economies and the pathologies of dependency this engenders (constructed during the colonial period) have proven markedly resilient. The root causes of Africa's underdevelopment have been the asymmetry between the role of the continent in the world and the degree to which powerful external forces have penetrated Africa. Broadly speaking, the international division of labor has not permitted African economies to move beyond their role as primary producers, for reasons that include a lack of access to technology, the comparative advantage of other economies in manufacturing, and the constraints of the fragmented African market. Walter Rodney captured this reality when he asserted that "African economies are integrated into the very structure of the developed capitalist economies; and they are integrated in a manner that is unfavourable to Africa and insures that Africa is dependent. . . . Structural dependence is one of the characteristics of underdevelopment."[22] In short, the economies of Africa essentially depend on two production systems that determine their structures and define their place in the global capitalist system: the export of "tropical" agricultural products and hydrocarbons and minerals. This has not radically changed since independence, yet such materiality has been overlooked in the excitement to both anoint Africa as the new frontier of opportunity for speculators and exaggerate the role of emerging economies as potential redeemers.

"AFRICA RISING"

Throughout the 2000s African per capita growth figures were relatively high and sustained. This was built upon "a commodity price boom that was unprecedented in its magnitude and duration. The real prices of energy and metals more than doubled in five years from 2003 to 2008, while the real price of food commodities increased 75%."[23] To a large degree this was intimately linked to new trading geographies and the emergence of nontraditional actors in Africa who were propelling demand; indeed, the commodity price hike of the first decade of the twenty-first century has generally been credited to the robust growth performance by emerging economies, particularly China, which were metals and energy intensive. The increase in emerging economies' activities across Africa were then said to be reshaping Africa's international relations and providing qualitatively better sets of relations for the continent: "Business conferences [were] filled with frothy talk of African lions overtaking Asian tigers,"[24] while some media sources claimed that "What took the UK centuries can now be a matter of decades, even years. . . . Today Africa has the greatest room to boom on the back of two centuries of global progress. . . . In other words, Africa is ideally poised to leapfrog centuries of industrial development. . . . It has an added advantage in that it does not have to carry baggage from the past."[25] Thus yet another commodity-driven boom in Africa, this time propelled by emerging economies, wiped the historical slate clean, made dependent relationships and unequal terms of trade vanish instantaneously and positioned the continent to reach OECD status virtually overnight.

In the context of depressed or stagnating economies in the core post-2007, at face value Africa's growth did look comparatively healthy. But it is now quite apparent that the tropes surrounding a notional Africa Rising fully reflected the point of view of capital, where poles of accumulation and sites of investment in Africa were identified by various actors (with asset managers at the fore) as spaces offering this or that opportunity for profit seeking. This has actually deepened Africa's dependent position in the global economy.

Growth in GDP as the central focus of talk about the "the hopeless continent," as *The Economist* put it in 2000, was spectacularly dropped, to be replaced by "A hopeful continent."[26] Yet the Africa Rising mania neglected a most fundamental context: "only for nine of the forty three [sub-Saharan] countries were growth rates during 1980–2008 high enough to double per capita income in less than thirty years, and only sixteen in less than one hundred years. Performance would have been considerably worse had it not been for the brief years of relatively rapid growth in the mid-2000s."[27] Africa needs to grow at least 7 percent a year for the next twenty or thirty years if any serious tackling of continental poverty is to be realized. However, growth induced by commodity price increases, new discoveries of natural resources, or increases in sources of foreign capital is simply neither sustainable nor practical.

What GDP growth did occur was characterized by the deployment and inflow of capital-intensive investment for extracting and exporting African natural resources. There was a distinct lack of value added on the African side. Problematically, although the mainstream development literature argues that higher rates of inflow of capital investment will have downstream effects on African employment, there is little evidence that this took place. The main reason for this was that the growth rested heavily on external foreign governments and corporations and their linkages with African state elites.

In late 2012 the deputy executive secretary of the Economic Commission for Africa noted that Africa's relatively good economic growth performance over the past decade had been driven mostly by nonrenewable natural resources and high commodity prices. Alongside this, deindustrialization had been a key feature, with the share of manufacturing in Africa's GDP falling from 15 percent in 1990 to 10 percent in 2008, going hand in hand with an increase in unemployment.[28] Manufacturing growth was near the bottom in twelve growth sectors—only public administration lagged behind. In fact, contra to the Africa Rising proponents who, apparently dazzled by new shopping malls and the proliferation of mobile phones, had declared that things had fundamentally changed, "If one disaggregates the countries into conflict-affected, and those not affected by conflict into petroleum exporters and others, the recovery during 2004–2008 appears less impressive. For the twenty-nine countries that did not export petroleum and were not burdened by severe conflict, the average growth rate in the second half of the 2000s was hardly different from the average ten years before."[29] Foreign direct investment into Africa increased—both in volume and in geographical spread—and as a result, volatile commodity prices became increasingly difficult for Africa to manage. After the boom it became quite clear that Africa had intensified its dependency on primary products.

Recent events simply confirm this reality, and the last ten years have highlighted just how unstable commodity prices are. The aggregate trend in prices for all primary commodities for the period 1995–2010 declined during the first half of the period, from 1995 to 2001, with prices down by one-third. From 2001, which coincided with the big upsurge of interest in Africa by the BRICS, commodity prices started to climb at accelerating speeds. This was stopped in its tracks by the 2008 crisis, with prices tumbling by nearly 40 percent by the year's end. Prices went up only to then crash again, with oil reaching below $30 a barrel in February 2016, a drop of almost 75 percent since mid-2014. Clearly, any planning dependent on receipts from commodities is extremely problematic given that international commodity prices are especially volatile, sometimes fluctuating by as much as 50 percent in a given year. This trend has only increased as the world has become more economically integrated.

Commodity dependence is typically measured by the share of export earnings of the top single commodity (or top three export commodities) in GDP, in total merchandise exports, and in total agriculture exports. The percentage of people occupied in commodity production and the share of government revenue accruing from commodities are also important measurements. "Examining trends in the share of primary commodities in total exports for the period 1995–2009," which coincides with the increase in interest in Africa by, among others, the BRICS, "shows that, despite a contraction between 1995 and 2000, the share of primary commodities in total exports rose rapidly between 2000 and 2009."[30] This development had particular implications for the African continent: "The share of primary commodities in exports increased across all regions of the developing world. . . . Africa—the region most dependent on primary commodity exports throughout the period—became even more commodity-dependent (the share of primary commodity exports was 72 percent in 1995 and rose to 81 percent by 2009)."[31] This super-cycle was largely—though not exclusively—driven by growth and industrial demand within the BRICS.

Using UNCTAD secretariat calculations, themselves based on UNCTAD's *UNCTAD Stat*, a diversification index using the Herfindahl-Hirschmann index can be developed.[32] An index value that is close to 1 indicates a very concentrated market (maximum concentration), whereas values closer to 0 reflect a more equal distribution of market shares among exporters or importers. The index shows the extent of the differences between the structure of trade of a country or country group and the world average. In other words, are countries or groups of countries more or less diversified than the world average? The figures demonstrate that Africa continues to be much less diversified than the rest of the world (see Table 5.2).

Clearly, "African economies exhibit very low level of diversification. By all measures and accounts, there has been limited diversification of exports by the

Table 5.2   Diversification Index: Africa's Regional Economic Communities Compared with the World's, 2000–2014

Area	2000	2005	2010	2014
Arab Maghreb Union	0.35	0.32	0.36	0.34
Community of Sahel-Saharan States	0.33	0.32	0.32	0.33
Common Market for Eastern and Southern Africa	0.35	0.35	0.33	0.34
East African Community	0.39	0.40	0.41	0.41
Economic Community of Central African States	0.41	0.45	0.40	0.43
Economic Community of West African States	0.39	0.40	0.39	0.38
Intergovernmental Authority on Development	0.41	0.41	0.41	0.41
Southern African Development Community	0.25	0.23	0.22	0.24
EU	0.08	0.10	0.12	0.12
MERCOSUR	0.25	0.22	0.24	0.23
NAFTA	0.13	0.14	0.17	0.16
Africa Average	0.27	0.27	0.28	0.28
Americas Average	0.11	0.13	0.14	0.13
Asia Average	0.18	0.20	0.17	0.16
Europe Average	0.09	0.10	0.12	0.12
Oceania Average	0.21	0.23	0.23	0.23

Source: UNCTAD, UNCTAD Stat, 2013, http://unctadstat.unctad.org.

African economies. Over the last 25 years or so, there has been very little change towards improved diversification in the African economies in general."[33] This is extremely problematic given that African economies have remained concentrated, whereas according to the UNECA, "The diversification of African economies is one way through which the recent economic growth achievements could be sustained . . . diversification is a *prerequisite* to achieving positive development in the continent."[34]

As the above diversification index shows, Africa more or less remained comparatively undiversified in its exports, remaining dependent on primary commodities. Half of the countries in sub-Saharan Africa derive over 80 percent of their merchandise export income from commodities (see Table 5.3).

The total share of fuels and mining products in Africa's total merchandise exports increased from 48.4 percent in 2003 to 70.6 percent in 2008. What this shows is that the upsurge of interest in Africa by the BRICS and other emerging economies coincided with and exacerbated the continent's increased dependency on primary products, particularly mineral products. As the IMF comments, the "BRICs' economic growth and rising demand for primary commodities have been key

Table 5.3   Commodity Exports as a Percentage of Total Merchandise Exports in Sub-Saharan Africa

UNCTAD region	Commodity exports as % of total merchandise exports
Eastern Africa	79
Middle Africa	92
Southern Africa	65
Western Africa	85.5

Source: UNCTAD Stat.

factors behind the growth of world trade and booms in international trade of primary commodities."[35] With the exception of Russia, resource-based commodities formed the bulk of African exports to BRICS. Although this certainly led to an increase in income for some African countries (or their ruling classes), "By diverting resources from non-raw material sectors and contributing to real exchange-rate appreciation, a price boom runs the risk of locking developing-country commodity exporters into what Leamer called the 'raw-material corner,' with little scope for industrial progress or skills advancement."[36] Leamer's triangle was a diagram illustrating both relative factor endowments and relative factor intensities with three factors and any number of goods.[37] Given that Africa's factor endowments are concentrated in commodities and the export profile and sector concentration is the same, the raw-material corner has been the continent's broad fate. The result has been what Issa Shivji terms *structural disarticulation*, where Africa exhibits a "disarticulation between the structure of production and the structure of consumption. What is produced is not consumed and what is consumed is not produced."[38] This disarticulation is not only a major feature of Africa's political economy but also a key factor behind the continent's underdevelopment.

As has been mentioned, the Africa Rising trope was built upon strong GDP growth rates in Africa. This fixation on growth stems from developments within the field of economics: "From the 1960s on, GDP conquered the political scene and affirmed itself as the supreme indicator of modernity and progress. Everything else (e.g., environmental sustainability, social justice, poverty eradication) were sacrificed on the altar of economic growth."[39] This measurement of one indicator of the economy as being the yardstick to measure progress enables pundits to ignore major developments in the economies of countries:

> In 1992, the GNP was superseded by GDP. . . . Traditional GNP referred to all goods and services produced by the residents of a given country, regardless of whether the "income" was generated within or outside its borders. This meant that, for instance, the earnings of multinational corporations were attributed to the country where the firm was owned and where the profits would eventually

return. With the introduction of the gross "domestic" product, this calculation changed completely. GDP is indeed territorially defined, which means that the income generated by foreign companies is "formally" attributed to the country where it is generated, even though the profits may very well not remain there. This conceptual evolution . . . was by and large responsible for the economic boom of many developing nations. Yet, it is obvious that the gains it revealed were more apparent than real.[40]

Given the capital-intensive nature of much investment in the resource sectors of Africa by foreign corporations (BRICS originated or otherwise), one can imagine how distortionary the effect is on the reporting of Africa's growth based on GDP rather than GNP. Yet it is precisely the GDP figures that were bandied about as evidence of Africa Rising by the World Bank, UNECA, investment bankers, and others.

Furthermore, it appeared that these international institutions (nor the actual governments of these African countries) gave little or no consideration to the long-term implications of how these growth rates had been accomplished. Resource extraction is by definition nonrenewable, and in the current milieu of dependent relations Africa's wealth continues to be taken out of the continent at an exponential rate by ever-diversifying actors, a process all the while celebrated as Africa's gain. Yet "GDP calculates such exports as a solely positive process (a credit) without a corresponding debit on the books of a country's natural capital."[41] The World Bank itself recommended in 2006 that subtracting the value of nonrenewable resources through extraction gave a superior indicator of actual gains through trade. This was termed "genuine saving" (GS), which is the measure of net investment in produced, natural, and human capital where negative genuine saving rates imply that total wealth is in decline. This has massive implications for the Africa Rising narrative given that the majority of this "rising" was built on nonrenewable extraction and that resource-rich countries are historically the poorest genuine savers. In fact, "With the exception of Algeria and Guinea, for whom GS was just above zero for the period 1970–2001, every country with an average share of fuel and mineral exports in total exports of over 60% had negative GS."[42]

The above is all missed in standard GDP measurements, despite the fact that "The policy implications of measuring genuine savings are quite direct: persistently negative rates of genuine savings must lead, eventually, to declining well-being."[43] Beyond this depletion of finite resources and subsequent negative debit on a country's stock, inequality has been re-inscribed during this boom. The IMF in fact admits that "higher inequality appears to have more than offset the positive impact of growth on poverty in Sub-Saharan Africa."[44] In a major understatement, the IMF notes that "higher GDP per capita growth appears to have been accompanied by higher inequality. Given the already high level of income inequality in the region, this is very concerning."[45] Even the Africa Progress Panel, which is invariably Pollyanna-ish in its assessment of Africa, admitted that "After a decade of buoyant growth, almost half of Africans still live on less than $1.25 a day. Wealth disparities are increasingly visible. The current pattern of trickle-down growth is leaving too many people in poverty, too many children hungry and too many young people without jobs. Governments are failing to convert the rising tide of wealth into opportunities for their most marginalized citizens. Unequal access to health, education, water and sanitation is reinforcing wider inequalities. Smallholder agriculture has not been part of the growth surge, leaving rural populations trapped in poverty and vulnerability."[46] The implications for attaining the Sustainable Development Goals are obvious and profound.

The above has gone hand in hand with, as has been pointed out, no serious structural change in the continent's economies; indeed, they are linked. The share of Africa in global manufacturing value added (MVA) actually fell: Africa's industrial sector declined as a share of GDP from 32 percent to 27.8 percent between 2005–2013, whereas the manufacturing sector has declined from 17.7 percent as a share of GDP to 11 percent in 2013.[47] Furthermore, compared to the rest of the world, African economies have on average shown the least change in their manufacturing base in terms of technological complexity of products over 2002–2011, the time when the BRICS involvement in Africa intensified. In 2012 resource-based manufacturing accounted for around 49 percent of total manufacturing value added, compared to 24.9 percent for low-technology manufacturing and 26.1 percent for medium- and high-technology manufacturing. These shares of low-tech and resource-based sectors combined accounted for about three-quarters of MVA, compared to an average of about 50 percent for East Asia and the Pacific (except China), for example. The picture is even more distorted if South Africa is discounted. Indeed, only 8.3 percent of total value added was accounted for in the medium- to high-tech manufacturing sector in the rest of sub-Saharan Africa, whereas the resources sector made up as much as 66.2 percent of MVA.[48]

In short, the much-vaunted recent economic growth in Africa was based on trade, not production. Such growth is problematic given that "production is the key to accumulation since the profits of all capital, even merchant capital that operates exclusively in the sphere of circulation, originate in the sphere of production."[49] The economic advantages of such trade accrue to the accumulation centers outside of Africa. The result is that the role of Africa was once again consolidated as being a source of cheap raw materials exported to feed external economies and/or processed up the value chain into finished products. This has long been a chronic problem for Africa given that building up capabilities in manufacturing and improving the productivity of agriculture are the levers to wealth creation, with suitable pro-poor policies aimed at equitable and sustainable development at the heart of long-term poverty reduction.

Of course, not all the BRICS involvement in Africa revolves around commodities—that would be a crude caricature. But developments inaugurated by colonization and imperialism reified the overall structure of Africa's insertion into the global economy. This is precisely what Timothy Shaw noted in separating structural and superficial features of Africa's economies. The superficial features can be identified in the GDP figures, industry, prices, debt levels, exchange, and so forth. "The *structural* features are, however, less apparent and more profound: Africa's changing place in the effective international division of labour."[50] Problematically, "Sub-Saharan Africa's international competitiveness in individual industries, especially in manufacturing and agro-processing, has seen little improvement over the last two decades. Its exports remained undiversified and their growth was overwhelmingly accounted for by natural resources. Sub-Saharan Africa's world market share in processing industries is not only low but has remained virtually unchanged."[51] Indeed, there is evidence of deindustrialization:

> Africa's current pattern of growth is that it has been accompanied by de-industrialisation as evidenced by the fact that the share of manufacturing in Africa's gross domestic product (GDP) fell from 15 percent in 1990 to 10 percent in 2008. The most significant decline was observed in Western Africa, where it fell from 13 percent to 5 percent over the same period. Nevertheless, there has also been substantial de-industrialisation in the other sub-regions of Africa. For example, in Eastern Africa the share of manufacturing in output fell from 13 percent in 1990 to about 10 percent in 2008 and in Central Africa it fell from 11 to 6 percent over the same period. Furthermore, in Northern Africa it fell from about 13 to 11 percent and in Southern Africa it fell from 23 to 18 percent. The declining share of manufacturing in Africa's output is of concern because historically manufacturing has been the main engine of high, rapid and sustained economic growth.[52]

Notably, "Africa—the region most dependent on primary commodity exports" became even more commodity dependent after the upsurge in interest in the continent by the emerging powers. "The basis of recurring growth in Africa has always been strong external demand. Growth has not been triumphant and the end of growth periods has ended with a combination of predatory rent-seeking and depressed external markets. The recent boom was one-sided, based on external market demand for natural resources."[53]

This is a serious issue. Without serious and credible policies, the diversification of dependency toward the BRICS and other emerging powers may further lead to negative outcomes for Africa, with history repeating itself. Relationships based on extraction have not historically worked as a catalyst for positive outcomes. This is perhaps why the governor of the Nigerian Central Bank, Sanusi Lamido Sanusi, asserted at the World Economic Forum in Davos in January 2013 that Nigeria should not content itself with being the producer of only raw materials for China. "How can we move up the value chain?" he asked. "China still uses raw materials from Africa, and Africa still buys Chinese manufactured products. . . . We have to get China to produce products on African soil. We have to take advantage of the Chinese market."[54] Sanusi correctly noted that unless Nigeria and other African countries start manufacturing products themselves, they would be stuck with 5 to 6 percent growth at best, a growth rate that would never allow Africa to develop.

CONCLUSION

Economic history proves that unless economies are moving up the value chain, they will be stuck in the rut of trading on commodities that simply provide diminishing returns in the medium to long term. Unless an economy is engaged in activities that deliver increasing returns over time, as found in manufacturing production, then the economy is not developing—it is just growing. The problem is that neoliberal economists argue that economies must integrate into the global economy using their notional comparative advantages, and if this means focusing on primary commodity extraction, then so be it. In this (entirely erroneous) reading the simple existence of upward GDP growth and flourishing trade volumes is seen as evidence of success. This is what the discourse about "Africa Rising" was based upon. But growth and trade in commodities do not equate to development and in fact may simply be the manifestation of an intensification of dependency. The vast majority of Africa's countries that were said to be on the rise instead remained locked into primary commodity sectors and evidenced very little progress toward engaging in value-added industrial production.

Jagdish Bhagwati recently argued that economic growth was the guaranteed way—if not the only way—to reduce poverty and promote development: "growth [will] pull the poor into gainful employment, thereby helping to lift them out of poverty . . . and that higher incomes [will] enable them to increase their personal spending on education and health."[55] This orthodox fetishization of growth and the neglect to link this to industrialization mean that the sort of far-fetched comparisons between Africa Rising and the experience of the East Asian Tigers is wholly specious. The claim that "The Next Asia Is Africa," based on an "African Growth Miracle," is a myth.[56] Commodities did not drive East Asian development; industrial policies did, along with massive transfers of capital from the United States and Japan in a crusade against the threat of communism. Industrialization develops countries, and extraction exploits them. No country can eradicate mass poverty unless it generates new employment opportunities in manufacturing and services. Resource-based exports can only promote development if there are strong and credible domestic policies to promote industrialization alongside commodity extraction, as found in the industrialized but resource-rich economies of the world such as Australia, Canada, New Zealand, Norway, and the United States. Development is, after all, fundamentally about structural change.

Obviously, countries moving up the value chain through industrialization and diversification do not simply abandon their natural resource assets. What matters for developmental realization is not whether a country continues to export commodities but rather what policy initiatives it introduces in conjunction with such exports to promote manufactures. When prices for commodities were high in the 2000s, prices for manufactured goods were low due to oversupply from Asia. This meant that commodities and energy exporters quickly accumulated capital, thereby entrenching dependency, while nascent manufacturing sectors and net energy importers across Africa suffered. True, African consumers benefit with cheap imported products, but this is not a sustainable model in terms of development.

The story of a rising Africa, bolstered by demand from the emerging economies such as the BRICS was just that: a story. In the discourse that growth for growth's sake was a manifestation of development and progress ("Africa Rising"), the agenda of industrialization and moving Africa up the global production chain was abandoned. Instead, reporting and analysis were hypnotized by the stellar growth rates (setting aside, of course, the fact that these were starting from very low bases anyway) and the upsurge of interest from the BRICS in Africa. How and why Africa could be said to be rising when a majority of its countries continued to export commodities but had to import almost everything else reflected the neoliberal fixation on global "integration" and economic growth as an indication of the robustness of a country's economic situation. Furthermore, according to a 2012 World Bank study, it continued to be the case that 47 percent of the population of sub-Saharan Africa still lived below the $1.25-a-day poverty line, and between 1981 and 2008 the continent's poverty rate declined only 4 percentage points. By contrast, East Asia saw dramatic drops in poverty, from 77 percent of the population in 1981 to 14 percent in 2008, with South Asia recording a decline in the percentage of its population in poverty from 61 percent to 36 percent. Data from the 2008–2011 African Economic Research Consortium (AERC) Collaborative Growth-Poverty Nexus project were analyzed, using data from African economists in eleven countries (Benin, Burkina Faso, Cameroon, Chad, Ethiopia, Ghana, Guinea, Kenya, Malawi, Nigeria, and Senegal). The key findings included that, with the exception of Ghana and Senegal, in all the other countries poverty reduction was modest or fluctuated, with poverty sometimes increasing. Yet among the five countries that provided information on severe poverty, Senegal's figures declined by 2.8 percent between 1995 and 2007, while Ghana's were reduced by only 2.1 percent. Ghana, which the IFIs routinely held up as a "success story" during the 2000s, experienced an increase in inequality during this period. Although some development indicators were positive, almost all were relative and from a very low base.[57]

Comprehension of the extent of the challenges facing the continent as well as the actual nature of Africa's insertion into the global order are vitally needed as is a more critical look at some of the "new" actors engaging in Africa. These nontraditional agents have been held up in some quarters as the new saviors of Africa, helping to construct a postcolonial and qualitatively better set of relations between Africa and the world. It is true that the emergence of new or nontraditional actors in Africa has opened up varying degrees of space for African elites to maneuver, yet how long will this last? As this chapter was written, severe economic and political crises were sweeping across the BRICS. In Brazil and South Africa the presidents faced calls for impeachment and prosecution, and China's economy is contracting. This last development has profound implications for the continent.

The huge growth of Chinese political and business interests in Africa was conceivably the most significant development for the continent's international relations since the end of the Cold War. Published trade figures alone bore evidence to the speed with which the Chinese economic presence in Africa developed. A desire to obtain sources of raw materials and energy for China's ongoing economic growth underpinned much of this expansion. New export markets for Chinese producers and traders, obliged to seek new markets by domestic dynamics within China's economy, also propelled the economic connections. The continuation of historic trends has meant, though, that when the external demand cools, the continent suffers. This is now becoming quite evident as China reorients its economy. The current regime in Beijing has made it clear that it wishes to restructure the Chinese economy so that it is based more on domestic consumption than on investment, as in the past. This means there are going to be many fewer mega-projects in China, which consumed massive amounts of imported natural resources, and more of a focus on other aspects of the economy. This "new normal," to use Xi Jinping's phrase, consists of the economy moving from the previous high-speed growth to a medium growth path, improvements and upgrades to the economic structure, and the economy being increasingly driven by innovation instead of input and investment (i.e., "developed in China" vs. "made in China"). Tertiary industry and domestic consumption demand are central to these new policies.

Of course, China will still need to import energy such as oil, but it is likely that the huge projects and the oil diplomacy that we saw in the 2000s will decrease. Xi Jinping's government has in fact de-emphasized Chinese investment in Africa's oil and gas sectors and instead prioritized infrastructural development—the so-called three networks in Africa: namely, a high-speed rail network, a highway network, and a regional aviation network. The commitment remains strong, just less spectacular. This policy of encouraging infrastructural development within Africa suits Chinese interests given that Chinese companies are famed for their competitive tendering. Now that infrastructure is not such a priority within China, the Chinese construction industry will require new markets. China's presence in Africa in these fields then is likely to increase.

The World Bank has in fact predicted that a slowdown in the BRICS's economies, of which China's is by far the largest, would have a greater effect on African economic growth than either drought or war, so Africa does face a tricky future in the immediate term. Significant revisions in price forecasts suggest that low prices are here to stay for some time, and it might be said that Africa faces the "new normal"—normal commodity prices, a "normal" Chinese economy. How its governments navigate this new situation is going to be central to debates about the continent in the next few years. But what the above informs us is that Africa

Rising was a blip based on high commodities demand, from the BRICS in particular, and a decline in conflict. The key issue for the continent remains that the post-colonial project of diversification and industrialization has to be made central. The diversification of dependency is not a coherent development project for the continent; policies must be put in place in Africa that "[meet] national needs; international economic relationships must be sufficiently diversified to promote this national economic development and control over economic growth must remain in national hands."[58] The continent needs to have its eyes wide open in dealing with the BRICS, as with all other external actors. Of course, external conditions are not propitious to true development—the WTO makes sure of that with multiple agreements that criminalize the industrial policy instruments used previously to nurture domestic capacities. This is likely to lock in the dominant position of the core capitalist countries at the top of the world hierarchy of wealth, with the BRICS countries expressly hoping to join such elite status. This is but a modern version of Friedrich List's "kicking away the ladder." In such circumstances a "rise" based on an intensification of resource extraction through diversifying partners, while inequality and unemployment increase and deindustrialization continues apace, hardly contributes to a qualitative turn for the continent and demolishes the Africa Rising narrative. For the continent's part, there are no external heroes waiting to rescue the continent, the BRICS included: "national liberation takes place when, and only when, national productive forces are completely free of all kinds of foreign domination."[59] That has to be the starting point for any true rise of Africa.

NOTES

1. Jim O'Neill, *Building Better Global Economic BRICs*, Goldman Sachs, Global Economics Paper no. 66 (New York: Goldman Sachs, 2001).

2. South Africa officially became a member nation on December 24, 2010, after being formally invited by the BRIC countries to join the group. BRIC then became BRICS.

3. Ruchir Sharma, "Broken BRICs: Why the Rest Stopped Rising," *Foreign Affairs* 91, no. 6 (2012), pp. 2–7.

4. R. Desai, "Dreaming in Technicolour? India as a BRIC," *International Journal* 62, no. 4 (2007), p. 785.

5. *Guardian* (London), January 17, 2010.

6. James D. Sidaway, "Geographies of Development: New Maps, New Visions?" *Professional Geographer* 64, no. 1 (2012), p. 53.

7. Richard Westra, *The Evil Axis of Finance: The US-Japan-China Stranglehold on the Global Future* (Atlanta, GA: Clarity Press, 2012), p. 168.

8. Antoine van Agtmael, "Think Again: The BRICS," *Foreign Policy* no. 196 (November 2012), p. 76.

9. Ibid.

10. Kaia Lai, "India-Brazil-South Africa: The Southern Trade Powerhouse Makes Its Debut," *Panama News* 12, no. 6 (March 19–April 8 2006), p. 627.

11. Alice H. Amsden, *The Rise of "The Rest": Challenges to the West from Late-Industrialising Economies* (Oxford: Oxford University Press, 2001).

12. Robert Chase, Emily Hill, and Paul Kennedy, eds., *The Pivotal States: A New Framework for US Policy in the Developing World* (New York: W. W. Norton, 1999).

13. Jeffrey E. Garten, *The Big Ten: The Big Emerging Markets and How They Will Change Our Lives* (New York: Basic Books, 1997).

14. Ian Morris, *Why The West Rules—for Now: The Patterns of History and What They Reveal About the Future* (London: Profile Books, 2011).

15. Dambisa Moyo, *How The West Was Lost: Fifty Years of Economic Folly—and the Stark Choices Ahead* (London: Penguin, 2012).

16. Richard L. Harris, "The Political Economy of Africa: Underdevelopment or Revolution," in *The Political Economy of Africa*, ed. Richard L. Harris (New York: Schenkman, 1975), p. 12.

17. Tatah Mentan, *The State in Africa: An Analysis of Impacts of Historical Trajectories of Global Capitalist Expansion and Domination in the Continent* (Bamenda: Langaa, 2010), p. xii.

18. Tamás Szentes, *The Political Economy of Underdevelopment* (Budapest: Akadémiai Kiadó, 1971), p. 163.

19. Peter Adamson, "A Measure of Progress," *New Internationalist* no. 460 (March 2013), p. 12.

20. Walter Rodney, *How Europe Underdeveloped Africa* (Oxford: Pambazuka Press, 2012), p. 14.

21. Claude Ake, *A Political Economy of Africa* (Lagos: Longman Nigeria, 1981), p. 139.

22. Rodney, *How Europe Underdeveloped Africa*, p. 25.

23. Bilge Erten and José Antonio Ocampo, "Super Cycles of Commodity Prices Since the Mid-Nineteenth Century," *World Development* 44 (2013), p. 14.

24. *Economist*, March 2, 2013, p. 5.

25. *African Business*, January 2013, p. 19.

26. *Economist*, March 2, 2013.

27. John Weeks, "A Study for Trade and Development Report 2010: Employment, Productivity and Growth in Africa South of the Sahara," unpublished paper, Centre for Development Policy and Research, School of Oriental and African Studies, University of London, 2010, p. 3.

28. *Addis Tribune*, December 8, 2012, p. 4.

29. Weeks, "A Study for Trade and Development," p. 6.

30. UNDP, *Towards Human Resilience: Sustaining MDG Progress in an Age of Economic Uncertainty* (New York: UNDP, 2011), p. 60.

31. Ibid.

32. The Herfindahl–Hirschman Index is a measure of the size of firms in relation to the industry and an indicator of both the amount of competition among them and the diversification levels within an economy.

33. H. Ben Hammouda, S. Karingi, A. Njuguna, and M. Jallab, "Africa's (Mis)-Fortunes in Global Trade and the Continent's Diversification Regimes," mimeo (n.d.), p. 11.

34. UNECA, *Economic Report on Africa 2007: Accelerating Africa's Development Through Diversification* (Addis Ababa: United Nations Economic Commission for Africa, 2007), p. 115 (emphasis added).

35. International Monetary Fund, *New Growth Drivers for Low-Income Countries: The Role of BRICs* (Washington, DC: IMF, 2011), pp. 12–13.

36. Ibid.

37. Edward Leamer, "Paths of Development in the Three-Factor, *n*-Good General Equilibrium Model," *Journal of Political Economy* 95 (1987).

38. Issa G. Shivji, *Accumulation in an African Periphery: A Theoretical Framework* (Dar es Salaam: Mkuki na Nyota Publishers, 2009), p. 59.

39. Lorenzo Fioramonti, *Gross Domestic Problem: The Politics Behind the World's Most Powerful Number* (London: Zed Books, 2013), p. 51.

40. Ibid., p. 41.

41. Patrick Bond, "Africa's 'Recovery': Economic Growth, Governance and Social Protest," *Africa Insight* 41, no. 3 (2011), p. 39.

42. Simon Dietz, Eric Neumayer, and Indra De Soysa, "Corruption, the Resource Curse and Genuine Saving," *Environment and Development Economics* 12, no. 1 (February 2007), p. 35.

43. Kirk Hamilton, and Michael Clemens, "Genuine Savings Rates in Developing Countries," *World Bank Economic Review* 13, no. 2 (1999), p. 352.

44. Daouda Sembene, *Poverty, Growth, and Inequality in Sub-Saharan Africa: Did the Walk Match the Talk Under the PRSP Approach?* (Washington DC: IMF, 2015).

45. IMF, *Regional Economic Outlook: Sub-Saharan Africa Dealing with the Gathering Clouds* (Washington DC: IMF, 2015).

46. Africa Progress Panel, *Africa Progress Report 2012: Jobs, Justice and Equity: Seizing Opportunities in Times of Global Change* (Geneva: Africa Progress Panel Foundation, 2012), p. 8.

47. UNIDO, *Sustaining Employment Growth: The Role of Manufacturing and Structural Change* (Vienna: UNIDO, 2013).

48. Isabelle Ramdoo, *Resource-Based Industrialisation in Africa: Optimising Linkages and Value Chains in the Extractive Sector* (Maastricht: European Centre for Development Policy Management, 2015).

49. Geoffrey Kay, *Development and Underdevelopment: A Marxist Analysis* (London: Macmillan, 1975), p. 71.

50. Timothy M. Shaw, *Towards a Political Economy for Africa: The Dialectics of Dependence* (London: Macmillan, 1985), p. 63, emphasis in the original.

51. World Economic Forum, the World Bank, and the African Development Bank, *The Africa Competitiveness Report 2011* (Geneva: World Economic Forum, 2011), p. 15.

52. UNCTAD, *The State of Commodity Dependence 2012* (Geneva: UN Conference on Trade and Development, 2012), pp. 2–3.

53. Morten Jerven, "African Growth Recurring: An Economic History Perspective on African Growth Episodes, 1690–2010," *Economic History of Developing Regions* 25, no. 2 (December 2010), p. 146.

54. Quoted in *Financial Times*, January 29, 2013.

55. Jagdish Bhagwati, "Does Redistributing Income Reduce Poverty?" *Chazen Global Insights*, November 3, 2011.

56. Howard W. French, "The Next Asia Is Africa: Inside the Continent's Rapid Economic Growth," *Atlantic Monthly*, May 21, 2012, p. 13.

57. Andy McKay, "Growth and Poverty Reduction in Africa in the Last Two Decades: Evidence from an AERC Growth-Poverty Project and Beyond," *Journal of African Economies* 22, suppl. 1 (2013).

58. Reginald Herbold Green and Ann Wilcox Seidman, *Unity or Poverty? The Economics of Pan-Africanism* (Harmondsworth: Penguin, 1968), p. 79.

59. Amílcar Cabral, *Unity and Struggle: Speeches and Writings of Amilcar Cabral* (New York: Monthly Review Press, 1979), p. 143.

In Pursuit of Autonomy: Civil Society and the State in Africa

Aili Mari Tripp

The 1990s marked a watershed in Africa with greater political opening and the beginning of a decline of major conflicts across the continent. By the 2000s the number of conflicts starting also declined, and the absolute number of conflicts began to drop. The political opening of the 1990s entailed the demise of one-party states in favor of multiparty regimes, greater freedom of the press, and more freedom of association. The number of countries considered democratic, semiauthoritarian, or hybrid peaked in 2005; there has since been a decline of democracy in many countries, while the number of authoritarian regimes has increased (see Table 6.1). Some countries have indeed improved their political rights and civil liberties since 2005, including Liberia, Nigeria, Cote D'Ivoire, Sierra Leone, and Burkina Faso. However, many more countries experienced declines, like South Africa, Burundi, the Gambia, Uganda, and Ethiopia. All of these openings and reversals in political rights and civil liberties influenced the capacity of civil society to function.

Such reversals in democratization have accompanied every wave of democratization historically, including the third wave, which started in Europe (Portugal) in the mid-1970s and spread to Latin America and the Asia Pacific in the 1980s and finally to East Europe and Africa by 1989.[1] Almost as soon as political liberation became evident in Africa, observers were noting its limits and reversals.[2] Many leaders used the façade of democratization to maintain power by manipulating multiparty elections and by allowing for a free press and civil society while

Table 6.1   Changes in Levels of Democratization Since 1975 in Africa

Years	Democratic regimes	Hybrid regimes	Authoritarian regimes
1975	8%	30%	63%
1985	4	28	69
1995	19	39	42
2005	23	44	33
2016	18	41	41

Source: Freedom House, www.freedomhouse.org.

constraining them indirectly. Hybrid regimes emerged that were neither fully au-thoritarian nor fully democratic. Some leaders even attempted to hang onto power after their legal mandate had expired by seeking to extend term limits through constitutional reforms. Others used outright repression to remain in power.

In the first three decades of independence, one-party states and military lead-ers sought to curtail, coopt, and sometimes shut down independent civil society. In other cases states and ruling parties formed their own mass organizations of women, youth, trade unionists, cooperatives, and even parents. These organiza-tions were often tied to the patronage politics of the single-party state, which lim-ited their agendas. Women's leagues and unions, for example, tended to focus on welfare, domestic, and developmental concerns while avoiding political engage-ment. At the grassroots level women's groups produced handicrafts, promoted lit-eracy, farmed, engaged in income-generating projects, and engaged in cultural activities and purposefully kept them depoliticized except to gain votes for the party in power and provide entertainment and food for political dignitaries and events. Their leaders were generally selected by the party, and their funding also came from the party.

After the 1990s civil societies in various countries increasingly played an im-portant role as service providers and as advocates for the poor, landless, women, LGBT groups, and other marginalized groups. Women's organizations, for example, became increasingly independent of government and the dominant political party. Women activists began to acquire their own resources, select their own leaders, and forge their own agendas. New women's networks and conferences organized around a broader agenda that included violence against women, peace, the envi-ronment, and reproductive rights. New women's organizations formed to improve leadership skills, encourage women's political involvement, promote women's polit-ical leadership, press for legislative changes, and conduct civic education. Although the older welfare-oriented and developmental agendas persist to this day, a new emphasis on political participation and advocacy emerged in the 1990s.

After the 1990s civil society organizations served as a watchdog of the gov-ernment in areas of corruption and transparency, advocated policy changes, and pressed for greater democracy and human rights. However, as political space became constricted, organizations continued to operate but shifted their orientation. Some movements gained momentum with the tightening of political space in the post-2005 period. Anticorruption coalitions and organizations have emerged throughout the continent, from Ghana's Anti-Corruption Coalition to the Anti-Corruption Coalition of Uganda, Civil Society Legislative Advocacy Centre (Nigeria), and United Against Corruption (South Africa). Such organizations are often accused of being antigovernmental and of encouraging political opposition. Many governments have increasingly sought to curtail civil society more generally through legislation regulating NGOs, media, and other sectors in order to provide oversight and control over their activities, even though the governments have signed the African Charter for Human and People's Rights (ACHR).

Uganda exemplifies these continent-wide shifts. It is a country that has a very active civil society, with eleven thousand registered NGOs and many coalitions and networks around debt, poverty, corruption, the environment, human rights, and women's rights concerns. It also has traditional organizations like monarchical formations (e.g., Buganda Lukiiko) as well as traditional associations such as burial societies and rotating credit associations. Uganda has many local associations for cultivating cultural expression and income generation in addition to professional associations, developmental associations, and special interest groups. The political space for civil society opened up in 1986 with the end of the "Bush War," when the government of President Yoweri Museveni took power. The war, which started in 1980, was between the National Resistance Army and various other militias, who fought against the government of Milton Obote. This was followed by fighting to depose his successor, General Tito Okello, in 1986. Some elements within civil society, including women's organizations, became especially active after Museveni came to power and were able to take advantage of the new openness.

Ever since Uganda opened up to multipartism in 2005, the political space has been closing. A 2006 NGO Act limited advocacy work and public policy activities. In 2013 a Public Order Management Act was passed, allowing the police to ban public meetings and decide on venues for public meetings. In 2015 another Non-Government Organizations Act was passed, permitting the government to refuse to register an NGO, restrict the employment of foreigners, and prohibit public meetings if they so desired. The 2016 NGO Act allows for imprisonment of up to three years, a fine of up to US$432, or both for what many consider "vague offences" as well as imprisonment of up to one year for denying access to or refusing or failing to comply with any order or direction of an inspector from an NGO Bureau. Nicholas Opiyo, executive director of Uganda's civil liberties group Chapter Four, said that the law "signals tough times" for NGOs and is the by-product of Museveni's prolonged stay in power of over thirty years, "which births paranoia and revulsion towards those critical of the state."[3]

During the 2011 and 2016 presidential elections the government banned social media amidst allegations of voter fraud while at the same time it detained the leading opposition candidate. After the 2016 elections the government banned all media coverage of the Defiance Campaign launched by the opposition party, Forum for Democratic Change, against President Museveni's reelection, which according to both local and international election observers, was marred by irregularities. A ban on political demonstrations was issued in advance of President Museveni's re-inauguration ceremony, restricting the media from any live coverage of opposition activities. All of these measures contravene the constitution, have made it incredibly challenging for civil society to operate, and reflect a gradual closing of political space since 2005 in what could be considered a hybrid regime.

Although most of the struggles in Africa have been between civil society and the state, there are also new tensions that have emerged between international and national NGOs over the way donors distribute funds. International NGOs generally contract out work to local organizations and individuals, whereas the national NGOs have most of the brainpower, do most of the work in a given field, and take most of the risk. They also engage in more culturally appropriate work and are generally better accepted by the local communities. Yet they receive a minimal proportion of donor funding while international NGOs capture the lion's share because they are believed to have greater capacity.

Several types of struggles have animated the civil society landscape since the 1990s, from struggles to keep presidential term limits intact to initiatives to prevent excessively restrictive regulatory legislation on NGOs and media. The first set of struggles are primarily defensive, to protect civil society freedoms from state encroachment and to protect gains made in political rights. The second set of struggles explored below are primarily aimed at gaining rights. New struggles have emerged around LGBT issues, women's rights concerns, and the environment. These contestations are explored in the following sections to illustrate the new political environment and what it has meant for civil society.

MOVEMENTS TO PRESERVE PRESIDENTIAL TERM LIMITS

There were only a few instances during the premultiparty period when presidents stepped down voluntarily. One could count them on one hand: General Olusegun Obasanjo in Nigeria (1979), Ahmadou Ahidjo in Cameroon (1982), Julius Nyerere in Tanzania (1985), and Leopold Senghor in Senegal (1980)—and these usually resigned only after they had held office for over twenty years. With the introduction of multipartyism, civilian rule, and the rewriting of constitutions in the 1990s, presidents were generally limited to two terms. With a few exceptions, the era of presidents for life seemed to be over. However, it did not take long for presidents to begin tinkering with the term limits imposed by these new constitutions. Today at least nine African countries have removed term limits as others seek to lift them, even though the majority of Africans (75 percent) support term limits according to the 2015 Afrobarometer survey.

The practice of prolonging the presidential term began in Namibia in 1998 when the Namibian constitution was amended to allow Sam Nujoma to have a third term. Term limits were also scrapped in Cameroon, Djibouti, Rwanda, Togo, Gabon, Guinea, Chad, Niger, and Uganda. A few other heads of state toyed with the idea of extending their terms but ultimately stepped down—for example, Benin's Mathieu Kerekou, Kenya's Daniel Arap Moi, Mozambique's Joaquim Chissano, Botswana's Festus Mogae, and Ghana's Jerry Rawlings. Senegalese president Wade got the Constitutional Court to permit him to run for a third term amidst resistance from opposition parties and street protests. But when he lost the second round of elections in 2012 to Macky Sall, he won praises from the international community when he conceded victory and graciously congratulated his opponent on his victory.

The preferred method of lifting term limits is for presidents with a comfortable majority in parliament to demand a constitutional amendment rather than risk a referendum. If this does not work, they go to the constitutional courts. If they use a referendum, they find ways to guarantee a favorable outcome through rigging or patronage. But many leaders have met with considerable civil society resistance to both legal and illegal manipulations.

Former Nigerian President Obasanjo's attempt to run for a third term in 2007 by using a constitutional amendment bill was blocked by the Senate Chamber and subsequently by the House of Representatives. Similarly, civil society vigorously thwarted attempts in Malawi and Zambia to extend presidential terms. In Malawi, where Hastings Banda had once declared himself president for life, civil society organizations and coalitions, including the Forum for the Defence of the Constitution, mobilized to resist efforts by President Bakili Muzuli to abolish term limits. In 2002 their parliament voted down a bill that would abolish term limits.

The new democrats are pressing for term limits and adherence to the constitution to avoid the past authoritarian practices in which leaders would monopolize power for extended periods of time, creating a zero-sum situation for other aspirants to power. In other cases proponents of term limits may have specific grievances against a head of state and wish to see a process in place that would allow for a change in leadership.

In Zambia the Law Association of Zambia in conjunction with key church coalitions, women's organizations, NGOs, and opposition parties successfully resisted President Frederick Chiluba's bid for a third term in 2001. Lawyers spearheaded the opposition, drawing on liberal principles of individual liberty, inalienable rights, and human equality to make their case. According to Jeremy Gould, their appeals were based on a liberal legal conception of rights and liberties. It was not so much a political discourse as much as a legalistic one drawing on the notion of the rule of law.[4] A coalition of opponents of extending presidential term limits met in the Oasis Restaurant in 2001 and drafted what came to be known as the Oasis Declaration, laying out the basis on which term limits could not be extended. The declaration is heavily laden with references to the constitution and is

uld has called a specifically "lawyerly" imagining of the state and a specif-
egalist" mode of authority, politics, and political morality.

cording to Gould, the three societal groups that were most outspoken in
Zambia around term limits included human rights and women's organizations
and other advocacy groups. A second group included the churches (Catholic,
Protestant, and Evangelical), with the Catholics in the forefront. The last was the
Law Association, which came in slightly later in 2001 to challenge the legal and
ethical implications of extending term limits. Similar patterns of activism and
actors can be found in other countries as well, although the press might also be
considered a contributing factor in these developments.

Where civil society has been crippled, the outcomes have not always been as
positive. Burundian president Pierre Nkurunziza sought to change the constitution in order to remain in power for a third term. He lost a parliamentary vote in
2014 but got the Constitutional Court to rule in his favor, unleashing protests and
an attempted coup, which pushed the country to the brink of civil war. Presidential elections were held under questionable circumstances in 2015 amidst international protests and domestic boycotts.[5]

In almost all cases the movements to limit presidential terms came from societal coalitions but required legislative support, which is indicative not only
of changing relationships between society and the legislature but also of the
strengthening of legislatures. It suggests a growing sense of responsiveness of the
legislature to popular pressures. Although it would be an overstatement to suggest
that there are close working relationships between civil society actors and parlia-
mentarians, legislators are paying greater attention to what civil society actors are
thinking and advocating. In the past, under single-party rule, parliaments used to
be rubber stamps and not worthy of study. This is rapidly changing, as there is a
fair bit of independence in the legislatures of Namibia, Mauritius, Ghana, Benin,
Botswana, Lesotho, Liberia, Senegal, Mozambique, South Africa, and Tanzania.

NGO REGULATORY LEGISLATION

Because so many NGOs became more advocacy oriented and began to explicitly
link human rights to developmental concerns, they became increasingly suspect
in many countries, leading governments in the mid-2000s to revive stalled efforts
that started in the 1990s to pass legislation regulating them. In the late 1980s and
1990s NGOs increasingly found themselves fighting for the right to autonomy
while opposing governmental legislative efforts to create agencies to monitor and
control NGO activities in Tanzania, Botswana, Ghana, Kenya, Malawi, Zambia,
Zimbabwe, Uganda, and other countries.[6]

Human rights, women, lawyers, environmental, and other groups opposed
efforts to pass these regulatory NGO bills containing restrictive provisions. Although these groups generally recognize the need to have an administrative
and regulatory framework for NGOs, they have resisted what they consider

heavy-handed infringement of their freedom to operate, even in countries calling themselves democracies. Bills regulating NGOs were drafted without sufficient transparency and without consulting NGOs or by consulting only the ones closest to the government. In the case of Uganda an NGO regulatory bill was hurriedly pushed through parliament without adequate time for consultation with NGOs.

In some countries like Zambia and Uganda the laws criminalize unregistered organizations. In Angola, Burundi, and DRC, the process of registering an NGO is unduly cumbersome. In Burundi some organizations are not able to travel to the Ministry of Home Affairs in the capital of Bujumbura in order to obtain the required registration documents, which are only available in Bujumbura. NGOs in Senegal must be approved by two different ministries, Social Development and Finance, and must regularly submit reports to the Ministry of Social Development, which evaluates their projects. In some countries NGOs must obtain government approval to carry out certain activities; for example, in Uganda NGOs must give seven days' notice before making "direct contact with people in any rural area of Uganda."

Some countries face outright bans on certain types of watchdog activity. Equatorial Guinea restricts NGOs from promoting, monitoring, or engaging in any human rights activities and requires government approval for gatherings with political purposes involving more than ten individuals. Angolan law prohibits NGOs from participating in "all activities of state organs; electoral processes; and from influencing national policy through the government or parliament."[7]

But even in the countries where such activities are not banned, NGOs rightfully fear that these regulatory bodies will suppress civil society organizations that are deemed too political, especially if they adopt positions that challenge or differ from the government's stance, regardless of how benign the issue. In most of these struggles NGOs have complained that the legislation assumed they were acting as opposition political parties, when in fact NGOs considered themselves nonpartisan—hence, excluded from restrictions on political parties. Developmental NGOs especially resent the assumption that they are seen as political. And although there are occasions when NGOs ally themselves with political parties to accomplish specific objectives, this does not warrant identifying them as political parties and therefore subjecting them to the same restrictions parties face.

One strategy for suppressing civil society is restricting international funding. Ethiopian civil society activists have come under particular repression. Since 2014 Ethiopia has restricted NGOs that receive more than 10 percent of their funding from foreign sources from participating in human rights and advocacy activity. The government strategy is to starve them of resources. The government restricts participation of charities and societies in activities that include the advancement of human and democratic rights, a focus on nationalities, the promotion of the rights of the disabled and children, and initiatives around conflict resolution or reconciliation or the promotion of the justice system. Civil society has sought to resist these restrictions through legal means, protests, and publicity as well as drawing international attention to them. Other impediments to operation include requiring reregistration at different intervals, while some countries have membership requirements. Once NGOs are registered, they may be subject to investigation by the government, restrictions, or even bans that may be placed on their activities and international management. Organizations in Ethiopia must notify the authorities seven days prior to a general assembly meeting.

Because of government suspicions of the political nature of NGOs, especially those involved in advocacy, NGOs themselves are sometimes hesitant to attach the term *political* to their activities. Nevertheless, Ghanaian Hamida Harrison argues that, for women activists, being political is unavoidable given the nature of advocacy around women's rights: "NGOs are supposed to be politically neutral, non-partisan and so on. And I think that many NGOs are afraid of the word 'political,' many of them actually say, 'we are not political,' while we in the women's movement are saying, 'This is politics.' The minute you start talking about power and resources and so on, it is politics. This is something that makes people within the NGO setting very uncomfortable."[8]

The NGO stance of claiming to be apolitical is understandable given the way NGOs are often treated. The 2003 Tanzanian NGO Act provides for criminal sanctions against NGOs that do not register with the government. It requires NGOs to align their activities with government plans and bans national NGO networks and coalitions. Tanzanian NGOs have strongly resisted these provisions, arguing that they contravene the Tanzanian constitution, the UN Declaration on Human Rights, and the International Covenant on Civil and Political Rights.

Some NGO activists have appealed on constitutional grounds regarding NGO regulatory legislation. In some countries they were able to stall the process for many years. In Zambia it took nine years before a regulatory bill was passed. In Uganda NGOs tried to preempt heavy-handed legislative restrictions, but in spite of strong protests from NGOs and donor countries, parliament passed a restrictive Non-Governmental Organisations (NGOs) Registration Act in 2006. For five years NGOs resisted the bill. They opposed the domination of the NGO board by government officials and security agents, the bill's stipulation that NGOs need to register on an annual basis, and the board's powers to deregister an NGO for violating any law. They felt this gave the board too much control that could be used for political purposes and undermined associational autonomy; it undermined advocacy work.

As leader of the NGO coalition Development Network of Indigenous Voluntary Organisations (DENIVA), Jassy Kwesiga reflected on one of the core concerns of NGO activists in Uganda but also throughout Africa: "As for denial of registration on the basis of incompatibility with Government policy, plans and public interest, what if the NGOs are expressing the will of the people that may be at odds with Government policy and Government definition of public interest? History in Uganda and elsewhere is full of many state inspired undemocratic misfortunes in the name of public interest."[9] Rather, state and society need to respect the "independence, rights and obligations of the other," writes Kwesiga.

What is emerging from these struggles is an understanding that it may be desirable to register and monitor NGOs so as to prevent duplication of activities and facilitate collaboration between NGOs or between NGOs and government, and there are, on occasion, NGOs that are set up for unscrupulous purposes. However, regulation in order to suppress advocacy that challenges government policy is incompatible with democracy and is a holdover from the past thinking and practice of one-party states. Attempts to characterize normal NGO advocacy or watchdog activities as antigovernmental and subject to controls have been resisted, as have efforts to curtail the autonomy of civil society more generally. Placing security personnel on NGO regulatory boards, for example, suggests that NGOs might pose a security risk of some kind.

Civil society activists are pointing to alternative ways of thinking about state-society relations. Many feel there needs to be more mutual trust built between governments and NGOs, with the understanding that a healthy democracy is built on productive synergies between the state and civil society. There needs to be room for societal activities that can help shape government policy through pressure and advocacy, serve as a check on corruption, and promote transparency. Civil society can also be an important resource for government, providing information, research, data, and other forms of knowledge to support government activities. It can also provide powerful societal backing for policies and mobilize people to participate in initiatives and campaigns.

The Ministry of Youth and Sports in Liberia, to take one example, works closely with youth and student organizations throughout the country, which have enthusiastically and actively lobbied the government around key issues, including corruption, transparency, and accountability, particularly in the education sector (e.g., grade buying). These groups play a watchdog role, monitoring the implementation of the 2011 education law, but they also act on other issues like policy regarding petroleum resources and their use. These types of productive synergies are only possible if they can be built in an atmosphere of trust and cooperation. The Liberia National Student Union complained to the president directly when her appointee as national youth advisor was not from the student movement and had come from out of the country. She was sympathetic to their concerns and appointed another liaison whom they approved.

Since Ellen Johnson-Sirleaf took over as president of Liberia in 2006 the human rights situation has improved dramatically; the press operates more or less freely with some important exceptions, as do NGOs and political parties; and a zero-tolerance policy for corruption is in place and enforced. The legislature and judiciary enjoy a level of independence rarely seen in Africa. NGOs have the confidence to operate freely because they know their advocacy will not be seen as antigovernmental, and they in turn do their best to support government when there is a need.

STRUGGLES FOR MEDIA AUTONOMY

In 1991 journalists from throughout Africa, UN groups, observers, intergovernmental bodies, and NGOs attended a conference organized by UNESCO, other UN bodies, the International Federation of Newspaper Publishers, the International Federation of Journalists, and the International Press Institute. After a long and frank discussion about the problems of the media in Africa, they adopted the Declaration of Windhoek on Promoting an Independent and Pluralistic African Press, popularly known as the Windhoek Declaration. The key and most-quoted principle in the Declaration states, "Consistent with Article 19 of the Universal Declaration of Human Rights, the establishment, maintenance and fostering of an independent, pluralistic and free press is essential to the development and maintenance of democracy in a nation and for economic development."

The document served as a rallying cry for some of the efforts to democratize in years to come. It was not only influential in Africa but was also the first such declaration in the world; other regions adopted similar documents in subsequent years, including central Asia (Alma-Ata Declaration), the Middle East (Sana'a Declaration), and Latin America and the Caribbean (Santiago Declaration), affirming the media workers' commitment to freedom of the press.

In more recent years numerous African countries have also signed international treaties pledging their commitment to freedom of information and the press. Between 2000 and 2016 nineteen African countries have passed access to information (ATI) laws, including some of the worst continuing violators of the law. The countries include South Africa, Angola, Zimbabwe, Uganda, Ethiopia, and Liberia.

As with NGOs, conflicts over media autonomy and freedom of the press have emerged over legislation to regulate media workers. These struggles have often placed media workers at the forefront of the civil society struggles for autonomy from government control and freedom of expression. Media workers in Angola, Botswana, Chad, Kenya, Gambia, Nigeria, South Africa, Uganda, and Zambia have debated existing or proposed bills regulating the media.

Of all nations in the world, Namibia has most improved its press environment, according to the World Press Freedom Index issued by Reporters Without Borders, and is now ranked seventeen. Africa overall has one of the most improved media environments in 2016, and it has the best media environment as a region after Europe. However, it still ranks low, which says more about the dismal overall state of journalism worldwide. Many countries in Africa experience routine arrests, detentions, imprisonment, killings, and exilings of journalists. There have been closures of important media houses, firing of media workers, and state control of broadcasting systems. Repressive laws curtail journalists' normal functioning.

Some of the worst infringements of the freedom of the press have occurred in Zimbabwe, where the independent media has been effectively silenced with the vigorous application of such legislation, including the Access to Information and Protection of Privacy Act (AIPPA) and the Public Order and Security Act (POSA). For example, in Zimbabwe in 2016 journalists were being arrested, a privately owned newspaper was closed down, and the state-owned radio had a monopoly in broadcasting.

In Uganda media workers have been threatened, attacked, and arrested. Their equipment has been confiscated and their offices raided. Many of these incidents occurred leading up to elections and have influenced citizens' ability to make informed decisions. According to Amnesty International, a journalist charged with the vague offense of criticizing government officials online and spreading false news about public officials in Gambia may face up to fifteen years of imprisonment and a large fine, according to the 2013 Information and Communication (Amendment) Act. In Cameroon journalists were arbitrarily arrested and faced unfounded terrorism charges. In Sierra Leone a journalist was arrested and detained for eleven days because of comments he made that were critical of the government response to the Ebola crisis. In Ethiopia media workers languish in prison and some have been convicted in absentia for being critical of the government. One journalist, Eskinder Nega, was found guilty of high treason for inciting terrorist acts and sentenced to eighteen years in prison simply for writing an article critical of the lack of freedom of expression. In Sudan the 2009 Press and Printed Materials Act imposed restrictions on the media in the interests of "national security and public order." Since January 2015 at least twenty newspapers have experienced confiscation of particular issues about forty-five times.[10]

In the early 1990s, as winds of political liberalization swept Africa and the media began to assert itself, various governments began to introduce new legislation to create regulatory councils to control media workers and their associations. The proposed legislation galvanized media workers to protect their professional interests as well as their freedom of speech.[11]

In Kenya, for example, media organizations successfully put on the back burner the Kenya Mass Media Commission Bill (1995) and Press Council Bill (1995), which sought to regulate and discipline journalists and media workers and oversee their registration. The bills were widely rejected on the grounds that they restricted the freedom of speech. However, in 2016 a media bill was passed that was much worse than the 1995 bills. It imposed harsh fines and two years in jail or both for a journalist found guilty of defaming the Kenyan parliament or its members. A joint statement issued by the Kenya Editors Guild, Kenya Union of Journalists, and the Kenya Correspondents Association slammed inclusion of the offensive clauses, saying they violated democratic ideals.

It is not only the independent media that is under attack. Social media is also now being targeted. Perhaps the most extensive and repressive regulations of this type can be found in Ethiopia, where such regulatory policies increased after the 2005 elections, when opposition candidates used social media and the Internet to mount a challenge to the ruling party. Relying on laws like the Mass Media and Freedom of Information Proclamation of 2008 and the Anti-Terrorism

Proclamation of 2009, the government uses filtering, surveillance, and blocking of contact to monitor and suppress numerous bloggers, activists, and journalists. Zimbabwe's Post and Telecommunications Act of 2000 and Interception of Communications Bill of 2006 allow the government to monitor email usage and require Internet service providers to provide information when requested.[12]

In Burundi the government forbade both public and private radio stations from broadcasting about the protests against the president's attempts to abolish term limits as well as shut down access to Facebook, Twitter, and WhatsApp from mobile phones, accusing the media of inciting rebellion.

LGBT MOVEMENTS

LGBT movements have become among the most active movements in Africa after the 2000s. A 2016 report, "We Exist: Mapping LGBTQ Organizing in West Africa," points to a rise in LGBT mobilization across the region amidst increasing religious fundamentalism and homophobia. The report finds that there have been not only increasing numbers of gay rights organizations but also newer organizations of lesbians and transgender people. There are new nationwide and regional networks and coalitions as well as new organizations focused on family mediation, working with the media, documenting rights violations, engaging law enforcement, providing emergency shelter provisions, facilitating safety and security trainings, and engaging in human rights literacy and legal aid.

The legal context in Africa is mixed and in flux. Homosexuality is illegal, and convictions carry jail time in thirty-four countries, with life imprisonment in Tanzania and Sierra Leone. Three countries have the death penalty for homosexuality—Mauritania, Sudan, and northern Nigeria—although the actual criminal prosecution of such cases is rare. It is legal in twenty-two countries, and Angola, Botswana, Mozambique, Seychelles, and Mauritius have some protections against discrimination based on sexual identity.

South Africa was the first country in the world to ban discrimination based on sexual orientation in its 1996 constitution. The clause is the product of lobbying by Zackie Achmat, the leader of the HIV-AIDS Treatment Action Campaign, along with other activists. Cape Verde in 2004 became the second nation on the continent to decriminalize homosexual acts over the age of consent (sixteen years).

Although levels of homophobia have escalated and have been evident in government policy, LGBT advocacy has slowly been having an impact. In 2016 the Botswana Court of Appeal unanimously delivered a crucial judgment in which it rejected the government of Botswana's appeal against a Gaborone High Court decision that allowed for the registration of the Lesbians, Gays and Bisexuals Organisation of Botswana (LEGABIBO). The Uganda Anti-Homosexuality Act of 2014 was initially passed by the Ugandan parliament, expanding the criminalization of same-sex relations to include the death penalty. It also included vague language about penalties for individuals, companies, and NGOs that aided and abetted homosexuality. As a result of pressures from gay and human rights activists, the Constitutional Court ruled the bill invalid on a technicality.

Civil society is divided on issues of LGBT rights, and religious institutions are sometimes at the forefront of opposition to LGBT reforms. In Malawi a coalition of pastors, the Young Pastors Coalition of Malawi (YPCM), lobbied to get the government to arrest four thousand gay people living in a northern Malawi town. In spite of the pastors' campaign, the Malawian government has said that it would not arrest nor prosecute gay citizens, and it announced plans to review existing antihomosexual laws. In 2012 the government committed itself to honoring regional, international, and fundamental human rights obligations. As a result, former president Joyce Banda imposed a moratorium on all arrests and prosecutions of consensual same-sex practices under the Malawian Penal Code.

Marc Epprecht has argued that accusations that campaigns for homosexual rights are a form of Western cultural imperialism have sometimes provoked patriotic defensiveness.[13] For this reason LGBT activists have focused primarily on health concerns that discreetly promote sexual rights, and they are having some success in challenging prevalent homophobic discourses. One way NGOs and governments have worked around societal prejudices is by avoiding naming the beneficiaries of health programs directed at the LGBT community. Thus, for those who don't know, it is hard to tell who these organizations are, serving with names like Alliance Rights (Nigeria), Freedom and Roam (Uganda), the Centre for the Development of People (Malawi), Matrix (Lesotho), Andiligueey (Senegal, meaning "men working together to help other men" in Wolof), Horizon Community Association (Rwanda), or Ishtar MSM (Kenya). This allows for these organizations to exist while avoiding stigmatization.

WOMEN'S RIGHTS MOVEMENTS

The 1990s saw the emergence of new women's movements, which served as catalysts for many of the new constitutional and legal challenges in women's rights that we are seeing today in Africa. These movements had new priorities, new leaders, and new sources of funding independent of state patronage networks, which older women's organizations in the past had depended on to a greater extent.

Women's rights organizations have drawn on international and pan-African treaties to advance their rights, especially the Convention on the Elimination of All Forms of Discrimination Against Women. Many of the post-1990 policies draw on the Platform for Action that emerged from the 1995 UN Beijing Conference on Women, which encouraged women to seek equal gender representation in political and other institutions, including legislatures, executives, judiciaries, nongovernmental associations, religious institutions, and other bodies.

At the pan-African level, women's organizations rely on such treaties like the African Union Protocol on Women's Rights to lobby around a new generation of policies that seek to protect women's bodily integrity through legislation around female genital cutting, domestic violence, and other such concerns as well as to address women's right to a livelihood through access to land, property, credit, inputs, and other resources.

Women activists have been advocating increases in their representation in legislatures through regional organizations like ECOWAS and the Southern African Development Community (SADC). In 1987 SADC set a goal of 30 percent female-held legislative seats by 2005, and in 2005 it set a goal for its member countries to attain 50 percent female representation in their legislatures by the year 2015. As a result of regional pressures, in 2012 non-SADC countries in Africa had on average 17 percent legislative seats held by women, whereas SADC countries had 24 percent.

Other women's rights issues have generated similar regional attention. In 2005 an African Parliamentary Conference held in Dakar focused on female genital cutting, and speakers and members of twenty African national parliamentary assemblies unanimously adopted a declaration calling for an end to the practice, arguing that "culture is not immutable and that it is subject to perpetual change, adaptations and reforms."[14] They pledged to work with civil society, traditional chiefs and religious leaders, women's and youth movements, and governments to adopt strategies to end the practice, drawing on a human rights framework by taking into consideration the education, health, development, and poverty dimensions of the problem.

Some of the pressures to end the practice are quite extraordinary. A group of distinguished Islamic scholars met at Al-Azhar University in Cairo and issued a statement calling female genital mutilation "a deplorable, inherited custom, which is practiced in some societies and is copied by some Muslims in several countries."[15] They concluded that "there are no written grounds for this custom in the Qur'an with regard to an authentic tradition of the Prophet" and acknowledged that "female genital circumcision practiced today harms women psychologically and physically." They insisted that the practice be stopped and called for it to be criminalized.

Since the 1990s women's organizations have been pushing for and often succeeding in getting constitutional reforms and legislative changes to protect their rights in ways that override customary laws and practices that violate women's rights, discriminate against women, or violate bill of rights provisions regarding gender equality. These are extremely profound challenges. They are, in effect, attempts to legitimize new legal-based sources of authority for rights governing relations between men and women, family relations, and women themselves. In the past, even when laws existed to regulate marriage, inheritance, custody, and other such practices, customary laws and practices coexisted and generally took precedence when it came to family and clan concerns. Today women's movements are challenging these norms through constitutional and legislative changes in ways that we have not seen in the past.

They have been actively chipping away at discriminatory customary laws through changes in family law/codes, land laws, and other such issues. They are also pushing through key legislation pertaining to women's bodily integrity involving violence against women and female genital cutting. These represent a new generation of policy measures to address women's status that are distinct from earlier legislation around marriage and inheritance, maternity leave, employment practices, and the taxation of women.

Since the 1990s new constitutions in countries like Namibia (1990), Ethiopia (1995), Malawi (1994), Uganda (1995), South Africa (1996), Rwanda (2003), Burundi (2005), and Swaziland (2006) have included nondiscrimination or equality provisions, prohibiting customary practices if they undermined the dignity, welfare, or status of women. These were new developments in African constitution making and can be contrasted with constitutions passed prior to 1990, in which customary law generally was not subject to any gender-related restrictions. Women's movements played an important role in ensuring that these clauses were included.

In terms of legislative change, one of the most important changes has been the involvement of women's movements in changing land laws to strengthen women's property rights. One of the most dramatic changes in land tenure reform today is that for the first time since the precolonial period, states are giving legal recognition to existing African customary tenure regimes, which are being treated as legitimate land tenure systems on par with the freehold/leasehold systems rather than being seen as systems to be eradicated or phased out. Unregistered customary tenure, which is the main system of land rights in Africa, is being recognized in the new policies. Ironically, at the very time that these gains are being won in the name of the rural poor, the pastoralists, women, and the landless, African women have mounted new movements to eradicate customary land tenure practices and fight for the rights of women to be able to inherit, purchase, and own land in their own name.

Some of these movements have targeted land grabbing, which has become a rampant form of corruption. In 2012 soldiers, police, and the Uganda Wildlife Authority guards evicted six thousand people from their homes in Apaa in northern Uganda's Amuru District. The land had been sold to a South African investor who intended to turn the area into wildlife hunting grounds. When a team of surveyors appeared in 2015, local residents demonstrated, resulting in the injury of eighty-two demonstrators.[16] Then on April 17, 2015, Acholi women from Apaa launched a protest, undressing before two government ministers who had come to try to pacify the population and assure them that no one was to be displaced from their land. The women, some stark naked, others baring their breasts, wept and threw themselves on the ground, revealing their utter contempt, frustration, and anger against state harassment and against the Uganda government's orchestrated evictions of families in Apaa. Female nakedness is the ultimate curse a woman can level against someone not only among the Acholi but also in many other parts of

Africa. Women's naked protest is the act of putting bodily symbols of motherhood and birth in the public space and, as such, the curse cannot easily be reversed, as it symbolizes social death. These forms of protest around land have become increasingly popular in Uganda.

Feminist lawyers working with these movements have argued that customary law in the present-day context has been used to selectively preserve practices that subordinate women. Rather than seeing customary land practices as a basis on which to improve women's access to land, they are advocating for rights-based systems that improve women's ability to buy, own, sell, and obtain titles to land. Since the time of colonialism bases of customary ownership have been eroded, making women's access to land significantly more precarious as the protections traditionally ensured by the clan system have been peeled away.

In recent years, with increased commercialization of land and problems of land scarcity, local leaders have felt mounting pressures to protect the clan system. In so doing they have placed even greater constraints on women's access to land, as the clan system they are seeking to preserve is often no longer one that affords women the supports it is once said to have guaranteed. For this reason women, both rural and urban, have responded to the renewed interest in protecting customary laws and practices through collective strategies, which in many countries have included movements to ensure women's access to and ownership of land. Women have also adopted individual strategies of purchasing land and taking their land disputes to court.

For example, in Uganda women of all classes have been purchasing and selling land throughout the country. Several studies by Makerere Institute for Social Research, carried out in 1995 and 2000 in the Lira, Mpigi, Mbale, Kamuli, Mbarara, Nebbi, Mubende, and Kabarole districts, show that between 15 and 20 percent of women own land in these districts, which are located throughout Uganda. A study of Mukono in 2002 showed that 45 percent of women owned land. Women's main concern in all these studies was difficulty in accessing land, which means that relying on their husbands was not a reliable strategy.[17] Purchasing land has in effect become a way of circumventing the traditional authorities.

Women have been active in a variety of land alliances and coalitions throughout Africa, many of which have arisen in response to legislative and constitutional changes in tenure laws. New land laws were enacted in Uganda, Tanzania, Zanzibar, Mozambique, Zambia, Eritrea, Namibia, and South Africa in the 1990s. Rwanda, Malawi, Lesotho, Zimbabwe, Swaziland, and Kenya are drafting land bills. Women have been at the forefront of organizations like the Uganda Land Alliance, the National Land Forum in Tanzania, the Zambia National Land Alliance, National Land Committee in South Africa, Kenya Land Alliance, Rwanda Land Alliance, and the Namibian NGO Federation (NANGOF), all of which have fought for the land rights of women, pastoralists, the landless, and other marginalized people. Regional networks like Landnet in East Africa have also formed to network between countries. At the same time, key women's organizations have been active around land issues in all these countries and have often played a leading role in forming the broader land alliances. At the regional level in East and Southern Africa, Women and Law in Development in Africa (WILDAF) has been active since the early 1990s on land and other issues, as has Women and Law in Southern Africa (WLSA) in seven southern African countries.[18]

The new movements have been galvanized by mounting land pressures and the placement of constraints on women, who generally do not have sufficient access to and control over land. Although the focus of the women's movements has been on customary land practices, they have also been concerned with the negative effects of the privatization of land and land grabbing as governments have increasingly sought foreign investment through tourism, mining, and other businesses. Women have joined forces with pastoralists, who have often found themselves shut out of vast grazing lands in many parts of East Africa, Botswana, and Namibia as a result of large land sales.[19]

The movements have taken up a variety of concerns. For example:

- Ugandan women's rights advocates have long fought to expand women's land rights. After facing numerous setbacks, in 2007 advocates from Law and Advocacy for Women in Uganda finally got the constitutional court to strike down key provisions of the Succession Act regarding women's right to inherit property. The law did not allow women to inherit property of a deceased person, including their husband, and this was found to be discriminatory and unconstitutional.[20] The Act provided only for male intestacy, assuming that women who died intestate had nothing to bequeath; it allowed for 15 percent of an estate to go to a widow and 100 percent to a widower, and it provided for the appointment of a guardian for any children, even though the widow could be appointed as guardian.
- Women's organizations were active in Tanzania, where they won the right to acquire, hold, use, and deal with land in the Land Act 1999 and Village Land Act 1999. These laws also ensure that women are represented in land administration and adjudication bodies. The Land Act overrides customary law if it denies women their right to use, transfer, and own land. Women's rights of co-occupancy are also protected.
- Women's organizations played a leading role in the passage of Mozambique's new land law in 1997. They were active in and led the Land Forum, a coalition of two hundred organizations that participated in discussions leading up to the passage of the land bill. The law not only protects customary tenure arrangements but also includes provisions that allow women to own land and protections that give them greater access to and control over land. Women still face enormous resource and social constraints in accessing land, but with this legislation many of the legal constraints have been removed.

ENVIRONMENTAL MOVEMENTS

Since 2000 environmental NGOs and others have responded to a series of environmental challenges on a scale not seen previously. Climate change has been an area of particular concern. African civil society actors have been involved in climate change issues since the UN environmental conference held in Rio de Janeiro in 1992 and at the Paris conference on climate change in 2015. They have been part of efforts to reduce the negative impacts of global warming, calling for governments to take measures to reduce harmful greenhouse gas emissions through the United Nations Framework Convention on Climate Change (UNFCCC). African countries have already been among the region's most affected as a result of the droughts, unreliable rainfall, flooding, and poor crop yields and grazing that result from such weather patterns. Changes in crop and animal disease patterns also accompany these problems. The continent is going to continue to face the most dire impacts.

Although civil society organizations do not have a role at formal UNFCC negotiations, they can be present as observers and make up about 15 percent of all participants. African constituencies make up the largest percentage of participants coming from environmental NGOs (ENGOs), business and industry NGOs (BINGOs), local government and municipal authorities (LGMAs), indigenous peoples organizations (IPOs), research and independent NGOs (RINGOs), trade union NGOs (TUNGOs), farmers, women and gender groups, and youth NGOs (YOUNGOs). African governments and civil society actors have already been able to shape the discussions to move away from strategies to prevent global warming to seeking strategies that also allow countries to adapt to new situations.

Environmental struggles have taken many forms:

- When the Ugandan government considered a request by the Mehta Group's Sugar Cooperation of Uganda Ltd. to take over seventy-one hundred hectares of Mabira forest to expand its sugarcane plantation and double sugar production, a broad coalition of NGOs protested the move.[21] They forced the cabinet to halt the proposed giveaway of the forest until a policy is developed to determine the use of such land. Mabira is the largest natural forest in the country and serves as a significant water catchment area for Lake Victoria. A broad range of environmental, religious, developmental, and human rights groups protested the move, arguing that it was a breach of the Constitution to degazette the forest reserve.
- In Sudan there has been a movement led by the Hamdab Dam Affected People to stop the construction of the Chinese-built Merowe dam, which will displace several communities of sixty thousand people and submerge archeological sites in proximity to the Nile within an area of 175-by-4 kilometers. The project is intended to double Sudan's power production.
- Protests broke out in Cote d'Ivoire with the news that a tanker ship of the Dutch Trafigura Beheer BV company had dumped around 528,000 liters of

liquid chemical waste in Abidjan in 2006, causing seventy-seven thousand Abidjan residents to seek medical treatment. At least ten were known to have died from the chemical dumping. Ivorian Human Rights League (Lidho) and officials of toxic waste victims associations sought compensation for the victims from the company. They have been pressing for and exploring changes in international legislation and monitoring mechanisms in order to avoid the recurrence of such environmental catastrophes in Africa.

- Kimarer-Sugutek Rights Group and other groups have protested pollution by Kenya Fluorspar Company as calcium fluoride was found to have been transported by the Kerio River into the gorges of the Kerio Valley, Rift Valley Province, making the water undrinkable for humans and animals.
- Earthlife Namibia, the National Society for Human Rights, and the German Oeko Institute raised concerns in 2005 about a uranium mining project carried out by the Langer Heinrich Uranium Mine. They were concerned about the polluting of ground and surface water sources, the emission of radioactive dust, and the ecological impact on plants and animals in the environmentally vulnerable Namib-Naukluft Park.

These are just a few of the many environmental movements that have sprung up across the continent and have resulted in the creation of linkages between various rights-based organizations.

CLASH OF RIGHTS

The new emphasis on rights-based approaches that emerged in the 1990s along with the political opening and subsequent growth of civil society have not only catalyzed new forces demanding rights they have also set various civil society groups onto a collision course by animating contradictory claims. With the new 1996 constitution in South Africa, women's alliances like the Women's National Coalition were able to lobby for and obtain key provisions ensuring the protection of women's rights. They gained greater representation at higher levels of government and in the legislature. Many women thought that with the end of apartheid and with the new constitution they would be free of discriminatory customary practices; however, the constitution not only guaranteed women's' rights but also provided for rights of traditional authorities who are now threatening women's bid for a new allocation of resources, especially of land. Both women and traditional authorities draw on the 1996 constitution to make claims for their rights, but in ways that potentially clash. One finds in other parts of Africa similar conflicts between those claiming the rights to religious and cultural freedom and women's rights advocates over issues like the family codes, polygamy, child marriage, and female genital cutting.

The political opening and democratization of South Africa not only provided space for women's mobilization but it also energized the traditional authorities. In the case of chieftancies in southern Africa, to take one example, the weakness or inaccessibility of the state or local government has led populations to seek more accessible traditional authorities. After 1994 a strong lobby of chiefs emerged, seeking legal recognition and protection. Rather than disappearing, traditional authorities (clan formations, elders councils like the *kgotla* in Botswana, the monarchical parliament in Buganda, hometown associations, women's and men's councils in eastern Nigeria, etc.) have become invigorated with political liberalization throughout Africa. These institutions exist side by side and interact with modern parliaments and local governments.

In Nigeria there are tensions between advocates for child rights who want to raise the age of marriage under the Child Rights Act of 2003 and the Supreme Council for shar'ia in Nigeria, which appeals to Islamic law for its authority. Federal laws that are passed at the national level are required to be passed within the State Houses of Assembly. By 2007 ten state assemblies had adopted the Act. The Islamic Supreme Council says that if state assemblies pass the Act, it will destroy the very basis and essence of the shar'ia and Muslim culture. The controversial sections of the Act include provisions that make it illegal for parents to marry off their daughter if she is younger than eighteen and to consummate a marriage with a child under eighteen years of age. Proponents of the law see the age limit as a way of ensuring that girls complete their schooling, which has implications for women's economic status and for development in the country more generally. The law also gives both boys and girls equal inheritance rights.

In other contexts the conflicts are not only between forces supporting or resisting women's or other human rights; there are also tensions between those who share a common agenda. At the end of military rule in 1999 women's groups in Nigeria found themselves with competing notions of rights and competing bases for appealing for women's rights. Some groups saw women's empowerment in terms of promoting family welfare, while feminists (e.g., the group Women in Nigeria) saw women's rights advancement as linked to equality and opposition to discrimination. For some Islamic women's groups women's empowerment was tied to educating people and building awareness among women of their rights under shar'ia. Still other Muslim women's organizations wanted to improve the rights of women and girls by appealing to Islamic law itself. The Federation of Muslim Women Associations of Nigeria (FOMWAN) sees Islamic family law as historically constituted with well-defined notions of rights that can be reformed, but they can only be reformed within the Islamic legal system.[22]

CONCLUSIONS

The 1990s saw the rise of new rights organizations in Africa based on human rights, including the rights of children, women, and the disabled along with environmental, economic, and other rights. Student protests rocked South African campuses in 2015 when the government announced a 11.5 percent tuition hike.

These protests cut across racial lines. As political space closed and reversals in democratization occurred in many countries, civil society organizations sought to preserve the autonomy of NGOs and the media, to limit executive power, and to preserve judicial and legislative independence. In spite of the constricting space, new movements emerged to tackle climate change, the rights of LGBT people, women, and other marginalized people. New tensions also emerged not only in relation to the state but also between domestic NGOs and international NGOs, both competing for the same funds but fighting to have their respective competencies and capacities recognized.

Competing definitions and sources of authority for rights emerged—for example, between groups fighting to define rights. Although there may be agreement on the adoption of rights-based approaches, not everyone agrees on their meaning. New democratizing constitutions invigorated not only women's and children's rights activists but also traditional authorities and religious activists who worked at cross-purposes when it came to issues like women's land rights and personal law, such as child marriage and polygamy.

Hybrid and authoritarian states have increasingly relied on legislative and constitutional sources of authority to rein in and control civil society and the media, whereas civil society has sought protection and autonomy using the same instruments. States prefer these legal manipulations over brute force, although force is also on the menu of tactics employed from time to time. Land and other property laws have been embraced both to protect the rights of marginalized groups and to unleash the forces of the market, creating forces that work at odds and establishing possible collision courses.

NOTES

1. The first wave began in the early nineteenth century and lasted up to 1922. The second wave lasted from the end of World War II up to 1962.

2. Larry Diamond, "Is the Third Wave of Democratization Over? An Empirical Assessment," Kellog Institute for International Studies, Working Paper no. 236. 1997, www 3.nd.edu/~kcllogg/publications/workingpapers/WPS/236.pdf; Samuel P. Huntington, "Democracy's Third Wave," *Journal of Democracy* 2, no. 2 (1991), pp. 12–34.

3. Amy Fallon, "Uganda's Repressive NGO Act," Inter Press Service, March 6, 2016.

4. Jeremy Gould, "Postcolonial Liberalism and the Legal Complex in Zambia: Elegy or Triumph?" in *Colonialism's Legacies: Variations on the Theme of Political Liberalism in the British Post-Colony*, ed. Terence Halliday and Lucien Karpik (Cambridge: Cambridge University Press, 2011).

5. Ken Opalo, "Term Limits and Democratic Consolidation in Sub-Saharan Africa: Lessons from Burundi," *Constitutionnet*, July 30, 2015, www.constitutionnet.org/news/term -limits-and-democratic-consolidation-sub-saharan-africa-lessons-burundi.

6. Emmanuel Gyimah-Boadi, "The Rebirth of African Liberalism," *Journal of Democracy* 9, no. 2 (1998): 18–31, 22; Stephen N. Ndegwa, *The Two Faces of Civil Society: NGOs and Politics in Africa* (West Hartford, CT: Kumarian Press, 1996); Michael Bratton, "The Politics of Government-NGO Relations in Africa," *World Development* 17, no. 4 (1989), p. 577.

7. Angolan Law of Association (14/91 of May 11, 1991), Article 8.

8. A. Mama, "The Ghanaian Women's Manifesto Movement: Amina Mama speaks with Dzodzi Tsikata, Rose Mensah-Kutin and Hamida Harrison," *Feminist Africa* no. 4 (2005), p. 129.

9. Jassy Kwesiga, "NGOs Call for Change," *Monitor* (Kampala) 6 (March 2001).

10. "Africa Media Freedom Seriously Threatened," Amnesty International, May 1, 2015www.amnesty.org/en/latest/news/2015/05/africa-media-freedom-seriously-threatened.

11. N. Alabi, Western African Regional Perspectives, Summary Review, Windhoek, The Windhoek Seminar: "Ten Years On: Assessment, Challenges and Prospects," May 3–5, 2001; C. Lingo and S. K. Lobe, Central African Regional Perspectives, Summary Review, Windhoek, The Windhoek Seminar.

12. Hilary Matfess, "Nigeria's Social Media Bill Follows a Trend of African Governments Keeping Tabs on Civil Society," Quartz Africa, December 9, 2015, http://qz.com/569372/nigerias-social-media-bill-follows-a-trend-of-african-governments-keeping-tabs-on-civil-society.

13. Marc Epprecht, "Sexual Minorities, Human Rights and Public Health Strategies in Africa," *African Affairs* 111, no. 443 (2012), pp. 223–243.

14. "Violence Against Women, Abandoning Female Genital Mutilation: The Role of National Parliaments," African Parliamentary Conference, 2005.

15. "TARGET's Breakthrough: Islam Outlaws Female Mutilation!" TARGET, November 24, 2006, www.target-human-rights.com/HP-00_aktuelles/alAzharKonferenz/index.php?p=beschluss&lang=en.

16. Okumu Langol, "Uganda Land Grab: Women Protestors, Facing Armed Soldiers, Unleash Secret Weapon—Nudity," *Blac Star News*, April 20, 2015.

17. A. Sebina-Zziwa, R. Kibombo, et al., *Patterns and Trends of Women's Participation in Land Markets in Uganda*, 8th International Interdisciplinary Congress on Women, Kampala, Uganda, Makerere Institute of Social Research, Makerere University, 2002.

18. Aili Mari Tripp, "Women's Movements, Customary Law, and Land Rights in Africa: The Case of Uganda," *African Studies Quarterly* 7, no. 4 (2004).

19. Robin H. Palmer, *Oxfam GB's Land Advocacy Work in Tanzania and Uganda: The End of an Era?* (Oxford: Oxfam, 1998).

20. "Implication of the Ruling on Adultery," *New Vision* (Uganda), April 8, 2007.

21. These included the Uganda Joint Christian Council, National Foundation for Democracy and Human Rights in Uganda, Uganda Land Alliance, Environmental Action Network, Advocates Coalition for Environment and Development, Uganda Forestry Association, the Advocacy Coalition for Development and Environment, Greenwatch, the Environmental Action Network, Environmental Alert, and the Anti-Corruption Coalition.

22. Nkoyo Toyo, "Revisiting Equality as a Right: The Minimum Age of Marriage Clause in the Nigerian Child Rights Act, 2003," *Third World Quarterly* 27, no. 7 (January 2006), pp. 1299–1312.

Democracy and the State in Sub-Saharan Africa

John W. Harbeson

Democracy's Third Wave in sub-Saharan Africa reached its twenty-fifth anniversary around 2015, an appropriate milestone for an overview of its progress and status over that period.[1] Although the wave of late-twentieth-century democratization preceded the end of the Cold War in southern Europe and Latin America and accompanied it in central and eastern Europe, democracy's Third Wave in sub-Saharan Africa followed in the wake of the Cold War.[2] Thus, democratization in sub-Saharan Africa displaced many long-running authoritarian regimes beginning early in the 1990s, newly undermined by withdrawn backing from the former principal Cold War adversaries, exposing at the same time the underlying weakness of many of the continent's postindependence, presumptively also postcolonial states.[3]

Post–Cold War African democratization and what has proven to be an ongoing crisis of the African state intersected with the international financial institution (IFI)–led demarche for economic liberalization, then in midpassage. Begun early in the preceding decade, the objective of this liberalization had been to rescue African and other developing economies from the consequences of their excessive and mismanaged direction by postindependence governments. The IFIs' prescription for these ills, supported by most Western governments, was and has been to liberate the countries' market economies from misconceived state direction, thereby also *inter alia* increasing their interdependence within an international economy still led at the time principally by the OECD countries. By the early

1990s, however, it had become apparent that this initiative had also reached a critical juncture. On the one hand, African and other governments had responded only incompletely to these internationally led economic liberalization initiatives, notwithstanding that they more or less reluctantly signed on to the objective under strong pressure to do so. On the other hand, what had been struck as an "implicit bargain" had been realized only weakly at best. This expected outcome of adherence to the IFI market-liberating guidelines was that Western investment would flow generously to the extent that African governments liberalized their economies. That bargain had been only weakly realized by the early 1990s.[4] At the same time, the IFIs gradually came to appreciate that their initiative needed adjustment to mitigate the poverty and environmental distress that economic liberalization had largely failed to alleviate.

THE CONTEXT OF DEMOCRACY IN SUB-SAHARAN AFRICA

A central premise of this essay is, on the one hand, that the progress and status of African democratization has been and continues to be intimately tied up with these parallel crises of economic reform and state strengthening and, on the other hand, that the dimensions of this interdependence have continued to be insufficiently specified, theoretically as well as existentially. Key to this interdependence has been the reality that these three processes have been launched *simultaneously*, where most received theory about all three, products largely of western European and North American experience, has presumed them to take place more or less *sequentially*. Thus, democracy has been presumed to be launched successfully on the foundation of an established state and significant levels of economic development, including a functioning democracy-minded middle class.

The questions then become: What have been the consequences for sub-Saharan Africa's first quarter-century of democratization because these prerequisites were largely missing at the outset, and to what extent have their trajectories thereafter been supportive, antithetical, or indifferent in their bearing upon the continent's democratic progress? Conversely, a parallel question is: To what extent and in what ways can it be shown that democratization processes have influenced economic development trajectories and the condition of sub-Saharan African states, for better or for worse over the course of this quarter-century? Thus, the evident complexity of sub-Saharan Africa's democratization progress in relationship to trajectories of stateness and economic development since the end of the Cold War at a minimum clearly implies the possibility that, for the countries of the region, processes of democratization have not necessarily been simply dependent upon the condition of the state and patterns of economic development; rather, presumptively they may also have influenced them in ways that may well bear on democracy's own sustainability over the long term. In the complexities and vagaries of these imperfectly understood relationships may also lie clues both to explanations for the stalling of the continent's democratization since the early years of the new century and pointers to how it may plausibly be sustainably resumed in the circumstances.

In the first years of the twenty-first century sub-Saharan African democratization has paralleled a largely unprecedented and lengthy period of sustained GDP growth, thanks at least in part to strengthened external investment, particularly from the BRICS and other emerging middle-income countries, complemented by partial success in meeting the UN-sponsored Millenium Development Goals (MDGs), launched to reduce significantly critically important dimensions of poverty by 2015.[5] Whatever the long-term sustainability of this economic growth trajectory, particularly given the trajectory of China's economy, the key questions have become: To what extent and in what ways have the contours of this decade-long growth spurt impacted democratization in sub-Saharan Africa for better and/or for worse? For example, the appearance of middle classes in the region in this century has been widely noted, though they have been defined primarily by their increased purchasing power and appetites for consumer goods. Insufficiently interrogated has been the extent to which they have become classes not only *in* themselves but *for* themselves in pursuit of their political interests with respect to the state and ruling regimes, as has happened elsewhere over the centuries. Similarly, the explosion of social media almost certainly has been redefining the political order in ways still only partially apparent and understood, albeit not necessarily in ways comparable to the influence of much earlier mid-twentieth-century communications revolutions on democracy.[6]

At the same time, significant democratic progress has occurred in the context of an arc of significant internal violence and civil war conditions, dramatizing state weakness, which began at the end of the 1980s, reached a peak at the end of the 1990s, and diminished, although by no means ended, in the new century.[7] Characterization of this phenomenon variously as state weakness, fragility, failure, or collapse has highlighted a definitional issue. Widely practiced in the academic and policy literatures alike has been a propensity to treat state and government as synonymous with one another, influenced by reliance upon Max Weber's classic definition of the state as a monopoly of the legitimate means of coercion within a compulsory territorial community.

Reliance upon that definition treats the government, specifically the civilian and security sectors of the executive branch, not only anthropomorphically but also as the *sole* state "actor." To do so, at least in the circumstances of sub-Saharan Africa, has been seemingly to ignore an important yet overlooked reality: if it is to be enduringly stable, the state must be broadly understood to consist in some senses in fundamental rules of the political game, to which ordinary citizens as well as ruling elites at least tacitly acquiesce and commit to upholding. A Washington think tank, the Fund for Peace, has assembled an annual failed states index that identifies the sources of state failure in the stressful conditions confronting citizens' lives at the grassroots, which call out for participatory formation of rules of the game to alleviate their situations as well as appropriate macro-level policies.

These sources of failure include demographic factors like natural disasters and pollution; refugees and internally displaced persons; group grievances over resources and religious and ethnic differences; riots, protests, and other forms of conflict; and a range of factors prompting emigration.[8]

On factors driving emigration, the tidal waves of migrants escaping Syria but also some African countries as this book goes to press have dramatized the obvious reality that, as a practical matter, political communities in the developing world are not completely compulsory. These waves of migration have also highlighted the extent to which ruling regimes' claims of legitimacy over their presumptive monopolies of coercion have come to hinge existentially upon the degree to which those rules of the game are effectively fashioned, promulgated, and widely accepted and honored within those societies.

The conjunction of newly democratizing processes in Africa with this arc of intrastate violence has helped to underscore a literature that has argued that unless African and other developing countries first await the emergence of strong states and significant levels of economic development, their democratic initiatives will be premature and, indeed, counterproductive to realizing those objectives.[9] But a closer reading of this literature reveals that it has tended in fact to presume that, before electoral dimensions of democracy have been introduced, the state must first already have incorporated other dimensions of democracy, such as a viable civil society and the rule of law, albeit without specifying just how the state has acquired these attributes. In other words, a fair inference is that certain dimensions of democratization closely associated with state formation, such as democratic establishment of fundamental rules of the game, actually are themselves prior foundations for stable states in developing countries, even as democracy's signature electoral component may need to come afterward.

Thus, it has appeared that where democratic processes of constitution making in sub-Saharan Africa preceded the introduction of competitive multiparty elections, these rule-setting processes contributed initially to state strengthening by state reform and, therefore, there was less parallel violence than where this prioritization did not occur, with economic conditions being a constant in the short term.[10] That this important initial correlation has faded in later years has spawned the question of to what extent, if rule-setting processes exemplified by democratic constitution writing had been more assiduously extended to a deepening and broadening of a constitutional culture within society at large, might a more sustained democratization momentum have resulted over the longer term?[11] As challenging, complex, and difficult at it would be in societies rent by corruption, ethnic and religious conflict, and other fracturing, perhaps a more robust and broadened commitment to instilling a constitutional culture, extending the models set by democratic constitution writing, may be some of what has been and remains required to restart and resume democratization momentum.

This essay offers preliminary observations on the progress and status of sub-Saharan African democratization and explores their possible ramifications for sorting out the complexities of democratization's interdependence with the condition of the state and patterns of economic development over the past quarter-century. Within the confines of a single essay it will be necessary to highlight the connections between state renewal and democratization rather more than those with evolving patterns of economic development, despite their importance.[12] Overall, the available evidence indicates that although perhaps most sub-Saharan African states have acquired at least some of the constitutional superstructure of democratic statehood, only about half have made at least partial progress toward realizing democracy in practice after a quarter of a century. Moreover, the same evidence suggests that even that level of democratic achievement remains somewhat precarious, as signs from about 2005 onward have consistently indicated that sub-Saharan African democratization has arrived at a plateau, with some demonstrations of democratic reversal.[13] At the same time, a number of African states have remained obdurately authoritarian in practice and generally weak, notwithstanding some adoption of varying elements of a constitutional façade of democratic accommodation. Noteworthy has been the collapse of Mali's long-presumed high level of democratization and the overt fracturing of the Malian state since 2012, from which only partial recovery has been achieved as this book goes to press. The case has challenged the predictive power and validity of quantitative measurements of democratic progress.

Significant variability in the conditions of democracy and states across the region renders doubtful the likely validity for even most countries of any single set of explanations for the apparent plateauing of democratization as well as the evident continuing weakness of most states in the region, not to mention the apparent democratic progress of a few countries. Nevertheless, among the critical factors, one has appeared to have been an overemphasis upon democracy's electoral competitive dimensions in practice and, indeed, in policy and academic literatures as well. This has occurred at the cost of an insufficient focus upon an equally indispensable dimension of establishing consensus on and upholding fundamental rules of the game, among the defining elements of stateness in contemporary sub-Saharan Africa. In short, what has appeared fundamentally missing in the literature and the practice of sub-Saharan African democratization has been sufficient emphasis on the principle that for democracy to be sustainable, consensus building is equal in importance and indispensability to free and fair political competition, even as it is also equal in importance to sustainable states to both establishing and legitimizing monopolization of coercive capacity in the hands of government, the traditional measure of state capacity.

It follows that building acquiescence on fundamental rules of the game has been and remains obligatory well beyond the democratic establishment of constitutions, legislation, and judicial processes. These macro-level processes of establishing the rule of law need to be models for society, enshrining normative expectations of dependable accommodation, inclusiveness, accountability, and transparent relations among individuals and communities to underpin market economies as well as bridging ethnic, religious, and subnational rivalries and antagonisms, and diminishing corruption. Admittedly, arriving at these terms of political engagement often is exponentially more difficult than establishing consensus on rules for multiparty democratic elections and other forms of political competition.

Evolving fundamental rules of the game in these larger senses places civil society organizations at the critical interface between vertical rules of the game defining relations between ruling elites and citizens, and horizontal rules of the game needed for bridging relations among these diverse social, cultural, and economic actors. Thus, recent African governmental demarches to co-opt and constrain civil society NGOs have predictably served to undermine promoting democracy in the longer term in horizontal senses among societal and economic actors as well as vertically between rulers and citizens.

SUB-SAHARAN AFRICAN DEMOCRATIC STATES AT TWENTY-FIVE

Now that sub-Saharan Africa has reached the quarter-century milestone of its democratic era, more reliable historical analytical consideration of its trajectory begins to be possible. Twenty-five years represents a *longue duree* of sufficient span to begin to glimpse some possibly enduring historical patterns in not only the region's democratic development but also that of the African states with which it has been so intimately connected over this period.

The clearest, starkest evidence for estimating democratic progress in the region has been largely quantitative, and for that reason it must be treated both carefully and tentatively for obvious reasons, not least because the methodologies by which these inescapably subjective observations are rendered as quantitative objective measures have, to a significant extent, remained the preserves of their creators. Nevertheless, that quantitative evidence can spawn intriguing, plausible hypotheses about what has actually transpired—hypotheses that then need to be checked against the unquantified estimates of other qualified observers.

The available evidence suggests that sub-Saharan African countries as a group are markedly—although sharply variable—more democratic in 2015 than they were in 1990. This upward trajectory crested around 2005, yielding to a plateau in the subsequent years, during which indications of actual regression have been more in evidence than those of further advances. The most widely relied upon evidence of democratic progress over the last quarter century has been that assembled by the respected organization Freedom House.[14] Freedom House relies upon expert testimony for all countries on twenty-five indicators of democratization. It aggregates these scores into seven broad categories: (1) electoral process, government functioning, and political pluralism and participation, further aggregated as political rights, and (2) freedom of expression, associational rights, rule of law, and personal autonomy rights, further aggregated as civil liberties. It scores political rights and civil liberties each from 1 (high) to 7 (low). Scores of 1 and 2 qualify as free, 3 to 5 as partially free, and 6 and 7 as unfree.

Table 7.1   Freedom House Measures of Civil and Political Liberties

	1985	1990	1995	2000	2005	2010	2015
All countries							
Political rights	4.54	4.29	3.75	3.64	3.50	3.60	3.53
Civil liberties	4.64	4.09	3.90	3.70	3.30	3.42	3.50
Sub-Saharan Africa							
Political rights	5.87	5.62	4.56	4.48	4.23	4.46	4.51
Civil liberties	5.80	5.11	4.58	4.70	3.98	4.19	4.39

Source: Freedom House.

Table 7.1 presents the overall average scores for all sub-Saharan African countries as a group at five-year intervals beginning in 1985, preceding the end of the Cold War by half a decade, and through 2015. The table attests that sub-Saharan Africa was markedly freer in 2015 than it was in 1990, when its democratic era began. Moreover, sub-Saharan Africa gained freedom during this quarter century at a faster rate than the world as a whole. The table also confirms the beginnings of a regression in democratic rights and liberties from 2005 to 2010 and a continuation of retreats since then in the civil liberties area as well as an earlier reversal on this score between 1995 and 2000, which appears to coincide with the worst outbreaks of civil violence mentioned earlier. These trends are also reflected in the worldwide averages, but the trends in African countries that make up more than a fourth of the total clearly influence them.

Another major democracy measuring system that has been in place as far back as 1990—indeed much further—has been Polity IV.[15] Where Freedom House's estimates have centered on personal rights and liberties, Polity IV's estimates have focused principally upon country executives whose authoritarian domination typified the continent's Cold War era. Polity IV gauges the extent to which effective constitutional restraints exist upon the exercise of presidential powers, and competition for these offices is open and free for all to participate in. Polity IV subtracts structural aspects of polities that permit the authoritarian exercise of executive power from favorable democratic dimensions, yielding scores from -10 (fully authoritarian) to +10 (fully democratic). Polity IV scores countries as democracies if their scores are +6 or higher, as authoritarian if they are -6 or lower, with those in between considered "anocracies" or systems of mixed authoritarian and democratic attributes, presumed to be inherently unstable for that reason.

The Polity IV data at five-year intervals shown in Table 7.2 traces patterns of increased democratic constitutionalism somewhat similar to but not identical to what Freedom House scores indicate for democratic rights and liberties. On the

Table 7.2   Center for Systemic Peace Polity IV Democratic Progress Scores

	1985	1990	1995	2000	2005	2010	2014
World	-1.45	0.70	2.60	3.02	3.71	3.94	4.28
Africa	-5.64	-5.02	0.00	0.69	1.88	2.39	2.70

Source: Center for Systemic Peace.

one hand, the Polity IV data show marked overall improvement from 1985 to 2014, with sub-Saharan Africa outpacing improvement by other countries of the globe as a whole.[16] Again, similar to the Freedom House data, they show that the greatest improvement took place from 1990 to 1995, with slower increases thereafter. The major difference is that the Polity IV data show a gradual improvement since 2005, where the Freedom House data describe retreats. A plausible reconciliation for this divergence would be that whereas constitutional and legal structural improvements may have gradually continued to be added in countries, systematic initiatives to achieve thorough adherence to those constitutional frameworks by those holding high political or civil service posts have been noticeably lacking, adding up to a marked rule-of-law deficit. It follows that rule-of-law deficits facilitate and themselves represent abuses of individual rights and liberties—that is, stagnating or regressing democracy.

Table 7.3 demonstrates clearly the presence of significant rule-of-law deficits continuing to impede progress toward democratic states in sub-Saharan Africa over the first quarter century of its democratic era. The table indicates that the Polity IV estimates, which appear to focus principally on the extent to which democratic constitutional structures are at least nominally in place, award democratic state status to many countries that Freedom House considers to have made only partial progress ("Partially Free Democratic States" in the table; Freedom House considers these countries only partially free, whereas Polity regards them as democracies). Freedom House estimates center on the status of democracy and the observance of democratic liberties in practice. Similarly, many of the states that Polity IV estimates to have transitioned from authoritarianism to anocracies ("Unfree Anocracies" in the table; unfree according to Freedom House but anocracies for Polity), Freedom House regards as still resolutely autocratic. Freedom House and Polity agree on the seven countries that are democratic, the three that are autocratic, and the six that are anocracies for Polity and partially free by Freedom House standards.

Thus juxtaposition of the Freedom House and the Polity IV data brings to the fore a connection between the actual practice of democracy and upholding liberties in sub-Saharan African states, on the one hand, and, on the other, the existence of democratic constitutional structures that may exist in these countries but are widely or wholly ignored in practice, comparable to their well-known fate

Table 7.3 Constitutional Structures and Democratic Practices Compared in 2015

Democracies	Partially free democratic states	Partially free anocracies	Unfree anocracies	Autocracies
Benin	Comoros	Burkina Faso	Angola	Gambia
Botswana	Kenya	Côte d' Ivoire	Cameroon	Equatorial Guinea
Cape Verde	Lesotho	Mali	C.A.R.	Swaziland
Ghana	Liberia	Nigeria	Chad	
Mauritius	Madagascar	Tanzania	Congo Rep.	
Senegal	Malawi	Togo	D.R.C.	
S. Africa	Mozambique		Djibouti	
	Niger		Ethiopia	
	Sierra Leone		Gabon	
	Zambia		Guinea	
			Mauritania	
			Rwanda	
			Somalia	
			Sudan	
			Uganda	
			Zimbabwe	

Sources: Freedom House, Center for Systemic Peace Polity IV rankings. Sao Tome and Seychelles excluded because not included in Polity IV rankings. Namibia, Eritrea, and S. Sudan excluded as countries not independent or in existence in 1985. Guinea-Bissau and Burundi fall outside the analysis because both qualify as democracies in Polity IV as of 2014 yet are listed as unfree by Freedom House for 2015. At this writing both probably would be unfree anocracies at best in updated rankings.

in many countries of other world regions. Thus, Table 7.3 indicates seven full democracies in 2015, sixteen partially democratic states ("Partially Free Democratic States and Partially Free Anocracies"), and nineteen states that remained largely or wholly autocracies ("Unfree Anocracies" and "Autocracies").

This conception of the democratic states as those where the rule of law is upheld and infused throughout society as democratically transparent rule-making and rule-abiding constitutional culture connects democratization to state strengthening and renewal in a way that the traditional Weberian conception inhibits. It posits an emphasis on the rule of law as a consensus-building, state-strengthening foundation for competitive multiparty democracy. By contrast the Weberian conception of the state on its face leaves to conjecture both how states might achieve monopolies of the means of coercion at all, let alone legitimately, or establish compulsory territorial communities except by coercion, and how, except through emergent internal divisions, democratic openings could occur. The implicit premise that only a weakened Weberian state could admit democracy clearly makes the case for a democratic rule of law emphasis, at least coterminous with the introduction of competitive multiparty elections, if not a precondition for them.

In part, this conception of democratic state-making follows Charles Tilly's understanding that once European states had been founded by war and war preparation, it is through institutionalized rules of the game that these states became enduringly sustainable.[17] For sub-Saharan Africa, perhaps ending the Cold War era–supported authoritarian regimes has been comparable to European states emerging from war and war preparation, the obligatory next step being the institutionalization of rules of the game comparable to that which Tilly found in Europe. But, in part, the difference has been that in sub-Saharan Africa's post–Cold War circumstances, democratization and state strengthening and reform have been simultaneous rather than sequential obligations. In a word, although the rule of law is always properly understood as a key dimension of democracy, it is also a dimension of the state in the larger sense proposed here, especially in sub-Saharan African circumstances. It follows that to pursue the rule of law is to pursue state strengthening and democratization simultaneously, whereas failure to do so weakens both.

Thus, failure to pursue the rule of law and, more generally, a constitutional culture in its support as vigorously as the launching of competitive multiparty elections plausibly appears to help to explain stalled early-twenty-first-century democratization in sub-Saharan Africa. As noted above, where sub-Saharan African states had the benefit of significant democratic constitutional deliberation preceding multiparty elections, democratization got off to a stronger start. But that was also true for the relative strength and stability of their states as well and has generally remained so to the present day for these states. The relatively few sub-Saharan states in this category benefitted from strong externally supported constitutional mediation (South Africa, Namibia, Mozambique, and Malawi) and the remarkable phenomenon of national conferences (Benin and Mali).

The model has not worked perfectly even in all of this limited number of cases. Eritrea's model constitutional development process would likely have produced a comparable result had it not been blocked by Issayas Afewerki, beginning his transition from visionary leader of the country's military campaign for independence from Ethiopia to the hard-core dictator he has become. Mali's model national conference outcomes decayed in subsequent years not least because it failed to maintain the participatory spirit of the conference and did not follow through on a bargain the conference struck with the pastoralist Tuareg in its northern region.[18] National conferences were not always conducted as democratically as necessary, as in Republic of the Congo (Brazzaville). At the same time, fairly durable embryonic democracies benefitted from South African mediation (Lesotho) and from an autocratic leader's constitutional epiphanies (Rawlings's Ghana).

Most sub-Saharan African countries lacked even these constitutional rules of the game-setting foundations for transitioning to competitive multiparty electoral democracy. Only a case-by-case review of each country's specific circumstances could establish whether this apparently optimal pattern was even envisaged or possible. In a larger sense, then, a corollary to the existential reality that democratization, state strengthening and reform, and economic development imperatives coalesced simultaneously rather than sequentially, as received theory would have it, has appeared to be that some elements of democracy, state strengthening, and reform optimally have needed to be introduced together but sequentially, before other elements of both, specifically the democratic setting of constitutional rules of the game. Thus, the apparent empirical support for this hypothesis in sub-Saharan Africa's settings has addressed the unarticulated presumption of the literatures that insist that state formation precede competitive democratic elections, that states must present some elements of democracy first—that is, democratic constitutional rule setting.

In the absence of this important step, both mandated and possible in post–Cold War sub-Saharan Africa, many countries of the region experienced political liberation without democratic constitutional rules of the game to produce orderly political competition; as a consequence, the previously mentioned arc of domestic violence and civil war affecting many countries ensued. The Center for Systemic Peace, which now continues the Polity IV project, has also tracked major episodes of political violence in Africa, the Middle East, and other world regions. It applies scores of 1 to 10 (where 10 is the most severe) to these episodes, depending on the severity of the ethnic and other political violence and outbreaks of civil war. Table 7.4 presents the findings for sub-Saharan Africa at representative four-year intervals from 1986 to 2012. In the table "Level" totals the number of episodes weighted by their severity.[19]

Table 7.4   The Arc of Violence in Post–Cold War Sub-Saharan Africa

	Level	No. states	Most affected states
2012	18	4	DRC(5), Somalia(5)
2008	27	5	DRC(5), Somalia(5), Sudan(5), Kenya(4)
2004	28	5	DRC(5), Somalia(5), Sudan(5), Burundi(4), Nigeria(4)
2000	89	11	DRC(6), Somalia(5), Sudan(6), Burundi(4), Angola(7)
1996	46	12	DRC(6), Somalia(5), Sudan(6), Burundi(4), Angola(7), Liberia(4)
1992	52	17	Somalia(5), Sudan(6), Liberia(4), Angola(7), Chad(4), Mozambique(6)
1988	44	9	Sudan(6), Somalia(5), Angola(7), Mozambique(6), Ethiopia(6), Chad(4)

Source: Center for Systemic Peace. Levels of violence in parentheses.

Table 7.5   World Bank Measures of Governance Quality in Sub-Saharan Africa

	1996	2000	2005	2010	2014
Political voice	28.9	29.8	31.2	30.7	32.1
Political stability	32.6	32.3	33.5	34.7	29.7
Governmental effectiveness	27.5	27.8	25.7	26.2	25.6
Regulatory quality	27.2	28.5	27.4	29.1	28.7
Rule of law	27.7	28.6	27.6	28.5	29.7
Corruption control	32.6	32.9	29.7	31.9	29.3
Overall	29.5	30.1	29.2	29.7	29.1

Source: World Bank, http://info.worldbank.org/governance/wgi/index.aspx#reports.

A third measure of progress in achieving democratic states over this period, the World Bank's Governance Indicators, dates from early in the post–Cold War democratization era but not its outset, notably after the most rapid democratization had already occurred, as attested by both the Freedom House and Polity IV data. But the Bank's interrogation of governance quality, begun in 1996, begins squarely in the middle of sub-Saharan Africa's arc of post–Cold War violent intrastate conflict. Thus, the Bank's governance indicators, especially in the early years, implicitly both gauge the effectiveness of sub-Saharan African governance practices in quelling this conflict and reflect the limitations in this regard.

The Bank's indicators draw on a very wide range of data sources to establish normed scores for all countries on six variables: political voice, political stability, governmental effectiveness, regulatory quality, rule of law, and corruption control. Initially released biennially, the scores have been produced annually since 2002. On each of these variables the Bank's data show African scores to have remained well below the median 50th percentile scores for all six and to have improved, collectively, only marginally between 1996 and 2014. Table 7.5 tells this story.

The table indicates marginal improvement over nearly two decades in political voice (comparable to the post-1995 increases revealed by the Freedom House) and in the rule of law (roughly tracking the evolution revealed by the Polity IV data). At the same time, the Bank data mark declines in governmental effectiveness, corruption control, and political stability, though all of the decline in stability occurred between 2013, not in the table, and 2014. The slightly contrary trajectories of political voice and the more specifically governmental variables portray the weakness of all the indicators by the Bank's estimates of global standards, but they also suggest that these low levels have been both relatively impervious to the ramifications of political liberalization and significantly ineffective in governing as well as supporting that liberalization.

A closer interrogation of the overall mediocrity of sub-Saharan governance quality by the Bank's estimates stands in marked contrast with sharp trajectories

Table 7.6 African Countries Advancing and Regressing in Governance, 1996–2014

Most improved governance Scores 1996–2014			Most regressed governance Scores 1996–2014		
Country	Avg.	Improvement rate	Country	Avg.	Regression rate
Rwanda	31.4	43.7	Zimbabwe	10.5	-22.6
Cape Verde	63.4	23.4	Mauritania	32.4	-22.2
Liberia	15.1	20.7	Eritrea	17.9	-20.4
Zambia	36.6	14.5	Madagascar	37.2	-16.0
Burundi	11.4	13.7	Sao Tome	40.7	-15.0
Ethiopia	21.1	13.0	Côte d'Ivoire	17.4	-13.7
Sierra Leone	20.3	11.7	Seychelles	57.8	-12.7
Niger	27.4	10.2	Mali	37.7	-10.6
Ghana	51.1	9.5	Benin	43.0	-9.6

Source: World Bank, http://info.worldbank.org/governance/wgl/index.aspx#reports.

of individual countries' advance and decline as well as sharp differences for each individual country in their performances on individual criteria. Table 7.6 identifies countries that, between 1996 and 2014, have both advanced and regressed by roughly half a standard deviation from the 50th percentile global mean. The table links the average total governance scores on all six variables over the eighteen years between 1996–2014 with the number of points for countries that have advanced or regressed the most.

The table indicates that countries have seen notable rates of improvement or regression at high, low, and middling overall levels of performance. The same pattern emerges on each of the six component variables on which the overall scores are based. On each of the individual variables about a quarter of the countries show significant improvement over the eighteen-year period. With the exception of Rwanda, which records significant improvement on all six variables, including political voice, the overall leaders all record regression in one or more areas, notwithstanding their overall leadership in governance improvement.[20]

The countries that have advanced the most overall in many cases have been those starting at the lowest ebb: Rwanda from its season of genocide, Liberia and Sierra Leone from near dissolution in civil war and restored with extensive United Nations assistance, and Ethiopia from the formation of the Ethiopian People's Revolutionary Democratic Front that was to overthrow tyrannical dictator Mengistu Haile Mariam in 1991. Some of the strongest and most sustained twenty-first-century GDP growth in Africa by Rwanda and Ethiopia has been accompanied by some of the worst suppression of democracy and civil and political liberties. They have been the focus, for Africa, of scholars who have advanced models of "developmental states" that focus upon rapid economic development while more or less undertaking to hold constant an authoritarian political status quo. Five of the nine governance leaders overall are also among the leaders in democratization: Ghana, Zambia, Liberia, Sierra Leone, and Cape Verde. Worrisomely, four of the poorest governance performers are also among the democratic leaders: Benin, Seychelles, and Sao Tome in addition to Mali. In general, however, the fourteen countries that have progressed the most in political voice by Bank estimates have been mostly in positive territory on the other five governance measures.

THE DECADE OF THE DEMOCRATIZATION PLATEAU

Freedom House and the Mo Ibrahim Index together have supplied both more extensive and fine-grained quantitatively expressed indicators of democratic governance performance since about 2005; this was when Freedom House especially began to warn that the gradual upward trajectory of sub-Saharan African countries on its measures of democracy and observance of liberties to that point had stalled, with indications of regression in evidence. As noted earlier, Freedom House builds its one-to-seven rankings each on political rights and civil liberties on seven subcategories, which it has made public since 2006. Noteworthy is a distinction Freedom House makes between "electoral democracy" and "liberal democracy." It designates as electoral democracies those that earn at least a 50 percent score (20 points out of 40) on political rights, including at least a score of 7 out of 12 on election quality, whereas to be a liberal democracy requires a score of about 65 to 68 out of 100 on all seven subcategory measures identified earlier.[21]

The Mo Ibrahim Foundation, established by a wealthy Sudanese communications industry entrepreneur, established an index in its founder's name early in the twenty-first century to measure African democratic governance performance. Unlike Freedom House and the other indices considered in this chapter, the index limits itself to African countries. It includes those of North Africa and the Maghreb. Also unique to the index among these indices is its inclusion of economic performance and human resources development as measures of governance.

Dimensions of Democratic Advance and Retreat

Freedom House data broken out by subcategories reveal that sub-Saharan African countries collectively have regressed on all seven of its indicators of democratic performance and at a more pronounced rate than for all countries worldwide between 2006 and 2015. Table 7.7 shows that sub-Saharan African countries collectively declined an average 4.5 points overall during the decade, compared to only 1.9 points for all countries. All countries worldwide declined slightly in all subcategories over the decade except for electoral process, while sub-Saharan African

Table 7.7   Sub-Saharan African Democracy Scores Compared, 2006–2015

	Possible score	2015		2006	
		World	Africa	World	Africa
TOTAL SCORE	100	60.4	44.9	62.3	49.4
Electoral process	12	7.8	5.8	7.7	5.9
Political pluralism, participation	16	10.0	7.4	10.1	8.0
Functioning of government	12	6.4	4.6	6.7	5.0
POLITICAL RIGHTS	40	24.3	17.7	24.4	19.0
Freedom of expression	16	10.9	9.2	11.5	10.1
Freedom of association	12	7.5	5.8	8.0	6.6
Rule of law	16	8.1	5.7	8.7	6.8
Personal autonomy/individual rights	16	9.5	6.6	9.6	6.8
CIVIL LIBERTIES	60	36.1	27.2	37.8	30.3

Source: Freedom House.

countries declined noticeably more in all seven subcategories. Significantly, the more pronounced African declines were in the civil liberties category, the greatest being in the area of rule of law (1.1 points) followed by freedom of expression (0.9) and freedom of association (0.8). Sub-Saharan Africa's rule of law score is the lowest of any of the seven subcategory indicators, except for functioning of government.

These declines may not leap out at the reader as earth-shaking, but they do clearly trace at best a loss of democratic momentum and perhaps, more realistically, a pattern of democratic regression. The three areas of greatest decline—rule of law, freedom of expression, and freedom of association—are interconnected. Governmental disregard for the rule of law has been clearly directed at groups, media, and individuals courageously attempting to exercise those freedoms that, in turn, undermine their capacity to push back against their abuse. Thus, a potential negative downward spiral may be in prospect.

This pattern adds up to a rule-of-law decline in more than institutional and strictly legal terms in the sense that courts are weakened and lack in independence and that there is poor, often corrupt law enforcement. Rather, this pattern reveals a lack of the rule of law in a larger societal and cultural sense, a deficit in diffusing adherence to fundamental rules of the game that enshrine transparent, inclusive, participatory decision making; tolerance of difference; and protection of minority views while the majority prevails.

As with the earlier analysis, the overall trajectory of stalled democratic momentum, if not actual decline, masks markedly divergent trajectories for individual countries. On the one hand, eight countries have remained solidly democratic throughout the entire decade, although both Botswana and South Africa have

Table 7.8   Democracies and Most Rapidly Democratizing Countries in Sub-Saharan Africa, 2006–2015

Sustained democracies		Most rapidly democratizing countries		
	2015 score		10-year average score	Change 2006–2015
Cape Verde	90	Côte d' Ivoire	40.0	30
Mauritius	90	Togo	29.2	25
Ghana	83	Zimbabwe	18.5	17
Benin	82	Benin	80.3	12
Sao Tome/Principe	81	Guinea	46.2	8
South Africa	79	Comoros	54.0	7
Namibia	77	Burkina Faso	52.4	6
Botswana	73			

Source: Adapted from Freedom House data.

witnessed significant declines. In addition, eleven countries, with varying average overall scores over the decade, have recorded significant improvement. Table 7.8 lists the democratic leaders and the most improved countries from 2006 to 2015 with their Freedom House scores. A notable feature of the sustained democracy list is that all are smaller countries by both population and land mass except for Botswana (population only). Notable on the list of most rapid democratizers is that all have been middling or weaker performers over the decade, with the exception of Benin, the only high performer to also improve markedly. Zimbabwe's presence on the list is startling in that it has quietly climbed into the list of partly free countries by Freedom House measures, notwithstanding the continuing autocratic proclivities of its leader since independence in 1980, Robert Mugabe.

On the other hand, twenty countries were unfree by Freedom House estimates in 2015, up from fourteen in 2006. More countries recorded democratic retreats than gains on all Freedom House indicators except for electoral process, and democratic regression was most pronounced in eleven countries. Table 7.9 presents the somber data.

A noteworthy dimension of the significant number of both relatively rapid democratizers and also those becoming significantly less democratic is the volatility that the two groups display collectively. The overall data showing stalled momentum to incremental regression masks a reality that nearly half the sub-Saharan African countries moved rapidly in one direction or the other over the past decade. That reality suggests a number of corollaries. First, this evidence of volatility is a reminder to eschew any teleological presumptions about the future course of democratization in Africa in any direction—positive, negative, or steady state. Second, it is a reminder that much depends simply on the extent to which elected leaders are committed to democracy beyond simply a way into office and power.

Table 7.9   Patterns of Democratic Regression in Sub-Saharan Africa, 2006–2015

	Countries advancing	Countries regressing	Country	10-year average	Democratic regression
Electoral process	18	15	C.A.R.	33	36
Pluralism, participation	15	26	Gambia	35	31
Government functioning	13	20	Mali	62	29
Freedom of expression	8	26	Ethiopia	26	21
Freedom of association	7	25	Burundi	38	20
Rule of law	8	27	Guinea	46	20
Personal autonomy	12	17	Kenya	56	15
			Somalia	8	13
			Eritrea	8	11
			S. Africa	84	9
			Uganda	43	9

Source: Adapted from Freedom House data.

In at least half the cases listed in Table 7.9, it would be problematic at best to say that country circumstances, as distinct from leaders' predilections, account for and explain democratic decline. Third, the volatility seems to say something about the limited degree to which the mores and political practices—the fundamental rules of the game—have been institutionalized and embedded in the political life of many countries. The less this institutionalization has occurred, the more vulnerable these and possibly other countries of the region may be to relatively major and abrupt swings in democratization one way or the other.

The Political Economy of African Democratization

The Mo Ibrahim Index (MOI) implicitly broadens the concept of democratic governance to include not only observance of the constitutional requirements of democracy but also what governments do or do not do to actually deliver socioeconomic as well as political goods to the citizens they are pledged to serve. A key feature of the MOI is at once a strength and a limitation: in limiting its scope to all African countries, including North Africa, the index escapes the criticisms implicitly leveled against other measuring systems that hold African countries accountable to standards and norms developed principally by mature Western democracies. By the same token comparisons of performance across regions on less prominently measured indicators that the MOI includes are not possible.

The MOI scores African governments on four broad areas: safety and rule of law, participation and human rights, sustainable economic opportunity, and human development. The focus on a broad range of deliverables to citizens appears in the sixteen subcategories, which include personal safety in the rule of law subcategory, infrastructural development and the needs of the rural sector in the sustainable economic development subcategory, gender progress in the participation and human rights subcategory, as well as health, education, and welfare provision in the human development category. Each of the 110 indicators are scored from 1 to 100, supporting the estimates for the sixteen subcategories and four overall categories. The Mo Ibrahim Index has developed over the course of the century's first decade. However, scores are in place for all indicators and categories back to 2000 for all African countries.

The MOI records significant improvement for all African countries as a group in the area of human development and incremental improvement in sustainable economic opportunity, which stands in contrast to more rapid overall rates of GDP growth over the same period. Thus, the trajectory of sustainable economic opportunity scores amounts to tacit recognition that, overall, strong rates of growth have been only partially translated in relief of widespread poverty between 2000 and 2015. The MOI also records essential but very incremental progress in the area of participation and human rights over the whole fifteen-year period, with slight retrenchment since 2006. Finally, for the category of safety and rule of law, the MOI scores are roughly in line with the other indices considered in this chapter, indicating a slight but noticeable regression since 2006.

Table 7.10   The Political Economy of African Democratic Progress, 2005–2014

	Rule of law/ safety	Participation and human rights	Sustainable economic opportunity	Human development	Overall
2000	52.7	47.2	39.4	45.4	46.2
2005	53.4	49.3	40.4	50.8	48.5
2006	53.8	49.9	40.8	51.4	49.0
2007	53.6	50.4	41.8	52.5	49.6
2008	53.9	50.5	42.8	53.3	50.1
2009	52.7	50.2	43.4	54.2	50.1
2010	52.9	50.6	44.0	53.5	50.2
2011	52.1	50.1	43.3	53.8	49.8
2012	51.8	50.0	43.5	54.6	49.9
2013	51.2	50.4	43.4	54.6	49.9
2014	51.8	50.1	42.9	55.2	49.4
Average	52.7	49.4	42.0	51.5	49.4
Std. Dev.	15.7	16.9	23.6	13.6	14.0

Source: Mo Ibrahim Index; www.moibrahimfoundation.org/iiag.

Table 7.11   Democratic Development Leaders and Regressors, 2000–2014

Leaders		Regressors	
Liberia	+20.2	Madagascar	-6.5
Sierra Leone	+14.3	C.A.R.	-4.2
Angola	+13.2	Eritrea	-3.0
Rwanda	+13.6	Mali	-1.3
Togo	+12.5	Niger	-0.7
Ethiopia	+11.0	Somalia	-0.7

Table 7.10 tells the story. To provide some statistical context for the overall category scores, the average and standard deviation for each category are listed based on all scores for each country for all years.

On closer examination, as is the case with the more detailed Freedom House data, MOI data reveals markedly divergent patterns among sub-Saharan African countries, but it's more prominent in two of the four categories: safety and rule of law and participation and human rights. Twenty-three of forty-seven countries displayed negative progress on safety and the rule of law, while fourteen of forty-seven were in negative territory on participation and human rights. All but six countries recorded some improvement in sustainable economic opportunity between 2000 and 2014 (Zimbabwe, Tanzania, Madagascar, Guinea, Eritrea, and Djibouti), and only Madagascar receded in the human development area.[22] Collectively, sub-Saharan African countries averaged only a 0.9 point decrease in the safety and rule of law category, in contrast to increases of 2.9 points on participation and human rights, 3.5 points on sustainable economic opportunity, and a hefty 9.8 points on human development.

Finally, Table 7.11 lists the countries that have progressed the most overall by MOI estimates and the six that have regressed overall between 2000 and 2014. The leaders include two countries set on their feet with major international assistance (Sierra Leone and Liberia) and the two principal exemplars of what some consider model "developmental states" that hold political liberalization constant while economic development surges (Ethiopia and Rwanda).

CONCLUSIONS

This chapter establishes that sub-Saharan African countries have made noteworthy progress in democratization and economic development but little if any progress in strengthening and reforming their states—the triple challenges they faced simultaneously with the conclusion of the Cold War. The most rapid and widespread democratization occurred in the first five years of the continent's democratic era, from about 1990 to 1995. In the same decade an arc of domestic violence and civil war put many of the region's postcolonial states at risk. This chapter's analysis suggests not that democratization per se is injurious to states before they gain strength but that some elements of democracy, specifically the rule of law, should infuse the state before its multiparty, competitive election dimensions commence.

This hypothesis calls into question the applicability to contemporary African circumstances of the conventional Weberian conception of the state as primarily only about the monopolization of legitimate coercion within a compulsory territorial community. Rather, a quarter-century of African post–Cold War experience suggests that the cultivation of the rule of law is an equally essential component not only in strictly legal and constitutional terms but also in the wider sense of a constitutional culture of democratically established fundamental rules of the political game enshrined by custom.

The chapter's quantitative evidence confirms a prevailing hypothesis that democratization in sub-Saharan Africa has reached a possibly unstable plateau, with hints of actual regression. The evidence suggests that weak or even negative progress in advancing the rule of law is a major factor in stalling democratization momentum. At the same time the overall evidence masks the reality of widely divergent patterns of democratic advance and regression since about 2005, indicative not only of states' weak institutionalization but also of the continuing need to restart democratization momentum, contingent upon both greater emphasis on the rule of law and wise, committed political leadership.

NOTES

1. The late Samuel Huntington employed the term democracy's "Third Wave" to identify late-twentieth-century democratization in Europe and Latin America preceding and following the end of the Cold War to distinguish this wave from its predecessors in the wake of the First and Second World Wars. See *Democratization in the Late Twentieth Century* (Norman: University of Oklahoma Press, 1991).

2. The focus of this essay—indeed of the essays in this and previous editions of this volume—on sub-Saharan Africa does not imply any fundamental disjunction between these countries and those of the Maghreb. Rather, this volume continues the prevalent recognition that, notwithstanding their connections, the countries of North Africa are significantly more consequently caught up in the politics of the Middle East.

3. Exposure of the weakness of the postindependence sub-Saharan African states prompted consideration of the deeper question of whether and/or to what extent polities over which of these authoritarian regimes had presided for the better part of thirty years even qualified as "states," as the term had been understood to that point, given their colonial antecedents. Crawford Young, whose chapter on the historical antecedents of African states appears in this volume, has written the leading treatises on the subject. His general conclusion has been that in most material respects, they did. See *The African Colonial State in Comparative Perspective* (New Haven, CT: Yale University Press, 1994) and *The Post-Colonial State in Africa: Fifty Years of Independence* (Madison: University of Wisconsin Press, 2012).

4. Thomas Callaghy has authoritatively written of these matters in the first four editions of this volume.

5. The expanded UN Sustainable Development Goals have launched, focused on ending poverty by 2030.

6. Seymour Martin Lipset, *Political Man: The Social Bases of Politics* (Baltimore, MD: Johns Hopkins University Press, 1981).

7. Center for Systemic Peace, Major Episodes in Political Violence, www.systemicpeace .org/.

8. http://global.fundforpeace.org.

9. Jack L. Snyder, *From Voting to Violence: Democratization and Nationalist Conflict* (New York: Norton, 2000); Edward D. Snyder and Jack L. Snyder, *Electing to Fight: Why Emerging Democracies Go to War* (Cambridge, MA: MIT Press, 2005).

10. John W. Harbeson, "Rethinking Democratic Transitions: Lessons from Eastern and Southern Africa," in *State, Conflict and Democracy in Africa*, ed. Richard Joseph (Boulder, CO: Lynne Rienner Publishers, 1997).

11. This concept was advanced some years ago in John Ferejohn, Jack N. Rakove, and Jonathan Riley, eds., *Constitutional Culture and Democratic Rule* (New York: Cambridge University Press, 2001). I suggest the concept merits revival.

12. This chapter leaves questions of economics more to the chapter by Todd Moss in this and the previous edition of this volume.

13. Freedom House, Freedomhouse.org.

14. Full disclosure: for several years I was a consultant to Freedom House on Africa.

15. The Polity Project is now maintained by the Center for Systemic Peace, www .systemicpeace.org.

16. The most recent year for which these data are available at this writing is 2014.

17. Charles Tilly, *Coercion, Capital and European States, AD 990–1992* (New York: Cambridge University State, 1992).

18. Harbeson, "Rethinking Democratic Transitions." The collapse of Eritrea's transition to constitutional democracy had not definitively occurred when this was written. The best account of Mali's remarkable National Conference and of the national conference phenomenon in general is Susanna Wing, *Constructing Democracy in Transitioning Societies of Africa* (New York: Palgrave, 2008).

19. The four-year intervals chosen unfortunately leave out the Rwanda genocide, most of which occurred in 1994.

20. Rwanda's eleven-point improvement in the political voice score stands in sharp contrast to Freedom House scores, which estimate Rwanda to be unfree, and Polity IV, which has consistently scored Rwanda as an anocracy.

21. The lowest score to be considered free is a score of 3 on civil or political liberties and a score of 2 on the other, or vice versa. The lowest score to earn a two on political rights is 30 out of 40 points and 44 out of 60 on civil liberties. The lowest scores to earn a three are 24 and 35, respectively. Depending on whether a state received a two on political rights and a three on civil liberties or the reverse, a state would need a minimum score of 65 or 68, respectively.

22. Sudan and South Sudan are not included because South Sudan has been in existence as an independent country only since 2011, and Sudan has only been included since 2011 to respect the preferences of the Sudanese founder of the Foundation and the Index.

IN SEARCH OF ELUSIVE STATE RECONSTRUCTION

In this section of the book two leading scholars and two distinguished former US ambassadors probe what has been arguably the enduring central problem of African politics: the condition of the state in this continent in the postindependence, post–Cold War era.

Notwithstanding widely recognized manifestations of fundamental state weakness, including instances of unambiguous state collapse, the question of the nature of and requirements for viable states in contemporary Africa has received much less systematic attention than it has deserved. The theoretical sufficiency of the widely implicitly recognized Weberian definition of the state—as a monopoly of legitimate coercive power with a compulsory territorially defined community— has rarely been directly questioned empirically in contemporary circumstances, at least not in those of sub-Saharan Africa. Crawford Young's authoritative work recognized that the colonial state embodied enough—if perhaps not all—of the properties required to merit the designation.[1] The enduring yet under-researched question has remained of how to define and achieve viable, truly postcolonial states in sub-Saharan Africa. The essays in this section approach this question.

The first quarter-century of the post–Cold War era in sub-Saharan Africa has yielded abundant evidence that manifest and pervasive weaknesses of the continent's states point to deeper conceptual issues concerning the basis of their viability. The Fund for Peace's annual global estimates of state weakness have drawn attention to an apparent reality that the political health of states is intimately bound up with the viability of the political and economic circumstances in which their citizens live, something quite missing in the Weberian conception.

The studies in this section chronicle three of the most comprehensive and profound cases of not only state weakness and disarray but, more important, the absence of viable visions and pathways for replacing and reforming still-surviving manifestations of the colonial state so as to realize sustainable postcolonial successors. Ambassador John Campbell's account of Boko Haram's assault on the validity of the very idea of Nigeria identifies the roots of the problem in Nigeria's failure to ground the postindependence state in legitimization by the people, and this was further exacerbated by the "isolation of the secular state and the northern elite from the mass of the population in northeast Nigeria."

In its wisdom, the Organization of African Unity resolved to live with the arbitrariness of colonially defined state boundaries, but Filip Reyntjens's essay on instability and worse in the Great Lakes region attests to the extent to which violent internal state conflict has spread across these artificial boundaries with impunity. He finds the core ingredients of the seemingly intractable conflict in the region that impede elusive postcolonial state formation, in addition to the weakness of the Congolese state and the territorial extension of neighboring states, to be shifting local alliances animated in no small measure by the profitability of war, linkage with enduring local issues, and pervasive impunity for egregious human rights violations. Ambassador Princeton Lyman, former US special envoy for Sudan and South Sudan, argues that efforts to reform the former state and build the latter have foundered because ruling parties in both have seen these initiatives as threats to their political survival. Effective change, he contends, can only come from within.

Finally, Will Reno writes that although efforts to promote democratic governance offer the prospect of long-term viable postcolonial state formation and economic well-being, they risk the collapse of the very states they undertake to reform given the pervasive patronage basis that has sustained them to this point.

NOTES

1. Crawford Young, *The African Colonial State in Comparative Perspective* (New Haven, CT: Yale University Press, 1994).

The International Factor
in African Warfare

WILLIAM RENO

Generalizing about recent wars and their global connections in a continent as diverse as Africa is a tricky business. The 1998–2000 Ethiopian–Eritrean border war looked like a classic interstate war, with trenches and front lines, field artillery and coordinated ground-air attacks as armies fought over the delineation of an international boundary. Around the same time wars in Congo and Somalia involved the collapse of state authority as ethnic militias, criminal gangs, religious ideologues, elements of old national armies, and armies of intervening states engaged in complex struggles. These wars have taken on new roles in global politics, too. After the September 11, 2001, attacks on New York and Washington, external actors began to view Somalia's conflict through the lens of counterterrorism. Congo's war appeared in international media as a humanitarian crisis. Some saw Sudan's counterinsurgency campaign in Darfur in the mid-2000s as an act of genocide, and fighting in South Sudan since 2013 has been seen in many quarters as part of a process of state collapse.

Amidst these diverse outcomes, distinct patterns emerge in the character of warfare in Africa, patterns rooted in changes in Africa's place in the international system. Most wars in Africa include "symmetrical irregular warfare" and the collapse of formal state institutions.[1] Large national armies play limited roles, and diverse armed groups dominate the scene as they pursue varied goals and agendas in often interlocking conflicts. Fighters use cheap, portable weapons. Few of these groups offer extensive political programs, and even if they do, they do not offer extensive programs of reform or propose to strengthen state institutions like rebels did in earlier decades. Civilians in war zones are likely to suffer from chronic insecurity amidst the collapse of effective central state authority, and many become refugees or internally displaced and encounter an international system of humanitarian aid and crisis management.

Most wars in Africa since 2000 have been fought across regions rather than solely within states and, thus, are fundamentally international wars. In 2016, for example, local issues drove conflicts in Congo, South Sudan, Sudan, Central African Republic, Nigeria, Mali, and Libya, but they also involved actors, relationships, and influences that spanned that region. Another regional complex appears in the Horn of Africa, with multiple armed groups inside Somalia's borders, some linked to ethnic kinsmen across borders and most involving global connections of some sort. Meanwhile armed groups associated with drug trafficking exacerbate political instability in several states in the region and have played a role in serious armed clashes in Guinea-Bissau.

This type of warfare in Africa defies conventional categories such as internal (civil) war and interstate war. It reflects the nature of political authority in parts of Africa where conflict is most prevalent. These conflicts often involve Africa's largest states, where formal state institutions are especially weak and regimes, instead, assert authority through political networks designed to control people's access to economic opportunities.[2] The political leadership manipulates the enforcement of their own laws to favor their political supporters and commercial partners as well as to manage external relations, giving some associates license to engage in predation and, in extreme cases, to seek out international criminals as collaborators. Resources such as international loans, proceeds from the sales of resources on global markets, foreign aid, and diplomatic and material support for siding with powerful states in initiatives such as the US-led War on Terror contribute to this store of political capital.

These "domestic" networks of political authority extend well beyond the formal institutional and physical boundaries of states, and thus, wars involving resources and political power connected to these networks take on global dimensions when measured against the grid of international boundaries. For example, when Tuareg rebels in Mali declared an independent state of Azawad in 2012 this appeared to be an internal affair. Some of these rebel factions relied upon weapons that fighters who supported Libyan leader Moammar el Gaddafi brought with them when Gaddafi was forced from power and they were driven from Libya. The appearance of foreign fighters in Libya was a further symptom of the regional dimension of this conflict, as UN investigators reported evidence of members of at least two factions of the Sudan Liberation Army and Sudan's Justice and Equality Movement in southern Libya. Meanwhile investigators found that Libyan groups were providing weapons to armed groups that included al-Qaeda in the Islamic Maghreb, Ansar Eddine, the Mouvement national de liberation de l'Azawad, and others that have been active in Mali, Niger, and elsewhere in the Sahel.[3] The distinctions between local uprisings, armed separatists, illicit commerce, and international terrorist networks become blurred.

In broad terms these wars are closely linked to the failure of twentieth-century state-building in the world's poorest countries. In the 1960s and 1970s many leaders who faced fiscal constraints and domestic political threats tried to build as large a coalition of supporters as possible while also building stronger state institutions. They used domestic resources and extracted as much as possible from the international community to sustain these sprawling patronage networks. The scarcity of domestic resources hindered this project from the start. Then these leaders faced a major shift to greater international scrutiny and criticism about how they governed that started in the 1980s and accelerated after 2000. This meant that old strategies of using patronage to build political coalitions, the banning of opposition parties, and economic policies that harmed producers were condemned as corrupt and repressive. Increased international interference into the details of governance made it much harder for these leaders to use these strategies, authoritarian and economically unsustainable though they may have been, to ameliorate political tensions with patronage and to repress their opponents to stay in power.

A new framework related to this crisis of patronage politics is needed to understand contemporary warfare in Africa and its place in world politics. The next section of this chapter explains how the crisis of patronage politics in parts of Africa is linked to how states and their opponents use violence. The two sections that follow then examine how changes in the international environment, particularly international intervention into the conduct of domestic politics in conflict zones, influence the conduct of warfare. In particular, threats of international sanctions and calls to abide by protocols to protect civilians change the distribution of resources and actors' calculations in warfare. Many of these measures strengthen the positions of armed groups and promote political fragmentation where formal state institutions already are very weak. Other international factors, such as US and European security aid to African states to combat terrorism, may increase state institutions' capacities when they already are fairly strong but can have an opposite effect where counterterrorism strategies rely upon the use of armed groups as proxies to identify and fight militants. The final section considers the future of warfare in Africa in terms of these global political links.

WARFARE AND THE CRISIS OF PATRONAGE POLITICS

Despite a quarter of a century of domestic and international pressure for reform, by various measures state institutions remain notably weak and regimes unstable across a wide range of African countries. Of the fifty-four member states of the African Union, only nine were rated as "free" in the 2016 Freedom House survey of political rights and civil liberties. Seven of these were situated on the continent's main landmass, much as a decade before.[4] This dearth of democratic governance, despite widespread adoption of laws and institutions associated with democracy, highlights the subordination of this visible institutional apparatus of the state to an underlying strategy of rule that undermines these institutions. Six of the ten countries that occupy the bottom of the 2015 Transparency International perceptions of corruption index, for example, are in Africa.[5] Violent, unconstitutional changes of government point to persistent political instability in many countries. Fourteen coups d'états occurred in seven sub-Saharan African countries from 2000 to mid-2016, and numerous other attempts failed. These violent changes of government highlight the instability of many patronage-based political systems in Africa and the tendency for the competition for power in at least some of them to descend into persistent conflict.

These examples are not meant to minimize important examples of successful reform in Africa and instead point to a growing divergence between countries in which institutions are increasingly stable and capable and countries where institutions grow weaker and political violence increases. For example, World Economic Forum estimates of the globe's ten fastest-growing economies include Tanzania (6.9 percent) and Senegal (6.6 percent), two countries that also have not experienced violent changes of government since independence in the early 1960s.[6] Ethiopia and Rwanda also maintained very high growth rates for the past two decades in what appear to be stable authoritarian political contexts. These cases illuminate different pathways out of a crisis of patronage politics, but as the reader will see below, elsewhere domestic crises and global pressures can lead instead to distinctive patterns of warfare.

Historically, political systems built on networks of patronage ties have been able to preserve a measure of political stability, if not economic prosperity. This is true when a single leader or a small coalition monopolizes the distribution of benefits. Stability also is contingent on this leadership's capacity to prevent potential challengers from mobilizing against them. As late as the 1980s it was still possible for notable scholars to propose that the president of Congo (then called Zaire) Mobutu Sese Seko was able to end large-scale political violence and turmoil by constructing a patronage system. Mobutu's system was fairly inclusionary at an elite level, so long as Mobutu was able to get the resources that he needed to co-opt important political figures. As long as his patronage network remained centralized at its apex, Mobutu's strategy reversed the collapse of authority and factional violence that affected Congo during its first five years of independence from 1960. To some observers this appeared to be one of the few ways to hold this vast country together.[7]

Rule that is based upon a leader's capacity to control access to economic opportunities usually exhibits little official regard for laws or systematic guarantees of human rights or any ethic of public allocation of resources, as the security and prosperity of the elite is subject to the personal decisions of the leader. This system of authority is hostile to private enterprise out of fear that those who do not owe their wealth to the ruler's favor may use these resources to oppose him. Thus, when opposition to the ruler does develop, it is most likely mobilized through the more ambitious members of the elite coalition rather than among political outsiders who can sustain a mass movement.

The main threat to leaders comes most often from within the incumbent elite coalition, and managing this threat occupies the leader's attention. Anxious leaders thus become preoccupied with manipulating contending factions at this elite level to keep ambitious individuals focused on struggle with each other rather than ganging up on their superior. Those who pose the greatest threat face the wrath of the regime as targets of corruption investigations or purges and, in some cases, are on the receiving end of direct applications of violence. Loyalty to the ruler often follows a pragmatic calculation: better to benefit from the protection of the regime than to be singled out for persecution, which fosters an image of great power that is tied to the leader's personal discretion. This system of governance is terrible for economies, but it can be effective for ensuring regime survival. In the late 1980s Jean-Francois Bayart wrote, "The salient feature of the last few decades south of the Sahara has been the absence of any collective agent capable or desirous of taking the lead in a social movement aspiring to a revolutionary alternative to the current grinding of the postcolonial state."[8] But as we will see, the sustainability of this system of governance is limited, with important consequences for the character of warfare in Africa and its global connections.

Patronage as a basis of authority, along with its negative consequences for economic development and accountable governance, appeared to be sustainable so long as the international community abided by the principles in Article 2 of the Charter of the United Nations that all states enjoy equality in their sovereignty. This principle protected governments from external intervention into their domestic affairs. Although it is true that superpower rivalries were played out through support for proxies in Africa, particularly in conflicts in Angola and Mozambique in the 1970s and 1980s, this international interference did not challenge the basic logic of patronage-based systems of political control. Moreover, leaders learned that they could trade their political support for an external patron to gain material assistance. In a notable test of this support, in 1982 the World Bank, the International Monetary Fund, private banks, and other creditors hired the German banker Erwin Blumenthal to investigate official-level corruption in Zaire (Congo). Blumenthal wrote in his report that it is "alarmingly clear that the corruptive system in Zaire with all of its wicked and ugly manifestations, its mismanagement and fraud will destroy all endeavors of international institutions, or friendly governments, and of commercial banks towards recovery and rehabilitation of Zaire's economy."[9] But US pressure ended creditor efforts to impose conditions on this debtor country. Zaire's real value was as a Cold War ally that provided a rear base for antigovernment rebels attacking Angola's Marxist government. Violations of human rights did not attract a great deal of international interference in internal affairs either. In 1977 the government of Uganda's President Idi Amin sat on the UN's Commission on Human Rights at the same time that his security forces were killing as many as a hundred thousand of his country's citizens. There was, as one scholar lamented, a sovereign "right to genocide," as massacres and other gross human rights abuses were considered domestic affairs.[10]

The end of the Cold War brought international demands that these governments modify their behavior. World Bank reports stressed that political reform would be added to economic reform as conditions for continued access to foreign loans. It made sense to target the core logic of patronage politics, such as the leader's personal control over the distribution of resources, the manipulation of laws to favor political supporters and their enterprises, and the suppression of economic enterprise. These reforms were supposed to foster the formation of a class of independent holders of wealth who would pressure governments to adopt better economic policies and more accountable and democratic governance.

Even before the end of the Cold War many African leaders were discovering that the external flow of resources from their own patrons had become less reliable. By the 1980s many Western governments had begun to share the view of Soviet officials that "involvement in sub-Saharan Africa represented an unacceptable drain on Soviet resources" and "that its manifold problems were peripheral to Soviet interests."[11] This withdrawal had the most dramatic impact on the fortunes of the continent's regimes that were most intensively reliant upon the manipulation of patronage and elite factional tensions to stay in power. Between 1980 and 1985 Liberia's government received about $500 million in combined US economic and military aid, which then dried up as the US Congress grew concerned about human rights violations.[12] The government of Zaire received about $2 billion in US aid from the mid-1960s to the end of the 1980s, but this, too, slowed to a trickle as Congo's strategic importance evaporated. By 1988 US aid to Somalia's dictator, totaling about $750 million over the previous decade, and massive aid to refugees that Somalia's government instead manipulated for political gain were ended as the US Congress investigated government massacres of about fifty thousand citizens.[13]

This sudden cut in the flow of resources to the three top African recipients of US aid in the late 1980s—Congo, Liberia, and Somalia—was followed very closely by the collapse of two of these governments and conflict between armed factions of the old incumbent elite. Civil war broke out in Liberia in late 1989 and, with interruptions, ended only in 2003, while state collapse and conflict has continued in Somalia with varying intensity since early 1991. Congo's Mobutu was able to delay the collapse for several years, but the sharp decline in external resources directly under his personal control (and advanced prostate cancer) also fatally weakened his authority over his political subordinates, and a complex multisided civil war with extensive armed foreign interventions started in 1996.

In each of these cases the trigger for warfare was the leader's loss of capacity to manage factional struggles as key elite members of each patronage network struck out on their own. Most of these leaders publicly acknowledged this anger and used it as a threat to convince foreigners to continue to provide financial and political support. Mobutu and Gaddafi were particularly fond of predicting that their removal from power would result not in reform but instead in the replacement of their political systems with open-ended violent multisided conflict amidst the collapse of the state. These predictions came true in many instances, as so-called warlords in many of Africa's conflicts had previously held significant positions in prewar political networks. These ambitious individuals no longer had a compelling reason to profess loyalty to their country's leaders, and the removal of their old patrons from power left them free to build their own political networks. The problem was that suddenly there were many such would-be leaders who now had to fight each other to realize their ambitions.

The focus of these new armed groups was on the appropriation of pieces of old patronage networks, including vital external commercial connections. This situation shaped how many viewed these struggles. Some scholars describe this as "greed-driven" warfare.[14] Although material gain appeared to play a major role in the purposes of fighting, the real objective of these wartime commanders was to seize the resources of old patronage networks and use them to assemble new versions of this kind of political authority. Capturing state power was still important, as the possession of sovereignty widened the scope of available resources. But greed in this context was as much about political authority as it was about personal enrichment, particularly as the resources of illicit trades in diamonds, timber, and other resources replaced Cold War–era foreign aid, loans, and other external resources as the material basis for this kind of political system.

Declining external support for patronage-based regimes in Africa in the 1990s challenged leaders to find new ways to manage patronage networks to ensure their survival in power. Angola's leaders proved adept at extending and adapting political networks to include nongovernmental organizations (NGOs). These NGOs, seemingly independent of the government but actually under the tight control of the regime's leaders, absorbed the energies of educated urban citizens and were useful as vehicles to solicit donations from foreign businesses that sought favor in the country's oil industry.[15] Other aspects of what at first glance appear to be societal resistance to the state also played roles in regime survival strategies. For example, the Gaddafi regime in Libya implemented economic reforms to create incentives for communities to smuggle goods and engage in other illicit commerce. This created an opportunity in which the "regime controlled key trafficking routes and used enforcement to reward some groups over others. The result was a controlled criminal market regulated by the state."[16] This manipulation of local competition and insecurity as instruments of central control intensified factional splits. Once Gaddafi's regime faced domestic armed opposition and a multinational intervention began in 2011, these factional tensions fed into the multisided armed factional struggle and state collapse that Gaddafi warned would be Libya's fate if he were removed from power.

Patronage-based personal rule also survived in many places against international and domestic pressures for democratic governance. In a pattern repeated elsewhere, Cameroon's incumbent president Paul Biya faced a competitive election in 1992, his first since coming to power in 1982. He won with about 40 percent of the vote, prevailing only because the opposition was split between two challengers and through the use of intimidation and other voting irregularities. The 1997 election was quite different, however, with Biya winning over 92 percent of the vote against a field of six other candidates. Though he won only 71 percent of the vote in 2007, Biya was able to exploit rivalries within his elite coalition to ensure that the rest of the vote was split among fifteen other candidates.[17] Thus, pressures for democratic reform in the 1990s led to the wide adoption of multiparty elections in Africa. By mid-2016 incumbent presidents of Equatorial Guinea and Angola (since 1979), Zimbabwe (since 1980), Cameroon (since 1982), and Uganda (since 1986) have weathered the introduction of formal multiparty electoral systems. Insofar as their regime survival strategies depend upon manipulating tensions between factions of the elite and the exploitation of local-level and even personal conflicts, these survival strategies lay the groundwork for the future fragmentation of political authority and possible multisided armed conflict.

In fact, many political networks do not survive as instruments of authority under central control, and the bulk of warfare in Africa from the 1990s has been connected to their fragmentation as the international relations of African states changed. This change has unleashed former clients in many places to manage their own external connections—such as to criminal gangs, humanitarian agencies, and diaspora groups—to attract their own supporters. Competition among aspiring patrons frequently spills over international borders. This happened in Congo when Rwanda and Uganda intervened, starting in 1996, to support various rebel groups. Ugandan army officers had a tendency to conduct business on their own account with rebel commanders.[18] Many militia leaders arose out of old Mobutu-era networks. Jean-Pierre Bemba, son of Mobutu's chief business partner and brother to the wife of one of Mobutu's sons, organized the Mouvement de Libération du Congo with help from Uganda's army, which also brought Sudan People's Liberation Army fighters across the border to fight against Chadian troops that had been lent to Congo's President Kabila. Then in 2002 Central African Republic's President Ange-Félix Patassé called upon Bemba to come to his aid to defeat a coup attempt.[19] This one slice of a very complex set of interlocking networks shows how the politics of patronage-based state regimes and the politics of collapsed states have been so closely connected. The Congolese warlord and the Central African Republic's president were fighting and ruling in much the same fashion. Then the successful coup of François Bozizé in 2003 in the Central African Republic brought Bozizé's network of Chadian fighters to the capital city to replace the Congolese networks.[20] Warfare in this context of state collapse seemed like a more violent and unstable version of the prewar authoritarian patronage-based rule rather than a huge change in how authority was exercised.

State collapse illustrates one outcome of a broad trend toward the equalization of the internal capabilities and the external relations of armed groups. This situation produces multiple armed groups that tend to be loosely organized under personalist commanders who serve as patrons to armed followers. Armed groups are held together on the basis of personal and community loyalties. Lacking strong centralizing organizational structures, these groups fight much like rival gangs, regardless of whether their leaders were part of the collapsed state's bureaucratic apparatus. This kind of conflict produces the symmetrical irregular warfare that is a common mode of warfare in many of Africa's conflicts. This development reflects the structure of domestic prewar political authorities. But especially after the September 11, 2001, attacks on New York and Washington, global pressures came to play a greater role in shaping the nature of warfare in Africa.

WARFARE, WORLD POLITICS, AND TWENTY-FIRST CENTURY STATE-BUILDING

US and European interest in the internal politics of African states rapidly intensified after the September 11 attacks. Even earlier, the simultaneous suicide bomb attacks in August 1998 on US embassies in Nairobi and Dar es Salaam killed more than 220 people and wounded over 4,000. Because the perpetrators of these attacks had found refuge in Somalia, US officials identified areas with weak or nonexistent state institutions as serious security threats. Then in 2002 US president George W. Bush highlighted the link between weak state institutions in Africa and threats to domestic US security, noting that "with our European allies we must help strengthen Africa's fragile states, help build indigenous capability to secure porous borders, and help build up the law enforcement and intelligence infrastructure to deny safe haven to terrorists."[21] Once viewed as undesirable candidates for external intervention, collapsed and weak states came under scrutiny for their lack of capacity or political unwillingness to provide guarantees to foreigners that the territory of these states would not be used to prepare new attacks. The American president warned that states that were unwilling or unable to provide this guarantee were candidates for armed intervention. In sum, the strongest states in international society now insisted that domestic governance in even the weakest states have come with responsibilities to govern in particular ways and that sovereignty was no longer a shield against external interference to correct deviations from this new standard.

This international shift has had substantial consequences for regimes that govern through patronage networks, particularly when these networks involve partnerships with illicit commercial operations or use violence against civilians. In Liberia, for example, UN experts who investigated Liberian president Charles Taylor's violations of an arms embargo detailed his business associations with arms traffickers, alleging that he used these connections to provide funding and weapons to Sierra Leone's rebels to conduct a reign of terror in an eleven-year war in which fifty thousand people died. The report also noted the extensive use of private bank accounts to conceal revenues and expenditures, suggesting that Taylor tried to hide his intimate ties to illicit networks that supplied his supporters with weapons in new security forces and supported allied armed groups.[22] Then a journalist showed how Liberia's illicit networks were linked to terrorist financiers from the Middle East.[23]

The recognition of a particular form of governance as a security threat essentially criminalizes regimes that rely extensively upon patronage networks to govern, especially if these networks involve illicit commercial transactions. Regimes like Taylor's in Liberia now faced serious international pressures in the form of sanctions and embargoes if they were seen as promoting conflicts as part of their strategies for exercising authority. This negative attention and its material consequences can make a country's leader appear to be more vulnerable in the eyes of domestic rivals. International concerns about illicit networks and their connections to security threats also can buy leaders latitude to act, provided these actions promise to address foreigners' anxieties. Events in Guinea-Bissau illustrate this international element in domestic political conflicts, even if exact impacts are difficult to trace in complex situations. In that country confrontations between army officers involved in drug trafficking and the prime minister led to a military coup on April 12, 2012. The prime minister wanted to rein in the military and relied instead on an Angolan security and training mission that appeared to be linked to Angolan government efforts to gain favorable treatment in commercial deals.[24] His efforts to target alleged drug trafficking may have bought the prime minister greater international tolerance for this approach. Once the coup leaders were in power, however, they faced serious international pressure to agree to a schedule for elections and were threatened with possible referral to the International Criminal Court (ICC) for prosecution.[25]

Regime involvement with illicit commerce and human rights abuses is not new in Africa,[26] but other states' willingness to intervene in the internal affairs of these states to halt this practice is a new development, often with major domestic consequences. For example, UN sanctions and US pressure forced Liberia's President Taylor to leave office in 2003 and eventually led him to appear before a tribunal in 2006. He was sentenced in 2012 for his role in atrocities committed during Sierra Leone's war, to which he was linked through clandestine political and commercial ties to Sierra Leone's rebels. Commanders of Congolese militias have attracted particular ICC attention, with seven of them having faced prosecution as of 2016 for crimes including massacres of civilians, use of rape as an instrument of war, and use of child soldiers.

The prosecution of Liberia's President Taylor in particular shows that international actors will withdraw their recognition of the sovereignty of leaders who stray from an increasingly complex set of norms. This right to intervene is accepted among many African governments, at least in principle, and is codified in the African Union's 2003 African Charter on Democracy, Elections, and Governance.[27] This has led to sanctions and diplomatic pressure being applied against regimes from other African governments, such as pressure applied to Senegal for harboring former Chadian president Hissene Habré. During the 1980s Habré's regime killed thousands of political opponents and members of their communities as part of his strategy to prevail over numerous armed factions up to his over-throw in 1990. During the 1980s the United States and France supported Habré as a counterbalance to Libyan influence. External support and domestic violence enabled Habré to maintain a modicum of control over an otherwise highly frag-mented set of political networks. But in 2005 Habré faced an indictment in Bel-gium for crimes against humanity. ECOWAS requested that he be tried before a special tribunal, and in 2015 his trial finally began.

Some regimes discover that external interference in their domestic affairs ac-tually gives them more means to strengthen the leadership's control over political networks. This happens most often when foreigners' security concerns outweigh concerns about human rights. This kind of intervention represents an import-ant global connection to wars in Africa, particularly when the leadership of one country or even a militia in a collapsed state can convince anxious foreigners that they are an acceptable security partner. Leaders in these circumstances discover that being included in international security cooperation can provide an excellent remedy to the crisis of patronage politics.

Security cooperation usually requires that leaders accept another set of ex-ternal demands to conform to a standard set of practices—in this case, in the realm of security. Outsiders' anxiety to counter security threats can be turned into a political resource for these regimes. A good illustration of this relationship can be found in the Combined Joint Task Force–Horn of Africa (CJTF-HOA), which deployed eighteen hundred US soldiers to Djibouti and became part of the newly established US Africa Command (AFRICOM) in 2007. AFRICOM operations, along with programs like the Pan-Sahel Initiative, focus on partnerships with US military and civilian agencies to train police and military personnel in African countries and to work with state agencies in these countries to implement re-form programs. CJTF-HOA describes these operations "as part of a comprehen-sive whole-of-government approach . . . aimed at increasing our African partner nations' capacity to maintain a stable environment, with an effective government that provides a degree of economic and social advancement to its citizens."[28] The UK's Africa Conflict Prevention Pool, established in April 2001, provided a model for coordinating the activities of African and foreign "partner" civilian govern-ment agencies and NGOs to operate alongside military forces to change local se-curity environments.

Drawing upon ideas about fighting irregular and counterinsurgency warfare, these partnerships lay the basis for preemptive counterinsurgency in African host states. This approach focuses on helping governments hold territory to deny ac-cess to armed groups. Engaging directly with local populations is an important step in achieving this goal. Where governments are weak, this can mean using foreign security support, humanitarian organizations, and a variety of NGOs and civic groups to extend services to local populations. As US secretary of state Colin Powell noted in 2001, "NGOs are such a force multiplier for us, such an important part of our combat team." Though officials subsequently downplayed this statement, the idea that it expressed is central to the concept of complex operations that leverage the knowledge and operations of many organizations to increase governments' capacities to behave like bureaucratic states.

Even though operations envision a step-by-step state-building enterprise, they actually are compatible with the underlying logic of patronage-based authority. Foreign political and material support can strengthen the leader's capacity to coerce subordinates to demonstrate obedience to his authority. The state's strengthened security and surveillance capabilities can give an authoritarian leader more leeway to marginalize and even use violence against groups that otherwise would have to be included in patronage networks. The improved capacity to detect dissent and, in some cases, to label discontent and opposition as terrorism means that some communities simply can be cut out of political bargains. Foreign aid to state agencies also helps to concentrate the allocation of resources into the hands of the ruler, particularly if the regime is able to turn elections into a façade of competition and address other concerns about standards of domestic behavior. These resources and visible external backing enhance the role of the ruler's personal discretion in political decisions. This creates the appearance of political stability that may seem to be successful foreign-supported state-building projects. Stability in fact may be the product of a leader's more centralized control over patronage and increased capacity to dictate the terms of membership in a political coalition centered on control of the state.

Uganda provides a good example of the intersection of internationalized war fighting in Africa and domestic patronage strategies. Yoweri Museveni has occupied Uganda's presidency since 1986, building a core coalition of security forces and key political associates while exercising careful personal control over the flow of resources. Domestic and international pressure to hold multiparty elections after 2005 threatened this control. The introduction of real competition for supporters gave subordinate members of this network and ambitious political outsiders an opening to challenge the president. This raised the price of co-optation back into the political network, as elections empowered some people to launch efforts to build their own political networks. International pressure at this stage caused what Joel Barkan called "inflationary patronage," which forced the president to distribute money in campaigns to co-opt viable opposition candidates, buy the support of communities, and maintain the loyalty of his associates, tasks that observers estimate cost up to $300 million in an election year.[29]

This external and domestic pressure for political reforms continues in Uganda. It undermines the stability of a centralized political network through weakening the president's hold over clients. Electoral violence in Kenya, Côte d'Ivoire, and elsewhere highlights how competition in the context of patronage-based politics can contribute to political fragmentation, often in a violent fashion—a link between international pressures to reform and an unintended outcome: African wars. The problem for reformers is that, although democratic governance may offer better prospects for long-term political stability and economic efficiency, it risks provoking the collapse of state authority where the logic of politics centers on patronage. Even Kenya, thought of as a relatively stable African state before the 2007 elections, suffered more than a thousand deaths in electoral violence in early 2008 in clashes of armed gangs aligned with politicians. Advocates of reform therefore have to consider carefully the paradox of their positions, caught as they are between a desire to fundamentally change these political systems to conform to global norms while still dependent upon what they see as the core problems of governance to provide short-term political stability. External actors are also caught in this bind, as the stability of patronage networks, even if they are implicated in illicit commerce and human rights abuses, is central to their desire to address security threats.

This paradox occasionally breaks out into the open. A US embassy official noted, "Many Ugandans believe President Museveni will never hold top officials . . . accountable for corruption, and Uganda's continued failure to seriously investigate and prosecute allegations of corruption involving senior government officials seemingly supports such conclusions."[30] Increased repression of those without political leverage involved human rights abuses that attracted more external condemnations.[31] These strategies, lamentable though logical in the context of patronage politics, led to reductions in what had been an annual $600 million in World Bank budget support through the decade to 2008, a serious blow to a government that relied upon aid for about half of its budget expenditures.

Uganda's government found salvation in security cooperation. The US government recognizes Uganda as a key ally in ensuring support for efforts to rebuild a central government in Somalia and particularly to contribute military contingents to the African Union Mission in Somalia (AMISOM) to provide military protection to the new government. Uganda has supported AMISOM since its organization in 2007, fielding more than five thousand infantry near Mogadishu. This willingness to serve in a multilateral African expeditionary force to fight Islamist enemies of the Somali government led to a reversal of the United States' cutoff of military aid. Aid had been halted in 2000 over Ugandan military abuses of civilians and involvement in illicit commercial operations in Congo. But since 2007 US military assistance has averaged about $200 million a year, supplemented with significant UK aid. The US State Department oversees contracts with private operators, some of whom include prominent Ugandans among their partners, for logistical support to Uganda's military. These arrangements contribute to the resources available to Uganda's president to support his political position.

Foreign training programs can help create a core of professional military officers, a key element of developing state institutions that can provide order and assert the authority of the government over the country's territory. Military training also is compatible with tightening executive control over armed forces within patronage-based political systems. Uganda's military includes armored units such as the Presidential Guard Brigades that remain under the personal control of the president and his son, who also received US military training (about which he wrote a book).[32] This distribution of tasks in Uganda's military enables a fairly effective institutional enclave to attract external resources to contribute to the president's personal authority.

Uganda's political establishment also benefits from international condemnation of the Lord's Resistance Army's (LRA's) use of child soldiers and commission of atrocities against civilians in northern Uganda and elsewhere in the region as well as US aid to Uganda's military to capture or kill the LRA's leaders. The LRA first appeared on the US State Department's list of terrorist organizations in 2001, partly due to pressure from advocacy groups. Aid to northern Uganda coordinated through the State Department, the Defense Department, USAID, while intelligence services provided logistical and intelligence support to the Uganda People's Defence Force and helped to build infrastructure and services for which Uganda's government could take local credit. Overall, US military assistance to Uganda amounts to about $170 million a year, with additional political benefits of visible American support for Uganda's role in AMISOM and its decision to contribute soldiers to a US-backed regional force designed for rapid intervention. As Ken Opalo notes, "the most obvious outcome of US cooperation is the privatization of the Ugandan army. It has become a lot more a tool of Museveni."[33]

In sum, Uganda's president benefits from external support to build institutions in ways that do not interfere with his personal role as a distributor of patronage and economic opportunity. His country's strategic interventions in wars elsewhere on the continent help to deflect international criticism of his domestic political strategies, particularly the failure to fully implement political reforms. US and European engagements with other governments for counterterrorism activities have provided regimes with long-serving presidents, such as Burkina Faso's Blaise Compaore (in office from 1987 until removed from power in 2014). Compaore received modest amounts of military aid, specialized training for soldiers, and, more important, the image of protection from a powerful external patron that prioritized security and stability, at least until mass protests in the capital challenged his hold on power and the military intervened to remove him and prepare for elections.[34] Idriss Déby Itno, president of Chad since 1990, continues this style of security cooperation, participating quite effectively in the Multinational Joint Task Force, a combined multinational force that includes units from Niger, Nigeria, Benin, and Cameroon to combat Boko Haram rebels in Nigeria and elsewhere in the region.

WARFARE, WORLD POLITICS, AND TWENTY-FIRST-CENTURY STATE COLLAPSE

Countries like Uganda show how regimes that control centralized networks of supporters and limit their uses of violence against critics and opponents are able to manipulate external aid designed to strengthen their domestic political positions. Regimes that struggle to control more fragmented patronage networks, however, are much more disadvantaged in Africa's new place in global politics.

Foreign criticisms of their desperate efforts to manage unwieldy coalitions and armed opponents, usually seen in terms of human rights abuses and gross corruption, undermine these regimes' desperate short-term survival strategies. Sudan, South Sudan, Central African Republic, Congo, Chad, Niger, and Mauritania as well as some small countries like Guinea-Bissau and Comoros have substantial histories of political instability and violent factional conflict. For decades rulers have struggled to prevent fragmentation of these coalitions, combining patronage (sometimes with considerable external financial assistance), palace intrigue, and episodes of considerable violence against opponents and their home communities to stay in power. This politics centers on the shifting alliances of strongmen and conflict-ridden center-periphery relations rather than reproducing an ideal model of governance. Thus, some of the conflicts that many regard as Africa's civil wars also are manifestations of conflicts within this kind of political system. Once serious fragmentation begins, local strongmen defy their president and call upon their home communities and various other kinship and commercial networks to join their fight.

Global efforts to limit the sovereign capacities of these rulers to manage their patronage systems as these rulers see fit can have the perverse effect of promoting further fragmentation and political disorder. Unlike Uganda's President Museveni, rulers like Sudan's President Omar al-Bashir who cannot convince outsiders that they are essential allies against terrorism face severe limits on external financial assistance to their treasuries, at least from US and European sources. As noted above in cases such as Guinea-Bissau, these rulers face sanctions and embargoes, further weakening their appeal to subordinates and regional powerbrokers that they can act as effective patrons. Al-Bashir, for example, faces an arrest warrant issued by the ICC in 2010 on counts of war crimes, crimes against humanity, and genocide after his government's bloody repression of a rebellion in Darfur. Al-Bashir had other options, however, and turned to Saudi Arabia, which gave Sudan $2 billion for joining Saudi Arabia's fight in Yemen. Much of this sum went into private bank accounts, lubricating the patronage-based system of authority.[35]

Alex de Waal points to Darfur's conflict as an example of such a "political marketplace" in Sudan in which international intervention has influenced warfare in ways that presented significant challenges to the incumbent regime. Local strongmen discovered that international condemnation of the head of the political network enhanced their own power. They then leveraged international negotiations as platforms for their otherwise insignificant rebel forces. Their attacks on government forces raised the price of their co-optation into a weakened patron's network. This international intervention into conflicts, argues de Waal, enables these armed local actors to instead negotiate deals with foreign critics of their government, multilateral peacekeeping forces, and global commercial networks.[36] Within Darfur's political marketplace, the ICC arrest warrants issued in 2007 for Ali Khushayb and Ahmed Mohammed Haroun for war crimes and crimes against humanity, committed while leaders of government-supported militias, further damaged the president's capacity to buy off his opponents, showing that using violence against them would further isolate the regime from the international community. Luckily for President al-Bashir, Saudi Arabia had different, more security-based criteria as it came into Sudan's domestic political scene.

The International Commission of Inquiry into Darfur, set up by the UN Security Council, concluded in January 2005 that Sudan's government was fighting a counterinsurgency campaign in Darfur. Historically this has been a customary right of governments, albeit not one that allows for wanton abuses of human rights.[37] In 2004, however, US secretary of state Colin Powell stated that "genocide has been committed in Darfur and that the government of Sudan and the Jingaweit bear responsibility."[38] This twenty-first-century response was quite different from the relatively muted responses in the 1990s as the Angolan government's counterinsurgency campaigns resulted in loss of life that exceeded the toll in Darfur.

International preferences for roundtable negotiations equip powerbrokers and local armed groups' commanders to drive hard bargains in negotiations with heads of patronage networks. Somali participants in peace negotiations, sometimes stretching over many years, found that they could buy preferential treatment in negotiations.[39] The costs of keeping them at the table for these negotiations rose in tandem with their capacities to display capabilities to fight and create mayhem in the field of battle. There are costs of this strategy that befall these beneficiaries, too, as their subordinates have the same incentives to break away and establish their own militias. Then they, too, gain entrée into negotiations and a role in potential settlements. In a demonstration of this tendency toward factionalization, the 2006 Darfur Agreement included only three rebel groups, whereas negotiations a year later involved over a dozen, with many of these soon splitting into multiple factions. This fragmentation in part reflected the Sudanese regime's efforts to make side deals with rebels to undermine their capacity to cooperate with each other while negotiations played their part in this proliferation of factions. Negotiations offer more direct benefits, too: even Uganda's LRA, noted above, in 2007 demanded $2 million from donors as their fee to participate in negotiations.[40]

Payments to members of armed groups for internationally sponsored disarmament and postconflict reconstruction in the context of fragmented patronage networks risk channeling resources to local commanders who have to be paid off to remain peaceful rather than national governments. These local strongmen then can use these resources to strengthen their own political networks. International support for administrative decentralization and grassroots civic action where state institutions already are very weak also can promote the fragmentation of the political networks that are the real basis of authority. In countries where leaders historically have had a hard time maintaining political coalitions and controlling the flow of patronage resources, these reforms that give more autonomy to local powerbrokers empower them to bargain more vigorously and demand a higher price for their support.

Not all leaders have to accept these reforms. Chad's President Déby Itno probably would not be in power in 2016 were it not for his decision to break his agreement with the World Bank consortium over the use of oil revenues. These revenues were supposed to be distributed, with 80 percent for economic development and poverty reduction, 10 percent for a sovereign fund, 5 percent for oil producing areas, and 5 percent for government revenues.[41] The deal fell apart in 2006 when Déby Itno decided to run for reelection right after a serious rebellion in the eastern part of the country that was connected to the conflict in Darfur. His decision to abrogate the agreement reaffirmed his position as the arbiter of a centralized patronage network, a status he underlined with his use of oil revenues to purchase weapons. Even with this advantage, Déby Itno was nearly overthrown in 2008 when rebel armies reached the capital. But with French support he held onto power, proving his worth later as an ally in the fight against Boko Haram, a terrorist group aligned with the Islamic State operating in northern Nigeria.

Déby Itno's survival as president of Chad highlights the importance to leaders of Africa's patronage-based political systems of leveraging their relations with external actors. Chad's army participates in the United States' Trans-Sahara Counter-Terrorism Initiative to monitor and block violent extremists' movements across the Sahara. The export of oil and the revenues that this trade generates support the president's efforts to keep rebel groups factionalized and weak. This dominance in patronage resources convinced some rebel leaders to change sides. Chad's president showed considerable skill negotiating a favorable position in the context of increased international scrutiny of the political strategies of African regimes, particularly when they are engaged in conflicts. This process shows how political strategies of African leaders and external actors alike promote factionalized conflict when war does break out. These strategies also demonstrate how warfare either can be a resource or a curse in organizing patronage politics, a dynamic that sheds light on the future role of African wars in world politics.

WORLD POLITICS AND THE FUTURE OF AFRICAN WARS

It is not likely that international pressure on patronage politics in the world's weaker states, usually defined in terms of corruption and human rights violations, will abate. Increasingly intense global exchanges of information and people contribute to demands for common standards and uniformity of behavior. Continued concerns about terrorism and security play their parts, too. Governments are called upon to certify that they are observing and protecting their borders, monitoring commercial transactions, watching for signs of extremism, and executing numerous other tasks. This intensifies a long-term trend. Since the start of the colonial era, globalization has supported the spread of states throughout Africa, even when some of these states exhibited little capacity to actually rule. More recently geopolitical shifts and exchanges of ideas have resulted in the universal spread of very specific forms of governance, such as multiparty politics; limits on uses of violence, particularly against citizens; and greater attention to suppressing corruption. Globalization in this fashion infringes on the prerogatives of African states' sovereignty. But this infringement has been part of a process of state construction and has reinforced the importance of the state as a basic unit of politics in Africa, as it has done so elsewhere as well.

The pages above show how this international engagement has expanded the resources available to some African states while also channeling more resources to some of their armed opponents. Though some state actors in Africa can manipulate and selectively shield themselves from global pressures to behave in certain ways, these pressures influence how warfare in Africa's future is likely to evolve. Meanwhile wars have become halting affairs, punctuated with cycles of negotiation and fighting. International intervention stays the hands of state actors while keeping nonstate armed groups politically and militarily viable for longer than might otherwise be the case. This has reduced the intensity of wars, including a decrease in death tolls, at the same time as it contributes to the absence of clearly defined war termination.

Conflicts short of war also have changed in ways that reflect international influences and point to future trajectories. The violent response of Guinea's government to September 2009 citizen protests against military rule, for example, resulted in the deaths of at least 150 people. Two decades earlier this would have been an unremarkable event. Perhaps at that time this event would lead to more confrontation and much greater violence, or it could have ended the challenge against this regime at that point in a decisive and bloody manner. Instead, African Union, US, and European Union pressure on President Moussa Dadis Camara and several dozen others to step down led to elections in 2010. In contrast, government repression in the 1960s and 1970s in Guinea resulted in the murder of fifty thousand people with little international comment.[42] This earlier event in a contemporary context would be viewed as alarming, a regionally destabilizing event with the potential to start a civil war. Now the principle that regimes are not allowed to systematically apply violence against citizens in the pursuit of political authority has reduced the incidence and intensity of warfare on the continent. At the same time, this response has reduced the capacity of regimes in Africa to manage splits and factional strife among members of their own elites. As this and other examples show, external intervention into the domestic politics of these states and their regimes can have some very positive benefits alongside effects that some might see as negative. In any event, this intervention has a major impact on the terms of state-building and the course of conflicts in Africa.

Prohibitions against some forms of government violence do not mean that all leaders in Africa will simply abandon patronage politics and refrain from using coercion to strengthen their hands in political bargains with critics and challengers. As noted above, leaders' capacity to use global political changes to their benefit varies widely. Those who can manipulate external pressures and manage intervention, such as Uganda's President Museveni, actually may strengthen personalist aspects of their authority at the expense of institutional development. They do this with considerable help from foreign patrons. Others, such as Sudan's President al-Bashir, face diminishing options. But even this president can sell his assistance to address other countries' security problems. And for the most desperate the threat that the demise of their regimes will lead to state collapse and open-ended disorder, with the danger that this will create a haven for terrorists, can cause some international actors to hesitate: Do they really want to launch far more expensive and politically risky interventions in the event that a president loses his political grip and factional fighting replaces his rule? The threat of political suicide, to be followed with state collapse—or more accurately, the collapse of a political network rather than state institutional collapse—is a political resource of a sort, too.

Recent changes in Africa's place in world politics have had an ambiguous impact on the character of warfare. States that already have relatively strong institutions can use these shifts to pursue reforms. Those that have very weak institutions may be prone to greater political fragmentation and violence. Some effects are more general. Governments hesitate to massacre their own citizens to degrees not seen in previous decades. But greater democratic accountability is illusory in many cases. As Uganda showed above, the domestic political consequences of global changes can reinforce patronage-based elements of regime politics.

Ultimately the evolution of patronage politics in many African countries and the turmoil that accompanies it highlights a tight link between African state-building, global politics, and African wars. Most recent wars arise out of contention within elite networks rather than challenges from rural farmers or the urban unemployed. They are products of the political systems out of which they emerge and rarely go far to reshape these political systems, even when accompanied by high levels of violence. Fundamental change in the character of warfare in Africa and in its links to global politics will have to await a fundamental change in the logic of politics and of state-building in Africa. That prospect is still far off in some of Africa's largest countries, such as Somalia, Congo, Central African Republic, South Sudan, Sudan, Chad, Niger, and Mali as well as in chronically unstable countries such as Guinea-Bissau. These countries see the bulk of conflict on this continent now and will continue to do so for the foreseeable future.

NOTES

1. Stathis Kalyvas and Laia Balcells, "International System and Technologies of Rebellion: How the End of the Cold War Shaped Internal Conflict," *American Political Science Review* 104, no. 3 (2010), p. 418.

2. This is an idea developed in part in Christopher Clapham, Jeffrey Herbst, Greg Mills, eds., *Big African States: Angola, DRC, Ethiopia, South Africa, Sudan* (Johannesburg: Witswatersrand University Press, 2006).

3. UN Security Council, *Report of the Panel of Experts on Libya Established Pursuant to Resolution 1973* (2011) (New York: UN, March 9, 2016), pp. 43 and 166–169.

4. Freedom House, "2016 Freedom in the World" (Washington, DC: Freedom House, 2016), https://freedomhouse.org/sites/default/files/FH_FITW_Report_2016.pdf.

5. Transparency International, "2015 Corruption Perceptions Index" (Berlin: Transparency International, 2015), https://thehomestead.net.

6. Joe Myers, "Which Are the World's Fastest-Growing Economies?" World Economic Forum, April 18, 2016, www.weforum.org/agenda/2016/04/worlds-fastest-growing -economies.

7. Thomas Callaghy, *The State-Society Struggle: Zaire in Comparative Perspective* (New York: Columbia University Press, 1982).

8. Jean-Francois Bayart, *The State in Africa: The Politics of the Belly* (Cambridge: Polity, 2009), p. 209.

9. Quoted in Thomas Callaghy, "The International Community and Zaire's Debt Crisis," in *The Crisis in Zaire: Myths and Realities*, ed. Georges Nzongola-Ntalaja (Trenton, NJ: Africa World Press, 1986), p. 226.

10. Leo Kuper, *Genocide: Its Political Uses in the Twentieth Century* (New Haven: Tale University Press, 1982), pp. 161–184.

11. Christopher Andrew and Vasil Mitrokhin, *The World Was Going Our Way: The KGB and the Battle for the Third World* (New York: Basic Books, 2006), p. 469.

12. Bill Berkeley, *The Graves Are Not Yet Full: Race, Tribe and Power in the Heart of Africa* (New York: Basic Books, 2001), p. 116.

13. US Congress, House of Representatives, Subcommittee on Africa, Reported Massacres and Indiscriminate Killings in Somalia (Washington, DC: Government Printing Office, July 14, 1989).

14. Most notably, Paul Collier and Anke Hoeffler, "Greed Versus Grievance in Civil War" (Washington, DC: World Bank Development Research Group, 2000), www-wds .worldbank.org/servlet/WDSContentServer/WDSP/IB/2000/06/17/000094946_00060205 420011/Rendered/PDF/multi_page.pdf.

15. Christine Messiant, "The Eduardo Dos Santos Foundation: Or, How Angola's Regime Is Taking Over Civil Society," *African Affairs* 100, no. 399 (2001), pp. 287–309; Ricardo Soares de Oliveira, "Business Success, Angola-Style: Postcolonial Politics and the Rise of Rise of SONANGOL," *Journal of Modern African Studies* 45, no. 4 (2007), pp. 595–619.

16. Mark Shaw and Fiona Mangan, *Illicit Trafficking and Libya's Transition: Profits and Losses* (Washington, DC: US Institute of Peace, 2014), p. 7.

17. Elections in Cameroon, African Elections Database, http://africanelections.tripod .com/cm.html.

18. UNSC reports and Republic of Uganda, *Judicial Commission of Inquiry into Allegations into Illegal Exploitation of Natural Resources and Other Forms of Wealth into the Democratic Republic of Congo—Final Report* (Porter Commission Report) (Kampala, 2002).

19. Gérard Prunier, *From Genocide to Continental War: The 'Congolese' Conflict and the Crisis of Contemporary Africa* (London: Hurst & Company, 2009), pp. 204–205 and 290.

20. Andreas Mehier, "The Shaky Foundations, Adverse Circumstances and Limited Achievements of Democratic Transition in the Central African Republic," in *The Fate of Africa's Democratic Experiments*, ed. Leonardo Villalón and Peter VonDoepp (Bloomington: Indiana University Press, 2005), pp. 147–148.

21. George W. Bush, *The National Security Strategy of the United States of America* (Washington, DC: White House, September 2002), pp. 10–11.

22. UN Security Council, *Report of the Panel of Experts Appointed Pursuant to Paragraph 4 of Security Council Resolution 1458 (2003), Concerning Liberia* (New York: UN, April 24, 2003).

23. Douglas Farah, *Blood from Stones: The Secret Financial Network of Terror* (New York: Broadway, 2004).

24. "Return of the Narco-State," *Africa Confidential* 53, no. 9 (April 27, 2012), p. 8.

25. UN Security Council, *Special Report of the Secretary-General on the Situation in Guinea-Bissau* (New York: United Nations, April 30, 2012), p. 7.

26. Jean-François Bayart, Stephen Ellis, and Béatrice Hibou, *The Criminalization of the State in Africa* (Bloomington: Indiana University Press, 1999).

27. Article 23, www.africa-union.org/root/au/Documents/Treaties/text/Charter%20on%20Democracy.pdf.

28. Combined Joint Trask Force Horn of Africa, www.hoa.africom.mil.

29. Joel Barkan, *Uganda: Assessing Risks to Stability* (Washington, DC: Center for Strategic and International Studies, 2011), pp. 8–9.

30. US Embassy Kampala, "Uganda's All-You-Can-Eat Corruption Buffet," Wikileaks cable, January 5, 2010.

31. Human Rights Watch, *Open Secret: Illegal Detention and Torture by the Joint Anti-Terrorism Task Force in Uganda* (New York: Human Rights Watch, 2009).

32. Muhoozi Kainerugaba, *Battle of the Ugandan Resistance: A Tradition of Maneuver* (Kampala: Fountain Publishers, 2010).

33. Ty McCormick, "Is the U.S. Military Propping Up Uganda's 'Elected' Autocrat?" *Foreign Policy*, February 18, 2016, http://foreignpolicy.com/2016/02/18/is-the-us-military-propping-up-ugandas-elected-autocrat-museveni-elections.

34. Craig Whitlock, "U.S. Expands Secret Intelligence Operations in Africa," *Washington Post*, June 13, 2012, www.washingtonpost.com/world/national-security/us-expands-secret-intelligence-operations-in-africa/2012/06/13/gJQAHyvAbV_story.html?hpid=z2.

35. "The Survival Imperative," *Africa Confidential* 57, no. 1 (January 8, 2016), pp. 4–5.

36. Alex De Waal, *The Real Politics of the Horn of Africa: Money, War and the Business of Power* (Cambridge: Polity, 2015).

37. *Report of the International Commission of Inquiry on Darfur to the United Nations Secretary General, Pursuant to Security Council Resolution 1564 of 18 September 2004* (New York: United Nations, January 25, 2005), p. 4.

38. BBC, "Powell Declares Genocide in Darfur," September 9, 2004, http://news.bbc.co.uk/2/hi/3641820.stm.

39. Otsieno Namwaya, "Somalia: Untold Story in the Peace Talks," *The Standard*, May 28, 2006, http://allafrica.com/stories/200605300784.html, accessed June 18, 2012.

40. BBC News, "Uganda Rebels Want $2m for Talks," July 30, 2007.

41. Jane Guyer, "Briefing: The Chad–Cameroon Petroleum and Pipeline Development Project," *African Affairs* 101, no. 402 (2002), pp. 109–115.

42. BBC, "'Mass Graves' Found in Guinea," October 22, 2002, www.washingtonpost.com/world/national-security/us-expands-secret-intelligence-operations-in-africa/2012/06/13/gJQAHyvAbV_story.html?hpid=z2.

Sudan and South Sudan: The Tragic Denouement of the Comprehensive Peace Agreement

PRINCETON N. LYMAN

THE UNFULFILLED PROMISE

In 2005 Sudan and the insurgent party of South Sudan, the Sudan People's Libera-tion Movement (SPLM), signed the Comprehensive Peace Agreement (CPA) that ended decades of civil wars between north and south, wars that had cost millions of lives and displaced millions more. The CPA, in addition to providing for South Sudan's right of self-determination, set an ambitious agenda for democratization of Sudanese politics and resolving other internal conflicts within Sudan. At the time the CPA was seen as a major success for diplomacy and in particular for the cooperative efforts of Western countries, the Arab League, the UN, and the mem-bers of the African subregional organization, the Intergovernmental Authority on Development (IGAD). Over the next six years these international groupings, with added leadership from the African Union, undertook intensive efforts to im-plement the agreement. Democratization fell by the wayside as elections in both Sudan and South Sudan served only to deepen the control of the ruling parties in each part of the country. But South Sudan achieved its right to a referendum on self-determination, voted for independence, and achieved it peacefully in July 2011. Over the next two years, through continuing intensive diplomacy led by the

African Union's High Level Implementation Panel (AUHIP), headed by former South African president Thabo Mbeki, Sudan and South Sudan resolved almost all the issues between them, including the division of oil revenue, citizenship, demilitarization of the border, assets and liabilities, and foreign debt. In a summit in September 2012 and in a reaffirmation in March 2013 the two countries pronounced their commitment to all these agreements and appeared to be on the threshold of, as President Obama frequently propounded, "living in peace side by side with prospects for development to the benefit of all Sudanese."[1]

And then the denouement. In December 2013 South Sudan fell into one of the most brutal, cruel, and disastrous civil wars seen on the African continent or anywhere else. More than two hundred thousand killed, 2 million people displaced— hundreds of thousands of them fleeing into UN compounds for protection, others fleeing into the bush or across borders—and massive human rights violations that are almost incomprehensible in their cruelty and viciousness. Members of IGAD, with UN and Western assistance, scrambled to bring about an end to the conflict but have achieved only a most fragile peace, with no end to the human rights violations being committed nearly every day.

In Sudan, if not on the scale of South Sudan, there has been no peace. Internal conflicts, in Darfur since 2003 and in the two areas of Southern Kordofan and Blue Nile since 2011, continue. The most recent effort to resolve them, a road map prepared by the AUHIP, signed by all sides in the summer of 2016, and designed to bring about a cessation of hostilities, humanitarian assistance, and a new national dialogue, has subsequently foundered as so many such efforts in the past. The president, Omar al-Bashir, remains in power despite being indicted by the International Criminal Court (ICC) for genocide, war crimes, and crimes against humanity. The press is intimidated, civil society is subject to arrest and restriction, and efforts to develop a national dialogue continue to fall victim to political rivalries and government manipulation.

How do we explain this outcome of what appeared to be a major diplomatic achievement in 2005? How do we explain how an agreement that appeared to be comprehensive in scope, addressing internal political developments as much as peace between contending parties, failed in so many respects? And how can the pieces of it be put back together to achieve at least that most essential missing piece: peace?

In its exhaustive report on the root causes of the civil war in South Sudan, the African Union's Commission of Inquiry put blame in part on flaws inherent in the CPA and its implementation:

> First, it is suggested that the CPA adopted or followed the dominant paradigm of "liberal peace-building," which in practice tends to privilege "negative peace," with its preoccupation with ending violence. The consequence is that democracy and structural transformation receive limited or cursory attention. With respect to both the North and South . . . the central focus on ending the

North-South conflict led the international community to overlook malpractices in the 2010 general elections as well as go easy on the GOSS in the post CPA-era in relation to commitments to democracy and transformation. Second the focus on marginalization and exclusion on a North-South axis ignored or glossed over similar concerns within the North and the South.[2]

This chapter accepts some of those conclusions. But the CPA did in fact include much more than "negative peace" provisions. The relevant criticism is that those provisions were not enforced. But the Commission may be making the error of mistaking the wish for the possible. It may be that in regard to the deep internal political dynamics operating in both Sudan and South Sudan, which undermined the CPA's objectives for democratization and institutional reform, outsiders have, in the end, only limited control. To have promised more may have been the real sin of the CPA. But if that were true, what were the alternatives, and what are they today in the wake of what has happened?

THE REALITIES OF DOMESTIC POLITICS

It may have been naïve to believe that international negotiations could dictate and even fundamentally alter the dynamics of politics within Sudan and South Sudan. In neither area in 2010 were the conditions ripe for multiparty politics. In Sudan several opposition parties were indecisive about participating in what they feared would be a rigged election and ultimately boycotted it. A major opposition candidate, Yasir Arman, entered the contest but withdrew under pressure from South Sudan. Many other politicians decided to throw their support to the government party, the National Congress Party (NCP), as a safe bet.[3] In South Sudan the ruling party, the SPLM, came down hard on any candidates challenging the government's choices, accusing them of disloyalty to the national cause. It was the beginning of a denial of political space in particular for Vice President Riek Machar, whose wife had unsuccessfully challenged the SPLM candidate for governor of Unity State, a precursor of the tragic events that would take place in December 2013. Whereas the CPA envisioned parliaments in each entity that would allocate 20 percent of the seats to opposition parties, the actual results were 5 percent.[4] Both entities came out of the elections more firmly controlled by one party.

International negotiators were torn about these elections. Although they were anything but fully free and fair and they hardly opened the door to multiparty democracy, the elections were an essential step in the CPA timetable for allowing South Sudan to exercise its right of self-determination in a referendum scheduled for January 9, 2011. Challenging the legitimacy of the elections could upset the peace process altogether. Nor was it clear that outside pressure would be sufficient to change the outcome. In the end, concerns about the elections were swallowed as attention turned to ensuring that Sudan would allow the South Sudan referendum to take place as scheduled. There was in fact considerable fear that Sudan would throw up obstacles to the referendum, and in that case the civil war would resume. In the end, following intensive diplomatic effort, the referendum took place on time, Sudan's government recognized the results—an overwhelming vote for separation—and South Sudan's independence came off peacefully on July 9, 2011.[5] The trade-off regarding the elections seemed to have been justified. Transformation would have to wait.

Other provisions of the CPA that addressed internal political dynamics also failed to realize their objectives. The situation in Southern Kordofan and Blue Nile was particularly difficult to resolve. Units of the SPLM's army (SPLM/A) from those provinces had been critical to the south's successes in the civil war. But the CPA maintained those two provinces within Sudan without a right to self-determination. Instead, the CPA provided for a process of "popular consultations" that would elaborate the political grievances of the people in those provinces and have them negotiated with the central government. But the process of popular consultations was ill-defined. It got under way in Blue Nile but was suspended in Southern Kordofan until the election of the governor there, which was delayed until 2011. Even if those processes of consultation had proceeded further, the issues in those provinces were more fundamental to Sudan than the CPA acknowledged and not easily addressed in so fuzzy a process. Those provinces desired more self-government and secular identity. This ran up against the national debate over central versus regional government, an issue basic also in Darfur and in the east, and it raised the issue of identity in a multireligious country that was, however, governed by an Islamic party. These were, in essence, issues about the very nature of the Sudanese state. Without a clear process for addressing these issues on a national or regional basis, the CPA formula in the two provinces was doomed to fail. Following a dispute over the gubernatorial elections in Southern Kordofan, the two provinces fell into civil war against the central government, a conflict that five years of negotiations have failed to resolve.

The CPA sought to resolve another difficult issue of great internal sensitivity: whether the province of Abyei should be in the north or south after separation. Residents of Abyei are predominantly Ngok Dinka, who have a strong desire to have Abyei become part of South Sudan. But the Misseriya, an Arab nomadic group that has regularly transited Abyei to water their cattle and as a pathway to further watering grounds in the south, are adamantly opposed. The issue was complicated by ties that each group has to the ruling parties respectively in South Sudan and Sudan, making the region a national issue and one constantly on the edge of conflict.

The CPA had sought to resolve this long-standing issue by providing for a referendum in Abyei to determine the inhabitants' wishes. But Sudan insisted that the Misseriya be allowed to vote in the referendum, to which the Ngok Dinka and the South Sudan government were bitterly opposed. In 2011 Sudan took over the region by force, triggering a major crisis that took months to resolve and then only with introduction of a new, Ethiopian-led UN peacekeeping force. No amount of diplomacy, innovative ideas, or employment of various pressures have succeeded in unlocking this dispute.[6] Abyei remains a source of tension and a potential source of armed conflict between Sudan and South Sudan.

And finally Darfur. In 2003, as the negotiations of the CPA were reaching their climax, a rebellion broke out in the western province of Darfur. Darfur had long been a neglected region of Sudan and in modern times had suffered from severe drought that intensified competition between herding populations, mostly Arab, and farming communities, mostly African. Rebel movements among the latter, such as the Justice and Equality Movement (JEM) and the Sudan Liberation Army (SLA), saw major concessions being given to the south in the CPA negotiations while their issues were not addressed at all. They launched attacks on several government installations with initial success. The rebellion took the Sudanese government by surprise. With most of its troops still occupied with South Sudan, the government engaged Arab militia, known as the Janjaweed, and were backed by Sudan air power to put down the rebellion. The campaign was so vicious against the rebels and their supporting populations that the United States declared it genocide, and the ICC later came to the same conclusion. In 2007 a joint UN-AU peacekeeping force, UNAMID, was dispatched to Darfur to protect the more than 2 million people displaced and to help develop a peace process. In all the years since, despite numerous peace efforts, the Darfur situation has remained unsettled, with flare-ups of conflict, millions still in IDP camps, others in refugee camps across the border in Chad, and now even conflict among some of the Arab militia.

A full account of the Darfur conflict is not possible here.[7] Darfur was not part of the CPA, but it did impact it. First of all, it changed dramatically the relations between the United States and Sudan. There was an informal understanding during the CPA negotiations that if Sudan agreed to peace and South Sudan were allowed the right of self-determination, the United States would remove Sudan from the list of countries supporting terrorism and lift other sanctions that had been placed on Sudan years earlier. All this changed in the wake of the Darfur rebellion. A strong grassroots movement, Save Darfur, began in the United States, mobilizing students, religious institutions, and celebrities on behalf of those being victimized in Darfur. Coming at the ten-year anniversary of the genocide in Rwanda, the possibility of another genocide taking place galvanized public and official attention.[8] The Bush administration responded. It determined Sudan's actions in Darfur to be genocide, then supported the referral of Darfur to the ICC, which in 2008 indicted Sudanese president Omar al-Bashir on charges of genocide, war crimes, and crimes against humanity. From that time on, US-Sudan relations have been deeply strained. The United States cut off direct contact with al-Bashir, which meant access at that level on issues related to the CPA was ended. In the run-up to South Sudan's independence the AUHIP and other observers believed that some rapprochement in US-Sudan relations was key to Sudan proceeding with the referendum and resolving other issues related to the south's pending independence and pressed the United States on the matter. The Obama administration took steps in this direction by agreeing with the Sudanese government on a road map for improvement. Thereafter, final agreements between Sudan and South Sudan were achieved.[9] But as long as Darfur remains unsettled, US-Sudan relations remain strained, sanctions remain in place, and US influence on remaining internal issues within Sudan is limited.

The second influence of Darfur on the CPA is that the conflict, as noted above, relates to the same issues of identity, decentralization, and accommodation as South Kordofan and Blue Nile. These conflicts became closely related when the Sudan People's Liberation Movement-North (SPLM/N), representing the insurgents in Southern Kordofan and Blue Nile, allied with three of the Darfur insurgent groups to form the Sudan Revolutionary Front (SRF) as both allies in the armed struggle and as a negotiating bloc. Ever since then the AUHIP has sought to address both conflicts—sometimes separately, sometimes together—all in an effort to encourage a major political transformation in Sudan. Sudan, however, has resisted major change to date. Separate peace agreements on Darfur, such as the Darfur Peace Agreement of 2006 and the Doha Darfur Peace Agreement (DDPA) of 2011, divided the Darfur rebel movements and produced little change in Darfur itself. Indeed, most recently Sudan has become confident that it has contained the threat from Darfur. JEM suffered serious casualties related to the civil war in South Sudan, a faction of the SLA under Minnie Minnawi took losses against the Sudanese military, forcing it across the border into Libya, and the SRF alliance has begun to fray. Sudan has launched a major military attack on the one Darfur rebel group with a territorial base, the SLA faction under Abdul Wahid. This campaign has displaced 133,000 people.[10] Neither UNAMID nor numerous UN Security Council (UNSC) resolutions against the bombing in Darfur have had any restraining effect. In a recent publication the government boasted, "The Darfur rebels and negative forces have lost their political and military vision, at the backdrop of military defeat on the ground, and political defeat in Darfur."[11]

Sudan today suffers from economic difficulties, aggravated by the continued US sanctions; continuing conflicts in Darfur and in Southern Kordofan and Blue Nile; and political opposition from an array of traditional and armed political parties. These are all issues that directly or indirectly were intended to be addressed in the unfolding of the CPA. Nevertheless, despite international pressure, dedicated effort by Thabo Mbeki and the AUHIP, and uneasiness even among the elite and the business community about the long-term viability of the state, the government is not yet willing to undertake a more fundamental transformation to an inclusive democracy. It has only agreed to a largely government-controlled "National Dialogue" to air grievances and recommend reforms, but there is little confidence yet that much will come from it. The leadership, especially within the security establishment and the presidency, appears to be determined to defend the current order rather than risk the uncertainties of change.[12]

SOUTH SUDAN: AN UNMITIGATED DISASTER

If the situation in Sudan is an unsettling and stark example of the difficulties of bringing about significant internal political reform through international negotiation, the situation in South Sudan is an example of the best intentions of the international community having gone disastrously astray. The overwhelming focus of the CPA and the actions in particular of the Western countries as well as the AUHIP was to end the decades of civil war between the north and south of Sudan. By 2010 it was clear that the option of forging a basis for unity between the two, given a six-year trial in the CPA, was not going to be viable. Following the death of SPLM leader John Garang in 2005 and the assumption of leadership in the south by Salva Kiir, SPLM's focus was totally on independence. Thus, the international community did much not only to prepare for South Sudan's vote on self-determination but, as the date for the referendum approached, also to help build the foundations of an independent state.

South Sudan's SPLM had in fact been given many of the resources and means for independence in the interim period from 2005 to 2011. These included administrative authority over the region, 50 percent of the oil revenue from the wells in the south, maintaining its liberation army intact, and the opportunity to develop state and local government institutions, a judiciary, and a parliament. Oil revenue under this arrangement between 2005 and 2011 reached as much as $10 to 12 billion. Significant foreign assistance was provided as well, totaling as much as $1 billion a year, with thousands of civil servants on loan from neighboring and Western countries; investments in education, health, and agriculture; the building of one of South Sudan's only major highways and rural roads; and a limited amount of non-lethal military assistance.[13] Humanitarian assistance was also significant: in 2012 the international community was feeding as much as one-third of the population and helping some two hundred thousand South Sudanese relocate from Sudan to the south, where they suffered from lack of housing and jobs on their arrival.

Everyone familiar with the civil war in Sudan knew that much of the fighting and most of the casualties had been from fighting among southerners, particularly from numerous ethnic-based militia supported by Sudan to fight against the SPLM. A pattern of shifting alliances, based largely on payments from one side or the other, characterized this period and created a pattern of "rentier rebellion" that would continue well after independence. There was a tendency to blame this civil war within the civil war on the Khartoum government, which certainly had encouraged and funded it. But underneath there were serious ethnic and political rivalries that could well surface in an independent South Sudan. Indeed, in 2005 the SPLA was a minority force, with those outside it three times as great. At first, however, in the run-up to the referendum, Salva Kiir demonstrated a remarkable ability to pull all these factions and separate militias together in support of independence. It augured well, it seemed, for the future. But it was superficial. Kiir did this largely by generous use of the oil revenue, buying the loyalty of leading rivals and giving out numerous high ranks in the national army so that soon the SPLA would have 745 generals. By 2011 security accounted for well over half the stated budget (which omitted many off-budget transactions); 80 percent of the defense budget was spent on wages and salaries. The army was not integrated but rather a coalition of militias, many ethnic based.[14]

If international observers looked at the brighter side of this apparent "unity," the rapid growth of corruption in the SPLM was another matter. Between 2005 and 2011 the SPLM's oil revenue was an extraordinary and unprecedented amount of wealth in a country of immense poverty and underdevelopment. Too much too soon. As Alex de Waal has detailed, at first the fighters were rewarded for their sacrifice, then gradually they all took more and more. Estimates by the government itself were that billions had been stolen or misused. But by this time the corruption had been institutionalized, built into the politics and the alliances that underlay the fragile state of unity within the government. Donors urged an accounting, recourse, better oversight, and responsibility. At a conference in Washington, DC, in December 2011, the South Sudan government pledged to establish a transparent system of accounts during the coming year. Donors thereafter put significant effort into developing stronger budget controls and, especially as the negotiations over oil payments between Sudan and South Sudan advanced, more transparency in the oil sector. Nevertheless, by the time the country descended into civil war at the end of 2013 little had been done to retrieve stolen money or to root out corruption. In the downward spiraling of the political situation during 2013 the Kiir administration fired and jailed the Finance Minister on whom donors counted most to bring order into the process.

Another factor at work during this period was the sympathy for the south that led many in the international community to want to overlook or downplay these underlying problems. From the early stages of southern revolt in the Anya-Nya rebellion in the 1960s, Americans had been drawn to the southern cause.[15] There was of course reason for it. The history of northern oppression, Khartoum's fomenting of armed groups and ethnic divisions, the seemingly purposeful underdevelopment in the south, the attempted Islamization of a non-Islamic population, and a history of slavery all made the southern cause the more sympathetic by far. When President George W. Bush appointed former senator John Danforth the first special envoy for Sudan and engaged the United States intensively in the CPA process, he was responding to pressure from both the evangelical movement in the United States, concerned about the rights of Christians in the south, and the Congressional Black Caucus, riled over Arabs' seemingly ongoing practice of kidnapping black southerners for slavery. The southern cause subsequently attracted celebrities like Mia Farrow and George Clooney and the support of a strong Sudan caucus in the Congress. After the genocide in Darfur, groups focused on that issue joined in the denunciation of the north and championing of the southern cause.

The problem with such support was that it inhibited focus on the shortcomings in the governance of South Sudan. The relations between the newly independent government of South Sudan and the United States were in fact rocky from the beginning, as South Sudan rebuffed President Obama's urging that it not continue to support the rebellion in Southern Kordofan and Blue Nile in Sudan. Attacks by the SPLA on minority ethnic groups, such as the Murle, and other human rights violations grew more serious in 2012 and worried the Obama administration. Yet advocacy groups and even some within the administration resisted public criticism of the South Sudan government. Such criticism was seen as giving support to the government of Sudan in its ongoing disputes and conflicts with South Sudan. When the administration did make such criticisms it was accused of "moral equivalency"—that is, implying that any faults in the south could possibly be equivalent to the more terrible ones of Sudan—or of moving wrongly from "advocacy [for the south] to neutrality."[16]

Only in the spring of 2013 did opinion begin to shift. Four of South Sudan's strongest advocates wrote a public letter to President Kiir expressing their concerns over human rights violations and other aspects of poor governance. Letters from Congress began to express similar concerns. Over the summer and fall, warnings were coming from the American Embassy in Juba and from those in Washington who were following events. Beyond the human rights violation and stifling of dissent, a political stand-off between Kiir and his vice president, Riek Machar, was threatening to get out of hand. In June, Kiir dismissed Machar from the vice presidency and fired several key members of the cabinet that had been vocal critics of the Kiir administration. Yet there was not a sufficient sense of crisis and not enough hard information. And perhaps it was too late. By then President Kiir was set on a policy of isolating his critics, silencing the press, and preparing for possible civil war.[17] In December a stand-off took place within the Presidential Guard between Dinka and Nuer soldiers. Kiir claimed Machar had attempted a coup, though subsequent investigations have cast doubt on that claim. Things quickly fell apart nevertheless. Kiir's soldiers went hunting Nuer throughout the city, killing many and sending thousands fleeing for their lives. Nuer elements of the SPLA broke away and moved to the center and north of the country, former vice president Machar with them. The war was underway.

Yet even if American and other international actors had been less chary of criticism, even if more pressure had been put on the Government of South Sudan (GOSS), it is not certain that war could have been avoided. The weaknesses of the institutions in that country, those that should have mitigated against civil war, and the predilections of the leadership may well have been deeper than outside influence or pressure could have overcome. The civil war that erupted in December 2013 has been more vicious, more rapacious, more lacking in a sense of responsibility by its leaders toward the general population than anyone had imagined likely. The Africa Union's Commission of Inquiry, the UN Panel of Experts, the UN Human Rights Commission, and Amnesty International have documented these terrible depredations. They make hard reading.[18] There is murder, massive rape, drinking of blood, forced humiliations, and much more. Famine now threatens half the country's population. And in a supreme irony at least two hundred thousand South Sudanese have fled to Sudan, some who had come back to the south from years in Khartoum with tears in their eyes at the dawn of the south's independence, now forced to seek refuge from their former overseers. The depth, horror, and bitterness of this conflict suggest a fundamental flaw in South Sudan's institutions of governance, political capacity, and sense of nationhood.

The African Union Commission of Inquiry report provides one of the most detailed analyses of the institutions of South Sudan, including the SPLM, the security sector, the judiciary, parliament, justice system, civil society, and the media. It dissects the weaknesses in each that kept them from preventing the collapse of the rule of law, the ineffectiveness of the political system in times of crisis, and the incidents leading up to the outbreak of civil war. It found the SPLM to be less an independent political party than a wing of the military, unable therefore to resist being sidelined by President Kiir in the confrontation with his party critics. It confirmed what has been described above as the SPLA having been an aggregation of militias rather than a professional unified army. It found that, in practice, there were no limits on the executive branch from either the SPLM or the parliament. Despite formal institutions of federalism, the states had been almost fully dependent upon and controlled by the central government. Judicial independence had been weak. Work on a permanent constitution had been stymied. The media had been oppressed. It is an illuminating if depressing report.

RETROSPECTIVE

As noted in the first part of this chapter, the AU Commission lays blame for the civil war in South Sudan in part on the CPA but more on its implementers for not paying enough attention to the institutional weaknesses that the report so clearly presents. There is some validity to that criticism. But those helping to implement the CPA did not ignore the issues of democracy, institution-building, a strengthened judiciary, state and local government, and civil society; indeed, there was assistance or offers of assistance in every one of these areas in South Sudan. The GOSS rejected or ignored some, such as the team from the National Democratic Institute sent to help with drafting a new constitution and those from the International Republican Institute to help strengthen the SPLM. The question arises, therefore: What were the means whereby the international community could have overcome the power dynamics within either South Sudan or Sudan that worked against both democracy and, in the end, against peace?

One could contemplate whether a more robust oversight of South Sudan, such as a degree of international management of the region in the period between 2005 and 2011, might have had some effect. In particular, if the oil proceeds had been placed in an escrow account, jointly managed by the international community

and the GOSS rather than turned over outright to a new and untested administration, it would have perhaps limited the pattern of gross corruption that came
into being. International oversight of the electoral process in 2010 might have
helped establish a system welcoming political competition that might have provided a different atmosphere for dealing with the subsequent political confrontation between Kiir and Machar. More difficult to contemplate, however, is how the
international community could have addressed the security sector. The many militias (some still getting support from Khartoum), the competition between them
for resources, the underlying land and resource disputes between various ethnic
groups on which such militias played—these are deeply ingrained problems that
would have required perhaps decades of oversight, resources, and reform to fully
address.[19]

But neither the East African countries, in their lead position in the CPA, nor any
other international grouping or institution was prepared to insist upon such a role
and force it on South Sudan. Nor is it clear that South Sudan would have accepted
such. Demanding a long-term system of "trusteeship" before independence would
surely have met with strong resistance from the SPLM. In fact, in the period of uncertainty over Khartoum's readiness to allow the referendum of 2011 to take place,
the GOSS was considering unilaterally declaring its independence, a step that would
have surely roiled the situation and perhaps led to more conflict. Nevertheless, these
considerations are pertinent to the situation that now faces the international community in South Sudan. The international community's willingness or readiness to
take oversight of the institutions of peace and reconciliation in South Sudan may
well determine the prospects for success of the peace plan currently being promoted
there. This issue is addressed in the final section of this chapter.

The possibilities that might have existed with regard to South Sudan nevertheless did not pertain to Sudan. It was virtually impossible for the international
community to take oversight of the 2010 election in the north nor to enforce
the institutionalization of multiparty democracy there. Sudan was a sovereign
country, a full member of the AU, and a major party to the CPA. It took exceptional pressure and dogged diplomacy to persuade Sudan to permit the self-
determination of the south and, thereby, the loss of 70 percent of its oil, close
to 90 percent of its foreign exchange earnings, a third of its population, and the
presence of a somewhat hostile neighbor to its south. To have demanded more
would have been fruitless. The thesis of this chapter is that the influence of outside parties—governments, international organizations, advocacy groups—on the
internal political dynamics of a country is limited, especially when recommendations for reform run up against what the ruling party sees as threats to its very
political survival. The AUHIP is charged under the CPA to continue to bring about
political reform in Sudan and works tirelessly on it, but with very limited results.
That does not augur well for Sudan, beset still with internal wars, economic crises,
and strong internal opposition. But the way forward has to lie there.

THE WAY FORWARD

Let us start with Sudan. There is some sentiment that the problem with US policy in Sudan is that it did not place sufficiently strong sanctions on the government. In the words of John Prendergast and Brad Brooks-Robin,

> Peace efforts in Sudan have failed in the past, in large part because of insufficient international leverage over the Sudanese government, but now the Obama administration has an unprecedented opportunity in its final months in office to make a policy investment that could pay big dividends. . . . U.S. leaders should adopt elements of the playbook used with Iran and other recent crises that are appropriate to the Sudanese political and economic context. Leaders should begin by immediately ratcheting up financial pressure and tightening sanctions enforcement on Sudan, deploying more focused, enhanced, and modernized sanctions that more sharply target the military and financial assets of those most responsible for continuing conflict, atrocities, and mass corruption in Sudan.[20]

The problem with this approach is that it assumes that outside pressure will force a regime to undertake reforms that it believes amount to political suicide. As already noted, the thesis of this chapter is that such is not likely. First, the circumstances of the experience with Iran, which the above authors cite, do not exist in regard to Sudan. With Iran, it was critical to develop an international consensus around sanctions and other pressures; otherwise there would be too many alternatives open to Iran to get around those sanctions employed by the United States. This was a singular achievement of the Obama administration. Second, the objective with Iran did not include changing the Iranian regime, nor did it address any of its internal policies or practices, which would have changed the negotiations entirely.

Sudan is a quite different case. There would be little international consensus for more sanctions on Sudan. Russia and China would never go along in the UNSC; indeed, there are problems with those countries in enforcing those already in place.[21] In addition, Sudan's shift in Middle East alliances in 2015, jettisoning its long-time relationship with Iran and providing troops to help Saudi Arabia in Yemen, has garnered al-Bashir new supporters in the Arab world and, most likely, new sources of financial as well as political support. Finally, the requirements for a just peace in Sudan, which would be the objective of more sanctions, go to the heart of Sudan's political system and would require the kind of fundamental change that outside pressures have consistently failed to bring about.

As frustrating as the situation in Sudan is, the change needed must come from within. It requires a consensus on political change that allows all sides to believe they have not only a stake but also a place in the outcome of transformation. There are some signs that such consensus is developing but also some serious backlash coming from those committed to the status quo.

The government of Sudan appears currently to run on two rather diametrically opposed paths. On the one hand, the government committed itself as far back as 2014 to a national dialogue that would examine all the major issues facing the country and pledged itself to implement the recommendations. However, the conditions over who would participate and how the recommendations would affect plans for elections in 2015 as well as the failure to bring in the armed opposition led to the official National Dialogue to be convened late in 2015 with largely government-selected participants and after President al-Bashir had already been reelected for another five-year term. Nevertheless, the National Dialogue has engaged hundreds of Sudanese in spirited debate over all the fundamental issues of Sudan, such as national identity, civil and human rights, economic policy, governance, and others. Unfortunately the conclusions have not been publicized, and the government's plans for follow-up are not clear. There is still a lack of transparency in the process and a lack of full countrywide participation. Nevertheless, there is a glimmer of hope that this process can be a stepping stone to a broader national dialogue and a genuine process of political reform.

Another glimmer of hope lies in the near agreement on implementing a road map between the government and the SPLM/N, which is fighting in Southern Kordofan and the Blue Nile under the auspices of the AUHIP. In the latest negotiations in March 2016 the government made several important concessions in those talks, especially allowing for a postponement, after a cessation of hostilities, of final security arrangements in those areas pending the outcome of political talks—an issue that has blocked agreement for some time.[22] The road map also provides for a process whereby the national dialogue can proceed from the current one to a broader one without jettisoning what has been done so far. The Sudan government and the SPLM/N have signed on to this proposal, but differences remain over how humanitarian aid will be provided to the conflict areas and on shaping a broader national dialogue.

Along with these more hopeful signs, however, the government has carried out a strong attack on civil society and the press, as well as launched a major attack on one of the armed opposition groups in Darfur.[23] It would seem that the presidency and leaders in the security sector are more focused on stifling dissent and maintaining the present political order than on giving free rein to a true national dialogue and achieving internal peace. Without commitment in those parts of the government, progress will be stymied. This is the most serious obstacle to reform, and it relates to that deep resistance in those key parts of the government to losing power, which undermines pressures for reform, whether coming from within or from abroad.

But there is a question also as to whether the armed opposition has to reconsider its stance. Years of fighting in Darfur and in Southern Kordofan and Blue Nile have not brought either peace or freedom for those in those areas. When the SPLM/N joined with the Darfur movements to create the SRF, the objective was to overthrow the Khartoum regime. The prospects for doing so were dim then and less likely today.[24] The SPLM/N can likely hold out in its territory for a long time, and the Darfur movements can continue to stage attacks, but whether more fighting is to the advantage of either region over the long term is questionable. As noted earlier, the situation in Darfur is not favorable today for the armed groups. Prospects for any major advances by the SPLM/N beyond the Nuba Mountains are questionable. Can the movements adjust their positions to take advantage of those glimmers of hope mentioned above?

Already there is an indication that the Darfur groups may be reconsidering. There are reports that they are looking at re-engaging, under the auspices of Qatar, in the DDPA, which they had refused to participate in earlier. That agreement has not lived up to its promises, but what might be the case if all the armed groups were part of it? The DDPA has suffered from the limited representation and, thus, the clout of the one group that signed. But by all assessments it is, on paper, a better agreement than the previous DPA. What it needs is full participation from all relevant parties, vigorous implementation by the government, and to be backed by the international community. For the people of Darfur this may be a way out of the long struggle and terrible price they have paid since 2003. Again, it is not starting from zero but building on months—indeed, years—of talks defining the issues and seeking solutions. It may be a long shot, but it is perhaps much better than continuing an armed struggle that seems, more than ever, unlikely for the armed groups to win.

The SPLM/N has also moved over the years to somewhat broadening its objectives. Although not formally giving up the objective of regime change, it has joined with unarmed opposition groups in various combinations, such as Sudan Call, to promote a clearer political platform and a path for reform that is not exclusively dependent on armed overthrow.

What lies in the way of these possibilities is the deep distrust between the government and nearly all the opposition movements, both armed and unarmed. There is such distrust that even what looks like progress on paper, such as the recent road map developed by the AUHIP, the SPLM/N perceives it as filled with "traps" that will lead to weakening the armed groups while offering no real progress on their political objectives. The actions of the government's security sectors against civil society, the press, and other forms of dissent, even as the government negotiates and promotes its National Dialogue, adds to this distrust. On the other side, the government not only distrusts but actively dislikes some of the opposition leaders and does not believe they have given up the hope of armed overthrow.

The value of the AUHIP and of other actors on the international side is that they continue to provide venues, ideas, and encouragement to the processes of peace and reform. It is unlikely that more sanctions or disengagement would help, much as this would seem justified by the government's continuing human rights violations. As noted earlier, sanctions only work if they are internationally enforced and have resonance within the affected country. There is no real prospect of UNSC or other international consensus for more sanctions on Sudan.

And the government seems immune to those now in effect. Instead, reform has to come from within. The international community should pursue every means of persuading the parties in Sudan that reform is not only possible but actually of value for all sides and should be pursued. The theme that reform need not be a zero-sum game is one that this author has sought to promote in the minds of the government and its supporters.[25]

As for South Sudan, the international community faces a choice, drawing on the lessons of the COI or going down a path similar to the CPA. The peace agreement IGAD put together to stop the recent civil war is proving extremely fragile. On the one hand, the peace agreement is quite comprehensive in the reforms it anticipates. On the other, it placed responsibility for carrying out those reforms on the very same leaders, Salva Kiir and Riek Machar, who had no respect for such matters before and who led their country into this disastrous civil war. To enforce the reforms that were needed, the international community would have had to assume some oversight authority in the country, but IGAD stopped well short of that. While establishing an internationally led monitoring and oversight mechanism (JMEC) headed by the former president of Botswana Festus Mogae, neither IGAD nor the AU was ready to establish the means of enforcement that would be necessary.

IGAD instead vacillated over asking the UNSC for, or enforcing itself, any sanctions against the leaders, most important an arms embargo that would possibly limit the slaughter of innocents and continuation of the war. It backed away from providing an African armed force to stand between the forces arrayed by both sides in the capital Juba as the proposed unity government was about to get under way. The AU has been slow in forming the Hybrid Court to examine the human rights violations in the war, an institution that might give Mogae some bargaining power with the leaders. There is as yet no oversight or control over the finances or budgeting of the government. All in all, the neighboring countries, IGAD, and the AU overall did not feel the underlying issues in South Sudan were worth moving to a precedent-setting takeover of South Sudan's principal governing mechanisms in order to bring about the development of the strong institutions that were so lacking in the previous period. The United States and other international players similarly vacillated over these issues, even on an arms embargo in the face of horrific human rights violations or after attacks on UNMISS patrols and protection sites as well as killing of humanitarian workers. In his statement to the JMEC plenary meeting on June 23, 2016, Mogae lamented that hardly any of the steps called for in the peace agreement had been implemented.[26]

President Kiir exploited this vacuum of enforcement to strengthen his position, extend his and his supporters' control over various parts of the country through constitutional change and armed force, and oppress dissent and a free press. In July 2016 the fragility of this peace process came into sharp relief. Fighting broke out between Kiir's and Machar's forces in Juba. At least three hundred people were killed, thousands fled, and even the UNMISS compound came under attack. Reports emerged of new roundups and beatings of suspected Machar supporters, as occurred in December 2013. Machar was forced to flee and is now in exile. Kiir installed Machar's erstwhile deputy Taban Deng as vice president, though Taban does not have nearly the level of support among opposition forces as did Machar. Fighting thus continued in several parts of the country. The peace agreement appeared on the verge of collapse. The international community once again scrambled for answers.[27] But the answers so far have been limited. IGAD recommended and the UNSC approved a four-thousand-person armed force to supplement the current UNMISS to keep Juba open and to protect civilians. But there is no change to the political framework under which this force will operate, and Kiir continues to chip away at its mandate before it is even deployed.

The question is whether the international community is prepared to take the much more challenging step of placing South Sudan under an international governance regime, as was done in Kosovo and East Timor, which would administer a process of institutional development that leads to a more stable independence In South Sudan, which is heavily armed not only within the forces of Kiir and Machar's allies but also in various militias, this would be a more difficult undertaking. It would require placing oil revenue in an escrow account to give the international community the ability to entice various armed units to stand down in order to get paid, enhancing UNMISS and its new reinforcement unit to deal with those armed units from the government or elsewhere who refused and especially to confront any such forces who blatantly attack civilians, removing effective power from both Kiir and Taban Deng, and other steps. It would take an enormous diplomatic lift from the United States, the AU, the UN, and interested European partners to accomplish this or even a more limited variation of it—and there is the rub. With the Obama administration coming to a close and changes underway in the leadership of both the UN and the AU this year, it is not at all clear that the diplomatic bandwidth is great enough, not unless all of these entities and their current leaders see this as one of the major crises in the world today that they must address and to do so in a way far more comprehensively than they have in the past or, at a minimum, to set such instruments of control in motion.[28]

Anything short of this will almost surely leave South Sudan for many more months in the throes of continuing conflict, with more terrible humanitarian crises, many more hundreds of thousands of refugees flowing into neighboring countries, and perhaps a destabilizing set of regional events as neighboring countries seek to cope with the situation. It may well be that some years from now we'll have another Commission of Inquiry that raises the same questions as this last one.

CONCLUSION

There has been much written about the conflict between peace and justice, whether the processes of accountability and punishment for gross violations of human rights should be sacrificed to obtain an end to war. Did the ICC indictment of

Joseph Kony, leader of the Lord's Resistance Army, blow up the peace agreement that he was ready to sign? Did the ICC indictment of Sudan's president for the crimes of Darfur create a block against political transformation in that country?

But there has not been much attention paid to the potential competition between peace and political reform. In almost every major conflict there is need to address the underlying sources of conflict to help prevent its reoccurrence or, at least, as James Dobbins has suggested as the objective of peacekeeping, the establishment of a situation that shifts conflict to political rather than armed competition. In some cases, like Liberia, where previous contending forces were largely defeated, the offending regime was removed and, where sufficient international peacekeepers were present, peace and reform were both able to progress.

Where the offending regime is in power, however, and is determined to remain so, pressures for peace can easily sacrifice the desire for fundamental political reform. Ending conflict and human suffering is surely a worthwhile objective. And that often requires working peace among the "guys with the guns," the ones with the power to enforce a peace and whose quest for power is part of the equation. The amount of pressure or direct control that would produce fundamental reform, thus overcoming the resistance to reform of those who have the power and are determined to keep it, is greater than most international actors are prepared to undertake. As such, peace agreements, however noble and far-reaching on paper, must depend on internal political dynamics to achieve those larger objectives.

Given that reality in Sudan, the international community can perhaps do more through engagement than the opposite, a combination perhaps of sanctions and awards as well as, in the end, engaging the political actors from all sides on the need and practicality of political reform rather than trying to force it.

For South Sudan the choices are starker. In the CPA the opportunity for achieving political reform through international control had been greater with the emerging South Sudan administration than with Sudan. That path was not taken. Now with South Sudan in such terrible disarray, that pathway seems more logical but, for the reasons cited above, may still again not be chosen. Those left in power there are at the same time defying principles of reform, human rights, and responsible governance more than ever. South Sudan was once thought to be the prospective model of democracy that would stand in contrast to the north. Ironically, the prospect for reform in Sudan, driven by internal forces, may be greater today than in the south.

NOTES

1. An in-depth account of the separation of the two Sudanese entities and the negotiations between them can be found in James Copnall, *A Poisonous Thorn in Our Hearts: Sudan and South Sudan's Bitter and Incomplete Divorce* (London: Hurst and Company, 2014).

2. AU Commission of Inquiry on South Sudan, Addis Ababa, October 15, 2014, pp. 37–38, www.au.int/en/auciss, hereafter AUCISS. An even harsher critique of international,

especially Western countries' role in the CPA has been made by Mohmood Mamdani, a member of the COI who dissented from some of its findings and recommendations. Mahmood Mamdani, "Who's to Blame in South Sudan?" *Boston Review*, June 28, 2016, https://bostonreview.net/world/mahmood-mamdani-south-sudan-failed-transition.

3. Yasir Arman was head of the Sudan (northern) wing of the Sudan People's Liberation Movement that had spearheaded South Sudan's fight for independence. With the likely independence of South Sudan in 2011, Arman looked to his future in the north and announced his intention to run for president of Sudan in the 2010 elections. But the SPLM leadership found this inconsistent with its focus on independence for the south and pressured Arman to withdraw.

4. Alex De Waal, *The Real Politics of the Horn of Africa* (Cambridge: Polity Press, 2015).

5. For a fuller description of the negotiations in this period and the sense of urgency about the referendum, see Princeton Lyman, "Negotiating Peace in Sudan: An American Perspective," *The Cairo Review of Global Affairs* (Spring 2011), www.thecairoreview.com/essays/negotiating-peace-in-sudan.

6. In 2010 the United States sponsored a weeks-long intensive negotiation beginning in New York and continuing in Addis Ababa to find a compromise voting formula for the referendum, but the effort failed. See Princeton Lyman, "Negotiating Peace in Sudan," for a detailed account of this effort. When it failed, Thabo Mbeki sought repeatedly to have Presidents al-Bashir and Kiir resolve the dispute, but they failed as well. In 2012 Mbeki finally put his own plan forward, accepted by South Sudan but bitterly opposed by Sudan. South Sudan negotiators had themselves underestimated the depth of national sensitivity in Sudan on this issue. For a long time South Sudan negotiators believed that at the climax of negotiations over all other issues between the two countries, a "grand bargain" would be struck trading oil from the south for Abyei. At the summit in 2012, when all the other issues were on the table, this effort failed. South Sudan had to accept agreement on all the other issues, including oil, without resolution of the Abyei crisis.

7. There are numerous books on Darfur. For general accounts of the origin and dimensions of the conflict, see Julie Flint and Alex de Waal, *Darfur: A Short History of a Long War* (London: Zed Books, 2008), Andrew Natsios, *Sudan, South Sudan and Darfur: What Everyone Needs to Know* (New York: Oxford University Press, 2012), and a forceful critique of Western interpretations, Mahmood Mamdani, *Saviors and Survivors: Darfur, Politics, and the War on Terrorism* (New York: Doubleday Religion, 2009). For accounts of the peace efforts see Harris Tordue Dera, *Conflict Resolution in Africa and the Role of the Africa Union in Darfur from 2004–2009* (Saarbrücken: Lambert Academic Publishing, 2012), and Alex de Waal, *The Real Politics of the Horn of Africa*, pp. 52–68.

8. Scott Strauss, *Fundamentals of Genocide and Mass Atrocity Prevention* (Washington, DC: United States Holocaust Museum, 2016), pp. 182–183.

9. The road map is discussed in detail in Lyman, "Negotiating Peace in Sudan: An American Perspective."

10. USAID/DCHA Sudan Humanitarian Update #52, April 4, 2016.

11. "Presence of Sudanese Rebels in Libya," undated document provided to the author by the Sudan Embassy in Washington, DC, March 16, 2016.

12. A fuller discussion of the prospects for political transformation in Sudan can be found in Princeton Lyman, "The Missing Piece: Where Is the Peace in the Comprehensive Peace Agreement?" speech delivered at the Peace Research Institute of the University of Khartoum, February 9, 2016, www.usip.org/the-missing-piece-where-the-peace-in-the-comprehensive-peace-agreement.

13. World Bank, "Public Expenditures in South Sudan: Are They Delivering?" *South Sudan Economic Briefing*, 2 (Washington DC: February 2013). See also Alex de Waal, *The Real Politics of the Horn of Africa*, pp. 100–102.

14. Alex de Waal, *The Real Politics of the Horn of Africa*, pp. 92–97.

15. Alan Reed was one of the first Americans to call attention to the plight of the south. Reed spent several years working in Sudan during and after the first civil war 1955–1972. He spent nearly a year walking throughout Southern Sudan with the Anya-Nya Liberation Movement, producing a documentary film for NBC-TV and conducting research on cross-border humanitarian assistance for World Council of Churches–affiliated NGOs.

16. For details of the relations between the United States and the government of South Sudan before the outbreak of civil war, see Princeton N. Lyman, "The United States and South Sudan: A Relationship Under Pressure," *The Ambassador's Review* (Fall 2013), www.americanambassadors.org/publications/ambassadors-review/fall-2013 /the-united-states-and-south-sudan-a-relationship-under-pressure.

17. As Kiir's confrontation with his Nuer vice president deepened, Kiir, a Dinka from the state of Bahr al Ghazal, began assembling a special military unit drawn from members of his home tribe to counter the threat he perceived from the largely Nuer population in the SPLA. This unit would go on to commit some of the worst human rights violations in the early days of the civil war that followed. US officials heard reports of this unit being created as early as September but lacked information about its size and purpose. Conversations by the author with former South Sudan and American officials. Even months later the African Union's Commission of Inquiry could not pin down the exact number of recruits into this unit, with estimates from 7,500 to 15,000. AUCISS, para. 53, p. 22

18. AUCISS; Final report of the Panel of Experts on South Sudan established pursuant to Security Council resolution 2206 (2015), www.un.org/ga/search/view_doc .asp?symbol=S/2016/70; Assessment Mission by the Office of the United Nations High Commissioner for Human Rights to Improve Human Rights, Accountability, Reconciliation and Capacity in South Sudan, A/HRC/31/49, March 10, 2016, www.ohchr.org/EN /HRBodies/HRC/RegularSessions/Sessions31/Documents/A-HRC-31–49_en.doc.

19. The Institute of Peace and Security Studies in Addis Ababa, Ethiopia, documented nine hundred local conflicts under way in South Sudan over land, cattle, boundary lines, or other issues—this before the outbreak of civil war in December 2013. Author's meeting with IPSS staff in Addis Ababa, February 6, 2016.

20. "Modernized Sanctions for Sudan: Unfinished Business for the Obama Administration," Enough Project, http://enoughproject.org/reports/modernized-sanctions-sudan -unfinished-business-obama-administration.

21. Jehanne Henry, "Dispatches: Inaction on Darfur Again," www.hrw.org/news/2016 /02/17dispatches-inaction-darfur-again.

22. For a fuller discussion of this long-standing obstacle in the negotiations see Lyman, "The Missing Piece."

23. Jennifer Charette, "Sudan: The Silent Crisis," Freedom House, October 7, 2015, https://freedomhouse.org/blog/sudan-silent-crisis; "Sudan Blocks Civil Society Participation in UN-Led Human Rights Review," Relief Web, April 4, 2016, http://reliefweb.int /report/sudan/sudan-blocks-civil-society-participation-un-led-human-rights-review. Several reports of oppression of the press and of individual journalists can be found in the report on Sudan of the Committee to Protect Journalists, www.cpj.org/mideast/sudan, March 2016.

24. The SRF's strategy was to have the SPLM/N army not only hold its own but also threaten the capital of Southern Kordofan and Sudan's only remaining oil fields nearby, thus forcing the GOSS to bring down additional forces that were protecting Khartoum. This would open the way for the Darfurian group JEM to march into Khartoum and lead the overthrow of the regime. The problem was that the GOSS, having previously allowed JEM to reach Khartoum for a short time, did not make the same mistake again; instead, it mobilized the same sort of militia as it used in Darfur, the Janjaweed, although now better organized and equipped in the Rapid System Force (RSF) to supplement its regular forces in Southern Kordofan. This made the war all the more brutal. After five years it is at a stalemate. Discussions by the author with leaders of the SRF.

25. Lyman, "The Missing Piece."

26. Joint Monitoring and Evaluation Commission, www.jmecsouthsudan.org.

27. "The Unraveling in South Sudan," *Washington Post*, July 15, 2016, p. A9; "The Tortured Infancy of South Sudan," *Financial Times*, July 14, 2016, www.ft.com/cms/s/0 /c418837a-49a8-11e6-8d68-72e9211e86ab.html; and reports to the author from persons in South Sudan.

28. For a fuller discussion of the peacekeeping issues and of alternative ways to achieve greater oversight of the peace process, see Princeton N. Lyman, "The Growing Crisis in South Sudan," Testimony Before the House Foreign Affairs Subcommittee on Africa, Global Health, Global Human Rights, and International Organizations, www.usip.org /publications/2016/09/07/the-growing-crisis-in-south-sudan.

Instability in the Great Lakes Region

F ILIP R EYNTJENS

INTRODUCTION

This chapter examines a quarter century of instability, violence, war, and extreme human suffering in Central Africa. Considered in the past as peripheral, land-locked, and politically and economically uninteresting, in the 1990s the African Great Lakes region found itself at the heart of a profound geopolitical recomposition with continental repercussions. Countries as varied as Namibia in the south, Libya in the north, Angola in the west, and Uganda in the east became entangled in wars that ignored international borders. However, the seeds of instability were sown from the beginning of the 1960s: the massive exile of the Rwandan Tutsi, who fled to neighboring countries during and after the revolution of 1959–1961, and the virtual exclusion of Tutsi from public life in Rwanda; the radicalization of Burundian Tutsi who monopolized power and wealth; and the insecure status of Kinyarwanda speakers in the Kivu provinces—all these factors were to merge with others to create the conditions for prolonged violence.

I argue that a unique and contingent combination of factors explains the pro-tracted instability and its dynamics. Although this combination of factors helps to understand the past, it may also have some value for assessing the future. Indeed, as long as these factors persist, the risk of conflict continues to exist. The factors studied here are (1) the weakness of the Zairean/Congolese state, (2) the territorial extension of neighboring countries' civil wars, (3) the shifting regional alliances, (4) the profitability of war, (5) the linking up of local stakes, and (6) the impunity for major human rights violations.[1]

The acute destabilization of the region started on October 1, 1990, when the Rwanda Patriotic Front (RPF) attacked Rwanda from Uganda with Ugandan support. After the collapse of the 1993 Arusha peace accord and following the genocide and massive war crimes and crimes against humanity, the RPF won a military victory and took power in July 1994. Over a million people died and over 2 million fled abroad, mainly to Zaire and Tanzania. Eight months earlier the democratic transition had ended in disaster in Burundi: tens of thousands of people were killed, and the country embarked on a decadelong civil war. At the end of 1993 some two hundred thousand Burundian refugees inundated the Zairean Kivu provinces, followed in mid-1994 by 1.5 million Rwandans. This was the beginning of the dramatic extension of neighboring conflicts, most prominently of the Rwandan civil war.

Given the complexity and abundance of events, I propose a brief time line here.[2] After the genocide and the overthrow of the Rwandan Hutu-dominated regime in July 1994, 1.5 million Hutu refugees settled just across the border in Zaire. Among them were the former government army, the Forces Armées Rwandaises (FAR), and militia. They launched cross-border raids and increasingly became a serious security threat for the new regime, dominated by the mainly Tutsi RPF. First under the guise of the "Banyamulenge rebellion" and later the "AFDL (Alliance des Forces pour la Libération du Congo-Zaïre) rebellion," the Rwanda Patriotic Army (RPA, the military wing of the RPF that became the national army after its victory) attacked and cleared the refugee camps during the autumn of 1996. Having security concerns similar to those of Rwanda, Uganda and Burundi joined from the beginning, later to be followed by a formidable regional coalition intent on toppling Zairean president Mobutu Sese Seko. In May 1997 Laurent Kabila seized power in Kinshasa. During the latter half of 1997 relations between the new Congolese regime and its erstwhile Rwandan and Ugandan allies soured rapidly.

In August 1998 Rwanda and Uganda again attacked, and they did so once more under the guise of a new rebel movement, the RCD (Rassemblement Congolais pour la Démocratie), which, just like the AFDL, was created in Kigali. The invading countries expected this to be to be a remake of the first war, only much faster this time. However, the swift action they expected failed to occur because of a spectacular shift of alliances, when Angola and Zimbabwe sided with Kabila against their former allies Rwanda and Uganda. This intervention made up for the weakness of the Congolese army, thus ensuring military stalemate along a more or less stable front line that cut the country in two. Considerable pressure from the region led to the signing of the Lusaka Accord in July 1999.[3] However, Laurent Kabila blocked its implementation, and only after his assassination and succession by his son Joseph in January 2001 was the peace process resumed. Again under great pressure, by South Africa in particular, and after cumbersome negotiations did the Congolese parties sign a "Global and All-Inclusive Accord" (AGI) in December 2002.[4]

It took three-and-a-half more years to implement the accord, a long and bumpy road replete with incidents, obstructions, negotiations, and renegotiations and constantly threatened by the resumption of the war. An informal international trusteeship, supported by a large UN peacekeeping force (MONUSCO) and the international and Congolese civil society, imposed elections on very reluctant political players. These took place in July through October 2006 in an overall free and fair fashion. Joseph Kabila and his party, PPRD, won the elections. Kabila was sworn in in December, both houses of parliament were installed in January 2007, and a new government was formed in early February, thus formally ending the transition.

However, the eastern part of the country remained unstable, and the Congolese government failed to establish full territorial control. Several local militias, captured under the general heading "mai-mai," as well as the Rwandan Hutu rebel movement, the Forces démocratiques pour la liberation du Rwanda (FDLR), remained active and were hardly hindered by the national army in their violence against local populations and the exploitation of natural resources.[5] In addition, Rwanda continued to back rebel movements in the DRC. The Congrès national pour la défense du peuple (CNDP) was created by Laurent Nkunda in December 2006, followed after it split in rival factions by the Mouvement du 23 mars (M23) set up in May 2011. As the UN Group of Experts and Human Rights Watch, among others, published precise information on Rwandan support for the M23,[6] countries like the United States, the UK, Sweden, and The Netherlands suspended part of their aid to Kigali. A UN-sanctioned and SADC (Southern African Development Community)-backed "Force Intervention Brigade," made up of troops from South Africa, Tanzania, and Malawi and sent in support of MONUSCO, finally defeated the M23 in November 2013. This effectively cut Rwanda's foothold in the DRC, while pressure from Washington and London prevented Kigali from resuming destabilizing activities there. However, in 2015 Rwanda started supporting Burundian rebels, as will be discussed below. The defeat of M23 did not, however, signal the full restoration of state control in eastern DRC: illegal exploitation of natural resources, taxation, and (cross-border) trade continue to flourish in a region characterized by hybrid governance.[7]

STATE FAILURE

Well before the start of the first war in the fall of 1996 Zaire had ceased to empirically perform a number of essential state functions, such as territorial control, public taxation, the provision of essential services, the monopoly of violence, and the rule of law. The gradual failure of the state preceded its collapse, and the first signs of a "shadow state" were visible in the 1970s after the "Zairianisation" measures allowed the transfer of large parts of the economy to political and military elites.[8] This heralded the putting into place of a prebendary and neopatrimonial exercise of power that profoundly corrupted official institutional norms and frameworks.[9]

Nzongola writes that "the major determinant of the present conflict and instability in the Great Lakes Region is the decay of the state and its instruments of rule in the Congo. For it is this decay that made it possible for Lilliputian states the size of Congo's smallest province, such as Uganda, or even that of a district, such as Rwanda, to take it upon themselves to impose rulers in Kinshasa and to invade, occupy and loot the territory of their giant neighbor."[10] Indeed, the void left by the state was filled by other, nonstate actors. Some of these—like NGOs, churches, local civil society, or traditional structures—assumed some functions abandoned by the state, but other less benign players also seized the public space left by the retreating state: warlords, (ethnic) militias, and "entrepreneurs of insecurity," both domestic and from neighboring countries.[11] This not only explains the extreme weakness in battle of the FAZ/FAC,[12] which were the mirror of the collapsed state, but also why a small country like Rwanda was able, without much of a fight, to establish extraordinary territorial, political, and economic control over its vast neighbor. What Achille Mbembe has called the "satellisation" of entire provinces by (much) smaller but stronger states was accompanied by the emergence of new forms of privatized governance.[13]

In eastern DRC most functions of sovereignty were thus privatized, as some examples show. In 1996 and again in 1998 the Zairean/Congolese government forces hardly engaged in combat; during the war that started in 1998 foreign and nonstate forces faced each other—the Angolan and Zimbabwean (and, at one point, Chadian and Namibian) armies and Rwandan and Burundian rebel groups on Kabila's side, and on the other the Rwandan and Ugandan armies with their RCD and MLC (Mouvement de Libération du Congo) proxies. Territorial control, the provision of (in)security, and the management of populations were taken over by militia, rebel groups—both domestic and from neighbors Rwanda, Uganda, and Burundi—and the armies of neighboring countries (and even the former Rwandan government army).

A UN panel monitoring an arms embargo reported compelling data on the state's absence in controlling cross-border traffic, including at ports and airports; indeed, "irregular aircraft practices are the norm."[14] The state's fiscal function, too, which was limited anyway, was profoundly eroded. Import and export levies collected by militias, rebel groups, and Rwandan and Ugandan "elite networks" funded the wars and lined individuals' pockets. Toll barriers (*péages*) were put up to extract resources from peasants taking their meagre surplus products to markets, so the possession of a gun was a sufficient means to impose internal taxation. In North Kivu travelers passing between the zones controlled by two opposing wings of the RCD were required to declare goods and pay duties at the "border."[15] There were annual taxes on vehicles and a panoply of charges for individual journeys, road "tolls," and "insurance."[16] The RCD taxed the coltan trade, sold mining rights, and demanded license fees, nonrefundable deposits, various export taxes, and a "war effort tax."[17] The panel documented a number of other examples showing that borders and their control became prized assets for armed groups and their sponsors in Rwanda and Uganda, allowing them the necessary revenue to maintain and resupply troops.[18] It concluded that "as an institutionally weak state, the DRC significantly lacks control over both customs and immigration."[19] Recent reports by the UN Group of Experts continue to make similar observations.[20]

TERRITORIAL EXTENSION OF CIVIL WARS

Although the sources of instability in the Great Lakes region were, in essence, domestic, reflecting as they did the political conflicts in Angola, Uganda, Rwanda, Burundi, the Kivu, and Zaire more generally, their repercussions were increasingly felt throughout the larger region. The geographic proximity of conflicts, the game of alliances, and population flows reinforced this regionalization of violence.

In the mid-1990s insurgent forces of several neighboring countries used the territory of Zaire as a base for attack and retreat. They included the Allied Democratic Forces (ADF) from Uganda, several groups (CNDD-FDD and Palipehutu-FNL in particular) from Burundi, and Angolan UNITA. From mid-1994 the most serious threat concerned Rwanda after 1.5 million Hutu refugees fled into North and South Kivu after the genocide and RPF's victory. Rwanda faced an increasing security threat after 1995, particularly in the three western préfectures, affected by commando operations emanating, at least in part, from Zairean territory.[21] Rwandan vice president and de facto leader Paul Kagame candidly told journalist François Misser that "if another war must be waged, we shall fight in a different fashion, elsewhere. We are prepared. We are ready to fight any war and we shall contain it along the border with Zaire."[22] Officials from the United States and The Netherlands, two countries close to the Rwandan regime, confirmed that they had had to dissuade Kagame on several occasions from "breaking the abscess" of the Rwandan refugees in Zaire the hard way.[23] During a visit to the United States in August 1996, one month before the start of the "rebellion," Kagame told the Americans that he was about to intervene,[24] the more so since, according to some sources,[25] the ex-FAR were preparing a large-scale offensive against Rwanda from Goma and Bukavu. Faced with the obvious unwillingness or inability of the international community to tackle this problem, Kigali's patience had reached its limits.

In September 1996, under the guise of the "Banyamulenge rebellion" first and later hiding behind the back of the AFDL created in Kigali, the RPA cleared the refugee camps around Goma and Bukavu. Thousands of civilian refugees were killed in the initial attack, hundreds of thousands were "voluntarily/forcibly" returned to Rwanda, and hundreds of thousands more moved westward, where they became the victims of a phased extermination campaign by the RPA.[26] Pourtier noted that "the strategic choice (of Kigali) to attack the camps clearly shows the fundamental objectives of a 'rebellion' that was no longer (a rebellion), because what really happened was the extension of the Rwandan civil war into Zairean territory."[27]

Faced with similar—though less vital—security concerns, Uganda and to a lesser extent Burundi participated in the war, thereby destabilizing the bases of their "own" rebel groups. By the end of 1996 Angola, another country facing a rebellion (UNITA) supported by Mobutu's cronies and operating in part from Zaire, realized that its security concerns had not been met by the situation created in eastern Zaire and decided to make a difference.[28] Luanda's position, which was to expand the ambitions of the rebellion to the whole of Zaire, eventually prevailed.[29] Angola provided the crucial impetus through the Katangese Gendarmes, known as the "Tigres."[30] During two weeks in mid-February 1997 several battalions (two to three thousand "Tigres" men) were airlifted to Kigali and taken from there by road to Goma and Bukavu. The Angolan army, obviously in close cooperation with Rwanda, supported this operation logistically. The entry of the Gendarmes and, later during the war, of other units of the Angolan army caused the "rebellion" to pick up speed. Whereas it took four months (October 1996 to January 1997) to occupy less than one-twentieth of the country, the remainder of Zaire was captured in the three months that followed the arrival of the Tigres (mid-February to mid-May 1997). The outcome of the war, namely regime change in Kinshasa, was the consequence of the merger of several civil wars that were intrinsically unlinked but that came together against the background of a weak state in Zaire, opportunistic alliances, and geographical proximity.

The support Rwanda later gave to the Congolese rebel groups RCD, CNDP, and M23 expressed this same logic of waging war on the territory of a vast but weak neighbor. More recently, in the context of strongly deteriorating bilateral relations and the violent unraveling of political conflict over Burundian president Pierre Nkurunziza winning a third unconstitutional term in office, Rwanda assisted in the recruitment, training, and arming of Burundian refugees on its soil with the intent to topple the Burundian regime.[31] At least some of these insurgents transited through South Kivu.[32] As with previous attempts by Rwanda to destabilize neighbors, this led to donors expressing serious concern, including the United States.[33]

SHIFTING ALLIANCES

The players in what became a regional civil war reasoned in the logic of "the enemy of my enemy is my friend." The fact that Mobutu had made many enemies explains the emergence of the formidable regional alliance that eventually defeated him. But that such a circumstantial alliance is also very fragile was clear during the second war, from 1998, when yesterday's friends became today's enemies almost overnight; indeed, coalitions shifted dramatically.

At the beginning of the resumption of the war in August 1998 Kabila was saved by Angola and Zimbabwe, who turned against their former allies Rwanda and

Uganda. Angola was concerned about two developments. Former Mobutu generals Nzimbi and Baramoto had been seen in Kigali before the new war broke out, and some politicians of the Mobutu era openly joined the rebellion, as did some former FAZ units. Because of their support for UNITA in the past, these elements were considered archenemies in Luanda. Moreover, Angolan intelligence was aware that there were contacts between UNITA and the rebel leadership and their Rwandan and Ugandan sponsors. Indeed, elements of UNITA later fought alongside rebel forces, the MLC in particular. Given the likelihood that the Angolan civil war would resume (which indeed materialized a few months later), for Luanda the choice was clear: those supporting UNITA were the enemy, and their enemies merited support.

The motives behind the involvement of Zimbabwe were diverse. The DRC had an important war debt outstanding toward Zimbabwe, and the Zimbabweans were worried about repayment in the event of Kabila being overthrown.[34] A second motive was also economic: Zimbabwean business interests had made efforts during the past year to penetrate the Congolese market and to invest in the mining sector, partly at the expense of South African ventures. Some of Zimbabwean president Robert Mugabe's business associates and high-ranking army officers stood to lose important assets if Kabila were defeated. Finally, the "old revolutionary" Mugabe saw the Congolese crisis as an opportunity to reassert some of his leadership in the region,[35] lost to President Nelson Mandela's South Africa, and to short-circuit the new leaders of the "African Renaissance," such as Yoweri Museveni of Uganda and Kagame,[36] who were being promoted—notably by the Americans[37]—much to Mugabe's dismay.

Other realignments soon occurred. Thus, the local mai-mai militias in the east, which had been fighting Kabila even before he came to power, now aligned with him in the context of an "anti-Tutsi" coalition.[38] Within the same logic an even more spectacular shift brought the ex-FAR and former Interahamwe militia into Kabila's camp, although less than a year earlier the Rwandan Hutu had suffered massive loss of life during and after the previous rebellion at the hands of Kabila's AFDL and his erstwhile Rwandan allies. FAR were brought in from neighboring countries, rearmed, retrained, and deployed on the northern and eastern fronts.[39] A UN report noted that "the changing alliances in and around the DRC have unexpectedly worked to the advantage of the former Rwandan government forces" because the ex-FAR and ex-Interahamwe "have now become a significant component of the international alliance against the Congolese rebels and their presumed sponsors, Rwanda and Uganda." The commission found it "profoundly shocking that this new relationship has conferred a form of legitimacy on the Interahamwe and the ex-FAR."[40] Likewise, the Burundian FDD's alliance with Kabila opened access to equipment, weapons, training, bases, and even a degree of respectability. They were headquartered in Lubumbashi, and troops recruited in Tanzanian refugee camps were transferred to the DRC.[41] The frailty of the alliances again showed when conflict erupted between Rwanda and a major section of the Banyamulenge, who had earlier sought the protection of Kigali while at the same time being used as a pretext for the Rwandan invasion in 1996. Already by the autumn of 1996 Banyamulenge leaders had realized that Rwanda was instrumentalizing them and that, rather than protecting their community, their close association with Kigali further marginalized and threatened them. This feeling of being used increased further when, in October and December of 1996, the RPA attempted to convince Banyamulenge leaders to resettle their entire community in Rwanda, an idea most of them rejected.[42] Disagreements with RPA commanders of the FAC over command positions and deployment of troops further exacerbated the tensions in the early months of 1998. When the second rebellion started in August 1998 the Banyamulenge were again faced with a crucial dilemma. On the one hand, they knew Rwanda was once again going to instrumentalize them and that this would worsen their relations with other groups even further; but on the other, they needed the physical security the RPA provided, including for their men in Kinshasa. As the war progressed, it became increasingly clear that those Banyamulenge (like Azarias Ruberwa, Moïse Nyarugabo, and Bizima Karaha) who had joined the RCD were a minority and that most Banyamulenge opposed the RCD and Rwanda.

The most dramatic shift occurred between the former core allies Rwanda and Uganda. In the words of Charles Onyango-Obbo, chief editor of the Ugandan daily *The Monitor*, in August 1999 "the impossible happened"[43]: the Rwandan and Ugandan armies fought a heavy battle in Kisangani, and more clashes followed later. In May to June 2000 the RPA and the UPDF again confronted each other in Kisangani; heavy weapons were used, and some 400 civilians and 120 soldiers were killed. The rift had several causes. Whereas Uganda wished to avoid repeating the mistake made in 1996–1997, when Kabila was parachuted into power without much Congolese ownership, Rwanda preferred a quick military solution and the installation of yet another figurehead in Kinshasa. Prunier noted that Kampala had no problem with an independent and efficient government in the DRC, a vision dramatically opposed to the view of a Kigali that wanted to keep its Congolese proxies under control.[44] In addition, "entrepreneurs of insecurity" belonging to the elite networks in both countries were engaged in a competition to extract Congolese resources (see below).[45] Finally, Museveni resented the geopolitical ambitions of his small Rwandan neighbor and the lack of gratitude displayed by Kagame, who owed his accession to power to the support of Uganda.

Just like the extension into the DRC of the Rwandan civil war, the conflict with Uganda was fought out on the soil of a weak neighbor and, in part, by proxy. Both countries supported rebel movements and (ethnic) militias in the context of an increasingly fragmented political-military landscape. They continuously traded accusations of supporting each other's rebel groups, which both sides indeed did. In March 2001 the Ugandan government declared Rwanda a "hostile nation." Despite attempts at appeasement during the following months, on August 28, 2001, Museveni sent a long and bitter letter to the UK secretary of state for International Development Clare Short "about the deteriorating situation in the bilateral relations between Uganda and the government of Rwanda, led by President Kagame." As a consequence Rwandan-Ugandan relations further worsened, and troops were massed on both sides of their common border. On November 6, 2001, Short summoned her two protégés to London to put an end to a situation that risked becoming a fiasco for the UK, just like the Ethiopian-Eritrean war of 1998–2000 had been one for the United States. Although relations did not become cordial, the threat of direct war subsided, and relations markedly improved in the mid-2000s.

PROFITABILITY OF WAR

A UN panel set up in 2001 published a number of increasingly detailed reports on the criminal practices of "elite networks," both Congolese and from neighboring countries, and identified elements common to all these networks.[46] They consisted of a small core of political and military elites and businesspeople and, in the case of the occupied territories, rebel leaders and administrators. Members of these networks cooperated to generate revenue and, in the case of Rwanda, institutional financial gain. They derived this benefit from a variety of criminal activities, including theft, embezzlement and diversion of "public" funds, underevaluation of goods, smuggling, false invoicing, nonpayment of taxes, kickbacks to officials, and bribery. International "entrepreneurs of insecurity" (among them Viktor Bout) were closely involved in this criminal economy, as the local and regional actors drew support from the networks and "services" (e.g., air transport, illegal arms dealing, and international transactions of pillaged resources) of organized international criminal groups.[47]

The linkage between military engagement and illegal economic activities was a clear trend. Indeed, pillaging was no longer an unfortunate side effect of war; rather, economic interests became war's prime driving force. Dietrich has drawn attention to the dangers inherent in what he calls "military commercialism," whereby a stronger state deploys the national military in a weaker neighboring country, supporting either the sovereign power (as did Zimbabwe) or insurgents (in the cases of Rwanda and Uganda) in exchange for access to profits.[48] Under these circumstances economic criteria invade military decision making, for example with regard to troop deployment and areas of operation.[49] In addition, if domestic resources are scarce or cannot be illicitly mobilized as a result of the scrutiny of the international community, cross-border predatory behavior, out of sight and/or hidden behind political and military concerns, provides an alternative resource. Finally, when control over resources has become a military objective in itself, this is a strong disincentive for troop withdrawal simply because the "expeditionary corps" and those they support, whether rebels or governments, need each other. Put simply by Samset, "war facilitates excessive resource exploitation, and excessive exploitation spurs continued fighting."[50] A panel monitoring the UN arms embargo confirmed that "the most profitable financing source for armed groups remains the exploitation, trade and transportation of natural resources. . . .

All supply chains from areas controlled by armed groups are compromised."[51] Crawford Young notes that this "ability to sustain themselves through traffic in high value resources under their control" distinguishes contemporary insurgents from their predecessors.[52]

Nowhere is this as clear as in the case of Rwanda, a small and poor country with few natural resources but with a large and efficient army.[53] In 2000 the revenue collected by the RPA in the DRC from coltan alone was believed to be US$80 to 100 million, roughly the equivalent of official Rwandan defense expenditure, which stood at US$86 million.[54] In a similar vein the UN panel found that in 1999–2000, "the RPA must have made at least US$250 million over a period of 18 months."[55] Marysse calculated that in 1999 the total value added of diamond, gold, and coltan plundered in the DRC amounted to 6.1 percent of Rwanda's GDP,[56] and to 146 percent of its official military expenditure.[57] The Kigali economy, which is virtually disconnected from the Rwandan economy as a whole, was largely dependent on mineral and other extraction in the DRC (as well as on international aid). Pillaging the Congo not only allowed the Rwandan government to beef up the military budget in a way that was invisible to the donor community but also bought much needed domestic elite loyalty.[58] Despite international condemnations, these practices continue—albeit on a lesser scale—as noted by the UN Group of Experts in 2015: "Mineral tracing tags . . . continue to be sold on the black market in Rwanda, which can allow minerals sourced in conflict areas in the eastern Democratic Republic of the Congo to enter the international market."[59] Jackson calls this the "economisation of conflict": a process whereby conflicts progressively reorient from their original goals (in the case of Rwanda, securing its borders) toward profit and through which conflict actors capitalize increasingly on the economic opportunities that war opens up.[60]

After officially withdrawing its troops from the DRC in September 2002 as a result of discreet but intense international pressure, Rwanda therefore changed tactics by seeking alternative allies on the ground and sponsoring autonomist movements in order to consolidate its long-term influence in eastern Congo and make the most out of the Kivu region.[61] In addition, even after its official withdrawal, Rwanda maintained a clandestine military presence in the DRC, at least until late 2013.[62] We have seen earlier that its support for the CNDP and the M23 caused serious conflicts with powerful members of the international community.

Uganda, too, greatly benefited from its military/commercial presence in the DRC. Although, unlike Rwanda, it did not set up an extra-budgetary system to finance its activities there, the UN Panel found that the "re-exportation economy" had a significant impact on the financing of the war in three ways: by increasing the incomes of key businessmen, traders, and other dealers; by improving Uganda's balance of payments; and by bringing more money to the treasury through various taxes on goods, services, and international trade.[63] By way of example, Ugandan gold exports totaled US$90 million in 2000—while the country produced practically no gold.[64]

The logic of military commercialism could also be seen in the strategies developed by domestic armed groups. Thus the Walikale region west of Goma became a battleground between RCD rebels and mai-mai, both supposedly integrated into the FARDC but who ceased to obey the FARDC eighth military region commander, an RCD general who himself refused to obey orders from Kinshasa. In their fight for control over Walikale's cassiterite mines, these ex-mai-mai units cooperated with FDLR troops. Small aircraft based in Goma collected the cassiterite "caught" by the RCD for purchasing agents; once it arrived in Goma, shares were distributed to local military and political authorities before being transported across the border to Rwanda, where a smelting plant is located near Kigali, or exported to South Africa.[65]

Clearly, criminal or informal regional integration was very real, and it was certainly more effective than the often-called-for formal integration. Cuvelier has shown how the support of Rwanda for the RCD heralded a growing cooperation between businesspeople, politicians, and high-ranking military on both sides of the border.[66] SOMIGL (Société minière des grands lacs) and the CHC (Congo Holding Company) were instruments set up by the rebel group and Rwanda to get as much financial benefit as possible out of the international interest in Kivu's natural resources. Two Rwandan companies with close links to the RPF and the army, Rwanda Metals and Grands Lacs Metals, were key in organizing the Congolese commercial ventures of the Kigali regime. What is novel about what Taylor suggests are "neo-imperialist" regional networks of violence and accumulation is that they are managing to develop their own links and ties to the international arena, often on their own terms.[67] The type of alliances and transboundary networks currently reconfiguring Central Africa may well, in his view, offer a prophetic vision of what may be in store for vulnerable and peripheral areas of the world.[68]

LOCAL DYNAMICS

These mega-conflicts developed against the background of several local-level conflicts. Problems related to identity in the Kivu region are ancient. Important migratory flows before, during, and after the colonial period; considerable demographic pressure; the uncertain status of (neo)traditional authorities; the political and economic dynamism of the region; its peripheral situation in the Zairean context; and its partial incorporation in the East African space are all factors that form the local background to events in Eastern Zaire. The most visible and violent expression of this was the situation of the Banyarwanda, the Kinyarwanda speakers living in the Kivu. They consisted of several groups: the "natives," established since precolonial days; the "immigrants" and the "transplanted"[69] of the colonial period; the "infiltrators" and "clandestines" before and after independence (1960); and the Tutsi[70] and Hutu[71] refugees. This mixture gave birth to conflict in the 1960s during the so-called Kanyarwanda rebellion, when the Banyarwanda faced the threat of expulsion from the North Kivu region.[72] After a long period of calm under the regime of Mobutu, whose influential director of the Political Bureau, Barthélémy Bisengimana, was himself of Tutsi origin, the problem came to the fore again during the National Conference (1991–1992), when representatives of civil society of North and South Kivu raised the question of the "Zaireans of dual or doubtful citizenship," a coded expression referring to the Banyarwanda.

Although the conflicts have older roots, this chapter picks up the story from early 1993 onward.[73] The events that started in North Kivu in March 1993 show how fluid ethnic categories are. Indeed, those who became the victims of a wave of violence waged by "indigenous" ethnic groups, such as the Hunde, Nande, and Nyanga, supported by their respective militias (the mai-mai and the Bangilima), were the Banyarwanda, Hutu, and Tutsi alike. Only two years later Hutu and Tutsi confronted each other in ethnic strife. There are various reasons for the violence that erupted in early 1993. First, the democratization process underway since 1990 opened up a new way of competing for power. As only nationals exercise political rights, citizenship became important, particularly in regions with a high proportion of Banyarwanda—in the extreme case of the zone of Masisi, they numbered 70 percent of the population. Second, in this relatively overpopulated part of Zaire, conflicts over land set groups against each other in two ways. On the one hand, as also seen elsewhere, two types of land use, agriculture and stock breeding, entered into competition with each other. On the other, two concepts of land tenure and access to land clashed: land use by members of a group that holds corporate ownership (the customary law regime) as opposed to the concept of individual ownership of the modern law type, which allows for contractual transactions in land. A third source of conflict, not unrelated to the previous one, concerned the position of customary authorities. Groups that are immigrant or presented as such tend to try to free themselves from the authority of local chiefs, thus threatening their position and differentiating themselves from "indigenous" populations. Pastoral communities of Tutsi extraction more frequently adopted this attitude of distancing. Under these circumstances the denial of citizenship became a means for politically and economically excluding the Banyarwanda, the Tutsi in particular.

The conflict came to the fore again during the Zairean National Conference, and confrontations had already taken place in 1991 and 1992, particularly in the zones of Masisi and Rutshuru. However, conflict spread dramatically in March 1993.[74] As the casualties show, a real war broke out with many deaths: "indigenous" and "immigrant" communities lost about one thousand each; tens of thousands more were displaced. In late 1993 to early 1994 North Kivu was pacified for a brief period through the deployment of the Special Presidential Division (Division spéciale présidentielle, or DSP) and a successful peace-making initiative by the local Catholic church and NGOs.

Only a few months after pacification North Kivu was flooded by over 700,000 Rwandan Hutu refugees who fled the civil war in their country and the victorious RPF, accompanied and to some extent controlled by those responsible for the Rwandan genocide. Concentrated in five huge camps (Katale, Kahindo, Kibumba,

Lac Vert, and Mugunga) on a limited area close to the Rwandan border, they completely upset the demographic situation and, therefore, the politics of the region. At the beginning of the 1990s approximately 425,000 Banyarwanda lived in the three zones (Masisi, Rutshuru, and Goma) where the refugees settled; out of a total population of about 1 million, this was about 40 percent. Obviously, as a result of this massive injection of people, the Banyarwanda and the Rwandan refugees suddenly constituted the majority of the regional population. In addition, the Hutu (both the Rwandan refugees and the Zairean Hutu) had now become largely dominant in numbers, thus breaking the fragile balance put in place earlier in the year. The alliance of Hutu and Tutsi Banyarwanda broke up, and as in Rwanda, the two groups entered into violent conflict. The massive arrival of refugees also had other destabilizing effects: the environment was thoroughly disturbed by deforestation, poaching, and pressure on water supplies; the economy was destabilized by dollarization and the dramatic decrease of livestock; and basic infrastructure, already very weak before the crisis, was badly damaged.

However, large-scale violence did not start until November 1995. Probably unwillingly, the Zairean government contributed to the instability in August 1995 by announcing that the Rwandan refugees were to be expelled; they were given until December 31, 1995, to leave the country. As a result, many refugees left the camps and attempted to settle in the zones of Masisi and Rutshuru, where they inevitably clashed with the "natives" and Tutsi Banyarwanda whose houses and land they threatened to occupy. On a more general political level these attempts at occupation heightened many Zaireans' fears that a "Hutu-land" was being put in place in North Kivu.[75] Incidents of uneven intensity in September and October 1995 were the prelude to a real war that started first in Masisi but rapidly spread to Rutshuru and Lubero.

The extension of violence was enhanced by the ambiguous attitude of the local authorities, used to manipulating ethnicity for plutocratic purposes. Thus in May 1995 the governor of North Kivu, Christophe Moto Mupenda, stated during a public meeting before a Hunde audience in the town of Masisi that "hospitality has its limits" and that it was necessary "to strike and strike now against the immigrants." During the following year two Goma-based radio stations fueled anti-Tutsi feelings while megaphones were used to call on residents to chase the Tutsi out of town; local authorities arrested Tutsi businessmen without specific charges.[76] In November 1995 FAZ chief of staff General Eluki declared publicly that "the Hunde, Nyanga and Batembo are right to fight for the land of their ancestors and to chase the foreigners away from it."[77]

Autesserre has shown that the relationship between local and national or regional tensions was not merely top-down and that issues usually presented as regional or national had significant local components, which fueled and reinforced the larger dimensions.[78] This reality was particularly strong in the region, as Hutu and Tutsi are found in both Kivus, Rwanda, and Burundi, a situation that is conducive to cross-border alliances, solidarities, and strategies.

IMPUNITY

Although an important factor, the practice of impunity for persistent gross violations of human rights can only be briefly mentioned. The humanitarian consequences of the conflicts in the Great Lakes Region over the last quarter century have been disastrous. Millions have died since 1990, of which well over a million were the victims of direct violence. Generally speaking, those responsible for crimes against humanity, war crimes, and even genocide have remained unpunished. The only justice at work in the region has been victor's justice meted out to the authors of the genocide in Rwanda, MLC leader Jean-Pierre Bemba, and a few Ituri warlords. However, the RPF, for instance, was not held accountable for the crimes it committed in Rwanda before, during, and after the genocide nor for those perpetrated in Zaire/DRC, particularly at the end of 1996 and the beginning of 1997. Although these crimes were well documented,[79] no prosecutions took place before the International Criminal Tribunal for Rwanda, before Rwandan or Congolese courts, or before courts in third countries on the basis of universal jurisdiction.[80]

This practice of victor's justice had a dual consequence. On the one hand, as impunity prevailed, it reassured criminals that they could commit new crimes without risk of judicial prosecution. For instance, it is likely that the RPA would not have massacred tens of thousands of civilian refugees in Zaire/DRC had those responsible for crimes committed in Rwanda in 1994 been prosecuted before the ICTR. On the other hand, biased justice created frustration and resentment among the victims of these crimes, thus creating a fertile breeding ground for new violence. Many Rwandan Hutu and Congolese remember what the RPA did to them, and they may well take revenge if and when the occasion presents itself.

CONCLUSION

This chapter has addressed the combination of factors that allows one to understand a long period of war and instability in the Great Lakes Region. Although this analysis has an explanatory function, it may also offer clues to future developments; indeed, if these factors are still present, one could conclude that a context favorable to continued instability prevails.

Although some steps have been made toward state reconstruction in the DRC, the state remains very fragile, particularly—but not exclusively—in the east, where earlier conflicts started. Territorial control is limited, private taxation continues, and the illegal exploitation and smuggling of natural resources go on.[81]

With regard to neighbors' civil wars, the one in Angola came to an end in 2002. The last remaining Burundian rebel movement, Palipehutu-FNL, laid down arms at the end of 2008 to become a political party under the name FNL. However, after several opposition parties rejected the outcome of the 2010 elections, some politicians, including former rebel leaders, went underground or fled abroad, but most later returned. At the time of writing, the country is facing renewed violence as a result of protests against Nkurunziza's election for a third, unconstitutional term. The Ugandan ADF continue to operate on both sides of the Congo-Uganda border in the Ruwenzori region. The LRA is no longer active inside Uganda, but it is still present in the DRC, though many of its fighters have relocated to the Central African Republic. The porous region straddling the DRC, the CAR, and South Sudan remains particularly open to insurgent activities. Although peace seems to have returned in Rwanda, this is only apparent. Structural violence is widespread, and an authoritarian regime attempts to keep a lid on the volcano.[82] Dissident Tutsi who once occupied very high positions in the Rwandan political and military establishment entered into open opposition in 2010. They created a political structure, the Rwanda National Congress, intent on overthrowing Kagame. The Hutu FDLR continue to be active in both South and North Kivu, and Rwanda has supported Congolese insurgent groups until 2013. It started aiding a Burundian rebel movement in 2015.

In a situation of relative regional peace, alliances between states have become less prominent, but they have not disappeared. Thus, after Tanzania suggested that Rwanda should engage in talks with the FDLR and played a large part in defeating Rwanda's proxy M23 as a contributor to the Force Intervention Brigade, relations between the two countries soured. A Kigali-Kampala axis now opposes a Dar-Es-Salaam-Bujumbura axis, which threatens the very survival of the East African Community. Alliances also continue to be concluded at more reduced scales. Thus, the Rwandan RPF dissidents are suspected of having been in contact with armed movements in Eastern DRC and possibly with elements of the FDLR while at the same time seeking support inside Rwanda.[83]

In the Kivu provinces in particular the national army, several armed groups, and Uganda and Rwanda continue to exploit Congolese resources. Despite attempts to tag some materials and to raise awareness in the business community of due-diligence guidelines, conflict around mineral and other wealth remains attractive. The UN panel of experts found that minerals continued to be transported through illegal border crossings between the two Kivus and Rwanda.[84] A recent UN Group of Experts report noted that this traffic continues up to the present day through the role traders from Rwanda play in "laundering" Congolese minerals by using Rwandan tags and certificates.[85]

Local tensions based on (ethnic) identity remain as intense as before, in Rwanda in particular, and cross-border alignments along these lines are still present. However, intra-Tutsi elite differences, as shown by the dissidence of the RNC and the fact that many Tutsi Banyamulenge are opposed to the regime in Kigali, may alleviate the ethnic divide, though other lethal alliances and the emergence of new violent strategies may replace this.

Finally, the issue of impunity has not been addressed seriously. For instance, the 2010 Mapping Report of the UN High Commission for Human Rights has not (yet) been acted upon. However, in March 2013 Bosco Ntaganda, a former warlord in Ituri and later leader of the CNDP and M23, surrendered to the International Criminal Court, where he stands indicted for war crimes and crimes against humanity. This is another instance of victor's justice though, as Ntaganda led a faction of M23 that was on the losing side, and he fled to the safety of The Hague in fear for his life.

Clearly, the conflict factors outlined in this chapter have not disappeared, although they have generally decreased in extent and intensity. Two of these factors need to be especially monitored. On the one hand, for both the development of the country and regional stability, state reconstruction in the DRC is an essential condition. Given the colossal nature of this endeavor, putting Humpty Dumpty together again will need to start with the main functions of sovereignty: regaining control over the state's territory and reestablishing links with the population; rebuilding public fiscal capacity, with revenues collected and spent in a transparent, efficient, and honest fashion as well as resources harnessed as public goods; and restoring legal security and the rule of law. Steps have been made since the end of the transition in 2006, but the DRC is still far from a properly functioning state. On the other hand, the Rwandan regime must address the country's severe problems of political governance and stop aiding and abetting violence in neighboring countries. Although the pre-1994 regime generally enjoyed good neighborly relations, its successor has been involved in military and/or diplomatic conflicts with all of its four neighbors. Rwanda has been at the origin of two major regional wars, and it could be so again if current authoritarian practices at home and aggressive behavior abroad are not amended.

NOTES

1. This text uses the name of the country at the time of the events that are analyzed—that is, Zaire before May 1997, Congo or DRC after that date.

2. Appendix 1 to this chapter summarizes the time line. Appendix 2 offers an overview of the main actors. For a fuller treatment of the war see Gérard Prunier, *Africa's World War: Congo, the Rwandan Genocide, and the Making of a Continental Catastrophe* (Oxford: Oxford University Press, 2009); Filip Reyntjens, *The Great African War: Congo and Regional Geopolitics, 1996–2006* (New York, Cambridge University Press, 2009); Jason K. Stearns, *Dancing in the Glory of Monsters: The Collapse of the Congo and the Great War of Africa* (New York, Public Affairs, 2011).

3. In addition to a ceasefire signed by the DRC, Angola, Namibia, Rwanda, Uganda, and Zimbabwe as well as by the Congolese rebel movements, the accord provided for an "open national dialogue" involving the government, the rebel groups, the unarmed opposition, and civil society. This was to lead to a new political dispensation.

4. The AGI provided for a two- to three-year transitional period, during which the executive branch was to be made up of a president, four vice presidents, and a government in which the rebel movements and the unarmed opposition were to be represented. A bicameral parliament included the same entities as those represented in the government.

5. In early 2015 the UN Group of Experts found that the Congolese government failed to authorize military operations against the FDLR and refused to tackle the old problem of

collaboration, at the local level, between the FARDC and the FDLR (UN Security Council, *Letter Dated 12 January 2015 from the Chair of the Security Council Committee Established Pursuant to Resolution 1533 (2004) Concerning the Democratic Republic of the Congo Addressed to the President of the Security Council*, S/2015/19, January 12, 2015, pp. 16–17).

6. UN Security Council, *Addendum to the Interim Report of the Group of Experts on the Democratic Republic of the Congo (S/2012/348) Concerning Violations of the Arms Embargo and Sanctions Regime by the Government of Rwanda*, S/2012/348/Add.1, June 27, 2012; Human Rights Watch, *DR Congo: Rwanda Should Stop Aiding War Crimes Suspect. Congolese Renegade General Bosco Ntaganda Receives Recruits and Weapons from Rwanda*, Goma, June 4, 2012.

7. Filip Reyntjens, "Regulation, Taxation and Violence: The State, Quasi-State Governance and Cross-Border Dynamics in the Great Lakes Region," *Review of African Political Economy* 41, no. 142 (December 2014), pp. 530–544.

8. W. Reno, "Shadow States and the Political Economy of Civil Wars," in *Greed and Grievance: Economic Agendas in Civil Wars*, ed. Mats R. Berdal and David Malone (Boulder, CO: Lynne Riener Publishers, 2000), pp. 43–63.

9. Gauthier de Villers, "La guerre dans les évolutions du Congo-Kinshasa," *Afrique Contemporaine* no. 215 (2005), p. 54.

10. Georges Nzongola-Ntalaja, *The Congo from Leopold to Kabila: A People's History* (London, New York: Zed Books, 2002), p. 214.

11. The expression is from Sandrine Perrot, "Entrepreneurs de l'insécurité: la face cachée de l'armée ougandaise," *Politique Africaine* no. 75 (1999), pp. 60–71. It refers to rational makers of cost-benefit analyses who realize that war, instability, and the absence of the state are more profitable than peace, stability, and state reconstruction.

12. Forces Armées Zaïroises until May 1997, Forces Armées Congolaises between 1997 and 2003. The national army was renamed Forces Armées de la République Démocratique du Congo (FARDC) as a result of the AGI.

13. Achille Mbembe, *On the Postcolony* (Princeton, NJ: Princeton University Press, 2001), pp. 92–93.

14. UN Security Council, *Report of the Group of Experts on the Democratic Republic of the Congo*, S/2004/551, July 15, 2004, para. 56.

15. In 1999 a wing known as the RCD-ML broke away in protest over Rwandan domination and placed itself under Ugandan tutelage. The RCD-Goma remained a proxy for Rwanda.

16. Amnesty International, *Democratic Republic of Congo: Rwandese-Controlled East: Devastating Toll*, London, June 19, 2001, pp. 16–18.

17. Ibid., p. 33.

18. UN Security Council, *Report of the Group of Experts*, para. 44.

19. Ibid., para. 31.

20. See for example, UN Security Council, *Letter Dated 12 January 2015*.

21. Thomas Turner (*The Congo Wars: Conflict, Myth and Reality* [London, New York: Zed Books, 2007], pp. 15–16) rightly points out that this threat applied to the regime but not per se to Rwanda as a whole. Indeed, the majority of the population may well have considered those posing this threat to be its allies and potential liberators. Likewise, when Kigali argued that it needed to protect the Congolese Tutsi, this may well have reflected the feelings of many Rwandan Tutsi but probably not those of many Hutu.

22. François Misser, *Vers un nouveau Rwanda? Entretiens avec Paul Kagame* (Brussels: Luc Pire, 1995), p. 121.

23. The EU Special Representative for the Great Lakes Region Aldo Ajello has confirmed this information to this author.

24. According to the then US ambassador to Kigali, Robert Gribbin, Kagame had already told him in March 1996 that "if Zaire continues to support the ex-FAR/*Interahamwe* against Rwanda, Rwanda in turn could find anti-Mobutu elements to support," adding that "if the international community could not help improve security in the region, the RPA might be compelled to act alone." Robert E. Gribbin, *In the Aftermath of Genocide: The U.S. Role in Rwanda* (New York: iUniverse, 2005), pp. 144–145.

25. The existence of this project was later confirmed by documents discovered in Mugunga camp in November 1996. Although these documents have never been published, some echoes can be found in extracts published in newspapers, for example *Le Monde*, November 19, 1996, and *Le Figaro*, November 20, 1996. It is surprising that neither the AFDL nor the RPA have kept these archives; on the contrary, they reportedly burned them. S. Boyle, "Rebels Repel Zaire Counter-Offensive," *Jane's Intelligence Review*, April 1, 1997. However, copies of a number of these papers are on file with this author.

26. On the fate of the Hutu refugees, see Reyntjens, *The Great African War*, pp. 80–101; Filip Reyntjens and René Lemarchand, "Mass Murder in Eastern Congo, 1996–1997," in *Forgotten Genocides: Oblivion, Denial, and Memory*, ed. René Lemarchand (Philadelphia: University of Pennsylvania Press, 2011), pp. 20–36.

27. R. Pourtier, "Congo-Zaïre-Congo: un itinéraire géopolitique au coeur de l'Afrique," *Hérodote* no. 86–87 (3rd–4th Term 1997), p. 27.

28. The more historical causes for the Angolan intervention in the war are addressed by T. Turner, "Angola's Role in the Congo War," in *The African Stakes of the Congo War*, ed. John Frank Clark (New York: Palgrave McMillan, 2002), pp. 77–81.

29. Thus, the Angolan weekly *Espresso* of May 3, 1997, affirmed that President Dos Santos insisted that Kabila should pursue his offensive to the end.

30. Having fled to Angola after the collapse of the Katangese secession in early 1963, a number of them were eventually integrated into the Angolan army, of which they—or rather, their sons—became the 24th Regiment in 1994.

31. As expressed by an astonishing post by Kagame on his Twitter account on May 8, 2015: "President #Kagame: If your citizens tell you we don't want you to lead us, how do you say I am staying whether you want me or not #Burundi." Coming from a president about the president of a neighboring country, the least one can say is that this very hostile communication was not aimed at appeasing bilateral relations.

32. Refugees International, *Asylum Betrayed: Recruitment of Burundian Refugees in Rwanda*, Washington, DC, December 14, 2015; UN Security Council, *Letter Dated 15 January 2016 from the Coordinator of the Group of Experts on the DRC to the Chair of the Committee*, S/AC.43/2016/COMM.2, January 15, 2016.

33. "US Accuses Rwanda of Stoking Violence in Burundi," *Daily Telegraph*, February 11, 2016.

34. The exact amount, due mainly to the state-owned Zimbabwe Defence Industries (ZDI), is unknown, but estimates range from US$40 million to US$200 million.

35. Zimbabwe happened to chair SADC's Organ on Politics, Defence, and Security. As Kabila's Congo had become a member of SADC, it benefited from a defense agreement providing for member states' assistance in case of an attack. However, South Africa and Botswana disagreed with the intervention in the DRC. Although presented as such by the coalition of the willing, it is doubtful whether the operation of Angola, Namibia, and Zimbabwe occurred under the SADC umbrella.

36. Other members of the club included Eritrea's Afewerki and Ethiopia's Meles Zenawi. All four eventually turned out to be just banal African dictators.

37. Addressing the Economic Commission for Africa in Addis Ababa on December 9, 1997, Secretary Madeleine Albright stated, without mentioning their names, that "Africa's best new leaders have brought a new spirit of hope and accomplishment to your countries—and that spirit is sweeping across the continent. . . . [Africa's new leaders] share a common vision of empowerment—for all their citizens, for their nations, and for their continent. . . . They are moving boldly to change the way their countries work—and the way we work with them."

38. Space prohibits a discussion of the mai-mai phenomenon. Suffice it to say that this is a generic term designating a wide array of local groups with very diverse organizational structures and ideologies, all claiming to protect the "indigenous" populations against exactions by "foreigners." A useful treatment can be found in Koen Vlassenroot, "The Making of a New Order: Dynamics of Conflict and Dialectics of War in South Kivu (DR Congo)" (PhD diss., University of Ghent, 2002), pp. 300–343. Vlassenroot insists on the fact that, although the mai-mai were also a resistance movement against foreign occupation, they can only be understood as an indigenous reaction to marginalization and exclusion. The theme of the mai-mai militias as an experience of more egalitarian forms of solidarity based social organization, with violence as its main discursive mode, is developed in Frank Van Acker and Koen Vlassenroot, "Les 'maï-maï' et les fonctions de la violence milicienne dans l'Est du Congo," *Politique Africaine* no. 84 (December 2001), pp. 103–116.

39. It is important to restate that, contrary to Rwandan claims (thus "justifying" the invasion by the RPA), this occurred *after* the beginning of the war. In other words, the Rwandan invasion was not a consequence of the involvement of "génocidaires" but rather its cause.

40. United Nations Security Council, *Final Report of the International Commission of Inquiry (Rwanda)*, November 18, 1998, S/1998/1096, paras 86–87.

41. International Crisis Group, *Scramble for the Congo: Anatomy of an Ugly War*, December 20, 2000, p. 19.

42. On this strange episode see Müller Ruhimbika, *Les Banyamulenge (Congo-Zaïre) entre deux guerres* (Paris, L'Harmattan, 2001), pp. 61–63: and Koen Vlassenroot, "Citizenship, Identity Formation and Conflict in South Kivu: The Case of the Banyamulenge," *Review of African Political Economy* no. 93 (2002), pp. 510–511.

43. *The East African*, August 30–September 5, 1999.

44. Gérard Prunier, "L'Ouganda et les guerres congolaises," *Politique Africaine* no. 75 (October 1999), p. 47.

45. A Congolese acquaintance of this author compared the fighting in Kisangani to two neighbors breaking into his house and then fighting in his living room over who would steal his television set.

46. The panel's early work was criticized on account of both its focus on the activities of the rebel groups and their sponsors as well as its definition of "illegality." Although these criticisms were not unfounded, the value of the panel's work is considerable: it has unearthed a large amount of empirical data and, in the later phase of its work, redressed the balance by inquiring into the predatory practices of the Kabila regime and its allies, Zimbabwe in particular.

47. UN Security Council, *Final Report of the Panel of Experts on the Illegal Exploitation of Natural Resources and Other Forms of Wealth of the Democratic Republic of the Congo*, S/2002/1146, October 16, 2002.

48. Christian Dietrich, *The Commercialisation of Military Deployment in Africa*, Pretoria, ISS, 2001; Christian Dietrich, *Hard Currency: The Criminalized Diamond Economy of the Democratic Republic of the Congo and Its Neighbours*, Occasional Paper #4 (Ottawa: Partnership Africa Canada, June 2002).

49. Several reports point to the direct link between the exploitation of resources and the continuation of the conflict. The UN Panel noted that the control of mineral-rich areas "could be seen primarily as an economic and financial objective rather than a security objective for Rwanda" (UN Security Council, *Report of the Panel of Experts on the Illegal Exploitation of Natural Resources and Other Forms of Wealth of the Democratic Republic of the Congo*, S/2001/357, April 12, 2001, para. 175); "Most of the fights between Rwandan soldiers and mai-mai have occurred in the so-called 'coltan belt'" (ibid., para. 176). Under the title "Rwanda's Unusual Tactics," the panel found that "attacks (by the RPA) seem to coincide with the period when coltan has been extracted and put in bags for evacuation by the mai-mai. Attacked, the mai-mai abandon their coltan, which is then taken away by small aircraft" (ibid., para. 177).

50. Ingrid Samset, "Conflict of Interests or Interests of Conflict? Diamonds and War in the DRC," *Review of African Political Economy* (2002), p. 477.

51. UN Security Council, *Final Report of the Group of Experts on the Democratic Republic of Congo, Pursuant to Security Council Resolution 1698 (2006)*, S/2007/423, July 18, 2007, para. 37.

52. Crawford Young, "Contextualizing Congo Conflicts: Order and Disorder in Postcolonial Africa," in Clark, *The African Stakes*, p. 25.

53. Indeed, post-1994 Rwanda has been called "an army with a state," rather than a state with an army. In the Kivus, the Rwandan army was nicknamed "Soldiers without borders," a wink to the international NGO "Médecins sans frontières."

54. Sénat de Belgique, *Rapport fait au nom de la commission d'enquête Grands Lacs par MM. Colla et Dallemagne*, session 2002–2003, February 20, 2003, no. 2–942/1, p. 72.

55. UN Security Council, *Report of the Panel of Experts*, para. 130.

56. This may seem a modest figure, but in light of the structure of the Rwandan economy it is gigantic. Indeed, in that same year, the production of export crops (mainly coffee and tea) only accounted for 0.4 percent of GDP (International Monetary Fund, *Rwanda: Selected Issues and Statistical Appendix*, IMF Country Report no. 04/383, 2004, p. 80).

57. Stefaan Marysse, "Regress and War: The Case of the DR Congo," *European Journal of Development Research* (2003), p. 88.

58. Of course, it was not really invisible, but the international community preferred to turn a blind eye to these practices. US Ambassador Gribbin, for one, candidly acknowledged this reality: "Rwanda had discovered during the first war that war in Congo was relatively cheap—even profitable. . . . [W]ell connected Rwandans . . . could seize opportunities . . . to accumulate wealth" (Gribbin, *In the Aftermath of Genocide*, pp. 282–283).

59. UN Security Council, *Letter Dated 16 October 2015 from the Coordinator of the Group of Experts Established Pursuant to Security Council Resolution 2198 (2015) Addressed to the President of the Security Council*, S.2015/797, October 16, 2015, p. 2.

60. Stephen Jackson, "Making a Killing: Criminality and Coping in the Kivu War Economy," *Review of African Political Economy* no. 93/94 (2002), p. 528.

61. International Crisis Group, *The Kivus: The Forgotten Crucible of the Congo Conflict*, Nairobi-Brussels, January 24, 2003.

62. UN Security Council, *Letter Dated 22 January 2014 from the Coordinator of the Group of Experts on the Democratic Republic of the Congo Addressed to the President of the Security Council*, S/2014/42, January 23, 2014.

63. UN Security Council, *Report of the Panel of Experts*, paras. 135–142.

64. Sénat de Belgique, *Rapport fait au nom de la commission*, p. 119.

65. UN Security Council, *Report of the Group of Experts on the Democratic Republic of the Congo*, S/2005/30, January 25, 2005, paras. 140–146.

66. Jeroen Cuvelier, "Réseaux de l'ombre et configurations régionales: le cas du commerce du coltan en République Démocratique du Congo," *Politique Africaine* no. 93 (2004), pp. 82–92.

67. Ian Taylor, "Conflict in Central Africa: Clandestine Networks & Regional/Global Configurations," *Review of African Political Economy* 30, no. 95 (2003), p. 48.

68. Ibid., p. 52.

69. The latter category of Rwandans was imported between 1937 and 1955 as workers as a result of deliberate policies by the Belgian colonial authorities, which even set up an agency (Mission d'immigration des Banyarwanda, MIB) to that effect.

70. These arrived mainly in 1959–1964, 1973, and 1990–1994.

71. These arrived massively in mid-1994.

72. See Jules Gérard-Libois, Jean Van Lierde, *Congo 1964* (Brussels: CRISP, 1965), pp. 79–80.

73. For details on earlier developments see, for example, Jean-Pierre Pabanel, "La question de la nationalité au Kivu," *Politique Africaine* no. 41 (March 1991), pp. 32–40; André Guichaoua, *Le problème des réfugiés rwandais et des populations banyarwanda dans la région des grands lacs africains* (Geneva: UNHCR, 1992); Patient Kanyamachumbi, *Les populations du Kivu et la loi sur la nationalité. Vraie ou fausse problématique* (Kinshasa: Editions Select, s.d., 1993); "Dossier: la 'guerre' de Masisi," *Dialogue* no. 192 (August–September 1996); Filip Reyntjens, Stefaan Marysse, *Conflits au Kivu: antécédents et enjeux* (Antwerp: Centre for the Study of the Great Lakes Region of Africa, 1996); Jean-Claude Willame, *Banyarwanda et Banyamulenge. Violences ethniques et gestion de l'identitaire au Kivu* (Brussels, Paris: Institut Africain-L'Harmattan, Cahiers Africains no. 25, 1997); Paul Mathieu, Jean-Claude Willame, eds., *Conflits et guerres au Kivu et dans la région des grands lacs: Entre tensions locales et escalade régionale* (Brussels, Paris: Institut Africain-L'Harmattan, Cahiers Africains no. 39–40, 1999).

74. For details see Willame, *Banyarwanda et Banyamulenge*, pp. 66–68, 124–131.

75. AZADO, *Nord-Kivu: Etat d'urgence*, Kinshasa, April 1996, p. 4. On August 3, 1996, the NGO SIMA-Kivu organized a conference in Brussels around the theme "Zaire-Rwanda-Burundi: Who Would Profit from the Creation of a Hutu-Land and a Tutsi-Land?"

76. US Committee for Refugees, *Masisi, Down the Road from Goma: Ethnic Cleansing and Displacement in Eastern Zaire* (Washington DC: June 1996), p. 16.

77. *ANB-BIA*, April 1, 1996.

78. Séverine Autesserre, *The Trouble with the Congo: Local Violence and the Failure of International Peacebuilding* (New York: Cambridge University Press, 2010).

79. Already in 1998 a UN investigative team concluded that "the systematic massacre of those (Hutu refugees) remaining in Zaire was an abhorrent crime against humanity, but the underlying rationale for the decision is material to whether these killings constituted genocide, that is, a decision to eliminate, in part, the Hutu ethnic group" (UN Security Council, *Report of the Investigative Team Charged with Investigating Serious Violations of*

Human Rights and International Humanitarian Law in the Democratic Republic of Congo, S/1998/581, June 29, 1998, para. 96). A mapping exercise conducted on behalf of the UN High Commission for Human Rights, published in 2010, confirmed and detailed a long list of atrocities uncovered earlier by UN panels, national and international NGOs, and investigative journalists. It concluded that the vast majority of the 617 listed incidents were to be classified as war crimes and crimes against humanity. On the issue of genocide it noted that "several incidents listed in this report, if investigated and judicially proven, point to circumstances and facts from which a court could infer the intention to destroy the Hutu ethnic group in the DRC in part, if these were established beyond all reasonable doubt" (UN Office of the High Commissioner for Human Rights, *Democratic Republic of the Congo, 1993–2003: Report of the Mapping Exercise Documenting the Most Serious Violations of Human Rights and International Humanitarian Law Committed Within the Territory of the Democratic Republic of the Congo Between March 1993 and June 2003,* Geneva, August 2010, para. 31).

80. See, for example, Victor Peskin, "Victor's Justice Revisited. Rwandan Patriotic Front Crimes and the Prosecutorial Endgame at the ICTR," in *Remaking Rwanda: State Building and Human Rights After Mass Violence,* ed. Scott Straus and Lars Waldorf (Madison: University of Wisconsin Press, 2011), pp. 173–183.

81. A report of the UN Group of Experts on the DRC offers ominous reading: UN Security Council, *Letter Dated 29 November 2011 from the Chair of the Security Council Committee Established Pursuant to Resolution 1533 (2004) Concerning the Democratic Republic of the Congo Addressed to the President of the Security Council,* S/2011/738, December 2, 2011. Also see Reyntjens, "Regulation, Taxation and Violence."

82. Filip Reyntjens, *Political Governance in Post-Genocide Rwanda* (New York: Cambridge University Press, 2013).

83. UN Security Council, *Letter Dated 29 November 2011,* paras 115–122, 284–288.

84. Ibid., paras. 484–492. For instance, the panel found that the house in Goma of General Bosco Ntaganda was on a street that crosses the border into Gisenyi, Rwanda, and that the entire area between the official border crossings was controlled exclusively by soldiers loyal to Ntaganda. The minerals were usually brought in vehicles into the neutral zone, after which they were carried to the Rwandan side, where they were loaded onto other vehicles. During smuggling operations Ntaganda's troops cut off all access to the area. Rwandan soldiers had sentry posts all along the border, and nothing could cross without their knowledge. The panel estimated that Ntaganda made about $15,000 per week by taxing at this crossing point (ibid., paras. 485–487).

85. UN Security Council, *Letter Dated 12 January 2015,* pp. 36–38.

Appendix 10.1: *Time Line*

1993
October 21. Coup d'état in Burundi; beginning of civil war.

1994
April–July. Resumption of the civil war in Rwanda; genocide against the Tutsi; RPF seizes power; 2 million Hutu, including defeated army and militia, flee to neighboring countries, Zaire in particular.

1995

Fall. Large-scale violence in North Kivu; hit-and-run operations by Rwandan Hutu refugees, operating from Zaire, against targets in Rwanda.

1996

September. Start of the "Banyamulenge rebellion" supported by Rwanda.

October. Creation in Kigali of AFDL, with Laurent-Désiré Kabila as its spokesperson.

October–December. AFDL, supported by Rwanda and Uganda, occupies a buffer zone in Eastern Zaire, stretching from Kalémie to Bunia.

1997

February. Angola joins the anti-Mobutu coalition.

May 17. Fall of Kinshasa.

May 29. Kabila sworn in as president of DRC, the new name of Zaire.

1998

August 2. Beginning of a new Congolese "rebellion" masterminded by Rwanda.

August 12. RCD rebel movement formally launched.

August 19. Deployment of Angolan, Zimbabwean, and Namibian troops in support of Kinshasa regime.

August 23. Fall of Kisangani.

November. Creation of another rebel movement, the MLC, with Ugandan support.

1999

May–June, August. Fighting between Rwandan and Ugandan armies in Kisangani.

July 10. Signing of the Lusaka Accord.

2000

June 5–10. Heavy fighting between Rwandan and Ugandan armies in Kisangani. Close to one thousand civilians killed. Widespread destruction.

2001

January 16. Assassination of Laurent-Désiré Kabila.

January 26. Joseph Kabila assumes office.

2002

February 25. Launch of the Inter-Congolese Dialogue in Sun City (South Africa).

September. Rwanda officially pulls out troops from the DRC but retains a covert presence.

December 17. Global and Inclusive Accord (AGI) signed in Pretoria.

2003

June. European IEMF force deployed in Ituri; replaced by MONUC Ituri brigade in September.

June–July. 1+4 Presidency, transitional government and transitional parliament in place.

2005

December 18–19. Constitution adopted by referendum.

2006

July 30. First round of presidential elections: Kabila 44.81 percent, Bemba 20.03 percent, Gizenga 13.06 percent; parliamentary elections: PPRD 111 seats, MLC 64, PALU 34, RCD-Goma 15.

October 29. Second round of presidential elections: Kabila 58.05 percent, Bemba 41.95 percent.

December. Creation of the CNDP rebel movement headed by Laurent Nkunda.

2008

August. Heavy fighting between FARDC and CNDP; Congolese government accused Rwanda of backing Nkunda; Rwanda denies.

2009

January. Joint DRC–Rwanda operation against CNDP; Nkunda replaced by Bosco Ntaganda and placed under house arrest in Rwanda.

March. Peace deal between DRC government and CNDP.

March–August. Joint FARDC-MONUSCO operation "Kimia 2" against FDLR.

2010

October. Publication of UN Mapping Report on gross human rights violations 1993–2003; claims a number of acts committed by AFDL/RPA might constitute genocide.

2011

January. DRC constitution amended, introducing relative as opposed to the previous absolute majority for presidential election.

November. Presidential elections: Kabila 48.95 percent, Tshisekedi 32.33 percent; parliamentary elections: PPRD largest party in highly fragmented parliament; legitimacy of elections contested domestically and internationally.

2012

April. Creation of rebel movement M23, an offspring of the CNDP.

October. UN Group of Experts accuses Rwanda and Uganda of supporting M23; both countries deny.

November. M23 briefly occupies North Kivu provincial capital Goma.

2013

March. Bosco Ntaganda surrenders to the ICC.

July. UN Force Intervention Brigade (FIB) deployed to disarm rebel groups.

November. M23 defeated by FARDC and MONUSCO/FIB.

2015

April. Burundi President Nkurunziza candidate for unconstitutional third term; announcement followed by violence; elections take place, but until the end of 2015 hundreds are killed and over two hundred thousand flee into exile.

December. Constitutional amendment allows President Kagame to run a third time in 2017 and possibly to remain in power until 2034.

2016

January. Several reports show Rwandan support for a nascent Burundian rebellion.

Appendix 10.2: Main Actors

Alliance des Forces pour la Libération du Congo-Zaïre (AFDL): Rwanda- and Uganda-backed rebel group led by Laurent-Désiré Kabila that overthrew the Mobutu regime in May 1997.

Banyamulenge: Congolese Tutsi group living in South Kivu; started the war in September 1996 with the support of Rwanda.

Banyarwanda: Kinyarwanda speakers living in Eastern DRC; both Hutu and Tutsi.

Jean-Pierre Bemba: Leader of the MLC rebel movement; unsuccessful presidential candidate in 2006; indicted by the ICC for war crimes committed in the Central African Republic.

Congrès National pour la Défense du Peuple (CNDP): Congolese Tutsi militia, formally integrated in FARDC, supported by Rwanda; its leader, Laurent Nkunda, arrested by Rwanda in early 2009, replaced by Bosco Ntaganda.

Force Intervention Brigade (FIB): Deployed from April 2013 in support of FARDC and MONUSCO to neutralize armed groups; troops contributed by South Africa, Tanzania, and Malawi; defeated M23 in November 2013.

Forces Armées Rwandaises (FAR): Former Rwandan government army that retreated to Eastern Zaire after its defeat in the summer of 1994 and conducted raids against Rwanda from the refugee camps in 1995–1996.

Forces Armées Zaïroises (FAZ)/Forces Armées Congolaises (FAC)/Forces Armées de la République Démocratique du Congo (FARDC): Successive names of the Zairean/Congolese government army.

Forces Démocratiques pour la Libération du Rwanda (FDLR): Rwandan Hutu rebel movement operating in Eastern DRC.

Joseph Kabila: Son of Laurent-Désiré Kabila, who succeeded his father as president in January 2001; elected president in 2006; reelected in 2011.

Laurent-Désiré Kabila: Leader of the AFDL; became president in May 1997; assassinated in January 2001.

Paul Kagame: Leader of the RPF/RPA; de facto ruler of Rwanda since 1994; became president in 2000; elected in 2003; reelected in 2010.

Mai-mai: Local militias operating in North and South Kivu; claim to protect local populations against "invaders."

Mobutu Sese Seko: President of Zaire from 1965 to 1997; overthrown by Laurent-Désiré Kabila in May 1997; died a few months later in exile in Morocco.

Mouvement du 23 mars (M23): Successor to the CNDP; created in April 2012 with Rwandan support; defeated by FARDC and FIB in November 2013.

Mouvement de Libération du Congo (MLC): Uganda-backed rebel movement created in November 1998; its leader, Jean-Pierre Bemba, unsuccessfully ran for president in 2006.

Yoweri Museveni: President of Uganda since 1986.

Bosco Ntaganda: Leader of the CNDP and general in the FARDC; indicted by ICC for war crimes committed in Ituri.

Rassemblement Congolais pour la Démocratie (RCD): Rwanda-backed rebel group that started a war against the Kabila regime in August 1998.

Rwanda Defence Forces: Rwandan national army (formerly RPA).

Rwanda Patriotic Front/Army (RPF/A): Tutsi-dominated movement that started a rebellion in October 1990 and took power in July 1994; de facto single party.

Uganda People's Defence Forces (UPDF): Ugandan national army.

União Nacional para a Independência Total de Angola (UNITA): Angolan rebel movement defeated in 2008.

Union des Patriotes Congolais (UPC): Main Ituri militia group; its leader, Thomas Lubanga, was the first to be convicted by the ICC in 2012.

UN Organization Stabilization Mission in the Democratic Republic of the Congo (MONUSCO): Known until 2010 as MONUC, a peacekeeping force established in 1999.

Boko Haram and Nigeria State Weakness

John Campbell

INTRODUCTION

Fighting between Boko Haram, a radical Islamist movement based in northeast Nigeria, and the Nigerian security services, mostly the army, killed at least 20,000 people between 2009 and 2016 and resulted in up to 3 million internally displaced persons. In 2014 the Institute for Economics and Peace (IEP) calculated that Boko Haram had killed 6,664 people that year, almost 600 more than the self-proclaimed Islamic State. IEP then characterized Boko Haram as the world's deadliest terror group.[1] The argument of this chapter is that weak governance, exploitive elites, a poorly developed sense of national identity, growing impoverishment, and an Islamic religious revival set the stage for Boko Haram.

In northern Nigeria the Islamic religious revival is influenced by rival theologies of Saudi Arabian and Iranian origin that are broadly critical of the secular Nigerian state and of the traditional Islamic establishment. Adherents do not so much seek to reform the secular nation-state as to replace it with Islamic governance in a new form. (They do not agree among themselves as to the practicalities of this new form, only that it should be Islamic.) Popular access to the Internet and social media as well as the increasing popularity of pilgrimages to Mecca have fueled this broader revival. They are an important part of the context for Boko Haram.

The struggle between Boko Haram and the official security services ebbs and flows. In March 2015 the Nigerian army, supported by Chadian troops and South African–led mercenaries, drove Boko Haram out of a territory about as large as Maryland. However, the movement has regrouped, and although it no longer focuses primarily on holding territory, it killed over two hundred in the months of January and February 2016. Increasingly, it attacks soft targets, often using female suicide bombers. In February 2016, however, Boko Haram once again used more conventional military tactics, including having its fighters wear military uniforms, while continuing its suicide bombing campaign. It remains to be seen what tactical direction Boko Haram will next take.

Boko Haram's stated goal is to establish God's kingdom on earth through justice for the poor, to be achieved by means of strict implementation of Islamic law, or shar'ia. To fulfill this vision Boko Haram seeks the destruction through violence of the current secular Nigerian state, which it regards as evil. What is unique about Boko Haram is that it kills those whom it regards as Muslim apostates—those Muslims who have "sold out" to and participate in the secular state. This includes much of the traditional Islamic establishment. If Boko Haram is in some sense a millenarian religious movement, it is also an insurrection against elites, and it does not hesitate to use criminal methods. It neither respects nor follows the traditional Islamic limits imposed on the use of violence during a "jihad," or the struggle to preserve true religion. For example, contrary to traditional Islamic practice during a jihad, women and children are often victims of Boko Haram.

There exists scant information on Boko Haram's internal structure and leadership. The media face of the movement has been Abubakar Shekau. Once highly visible, not least in grisly videos featuring beheadings, he disappeared from sight in 2015–2016. In the summer of 2016 he reappeared when the Islamic State, to which he had pledged allegiance, demoted him as the leader of its West African province. Since then there have been at least two Boko Haram factions that often fight each other. One is led by Shekau; the other by the Islamic State–imposed leader, Abu Musab al-Barnawi. Shekau, however, has not renounced his allegiance to IS. Although there may be a supreme council, or *shura*, its membership is unknown, and evidence of even its existence is not definitive. Little also is known about the depth of popular support Boko Haram enjoys. However, a 2015 poll by the Pew Research Center found that about one Nigerian Muslim in five was favorably inclined toward the Islamic State.[2] An earlier 2014 poll indicated that around 10 percent of Nigerians of all religions were favorably disposed toward Boko Haram.[3] If that is true, Boko Haram sympathizers would number in the millions.[4] Hence, it is likely that the movement can draw on a deep reservoir of support or acquiescence.

Although Boko Haram's killing of Christians has been widely publicized in Europe and the United States, estimates are that about two-thirds of its victims have been other Muslims. Human rights organizations estimate the security services have killed at least eight thousand people between 2011 and 2016, and too often they fail to differentiate between civilians and Boko Haram fighters. Security service abuse of the civilian population appears to be an important driver of Boko Haram recruitment.[5]

The struggle in northern Nigeria should be understood as a civil war between two approaches to Islam: that of Boko Haram and some of the dispossessed, and the traditional, broadly tolerant Sufi Islam that has been characteristic of West Africa. The latter is closely associated with the Sultan of Sokoto, the Shehu of Borno, the traditional Muslim establishment, and Muhammadu Buhari, inaugurated president of the Federal Republic in 2015. Sufi Islam focuses on individual spirituality and is infused by an African traditional culture far removed from that of the Middle East, and its adherents fully participate in the secular state.

ELEMENTS OF STATE WEAKNESS
Weak Nigerian Governance

How can we account for the rise and persistence of a murderous movement, ostensibly Islamic, in its own eyes at least, that seeks to destroy Nigeria as a state and make war on the traditional Muslim elite in the northeast? For adherents to Boko Haram, the concept of Nigeria, Nigerian national identity, and the Nigerian federal government are not Islamic and have no validity. Similarly, in its view the Muslim elites that support the secular state are not genuinely Islamic. From Boko Haram's perspective, those who participate in governing the Nigerian state are nothing less than apostates. As such, following seventh-century Islamic texts, Boko Haram deems them as deserving to die or, if female, to be sold into slavery.

Since the 1999 restoration of a nominally civilian government after a generation of military rule, the secular Nigerian state has failed to deliver good governance ("justice for the poor"). Failed by the secular state, northern Nigerians—Christians as well as Muslims—have turned to religion: among Muslims the most radical form of Salafist Islam; among Christians, varieties of "African" and Pentecostal churches.

Especially in the aftermath of the 1967–1970 civil war over the Biafra secession attempt and the coming of oil riches that accelerated during the Babangida, Obasanjo, and Jonathan administrations, Nigeria has had the misfortune of a political system shaped by fraud, embezzlement, and violence. Much of the criminal behavior has its roots in politics, and perpetrators are often elites connected to the secular state and isolated from the people that Islam charges them to support and lead. Poor and corrupt governance on the backs of the poor prepares the way for an antigovernment, anti-establishment movement such as Boko Haram.[6]

A root cause of Boko Haram's persistence is the isolation of the secular state and the northern elites from the mass of the population in northeast Nigeria. Many Nigerians who do not resort to the violence characteristic of Boko Haram share a similar sense of alienation from the secular state. Boko Haram is largely an indigenous movement, though it is influenced by theology and rhetoric from the Middle East. (The Saudis, especially, were responsible for the propagation of their Salafist interpretation of Sunni Islam across the Sahel and the Iranians for the introduction of Shia Islam, both of whom reject the traditional, tolerant, Sufi-inspired Islam once characteristic of northern Nigeria and supportive of a secular state.)

The quality of Nigerian governance has varied considerably since independence in 1960. However, its trajectory has been especially negative during the period in which Boko Haram has been active. Corruption has long been endemic in Nigeria. It accelerated during the 1967–1970 civil war and especially after oil distorted and transformed the economy for the worse, also starting in about 1970. Already salient during the days of military rule, corruption worsened during the 1999–2007 administration of Olusegun Obasanjo and the 2007–2010 Umaru Yar'Adua interlude administration. But during the 2010–2015 Goodluck Jonathan administration, new kleptocratic thresholds were breached.[7] Corruption diverted so much funding intended for the security services that soldiers went into combat against Boko Haram without sufficient ammunition. It remains to be seen whether the reform agenda of President Muhammadu Buhari will reverse the downward direction of the Nigerian state and its security services that provides such fertile ground for Boko Haram.

Weak Nigerian Identity

The euphoria at independence in 1960 and the optimistic national mood before the military handover to civilians in 1979 and again in 1999 as well as the popular excitement following Buhari's election victory in 2015 masked the historical and structural weaknesses of Nigerian identity.[8] There was little commonality inherited from the past to support a nation-state on the Western model. Instead, Nigeria's postindependence, first-generation political leaders looked to establish something new in Africa: a multiethnic, multireligious state based on democracy and the rule of law at home and with the heft to give Africa a seat at the international table. For them Nigerian national identity would be newly created. Rather than a shared history, culture, or religion, it would be based on shared ideals. As elsewhere in Nigeria, only some among the northern Muslim elites bought in to this vision. For the vision to have been achieved would have required a high level of governance and exceptional political skill on the part of elites, perhaps the equivalent of George Washington and America's other eighteenth-century founding fathers. Alas, for Nigeria such leaders have been lacking.

Parts of the current territory of Nigeria were the location of culturally rich precolonial civilizations. There was a succession of Hausa-Fulani, Yoruba, and other empires before the British completed their conquest of the present territory of Nigeria. Ancient civilizations and empires shaped the peoples where they held sway. But none of the early empires incorporated into a single political unit all or even much of the territory of the present state. Nor, unlike in the period of the American founding fathers, was there an overarching cultural unity among the hundreds of different ethnic groups that are present in the current Nigeria: the American founding fathers identified themselves as being of one ethnicity— British, speaking one language, English, and with one or two exceptions were of one religion, protestant Christianity. By contrast, Nigeria was and is made up of some 350 different ethnicities and languages, with the population now divided between two world religions, Christianity and Islam, and myriad traditional religious practices. Nigeria's competing and cooperating elites never really adopted a vision of a national identity based on shared ideals. The vision of Nigeria as a nation-state in the Western sense had little resonance.

The Colonial Legacy

The nation and the concept of a Nigerian national identity are British creations. In 1914, for administrative expediency, the British cobbled together their Nigerian colony out of disparate but adjacent territories acquired over a century, the acquisition of which had been motivated by a mixture of commercial, strategic, and humanitarian concerns. As was generally the case with colonial rule in Africa, British decisions about governance were made without reference to the indigenous populations. They gave little consideration to the long-term political and social consequences of amalgamating highly diverse populations and cultures into a single political entity, and they exhibited no interest in creating a Nigerian identity.[9]

At the time the main argument for amalgamation was administrative convenience. It would allow the governor-general to create a single budget for all the geographically adjacent territories acquired by the United Kingdom since 1861. The British goal was to keep the costs of governance to a minimum. Amalgamation did achieve that goal, and governance of Nigeria was almost entirely paid for by itself, not the British taxpayer. The name "Nigeria" is credited to the colonial editor of the *Times* of London, Flora Shaw, who later married the new entity's first royal governor, Lord Frederick Lugard. The moniker stuck.

As in their Indian empire, the British followed the principle of "indirect rule" in Nigeria. They imposed a colonial administration on top of indigenous emirates, kingdoms, and tribal structures. In principle, the colonial government dealt with foreign affairs and the development of national institutions. Local, traditional authorities would carry out judicial and policing tasks, raise local revenues, and implement "development" as determined by the colonial authorities. The idea was that by such a division of responsibilities, traditional society would advance gradually toward modernization, self-rule, "Western civilization," and, ultimately, independence but only far in the future. Where no traditional rulers existed, the British did not hesitate to create them, even if they generated little popular respect locally. In the meantime indirect rule facilitated the economic development and exploitation of Nigeria's resources for the benefit of British finance and industry.

The authority of traditional rulers was based on their ethnic group's cohesiveness and distinctiveness from other groups. Hence, indirect rule tended to reinforce the most conservative elements of traditional behavior and discouraged supra-ethnic cooperation. Colonial officials found themselves balancing the policy of indirect rule, with its dependence on indigenous authorities, and the need to enforce British law that in turn reflected British standards not necessarily shared by the people they ostensibly governed. In northern Nigeria British conquest followed by indirect rule paradoxically strengthened the emirate system and tied local elites to the British administration.

Indirect rule implies a partnership between the British and local elites, albeit one heavily weighted in favor of the colonial administration. Especially in northern Nigeria, traditional rulers were the final link in the colonial administrative chain. It was through them that decisions made in London and Lagos were enforced locally. In northern Nigeria, traditional rulers were aristocratic and autocratic. Unlike in other parts of Nigeria, it was easy for the British to identify indigenous partners for indirect rule. Though hard to quantify, there was an affinity between many British administrators and northern, traditional rulers, and vice versa. Both often identified with aristocratic ideals and, horses were an important part of their lives for both.

Indeed, northern traditional rulers' power and authority has steadily declined with the end of British rule. With independence, in effect, the dependence of traditional rulers shifted from the British to Nigerian politicians, many of whom were unsympathetic. Under the current republic the formal responsibilities of traditional rulers are almost entirely ceremonial.[10] However, they retain considerable local influence in some areas. When Boko Haram was occupying territory, it often marked for killing the local emir as well as the local imam. It has attempted to kill both the Sultan of Sokoto and the Shehu of Bornu, the most senior of northern traditional rulers.

Hence, the British created Nigeria, but not a Nigerian nation. There were no real national institutions until near the end of the colonial period, when the British established the Nigerian army and police, a small number of high-quality secondary schools that drew students countrywide, and a university college. In the north the British established a handful of schools intended for the children of the traditional elites and reflecting Western values. These also served to encourage the separation of elites from the mass of the northern population, and at present they are a focus of Boko Haram rage. Even now, sixty years after independence, primary and secondary education for nonelites in northern Nigeria is weak, much weaker than in other parts of the country. To fill the void, many turn to Islamic schools, or madrassas, where the focus is on memorization of the Qur'an and, in effect, a rejection of Western education and values as not Islamic. Today those schools enroll up to 12 million students that are ill-prepared to participate in a modern economy.

Also discouraging the emergence of national politics that might have supported the growth of a Nigerian common identity, the structure of governance varied within the new country; British rule in the north was very different from that in the south. In the north, to maintain the emirate system, the British discouraged Christian missionary activity. This meant no Western schools in most areas (except for the elites) and few hospitals or clinics. The British also left in place shar'ia, the traditional Islamic legal system. These measures in effect perpetuated much of the north's precolonial civilization.

In the run-up to independence the British promulgated a variety of constitutional instruments, but there was no process of popular ratification of a constitution. Colonial masters imposed governments—they did not evolve from the people. Politics was regionally and ethnically based rather than national in nature. There never was a nationwide independence movement fueled by a shared idealism and vision for the future. As early as 1944, sixteen years before independence, US consul Andrew Lynch traveling in northern Nigeria wrote, "I have formed the opinion that . . . [for] the majority of the Africans I have met . . . self-government offers simply an unparalleled opportunity for self-advancement. Personal gain seemed to be the controlling motive and they have not developed that sense of responsibility toward their own people which, after all, must be the first qualification for self-government."[11]

Many of the characteristics of postindependence Nigerian governance emerged from the British colonial experience. After independence the pattern has been national and state governments imposed on the population by elites, local and national. These national governments have not been accountable to the Nigerian people any more than the colonial administration had been. Politics has largely been a process of elite bargaining. National governments have encouraged the establishment of states, now numbering thirty-six, that seemingly reflect the principle of federalism and the fragmentation of the population into hundreds of different ethnic groups. But for most of Nigeria's postindependence history the central government has kept the states under its control because it is the primary source of their revenue. For many Nigerian critics the country remains essentially a colonial state, with local elites having merely replaced the British and politicians the traditional rulers. For Boko Haram that reality is fundamentally contrary to Islam and must be destroyed.

Poverty

Poverty is the context in which most Nigerians live and in which Boko Haram operates. However, poverty cannot be seen as the sole or even predominant cause of Islamic radicalism. Most Nigerians are poor, but most are nonviolent and eschew radicalism. Rather, poverty interacts with other, more abstract factors, such as religion, ideology, and a wider sense of political marginalization. How that interaction occurs varies from individual to individual as well as from community to community.

British administration—based on the rule of law, effective policing, and, eventually, a strong civil service—did promote economic development. The country became the breadbasket of West Africa, and a significant manufacturing sector emerged. Railways and roads were built. By the time of independence Nigeria's level of economic development was seen as similar to that of Taiwan, Malaysia, and Thailand. However, after 1970 Nigeria became a victim of the "oil curse." Oil sucked up the capital from other parts of the economy. Very high oil prices resulted in the overvaluation of the currency, which made imports cheap and exports expensive. (Elites became notorious for their taste for imported goods, such as French Champagne.) At independence Nigeria had a sizable agricultural export sector; now Nigeria is a net importer of food. Indigenous manufacturing also collapsed, no longer competitive in the international market. Oil is a commodity and, thus, subject to price booms and busts. In periods when oil was high the Nigerian state spent massively; when oil prices fell, it borrowed, resulting in high levels of indebtedness.

Because oil is the property of the state, the way to get rich was to capture the state, not through productive economic activity. The federal government distributed a significant portion of the oil revenue by formula to each state and to local governments. (The oil-producing states received a larger percentage than the others.) All over Nigeria, but especially in the north, a tiny elite with government connections and access to oil revenue through favorable contracts became richer and richer while the mass of the population became poorer and poorer. In the northeast a very high birthrate and a youth bulge are causes of unemployment and poverty. So, too, is agricultural decline, resulting from underinvestment exacerbated by climate change, water shortages, and the Sahara's march south into what had been productive grazing lands.

Religion

From a secular, Western perspective, religion in the Sahel is turbocharged. Causation of events, large and small, is ascribed to the divine. The end times are near, among Christians as well as Muslims. Almost everybody in what Westerners would regard as secular circumstances uses faith vocabulary.[12]

In northern Nigeria popular protest against the established order and state corruption usually takes the form of radical Islamic renewal. One of these movements was Izala, founded in 1978.[13] It was followed by the Maitatsine and Kalo Kato.[14] The most recent is Boko Haram, which became politicized after an elite faction enlisted it to support a gubernatorial candidate in return for influence over local religious policy.

Since the end of the civil war in 1970 Islam in northern Nigeria and the broader Sahel region of West Africa has come more and more to resemble Saudi Arabia's Wahabism, with its literal reading of the Qur'an and other sacred texts.

Saudi missionaries and Saudi money helped strengthen that approach by building mosques and Islamic schools. Those influenced rejected the alleged "accretions" to Islam from African traditional religions that Sufism would tolerate, such as veneration of local saints. Hence in Timbuktu, Mali, in 2012 Salafist radicals destroyed the ancient tombs of such saints, which were UNESCO World Heritage Sites.

BOKO HARAM
History

The group now known as Boko Haram emerged in Maiduguri, the capital of Borno state in the northeast of Nigeria late in the decade of the 1990s. It was hostile to the secular state from its very beginning. The moniker *Boko Haram* was first applied in the Railway Quarter, a Maiduguri neighborhood, to the followers of a radical malam, Mohammed Yusuf. Boko is the Hausa word for "book" and commonly refers to Western education. Haram is the Arabic word for "forbidden." Some members of Yusuf's movement styled themselves as "People Committed to the Prophet's Teaching and Jihad." Others, however, have observed that the broader movement had no overarching name for itself. Instead, local people called it by many different names. The Nigerian government and the media employed the moniker Boko Haram, applying it to virtually all antigovernment activity in the north, thereby imposing undue coherence on a diffuse, often localized revolt.[15]

Mohammed Yusuf's specific group started as a small and marginal part of the larger movement of Islamic protest in the north, which was usually nonviolent.[16] Boko Haram's transformation from a largely peaceful into a violent movement was encouraged if not entirely caused by security service brutality, especially the army and police murder of Mohammed Yusuf and some eight hundred of his followers in 2009.[17] (Al-Barnawi, the leader of the faction opposed to Shekau, is probably a son of Mohammed Yusuf.)

A New Revolution

With its highly diffuse, religious, even millenarian dimensions, Boko Haram (including Yusuf's followers and successors) might constitute a new type of "revolution" in Nigeria because it aims at creating a polity through violence and rage but without a political program or even much of a structure. Intensely parochial, it defies conventional analysis based on the precedents of the French, Russian, or even Iranian revolutions. It also does not fit with the Arab Spring, lacking any democratic aspirations. Nor does it fit into the internationalist al-Qaeda or jihadist framework, though it shares the same Islamic rhetoric. In March 2015 Yusuf's surviving followers, led by Abubakar Shekau, swore some type of allegiance to the Islamic State, but it is unclear whether that act has any practical consequence.

Boko Haram in 2016 appears to be embedded in northeastern Nigerian society. In February the Nigerian military announced it was closing certain markets because they were the venues where Boko Haram traded. The Nigerian army claimed Boko Haram was selling smuggled goods to acquire the supplies that it needs. Apparently the trade was open and seemingly involved the larger community.

Since its reemergence in 2011 Boko Haram's operations have primarily been in Borno, Yobe, and Adamawa states. However, it has carried out successful attacks in Abuja and Kano and occasionally operated in the Middle Belt, the borderlands between Nigeria's predominately Christian and predominately Muslim populations. There have been no reported operations in the oil patch and only one in Lagos. The oil patch has its own, indigenous insurrection, and there is little evidence of it cooperating with Boko Haram. Perhaps half of the population of Lagos is Muslim, but it appears to have little interest in radical jihadi movements. Up to now Boko Haram's focus has been mostly on the predominately Islamic north. If Boko Haram and the Islamic State do draw closer together tactically and strategically, that could change, and Lagos and the oil patch could become a venue of terrorist attacks.

Beliefs and Ideology

Boko Haram's belief system is Salafist. A central religious principle is what the Islamic State describes as "prophetic methodology." This principle requires following in punctilious detail the seventh-century prophecies and behaviors of the Prophet Muhammad and his closest associates. This includes dress, family life, punishments, and warfare, including methods of execution that vary according to the crime or the nature of the apostasy from Islam. In this way Boko Haram resembles the way of thinking propagated by the Islamic State in Syria and Iraq.

For the Islamic State, Boko Haram, and other radical Salafist movements, there are many acts that remove a Muslim from Islam. They include selling alcohol, wearing Western clothes, voting in an election, and, especially for Boko Haram, participating in secular education. A person excommunicated is an apostate, an infidel. The seventh-century penalty for an infidel was death, and women associated with infidels or were infidels themselves were war booty and to be sold into slavery. And so it is today, with Boko Haram as well as the Islamic State.

But Boko Haram has a specifically Nigerian flavor. Its terrorism is a reaction to Nigeria's corrupt political economy, exploitation of the poor, and security service abuses. Boko Haram's rhetorical focus on providing for the poor highlights that it is, among other things, an insurrection of the poor against the rich, within a specifically Islamic context. However, it has published no concrete plan for economic development or poverty alleviation. In that sense it resembles more a religious cult than a political party.

Between 2011 and early 2015 Boko Haram destroyed federal, state, and local authority in the territory it occupied. However, little is known about how Boko Haram administered the territory it occupied, beyond establishing shar'ia courts. It is even unclear whether Boko Haram sought to collect taxes in any systematic way. However, in the run-up to the March 2015 elections the Nigerian military, making use of South African mercenaries, along with Chadian and Nigerian forces drove Boko Haram out of the territories it had occupied. Boko Haram's withdrawal led to the emancipation of several hundred women and girls who were being held as slaves, but not the famous Chibok schoolgirls.[18] Boko Haram nevertheless continued to kidnap girls and women.

Boko Haram and the Islamic State

The Islamic State is, among other things, a Middle Eastern terrorist organization with millenarian goals espoused by some of its leaders, especially Abu Bakr al-Baghdadi. It is shaped by the politics of the aftermath of the Iraq war and the civil war in Syria as well as by a millenarian vision. In contrast, Boko Haram more resembles a peasants' revolt against the Nigerian political class that uses Islamic vocabulary and imagery.

Thus far Boko Haram's links to the Islamic State have little strategic importance and do not extend much beyond a rhetorical and theological similarity. The Islamic State and Boko Haram do make use of similar symbols, reflecting their common Salafist heritage. Boko Haram appears to have borrowed images from the Islamic State for its social media campaign. Otherwise there is little if any evidence of strategic or tactical cooperation, much less coordination between the two movements. Nor is there evidence that the Islamic State provides financial subsidies to Boko Haram.

But what about Boko Haram's swearing of allegiance to the Islamic State in March 2015 and Shekau's 2016 demotion as leader of its West African province? What does that mean? It was Abubakar Shekau who did the swearing. It has never been clear what authority he actually has within the movement. One credible but unproved hypothesis is that it was he only who swore allegiance to the Islamic State in Syria, having little or no impact on the Boko Haram movement in Nigeria.

There is also a difference of focus. Boko Haram's stated goal is the destruction of the Nigerian secular state. It does not seem to share the much broader, internationalist goals of the Islamic State. Boko Haram is not much interested in the United States or the West in general. There have been no attacks on Western facilities, which, it is true, are thin on the ground in northern Nigeria. There is no equivalent in Boko Haram of the former supporters of Iraq's Baathist regime in the Islamic State. Unlike the Islamic State, Boko Haram has attracted no European or American fighters. Within Boko Haram the end-times or millenarian vision of the Islamic State's spiritual leader al-Baghdadi is much muted.

RESPONSES TO BOKO HARAM
President Muhammadu Buhari

In his 2015 inauguration address, Muhammadu Buhari sketched out his approach to Boko Haram. As does President Obama, he denies that Boko Haram is an authentic form of Islam. He said, "Boko Haram is a mindless, godless group who are as far away from Islam as one can think of." For President Buhari, Boko Haram is a criminal movement that uses terror, and it can be destroyed by conventional, military means.

President Buhari laid out certain new practical steps. The most important was an overhaul of the security services' rules of engagement to reduce human rights violations in operations. He said that his administration will improve operational and legal mechanisms so that disciplinary steps are taken against proven human rights violations by the armed forces. He also said that the military campaign's headquarters would be moved from Abuja, the national capital, to Maiduguri until Boko Haram is defeated. He announced the establishment of a new military unit to be based in Maiduguri. He also appointed the well-regarded retired general Theophilus Danjuma as a tsar in the northeast to coordinate military and civilian responses to Boko Haram and the horrific humanitarian challenges.

Buhari is also addressing the widespread corruption within the Nigerian military. He has ordered the investigation of a former national security advisor and a host of retired senior officers who may have siphoned off funding intended for the military effort against Boko Haram. Buhari's approach to Nigeria's notoriously bad governance is not structural reform of government institutions; rather, it is putting good people into high office and holding them accountable.

Multinational Cooperation Against Boko Haram

Nigerian-led coordination of Chad, Cameroon, and Niger in the fight against Boko Haram—a signature Buhari goal—is inherently difficult to achieve. There is long-standing suspicion of Anglophone Nigeria by Francophone Chad, Cameroon, and Niger, not least because of its size. Early in his career Buhari himself was involved in a military response to Chadian incursions on Nigerian territory. There is not the culture or habit of operational cooperation among the four states. They are not even all members of the same regional organization: Nigeria and Niger are members of the Economic Community of West African States (ECOWAS), and Chad and Cameroon are members of the Economic Community of Central African States (ECCAS).

Chad and Cameroon especially are also characterized by poor governance. Chadian president Idriss Déby Itno has been in office for twenty-five years. Chad and Niger are subject to attempted military coups—apparently there was an attempted coup in Niamey, the capital of Niger, in early 2016. Cameroonian president Paul Biya has been in office thirty-three years. His Christian government has marginalized Muslim northern Cameroon. Indigenous support for Boko Haram in Cameroon and Chad cannot be ruled out, with a common ethnic and religious identity to be found among adjacent districts in the two states as well as with northeast Nigeria.

Finally, all four countries are desperately poor. Niger and Chad are much poorer than Nigeria and are among the poorest countries in the world. It says something about the quality of their governance that Chad's Déby Itno's personal wealth is estimated at $50 million, while Cameroon's Biya's is estimated to be $200 million. Despite the wealth of the chiefs of state, sustained military effort will require massive foreign assistance. It is unclear whether the United States, the UK, or France, the most likely donors, have the political will to deepen their involvement in the Sahel.

THE FUTURE OF BOKO HARAM

It is difficult to see how the Boko Haram movement will end. Unlike other insurrections, it has not moved to create an alternative government, even when it occupied significant amounts of territory. In the past, millenarian religious movements in northern Nigeria have burned themselves out. But if little is done to address the core grievances of the north, even if the Nigerian government destroys the current, splintered Boko Haram leadership, about which we know remarkably little, it will endure in some form as a violent movement with a populist base.

President Muhammadu Buhari charged the security services to defeat Boko Haram by December 2015.[19] That month President Buhari declared victory, by which he meant that Boko Haram had been dislodged from the territory it had once occupied. Since then Boko Haram activities, especially killings, have continued. Yet the Nigerian military reports one success after another. On October 26, 2015, Lieutenant General Tukur Buarati, the chief of army staff and an appointee of President Buhari, made public reference to the "new" brigade deployed in the northeast, though it is not clear whether this is the augmentation of military strength promised by President Buhari or a redeployment. The Nigerian media reports that in remarks to his soldiers he said, "You are better trained and equipped than the criminals and you have to be professional and responsive. You should have no excuse not to be on patrol, ambush, or raid operations." He went on to say, "We have to maintain the momentum to achieve Mr. President's deadline. We must eradicate insurgency and make Nigeria peaceful."[20]

The alternative narrative starts with ongoing Boko Haram terrorism. As late as 2014 there were attacks in Abuja and in Kogi state, not where Boko Haram usually operates. However, more recently attacks have been concentrated in Borno and Yobe states. The security services claimed to have arrested a Boko Haram cell in Lagos.[21] If true, that would indicate that Boko Haram is trying to build a capacity to operate in Africa's largest city. It is not clear whether the army has entirely dislodged Boko Haram from the territory it occupied, as the Abuja government claims. Borno state governor Kashim Shettima said on October 26, 2015, that Boko Haram occupies two local government areas in his state, Abbam and Mobar, and partially controls a third, Marte.[22] But he also said that in the past Boko Haram had "overrun" twenty of the twenty-seven local government areas in the state, an indication that the territory the movement directly controls is much reduced. In the meantime Boko Haram's depredations make it difficult for the

Buhari administration to provide humanitarian assistance to the internally displaced and, over the longer term, to address the social and political and economic drivers of repeated waves of radicalism. Buhari's signature focus has been on suppressing corruption. In so far as he is successful, he is laying the groundwork for addressing the grievances of the north. But as celebrated US Supreme Court Justice Louis Brandeis said, "If the government becomes a lawbreaker, it breeds contempt for the law." Participants in Nigerian governance have long been the principal lawbreakers.

In his new book, *This Present Darkness* (2016), Stephen Ellis suggests that a failing state is like a very sick patient rather than an automobile that has broken down. Recovery, not repair, is required. The return to health is by fits and starts and takes a long time. The poor governance, corruption, and brutality of the security services that provided the environment for Boko Haram will take a long time to cure. Hence, Boko Haram in one form or another is likely to be around for a long time.

NOTES

1. "Global Terrorism Index 2015: Measuring and Understanding the Impact of Terrorism," Institute for Economics and Peace, November 2015, pp. 2–3.

2. Jacob Poushter, "In Nations with Significant Muslim Populations, Much Disdain for ISIS," Pew Research Center, November 17, 2015, www.pewresearch.org/fact-tank/2015/11/17/in-nations-with-significant-muslim-populations-much-disdain-for-isis.

3. "Nigerian View of Boko Haram," Pew Research Center, June 30, 2014, www.pewglobal.org/2014/07/01/concerns-about-islamic-extremism-on-the-rise-in-middle-east/pg-2014-07-01-islamic-extremism-04. It is highly unlikely that any Christians have a favorable view of Boko Haram.

4. Nigeria's population was estimated to be about 183 million in 2015.

5. John Campbell, "Nigeria Security Tracker," Council on Foreign Relations, March 2015, www.cfr.org/nigeria/nigeria-security-tracker/p29483.

6. Stephen Ellis, *This Present Darkness: A History of Nigerian Organized Crime* (London: Hurst & Company, 2016). Ellis provides an analysis of the progressive criminalization of Nigerian governance.

7. For example, in 2014 Central Bank Governor Lamido Sanusi credibly accused the national oil company of diverting billions of US dollars in oil revenue from the national treasury. President Goodluck Jonathan fired him. Investigations carried out by the Buhari government have largely confirmed what Sanusi said.

8. In 1979 the military government under General Olusegun Obasanjo organized elections and then turned over the government to elected civilians. In 1999, following the death of the then military chief of state Sani Abacha, the military again organized elections and turned over governance to civilians.

9. Richard Bourne, *Nigeria: A New History of a Turbulent Century* (London: Zed Books, 2015), pp. 1–15.

10. However, the Sultan of Sokoto is usually listed first in official Nigerian protocol order.

11. Ellis, *This Present Darkness*, p. 48.

12. John Campbell, *Nigeria: Dancing on the Brink* (Lanham, MD: Rowman & Littlefield Publishers, 2013), p. 45.

13. See "Islamic Actors and Interfaith Relations in Northern Nigeria," Policy Paper no. 1, March 2013, Nigeria Research Network, University of Oxford.

14. For a review of scholarly views on Maitatsine, see Mervyn Hiskett, "The Maitatsine Riots in Kano, 1980: An Assessment," *Journal of Religion in Africa* 17, no. 3 (1987).

15. On the origins, theology, and trajectory of Boko Haram see John O. Voll, "Boko Haram: Religion and Violence in the 21st Century," *Religions* 6, no. 4 (2015), pp. 1182–1201.

16. It was involved, however, in occasional murders, especially of rival imams and malams.

17. Virginia Comolli, *Boko Haram: Nigeria's Islamist Insurgency* (London: Hurst & Company, 2015), p. 53.

18. In 2014 Boko Haram kidnapped more than two hundred school girls gathered at a boarding school to take their final examinations. The magnitude of the kidnapping produced a worldwide reaction, with futile calls on the Abuja government "to do something."

19. "Boko Haram Crisis: Nigerian Military Chiefs Given Deadline," BBC, August 13, 2015, www.bbc.com/news/world-africa-33913305.

20. Adekunle, "Army Establish Task Force Brigade in Borno to Fight Boko Haram," *Vanguard*, October 26, 2015, www.vanguardngr.com/2015/10/army-establish-task-force-brigade-in-borno-to-fight-boko-haram.

21. AFP, "45 in Custody over 'Boko Haram Plot' in Lagos: Sources," Yahoo! News, October 25, 2015, http://news.yahoo.com/45-custody-over-boko-haram-plot-lagos-sources-175635962.html.

22. PM News, "Boko Haram Controls 2 Local Councils on Borno, Shettima Reveals," *Sahara Reporters*, October 26, 2015, http://saharareporters.com/2015/10/26/boko-haram-controls-2-local-councils-borno-shettima-reveals.

PART IV

ENGAGING THE INTERNATIONAL COMMUNITY ANEW

The first decades of the twenty-first century have witnessed a seismic shift in the relationships of sub-Saharan African countries with the major actors in the global economic and political order, a widening array of midlevel and major powers as well as the United Nations and the multilateral international financial institutions (IFIs). In no small measure this has been because of major transformations in the power structures and alignments of the international order itself.

The first post–Cold War decade, the 1990s, was the last when the relative hegemony of Western powers, buttressed by the United Nations and the multilateral IFIs, enabled them to project political and economic liberalism across much of the globe relatively unimpeded. Sub-Saharan African countries continued to be recipients of pressures to liberalize their economies, somewhat moderated by newer attention to poverty and environmental sustainability, to which was added strong encouragement to embrace democracy.

The rise of the BRICS and other emerging mid-level economic powers, led by China as well as state-sponsored and non-state-based terrorism and global counterterrorism campaigns, both profoundly influenced by revolutionary information technology, has transformed the global political and economic order in the twenty-first century. Heavily influenced by these circumstances, sub-Saharan African countries have increasingly borne responsibility on their own for charting courses in dealing with them, even as their states remain predominantly weak and their economies are still burdened by poverty, inequality, and other weaknesses, notwithstanding unprecedented levels of GDP growth in many cases.

A common theme in the four essays of this final section of the book is that rich architectures of diplomatic structures and processes have evolved in and for sub-Saharan Africa for addressing these emergent contours and challenges.

Although beneficial and even necessary, the authors recognize that these elaborate arrangements are insufficient in and of themselves for the purposes they are to serve. I. William Zartman's essay on the diplomacy of African conflicts argues that the richness of diplomatic resources for resolving African conflicts offers opportunities for comparing their relative effectiveness in particular circumstances while presenting the danger that competition among many eligible diplomatic actors can become a dimension of those very conflicts.

Carrie Manning and Louis-Alexandre Berg make the central point that bilateral donors with deep connections and ties in conflict countries can compensate for the limitations of multilateral actors' resources in addressing those conflicts, even as they may also have interests that can complicate collaborative bilateral-multilateral diplomatic efforts.

Ulf Engel pinpoints the priorities and continuing challenges for making the African Peace and Security Architecture of the African Union effective in conflict situations along with the expanding and overlapping African regional economic communities.

Finally, Ambassador Francis Deng offers a first-person account of the emergence of the doctrine of the Responsibility to Protect (R2P) over his two-decade post–Cold War career, first as special representative of the UN secretary general on displaced persons and then as special advisor on genocide prevention. His thesis is that the principle of state sovereignty on which the United Nations is founded has come to entail responsibility for and, in principle, enforceable accountability to the international community for protecting citizens' liberties and welfare. He argues that responsible sovereignty in this sense has become a key to preventing and ameliorating major humanitarian crises that originate with states but spill across borders and that underlie so much violent conflict across the globe.

The Diplomacy of
African Conflicts

I. WILLIAM ZARTMAN

African conflict diplomacy has overcome some enormous problems. It has essentially eliminated border, secessionist, and territorial conflicts, classified as the major sources of interstate wars.[1] Some lingering evidence of these types of conflicts remains, to be sure, but most of Africa's conflicts are internal, with an interstate overhang. African diplomacy finds its place in a system of subsidiarity, and the suborganization of the continent into (sub)regional organizations of security and cooperation facilitates (but also complicates) that distribution of tasks. There is therefore much to appreciate in African conflict diplomacy. It should ready itself to face new types of challenges: from conflicts over major scarcities of resources and from fanatical nonstate movements that do not govern but only destroy.

SUBSIDIARITY

Africa's conflicts are handled by collective diplomacy—institutions and mediation. The Peace and Security Architecture of the African Union (AU) has a number of figurative floors, in a relationship referred to as subsidiarity: this indicates that conflicts are to be handled at the lowest level and, if that does not work, are promoted to the next for attention, and so on. The main floor in the middle of the ladder is occupied by the Peace and Security Council (PSC) and is extremely active, with over six hundred meetings by mid-2016. Although it can make decisions on its own, it relies on the responses of member states for action. The Architecture operates under the authority of the heads of states' annual meeting but also works in cooperation or competition with the continent's important subregional organizations (SROs, sometimes referred to as RECs, regional economic communities). These make up the next lowest level, which is independent of the AU and often have minds of their own. The top level of last resort is the UN Security Council, on which the PSC was modeled and that generally tries to leave African problems to African states. Conflicts are often remanded to the continental or regional level, or endorsed at those subsidiary levels, but can also be handled directly, often through the Secretary-General's Special Envoy (SESG) or Special Representative (SRSG). Hovering around the top rung are also the European Union (EU), the Franco-African Summit, the Organisation de la Francophonie (OIF), particularly interested in Africa because of its colonial past, and also the Organization of the Islamic Conference (OIC), which has been less involved.

Off to the side of the ladder of subsidiarity are a host of nongovernmental organizations (NGOs), generally operating with the authorization of the states as Track 2 or Track 1½ (as opposed to Track 1, or official diplomacy), such as Sant'Egidio, Conflict Management Initiative (CMI), Center for Humanitarian Dialog (CHD), Mo Ibrahim Foundation, Carter Center, and HTL Strategies, among others, as well as individual statesmen, often retired, institutionally anointed or not. A characteristic of the operations of all these groups is that, when involved, they want to be in charge; the reaction is natural, as each has its own angle on diplomacy and all want to avoid outbidding, but it gives rise to some jostling until the mediator-in-charge is decided. If official mediators for the most part are directed by an interest either in the conflict or in getting it off the table, NGOs are driven by an interest in enhancing their reputation as conflict managers. Their knowledge is often broad, their ability to extend contacts beyond the official reach is often quite useful, and their patience is often greater than that of officialdom, but their work needs to be coordinated with official efforts. The classic case of Sant'Egidio's delivery of a Mozambican peace agreement in 1992 after the failure of several African attempts shows how a Track 2 NGO can work with Track 1 negotiators to produce good results.[2]

At the regional level the recognized organizations (ROs) are the Common Market for Eastern and Southern Africa (COMESA), the East African Community (EAC), the Economic Community of Central African States (ECCAS), the Economic Community of West African States (ECOWAS), the Intergovernmental Authority on Development (IGAD), South African Development Community (SADC), the Eastern African Standby Brigade Coordination Mechanism (EASBRICOM), and the Community of Sahel-Saharan States (CEN-SAD), some of which have overlapping membership and jurisdictions. The Peace and Security Architecture of the AU-RO system follows the practice of the former Organization for African Unity (OAU) by creating ad hoc commissions of neighboring and other interested states to handle individual conflicts.[3] Current examples are the Joint Follow-up and Support Group for the Transition in Burkina Faso, the Abyei

Joint Oversight Group, the Commission on the Official Results of the Election in the Federal Republic of Nigeria, and the Mediation Team of IGAD for South Sudan, and so on. The practice may be seen as the modern institutionalization of the traditional African use of palaver: talking out disputes without a deadline until everything has been heard and a consensual decision is reached.[4] The practice can work to produce harmony and inclusion, as it is supposed to do, but it can also work against clear decisions and the timely adoptions of resolving outcomes. Regional attention includes parties who know the territory and can facilitate resolution but who also have their own axes to grind in the conflict; if the regional level of subsidiarity avoids international great power interference in African affairs, it does include African great powers' involvement for their own interests. Conflicts do not freeze while talking is going on, and diplomacy is part of the conflict.

Sometimes these multiple actors get in each other's way, opening the possibility for competitive intervention and outbidding; however, the situation also has the contrary effect of allowing successive attempts at resolution and mediation at different levels, opening the subject for an analysis and debate of the best features for different conflicts. In sum, the choice of the mediator from among the many available is a matter of the conflict itself. It is scarcely possible to indicate which level or agency at any one level is most appropriate, but it is certain that the availability of many subsidiary levels affords African conflicting and resolving parties the possibility to work at a choice.[5] The African system provides the maximum flexibility, even if it requires some patience and political footwork. Although the term comes from the European experience, subsidiarity is roughly equivalent to the segmentary system that governs many traditional structures in Africa. Segmentarity refers to conflicts: myself against my brother, my brother and I against our cousins, we cousins against the outside world. On the international level conflicts are bounced back and forth among various institutions, often tripping over each other's jurisdictions because of individual state members' preferences and interests and jurisdictional disputes but also reflecting divergent competencies.

In practice the subsidiary system does not work as it should. Instead of providing clear procedural priorities, it tends to produce rivalries among levels and mediating agencies rooted in the interests of particular state members, whether parties to the conflict or otherwise concerned. Like everything in life, this has advantages and disadvantages. It assures interested parties ownership in the proceedings and outcome, and it sends the conflict into the hands of the most appropriate and even knowledgeable agency. By the same token, it also removes neutrality from the proceedings and introduces neighbors who know the situation all too well and have their own interests in it, leading to a secondary conflict over the proper mediating agency and outbidding among mediators, which delays solutions. Fabienne Hara argues that "every political tendency in Burundi has found a temporary ally among the international negotiators, who, in turn, have become part of the problem."[6] An exchange of two former Mobutu ministers over the choice of mediators in the Congo crisis in 2001 is revealing: "Ketule Matsire does not handle his job appropriately. Is it because he is an English-speaker and from southern Africa? This former president doesn't grasp all the elements of the crisis. First, he doesn't seem to have the same vision of the problems as we do. What seems unimportant to us seems important to him; what is important for us is negligible or him. This is why we feel . . . that the president of Gabon should be appointed the facilitator."[7] In fact, Matsire did work out quite well in the Gabarone phase of the mediation series.

A good example of subsidiarity in action has been the mediation of the Central African conflict in 2013, where ECCAS, the EU, the AU, and the UN were all involved in the jostling.[8] Chadian president Idriss Déby Itno and Congo-Brazzaville president Denis Sassou Nguesso brought ousted CAR president François Bozizé to sign an agreement passing powers to the new coup forces; when Kenya was brought in as a mediator the new CAR regime refused, with weighty support from South Africa, Nigeria, and the two Sudans. France urged EU and then UN involvement, and a succession of UN missions (whose changing nomenclature illustrates the bureaucratic and political confusion) were sent to protect populations and restore order: MISAB (Mission interafricaine de surveillance des Accords de Bangui), MISCA (Mission International de Soutien à la République de l'Afrique Centrale), MINURCA (Mission des Nations Unis à la République de l'Afrique Centrale), FOMUC (Force Multinationale en Centrafrique), MICOPax (Mission for the Consolidation of the Peace in Central African Republic), BINUCA (UN Integrated Peacebuilding Office in the CAR), and finally MINUSCA (UN Multidimensional Integrated Stabilization Mission in Central African Republic), with EUFOR RCA (European Force in CAR) somewhere in between. Chad pressed for the involvement of ECCAS, the regional organization, and finally the AU to keep conflict management in African hands. Meanwhile the conflict continued. It is hard to say that the final designated diplomatic agencies were the most appropriate; by the same token it is hard to establish a basis for judging appropriateness.

CONFLICT

African conflict diplomacy concerns above all internal or intrastate conflicts, although most intrastate conflicts rapidly acquire an interstate dimension. Direct interstate wars over coveted territory are rare; they are too costly and not worth the effort. Conquering neighboring territory was declared illegitimate by the OAU since 1963 and 1964, reasserted by the AU, and would be likely to contain restive minorities. Arguably the last major territorial claim, not just a border strip, was the dispute between Nigeria and Cameroon over the potentially oil-rich Bakassi Peninsula, settled in favor of Cameroon by a judgment of the International Court of Justice in 2002 that was finally implemented by 2008. The last major African border war over territory, the enormously costly Eritrean-Ethiopian war of 1998–2000, illustrates an important lesson of African border relations: when states break apart, if the border is not settled before the breakaway unit becomes independent, there will be a border war afterward. A number of minor border issues that currently exist do not constitute causes for serious conflict, but they call for the diplomacy of adjustments lest they become a trigger for escalation. The AU adopted a Border Program (AUBP) in 2007 and the further Declaration and Implementation Modalities for peaceful border relations in 2010, an important action that mirrors and perhaps contributes to the lowered salience of border issues in Africa.

South Sudan

Many of these characteristics are found in the civil war in South Sudan and its related unresolved border disputes in Abyei, the Blue Nile region, and the Nuba Mountains as well as the related conflict in Darfur, all of which constitute a major conflict, now internal but with complex interstate complications emanating from unresolved elements in a conflict of secession that has occupied all the levels of subsidiarity in African diplomacy. The continued hostilities between (North) Sudan and South Sudan after the latter's independence in 2011 provide the latest evidence that the lesson of boundaries has not been learned.

South Sudan and the related conflicts have their deepest origins in two basic elements in traditional relations that remain salient in contemporary Africa: the struggles between the herder with his need for seasonal pastures and the farmer with his need for fixed cultivated land, and the conflicts over scarce resources between neighboring ethnic groups that have become internalized as historic rivalries. Darfur, Abyei, and other parts of South Sudan have long been rent by the first type of conflict, and the major part of the country is dominated by the deep conflict between the two major tribes, Dinka and Nuer, along with other groups that often overlap the first type. As such, such elements present a deep social basis for conflicts that are highly personalized through key individuals who then represent and incarnate the social forces. Doudou Sidibé observes, "It is practically impossible to make peace when there is a personal problem between the two parties to the conflict."[9] Although they have attracted an ineffective combination of subsidiary levels of attention, the local forces of conflict have shown themselves to be much stronger than the agencies of diplomacy in their ability to ignore summons to cease hostilities.

As independence was approaching in Sudan in 1955, the ethnic and religious difference between north and south broke out into deep conflict. When fatigue set in on both sides after seventeen years of war, peace was negotiated under the mediation of a combination of continental and nongovernmental organizations—the OAU (and Emperor Haile Selassie of neighboring Ethiopia) and the African Council of Churches. But the 1972 Addis Ababa Agreements provided for a federation that allowed Sudanese president Jaafar Numeiry to play on the ethnic division in the south, pitting Nuer against Dinka in a revised federal system and trashing the agreement. So a decade later, in 1983, war broke out again under the charismatic leadership of Dr. John Garang and his Sudanese Peoples' Liberation Movement (SPLM) and Army (SPLA), fighting for a united, revolutionized Sudan rather than secession. The government of Sudan again played on internal tribal divisions in the Movement and encouraged a Nuer faction under Riek Machar to work for a separate deal; a massacre of hundreds of Dinka at his hand in 1991 sowed an irreconcilable thirst for revenge. It also used the farmer-herder setting for attacks on a restive population in Darfur on its western border, escalating to Libyan and Chadian involvement and to calls in the UN for a reaction to genocide. At the turn of the millennium stalemate again set in in South Sudan; under heavy pressure from the outside world, including the United States, itself under heavy pressure from Christian groups, negotiations mediated by the Inter-Governmental Agency for Development (IGAD), the regional organization of the Horn of Africa, methodically produced a Comprehensive Peace Agreement (CPA) in 2005. The CPA provided for a six-year period of cohabitation between the North and South to test whether unity was possible. In 2011 a referendum confirmed that it was not, and South Sudan became independent.

For the ensuing half decade (and more) the tribally based personally led factions of the SPLM/A waged a vicious civil war. Full violence broke out in 2013 when President Salva Kiir (successor to Garang) fired Vice President Machar, who had announced he would run for president, with charges of a plot that grew out of ethnic violence between militias of the two leaders. Support for the new government was immediately offered by the UN, who established a broad Mission for South Sudan (UNMISS) with a small peacekeeping force, which shifted to a limited role of protection for the internally displaced persons (IDPs) who had taken refuge in UNMISS camps. The AU cooperated with the UN in adding peacekeepers but handed jurisdiction over conflict diplomacy to IGAD. But the involvement of two neighbors in the conflict reduced the regional organization's effectiveness: Uganda put troops in Juba to protect the government of Kiir against the Machar rebels, whom Sudan supported (as before) in fear that Uganda would press its hostility against the government in Khartoum itself. The AU commissioned a report by former Nigerian president Olusegun Obasanjo in 2015 (never officially released) that castigated both sides and urged a transition process free of both leaders. In July in Nairobi, President Obama summoned regional leaders to move on a neutral transition or face UN sanctions; instead, in August 2015 IGAD called for power-sharing, which had been the arrangement that produced the original outbreak. Kiir was "reelected" for an additional three-year term in 2015, and Machar finally and gingerly returned to Juba in April 2016 as vice president in the power-sharing transition. But the civil war broke out again over confrontations of the two leaders' troops, and resolution, despite periodic ceasefires and hortatory statements, is not in sight. The Juba government continues to support imitators of the SPLA in Darfur, South Kordofan, and Blue Nile areas on the Sudanese border, impervious to any of the subsidiary levels' attentions.

The few territorial issues that still remain on the continent tend to be frozen or dormant. Two examples, probably the most alive among these frozen conflicts and typical of their category, are the Casamance and the Western Sahara. The two have been given over primarily to opposite levels of the subsidiarity ladder of African diplomacy—Casamance to government-engaged NGOs and the Western Sahara to the UN Security Council. Both are in remission on the ground but still constitute unresolved issues of international and domestic diplomacy. Both pose diplomatic challenges for their impacts on neighboring relations, Casamance between Senegal and Gambia (and to a lesser extent Guinea Bissau) and the Sahara between Morocco and Algeria.

The Casamance Conflict

The Casamance conflict is a case of calls for decolonization of an isolated enclave from domination by elites and policies from the capital. It broke out into violence in 1982 when a peaceful demonstration for self-government by representatives of the southern region of Senegal—largely cut off from the rest of the country by Gambia—organized into the Movement of the Democratic Forces in Casamance (MFDC) was violently repressed. The MFDC continued its militant rebellion for secession while its political wing attempted to negotiate directly with the government of President Abdou Diouf and finally produced a series of ceasefires in the early 2000s; a former French ambassador was one of the attempting mediators. Perhaps the most farsighted diplomatic venture was Diouf's initiative soon after his accession to the presidency in 1981 to establish a SeneGambian Confederation, initially to protect the Gambian regime of Dawda Jawara against a coup. Had it been maintained, it would have effectively eliminated the colonial anomaly of Gambia and ended the enclavement of Casamance; instead, Diouf canceled it in 1989 because of Gambia's refusal to integrate more meaningfully in a customs union.

Abdoulaye Wade defeated Diouf in 2000, and although ceasefires were produced with the MFDC, the government considered conflict management to be the same as conflict. It never moved further to handle the grievances of the rebellion, which included underdevelopment, neglect, and economic and political domination from the capital of Dakar, all compounded by growing distrust of the government and its promises. Rebels found sanctuary and illegal trade outlets from neighboring Gambia and Guinea-Bissau. Yet the rebellion grew tired of both government inattention and its own ineffectiveness.

When Macky Sall defeated Wade for the presidency in 2012 he, too, promised early resolution of the conflict. He adopted Wade's notion that development would replace independence, but with limited means and pressures for attention elsewhere, the plans for economic improvement proceeded only slowly, feeding the memories of neglect. However, the government also engaged two important NGOs to deal with the two more prominent MFDC leaders—the Geneva-based

Center for Humanitarian Dialog (CHD) to work with the faction of Cesar Atoute Badiate and the Rome-based Sant'Egidio to deal with the Salif Sadio faction. The United States offered ambassadorial support on a special mission, the EU funded the CHD, and Badiate engaged the Cardinal of Dakar.[10] The Senegalese government worked with the rather unstable government of Guinea-Bissau to close the border to the rebels, but Gambia lives off the illegal trade across its border, and the leaks continue; Gambia also has refused for two decades to build a bridge across the Gambia River, for which World Bank funding is available, that would go far to overcome the isolation of Casamance from the rest of Senegal. Four years after the Sall regime entered office, there were no visible effects of the mediations. Although the militant advocates of independence have lost their steam, the socio-economic grievances continue to slow the political process of resolution.[11]

The Western Saharan Conflict

The Western Saharan conflict is the last major case of decolonization in Africa, where a nationalist guerrilla movement operating out of neighboring Algeria has contested the integration of the former Spanish colony into Morocco.[12] When Spain left in 1974 a civilian Green March supported by the Moroccan army led the takeover of the territory, but the Polisario Front (Popular Front for the Liberation of Saqiet al-Hamra and Rio de Oro, the territory's two constituent provinces) contested the Moroccan presence. A complex series of military engagements led to a UN-sponsored ceasefire in 1991 and the installation of a mission (MINURSO) to supervise a referendum on independence or integration into Morocco. However, the two parties were unable to agree on a voters' list, and in 2007, when Morocco proposed a compromise solution of autonomy within Morocco, the UN Security Council declared the referendum to be a dead plan and autonomy a credible and realistic alternative. The Polisario and, behind it, Algeria refused.

The UN Security Council gave MINURSO its annual renewal on April 30, 2016, and the special envoy of the secretary-general, presently Christopher Ross, has been attempting various confidence-building and even substantive discussions among the parties to no avail. A referendum has not been mentioned in the UN resolutions since and autonomy has been referred to as the "serious and credible" alternative, to be achieved by direct negotiations. More than an issue over whether the former Spanish colony has been decolonized or not and how its permanent status should be determined, the Western Saharan conflict is the most immediate evidence of the rivalry over rank and relations between the two leading states of the Maghreb. Each side enjoys a form of winning—Morocco by its possession of the territory and Algeria-Polisario by its claims of recognition and legitimacy—and each side suffers a fear of serious, even existential loss if the other side's solution is pursued. In this situation international mediation has no purchase on the parties, there is no confidence to be built, and the conflict teeters on the edge of a destabilizing accident. It is further locked in its current impasse by the frozen political situation in Algeria, where the limited capacity of President Abdulaziz Bouteflika prevents any constructive movement.

As a result, most diplomacy over the Saharan conflict is slow-moving shadow-boxing conducted in the organizations of the EU and occasionally in the UN. Because Morocco has left the AU and the regional organization, the Arab Maghreb Union, is officially "frozen" from meeting because of the Saharan issue, the standard levels of subsidiarity are blocked. Diplomacy in the organisms of the EU concerns such side issues as human rights in the territory and in the Polisario camps in Algeria as well as disposition of natural resources of the region, such as fishing rights. Diplomacy in the UN concerns renewal of MINURSO or human rights issues. Neither instance is of any direct relevance to the mitigation of the conflict itself, and although the Security Council and previous SRSGs and secretaries-general have expressed support for the autonomy idea, recognition of the proposal as a solution to the conflict has not been formalized.

The types of conflicts discussed thus far have all involved military action, so the term implicitly refers to "violent conflict." There are, however, also major conflicts where violence may only be on the horizon and the challenge to African diplomacy is nonetheless great. These may include territorial, border, ethnic, or secessionist conflicts of the types discussed; it was noted long ago that "Any African State can have a border conflict if it wants to."[13] However, much more challenging are the impending crises of scarce resources, of which water is the most important. Population growth, where Africa leads the world, and climate change, where Africa will experience a heavy impact, make large swaths of the continent—above all, North Africa and the Sahel, and southern Africa—water deprived, already now and increasingly in the future. African diplomacy will be tasked with apportioning a resource formerly deemed unlimited, as African domestic politics will be faced with limiting its consumption.

The Politics of the Nile

The politics of the Nile constitute the largest and most immediate form of this type of diplomatic challenge. The Nile waters have been apportioned since 1929 by a treaty negotiated under British rule between Egypt and Sudan and updated in 1959; upriver riparian states were assumed be willing contributors, the originators of the flow and not its consumers.[14] At the turn of the millennium, with the riparian states all sovereign with their independent interests, those outside the original treaty proposed a new repartition of the Nile waters and adopted the treaty among themselves over Egyptian objections, despite active diplomatic exchange among the parties; Egypt was busy with the instability of the Egyptian Spring at the time. At the same time, Ethiopia began constructing the Grand Ethiopian Renaissance Dam (GERD) and its saddle-dam backup, which would help protect the Aswan Dam from silting but would also heavily impact the Egyptian agriculture below it. In 1999, nine riparian states established the Nile Basin Initiative designed to include the Upper Nile states in the water distribution, and in 2010 six states—not including Egypt, Sudan, and the DRC—established the Nile Basin Cooperation Framework Agreement. In March 2015, however, the two downstream holdouts and Ethiopia signed a Definition of Principles Agreement. Arguments of justice and power are the weapons of the diplomacy, which is not yet over. Much depends, too, on the weather: a long dry spell will heighten the conflict, just as a long period of normal rain will lighten the tension.

MEDIATION AND DIPLOMATIC INTERVENTION

Conflicts vary in their tractability to diplomatic efforts. Conflicts can be risky and costly, but third-party efforts at conflict diplomacy can also be troublesome, expensive for the mediator, and prolonging for the conflict. Third-party attitudes are more a lagging matter of "it's about time we finally did something about this" rather than rushing in with fire brigades at the first sign of smoke. There are many reasons why early warnings are ignored, but even if early action were the automatic reflex to the first signs of an early warning, a rush to mediation could be precipitous.[15] Thus, the question of when to seek entry into a conflict is an important judgment call. The doctrine of Responsibility to Protect (R2P), which has its origins in Africa,[16] contains three "pillars": (1) each state's responsibility for the welfare of its own people, (2) third state responsibility to help home state efforts for citizen welfare, and (3) third state responsibility to take on citizen welfare in case of home state inaction or irresponsibility, with mediation placed somewhere between Pillar 2 and Pillar 3. Mediation and diplomatic intervention are not simply a matter of helping the government to overcome rebellion but rather of recognizing that rebellion, right or wrong, is a symptom of a problem. The reflex of the subsidiary African levels, as clubs of chiefs, is generally to assume that rebellion is wrong and so to ignore the causes that are key to a solution.

When a party feels that it is engaged in a Final Solution effort to once and for all eliminate an opponent, or a zero-sum existential conflict, or is following a divine order to eliminate the other, it is a bit difficult for a mediator to find any space for entry.[17] Even when parties feel caught in a security dilemma, a vicious circle where one party's effort to increase its security only decreases the other's security, it takes great efforts of persuasion to convince the parties that they are really not in danger of elimination. Once the cycle has become physically vicious, as in Kigali in 1993 or Brazzaville in 1997 or Juba or Darfur in 2013 and earlier, it is difficult to overcome the tangible evidence of its reality. It takes a combination of loud official statements, NGO-led dialog groups, and heavily and neutrally policed local separation of populations to unwind the cycle, as Ahmedou Ould-Abdallah did in Burundi in 1993 and as has been attempted in Central Africa with still-limited success.[18]

Another type of conflict highly resistant to diplomatic efforts at resolution has been called an "S5 situation"—a soft, stable, self-serving stalemate—where the parties are not really uncomfortable in the immobility of the conflict, each hold-ing some advantage and in fact some parties on either side making money out of it, but each fearsome of losing the benefits of their current situation, however imperfect, if they take part in a diplomatic move to resolve it. This is what pros-pect theorists call risk aversion, and it is a powerful factor in freezing conflict, even—or especially—at a low level of violence. The risk—danger plus cost—of loss is feared much more than whatever pain and cost the present level of the conflict might entail.[19] The display case is the Western Sahara dispute, discussed above: a loss could be fatal to the monarchy in Morocco, and a corresponding loss would be fatal for the Polisario organization and elites and might be troublesome to the Algerian army. At the moment there is no other conflict in Africa of equal intensity and low level at the same time.

Handling conflicts of this type diplomatically, where the parties feel they dare not compromise for fear of losing everything, requires turning the parties' exter-nal support into pressure for mutual movement from competing salient solutions to a single salient solution between the extremes and using external assistance to ensure that all will not be lost and to guarantee the outcome. UN mediators did this in 1992 when the agreement between the Renamo rebels and the Frelimo gov-ernment managed the Mozambique civil war and turned the two movements' ri-valry from violence to elections. In the Western Sahara the single salient solution has been identified as the autonomy proposal, but the external supporters—nec-essarily in the UN, as Morocco is not a member of the AU—have not put their full weight behind it. The situation of risk aversion carries the further trap that if one party makes a conciliatory move, it is taken as the new extreme, and the compro-mise point in between is then moved closer to the unyielding side.

When victory seems within the reach of one party, diplomatic activity would aim either to stop the victory drive if it is deemed undesirable or to slow it down enough to protect the losing side and populations. It would be first necessary to establish a balance and block the certain victory, a heavy challenge for a medi-ator in a manipulative role. This was the problem that faced the Carter media-tion effort in Ethiopia in 1989 when the government was on the ropes, the EPLF (Eritrean Peoples' Liberation Front) was on a roll, and there was little prospect of any effect for third-party efforts.[20] The best that could be done was seen later in the intervention of Assistant Secretary Cohen to have Addis Ababa declared an open city. Such moments evolve. When the Carter Center began mediating among the three presidents of Congo-Brazzaville in the summer of 1997 the invitation came as a result of the stalemate that existed among three forces.[21] But by October the rebel forces had gotten discouraged in the stalemate and lost their nerve; the ripe moment had passed, and the mediation collapsed (to be taken up later by Sassou Nguesso's son-in-law, Gabonese president Omar Bongo, who arranged a deal—never consummated—for the rebels with the government).

The key to mediation is stalemate, either from fatigue or from active dead-lock on both sides, and the major challenge of diplomacy is to ripen the parties' perception of the conflict so that mediation can be possible.[22] The effort is not often recognized as a part of the mediator's job, but it in fact occupies most of mediation activity and should in no way be considered as a separate or "pre-"mediation. The four years' blockage to peace and reconciliation in the South Sudanese civil war has been the result of the inability of either of the two leaders to admit that victory is not possible and that their impasse is doing damage to their own communities. Assistant Secretary Chester Crocker spent six years ripening the parties' (and Washington's) understanding that refusal to see the linkage between the presence of both South African and Cuban troops was blocking a solution, and then he spent one year actually working out the solution.[23] Ripening is above all a matter of persuasion and a test of the skill of the diplomat in charge.

Persuasion is, however, also aided by objective support for the subjective appreciation of the situation.[24] NGOs have little purchase on the objective referents of those perceptions, but persuasion can be within the reach of NGO mediators, who can be particularly effective in changing conflicting parties' perceptions of their chances in conflict. The primary source of a hurting stalemate—one that causes unbearable cost to the parties—comes from the conflict itself. If the mediator has some hard data to underscore the feelings of the hurting stalemate he is working to raise, entry into the operative phase of mediation is facilitated. Body bags with white bodies, recent offensives beaten back on both sides, and threats of hot pursuit, as in Namibia, make it easier to get both parties' attention to focus on a negotiated outcome. A drought around 1990 in Mozambique brought home the damage that the civil war was causing and the inability of either of the parties to win. Yet objective facts are only a referent: the tremendous losses in people, property, and prosperity in Central African Republic and South Sudan have taken a long time to make their impact on leaders' perceptions.

In the absence of faits accomplis, the mediator can also use threats of escalation to ripen perceptions, although they run up against both credibility and retaliative problems. Again in Namibia, the Cuban threat of hot pursuit was effective in attracting the South Africans' attention to the mediator's efforts, and the South African potential to bury any Cubans who crossed the front helped to get the Cubans' attention. The Malagasy politicians' persistent refusal to live up to the 2009 Maputo agreement and put their house in order was the cause of AU suspension but, unusually, also of threats to do worse; SADC and the Francophonie also suspended the Malagasy Republic, and the two squabbling leaders were warned, initially by France and then, too, by SADC, not to run in the 2014 elections[25]; despite the fact that several subsidiary levels weighed in, the rivals ran in the election anyhow.

There are instances when the mediator does orchestrate reinforcement as well as perception of the stalemate. France, in mediating a ceasefire and political accord between the parties in the Ivorian dispute at Linas-Marcoussis in 2003, also exerted military pressure on the government; it was a case of strong-arm mediation, and the mediator's bona fides were questioned, ending up with inconclusive results. One step away from the mediators itself, the United States, assisting the IGAD in mediating the CPA for Sudan, put serious pressures on the North in order to make and keep the moment ripe until agreement was reached, ending in 2005 with greater success. Side payments require considerable resources and engagement from the mediators, thus they are rarely made and certainly not the key to successful mediation. Yet when the outcome is not large enough to provide sufficient benefits for both parties or to outweigh the present or anticipated advantages of continued conflict, some source of additional benefits is needed. Side payments may be attached to the outcomes themselves, such as third-party guarantees of financial aid for accomplishing changes required by the agreement, or they may be unrelated to the outcome itself, simply additional benefits that make agreement more attractive. For example, the United States and six African leaders of the region called on South Sudanese leaders in July 2015 to end their conflict and move toward a transition, on pain of sanctions.

In the end leverage derives from the mediating skills of the mediator, the organizational side of persuasion. These include identifying appropriate subjects to be covered and precedents for handling them, including relevant and necessary parties and the excluding of nondangerous spoilers, creating a sense of ownership of the process and agreement, developing a formula to give coherence to the haggling over details, managing the process of a rolling agreement where hold-outs can be folded in later on, early testing of the introduction of a ceasefire with final adoption toward the end when the parties can see what they are ceasing fire for, and using deadlines tactically as well as ensuring continued support from deciding authorities and mandate sources outside the process, among others.[26] African mediations can provide ample examples of the importance of these elements. The best example is found in the extraordinary personal charisma of African president Julius Nyerere, until his death in October 1999, and then of Nelson Mandela in mediating the Burundi conflict, before the process fell apart to multiple mediation. Unfortunately many African mediation efforts are undertaken by figures— possibly eminent in their own right—who are inexperienced in mediation and lack (or refuse) the support of professionally trained mediators.

More frequently, the objective ingredients for ripening come from the surrounding international community that has implicitly designated the mediator. The simplest form is through UN resolutions and other statements of support for the mediation to indicate that a facilitated negotiation is preferable to continued conflict and that the time of support for one party or the other is over. Ostracism, through the suspension of membership in an international organization, is an indication that the current course of action is blocked and will not be tolerated by the party's peers and so the path of mediation is indicated.

The AU's ostracism system, based on the Lome Declaration of 2000, has been called "minimalist, automatic, and conservative."[27] It has suspended governments (specifically not states) for overthrowing elected rulers, including CAR (2003–2007, 2013 on), Malagasy (2002, 2009–2013), Guinea (2008–2010), Mauritania (2005–2007, 2008–2009, 2010–2012), Egypt (2013 on), Niger (2009–2011), Ivory Coast (2000, 2010–2011), and Guinea-Bissau (2010–2011), Mali (2012), and Togo (2005), and it has succeeded in all cases except those that are ongoing. It has also suspended members for nonpayment of dues, and it can in addition suspend members for nonobservation of AU decisions, but it has never done so. Ostracism works, although there are ways about it; the rule had to be revised in the 2007 Addis Ababa Charter on Democracy, Elections and Governance to prohibit an overthrowing usurper from running in the restored election, and that has not been foolproof.[28] But except for the implied insistence on undoing the unconstitutional government change, the move has almost never been combined with policy recommendations for serious punishment. Sanctions put muscle behind ostracism and are a stronger way of making a stalemate hurt, but they have been little used beyond the prohibitions of participation in AU affairs and contact with member states; AU sanctions and suspending foreign aid in the Malagasy case are an exception. Ostracism, it is assumed, carries its own punishments that need not be intensified.

Ultimately the international community and its agencies can make stalemate hurt through indictment by the International Criminal Court (ICC). The effect has been the opposite of that intended, however: indictment makes conflict management mediations improbable, as once the negotiations are over, the subject faces judicial proceedings. Joseph Kony broke off negotiations with Uganda and the Carter Center because the indictment was hanging over his head, and al-Bashir has taunted the Court with his international travels with impunity; President al-Bashir in Sudan has taunted the ICC indictment by traveling to signatory countries and dared them to send him to The Hague. The threat of indictment is the only effective measure, with indictment itself useful only when the subject is in the hands of the law. But threats rest on effectiveness and depend on credibility, currently missing elements whose absence has besmirched the ICC, particularly as an adjunct to mediation.

Once the push factor of a hurting statement is achieved, that is only half the way to creating a ripe situation. The mediator must elicit a willingness to negotiate from both parties and make sure each sees the other's intent to seek a way out (WO) of the conflict. Until 2002 the parties representing the two halves of Sudan quite correctly did not feel that the other party was ready to negotiate an end to their conflict, but thereafter, under pressure from third parties, including the United States, the AU, and IGAD, they saw a mutual appreciation of a way out and engaged in negotiations mediated by Kenyan General Lazaro Sumbeiywo, leading to the Comprehensive Peace Agreement (CPA) in 2005. Only then does the mediator's substantive job begin, helping the parties turn that willingness into an outcome that constitutes a mutually enticing opportunity and pulls them to final agreement.

The mediator is generally not only unwelcome, viewed by the parties as a meddler, but also powerless. S/he cannot command an agreement, and attempts to do so that outrun the effects of persuasion generally fail, again as in Abuja on Darfur. The mediator can threaten to withdraw and leave the parties to their own devices and their continuing conflict, but the impact of withdrawal is entirely in the hands of the disputing parties. They may be happy to see the mediator leave, but if their security point is low, they will be sensitive to the threat of leaving. However, if the mediator needs a solution more than the parties do, s/he will be unable to threaten termination credibly. President Carter told parties of the possibility of termination at the beginning if they did not play by the rules; he threatened it in dealing with the Ethiopians and Eritreans and expressed his unhappiness when the SPLA/M broke "his" guinea worm truce, but he continued working for a result. Often, the mediator's leverage comes from his ability to claim that his efforts are the only game in town. On many occasions this is true, as, given the uncomfortableness of the mediator's position, no one else wants the job, but on other occasions competitive mediators and outbidding make the only-game claim difficult to sustain. The UNSC designated ECOWAS as mediator in Mali, Mauritania as AU president in 2014 stepped in, but it was Algerian Foreign Minister Lamamra who simply took over with his country behind him to produce the Algiers accord of March 2015.

Leverage derives from the mediator's ability to tilt toward (gratification) or away from (deprivation) a party and thereby to affect the conditions of a stalemate or of movement out of it. The activity may be verbal, such as a vote of condemnation, or more tangible, such as side payments. The point of this leverage is to worsen the dilemma of parties rejecting mediation and to keep them in search of a solution. The mediator might shift weight in order to prevent one party from losing the conflict because the other's victory would produce a less stable and, hence, less desirable situation. Such activity clearly brings the mediator very close to being a party in the conflict. As weight shifts affect the continuing conflict, side payments may be needed to augment or enhance the outcome to one or more parties. In sum, mediation depends on mediators' interests but more so on conflicting parties' interests, above all determined by their perceptions of ripeness. The challenge of the mediator is to bring out that perception, through persuasion but also through manipulation of the objective elements underlying that perception, by the mediator but mainly by the conflicting parties themselves and by the international community.

CONFLICTS BEYOND DIPLOMACY

Africa holds a number of conflicts of different types that are rather impervious to diplomacy. The swath of conflicts from Somalia through Uganda–South Sudan, northern Nigeria, Mali and Niger, Libya, and the Algerian Sahara led by al-Qaeda (now al-Khilafa, the Islamic State—IS, or *da'esh*) franchises, notably al-Shabab, Beit al-Maqdis, Boko Haram, and the North African Wilayat are thinking neither of ripeness nor mediation, nor subsidiarity, nor territoriality at the moment. These conflicts are not contests for state control (despite IS's name) or territorial acquisition or separation, nor do they represent particular ethnic or national groups. They thrive on and promote state collapse and are conducted by nonterritorial nonsovereign bands of fanatics. They therefore constitute an additional level of difficulty beyond even the most long-lasting of the conflicts already mentioned. It is hard to see possibilities for mediation with Boko Haram, al-Shabab, or Beit al-Maqdis, or other al-Qaeda or Khilafa (IS) franchises; at best, efforts other than military defeat can include deconversion of individual leaders and members, as is being tried in Nigeria.[29]

Conflict diplomacy in such cases focuses, on one hand, on building responsible military cooperation among states and within regional organizations, and on the other, on building responsible and accountable state apparatuses winning popular support by meeting popular needs—two goals that can work together or in opposition. Regional military cooperation has characterized responses to al-Shabab in Somalia, against the Lord's Resistance Army in northern Uganda, and against al-Qaeda in the Islamic Maghreb (AQIM), Ansar al-Din, and the National Front for the Liberation of Azawad (FNLA), with varying degrees of sporadic international—mainly US and French—involvement. The result has not been a high degree of effectiveness, and in all cases the movement has spilled over into some spectacular raids against neighboring countries.

A notable case is the formation of West African military cooperation against Boko Haram. In 2015 the AU redirected a low-level cooperation effort established in 1998 as the Multinational Joint Task Force (MNJTF) among Nigeria, Chad, and Niger by the Lake Chad Basin Commission to fight Boko Haram.[30] Although some nine thousand troops are provided, that is only the first step. It took two years and a presidential election in Nigeria to focus on Boko Haram and another year to become operative; military coordination has been minimal and suspicious, both among parties and within the Nigerian military. Although there has been some reduction of the insurgent activity, early hostages have not been released and the rebel command structure remains intact. Although the record of the rest of the world in similar cases is not exemplary, it would be good if African states could learn to cooperate militarily more effectively among themselves on a given level of subsidiarity, the same lesson that stands out between the levels.

CONCLUSION

There are many cases and even types of conflict diplomacy that are not specifically reviewed here, such as the Kenya elections, the leftover eastern Congo rebellions, the civil war in Central African Republic, and others. The characteristics of African diplomacy in these cases are similar to those noted in the preceding discussion. Africa is run by a fraternity of chiefs, which, under various circumstances, may facilitate or impede diplomacy. Given its proliferation of conflicts among new, developing—or underdeveloping—states, Africa's record is not markedly worse than other regions. The nearly total elimination of territorial claims and the great reduction of secessionist demands are notable achievements, requiring about a century less than it took in Latin America. The normative development of the AU is striking, even if the norms (as elsewhere in the world, including about people and within families) are not scrupulously observed. For example, overthrow of elected regimes and disregard of two-term limits are condemned and frequently adhered to, although leaders who infringe the rules need indeed to be ostracized from the club of chiefs, with sanctions in support. The existence of a ladder of institutions to handle conflict diplomacy is a useful asset; the levels of subsidiarity can easily get in each other's way, and subsidiarity itself should not be taken as a fixed rule of precedence, although it does provide useful alternatives for diplomacy. Mediation is part of the African traditional culture of conflict management, and Africans make use of it in their modern diplomacy—practice makes perfect, or at least gives lessons on how do so.

NOTES

1. Jacob Bercovitch, Victor Kremenyuk, and I. William Zartman, eds., *SAGE Handbook on Conflict Resolution* (London: SAGE, 2009).

2. Ibrahim Msabaha, "Negotiating an End to Mozambique's Murderous Rebellion," in *Elusive Peace: Negotiating an End to Civil Wars*, ed. I. William Zartman (Washington, DC: Brookings, 1995).

3. Yassin El-Ayouty and I. William Zartman, eds., *OAU After Twenty Years* (New York: Praeger, 1986).

4. Robert Armstrong, ed., *Socio-Political Aspects of the Palaver in Some African Countries* (Paris: UNESCO, 1979).

5. Laurie Nathan, "Will the Lower Be First? Subsidiarity in Peacemaking in Africa," in *Minding The Gap: African Conflict Management in a Time of Change*, ed. Pamela Aall and Chester A. Crocker (Waterloo, Canada: Center for International Governance Innovation, 2016).

6. Fabienne Hara, "Burundi: A Case of Parallel Diplomacy," in *Herding Cats: Multiparty Mediation in a Complex World*, ed. Chester Crocker, Fen Osler Hampson, and Pamela Aall (Washington, DC: US Institute of Peace Press, 1999), pp. 149–150.

7. R. Ndiaye, "Qui a peur du dialogue intercongiolais?" *Afrique internationale* 438 (November 2001); RDC, "Dialogue intercongolais: l'heure du doute," *L'autre Afrique* 9 (2001), p. 29.

8. Martin Welz, "Contested Peacemaking: Insights from Madagascar and the Central African Republic," paper presented to the International Studies (ISA) annual meeting at New Orleans, February 20, 2015.

9. Doudou Sidibé, "La négociation diplomatique dans le conflit de la République démocratique du Congo: insuffisances et instabilité des accords," *Manuel interdisciplinaires des modes amiables de résolution des conflits* (2014), p. 624, speaking of Congo.

10. James R. Billington, *Expeditionary Diplomacy in Action: Supporting the Casamance Peace Initiative* (Bullington, 2015).

11. I. William Zartman, ed., *Understanding the Casamance Conflict* (Baltimore, MD: Conflict Management Program, Johns Hopkins University Press, 2016).

12. Anouar Boukars and Jacques Rousellier, eds., *Perspectives on Western Sahara: Myths, Nationalisms, and Geopolitics* (Lanham, MD: Rowman & Littlefield, 2014).

13. I. William Zartman, "The Foreign and Military Politics of African Boundary Problems," in *African Boundary Problems*, ed. Carl Gösta Widstrand (Stockholm: Scandinavian African Institute, 1969), p. 79.

14. John Waterbury, *Nile Basin: National Determinants of Collective Action* (New Haven, CT: Yale University Press, 2002).

15. I. William Zartman and Guy Olivier Faure, eds., *Escalation and Negotiation in International Conflicts* (Cambridge: Cambridge University Press, 2005); I. William Zartman, *Preventing Deadly Conflict* (Cambridge: Polity, 2015).

16. Africa Leadership Forum, Organization of African Unity, UN, and Economic Commission for Africa, *The Kampala Document: Toward a Conference on Security, Stability, Development, and Cooperation in Africa, 19–22 May 1991, Kampala, Uganda* (Abeokuta, Nigeria: Africa Leadership Forum, 1991); Francis Mading Deng, *Sovereignty as Responsibility: Conflict Management in Africa* (Washington, DC: Brookings Institution, 1996); Francis Deng and I. William Zartman, *A Strategic Vision for Africa: The Kampala Movement* (Washington, DC: Brookings Institution, 2002), pp. 113–122.

17. Carolin Goerzig, "Mediating Identity Conflicts," Berghof Occasional, Paper 30, 2010.

18. Ahmedou Ould Abdallah. *Burundi on the Brink, 1993–95: A UN Special Envoy Reflects on Preventive Diplomacy* (Washington, DC: US Institute of Peace, 2000).

19. Rose McDermott, "Prospect Theory and Negotiation," in *Negotiated Risks: International Talks on Hazardous Issues*, ed. Rudolf Avenhaus and Gunnar Sjöstedt (Berlin, London: Springer, 2009).

20. Marina Ottaway, "Eritrea and Ethiopia: Negotiating in a Transitional Conflict," in Zartman, *Elusive Peace*.

21. I. William Zartman and Katharina Vogeli, "Prevention Gained, Prevention Lost," in *Opportunities Missed, Opportunities Seized: Preventive Diplomacy in the Post–Cold War World*, ed. Bruce Jentleson (Lanham, MD: Rowman & Littlefield, 2000).

22. Mohammed Maundi, I. William Zartman, Gilbert M. Khadiagala, and Kwaku Nuamah, *Getting In: Mediators' Entry into the Settlement of African Disputes* (Washington, DC: US Institute of Peace, 2006). For a fuller discussion see I. William Zartman, "Beyond the Hurting Stalemate," in *Conflict Resolution After the Cold War*, ed. Paul C. Stern and Daniel Druckman (Washington, DC: National Academy Press, 2000); I. William Zartman, "Mediation and Political Tools in Africa," in Aall and Crocker, *Minding the Gap*.

23. Chester A. Crocker, *High Noon in Southern Africa: Making Peace in a Rough Neighborhood* (New York: W. W. Norton, 1993).

24. I. William Zartman and Alvaro deSoto, *Timing Mediation Initiatives* (Washington, DC: US Institute of Peace, 2010).

25. Laurie Nathan, *A Clash of Norms and Strategies in Madagascar* (Center for Mediation in Africa, University of Pretoria, 2013).

26. Crocker, Hampson, and Aall, *Herding Cats*; I. William Zartman, *Ripe for Resolution: Conflict and Intervention in Africa* (Oxford: Oxford University Press, 1989); Sean Brooks, "Enforcing a Turning Point and Imposing a Deal: An Analysis of the Darfur Abuja Negotiations of 2006," *International Negotiation* 13, no. 3 (2008), p. 415–442; Vasu Gounden, *Conversations with Ahtisaari* (Umhlanga Rocks, South Africa: CMI, 2012); Tanja Tamminen, ed., *Strengthening the EU's Peace Mediation Capabilities: Leveraging for Peace Through New Ideas and Thinking* (Finnish Institute of International Affairs, 2012), www.fiia.fi/en/publication/296/strengthening-_the_eu_s_peace_mediation_capacities; Lakhdar Brahimi

and Salman Ahmed, *The Seven Deadly Sins of Mediation* (New York: NYU Center on International Cooperation, 2008); *Guidance for Effective Mediation* (UN, 2012); Isak Svensson and Peter Wallersteen, *The Go-Between* (Washington, DC: US Institute of Peace, 2010); I. William Zartman and Saadia Touval, "International Mediation," in *Leashing the Dogs of War: Conflict Management in a Divided World*, ed. Chester Crocker, Femn Osler Hampson, and Pamela Aall (Washington, DC: US Institute of Peace, 2007).

27. Elin Hellquist, "Regional Organizations and Sanctions Against Members," Working Paper no. 59, KFG, Free University, Berlin, January, 31. 2014.

28. Konstantinos Magliveraa, "The Sanctioning System of the African Union," paper presented to the Institute for Security Studies meeting in Addis Ababa, October 11–13, 2011.

29. Tanimu Turaki and Alhaji Kabiru, "Conversation with Nigerian Minister of Special Duties and Intergovernmental Affairs," CHD Oslo conference, 2014.

30. Alex Thurston, "West Africa's Regional Forces Against Boko Haram Is a Political Prop," *World Politics Review*, April 27, 2016, worldpoliticsreview.com/articles/18605/west-africa-s-regional-force-against-boko-haram-is-a-political-prop.

Bilateral vs. Multilateral Peacebuilding in Africa

CARRIE MANNING AND LOUIS-ALEXANDRE BERG

INTRODUCTION

Conflict, especially intrastate conflict, and efforts by outside actors to help resolve it have been influential in shaping politics in sub-Saharan Africa. Since 1989 African armed conflicts have accounted for roughly one-third of the global total each year, with an average of thirteen armed conflicts per year from 1989 to 2014.[1] During the same period no fewer than twenty-two UN-led peace operations were carried out in the region, and seven more are ongoing.[2]

Although much of what we know of peacebuilding focuses on the successes and failures of these multilateral missions, this chapter explores the role of bilateral donors in postconflict peacebuilding processes. We argue that the success or failure of complex, multidimensional peace operations is too often assumed to hinge on the UN mission itself. However, bilateral donors have also played a critical role in securing successful outcomes and perhaps also in contributing to the failure of peace missions, though this has not been extensively examined. Of particular interest is how bilateral aid interventions may affect both the capacity and the political will of domestic political actors by offering credible commitments to reduce the costs to local actors of embracing postwar democratic politics.

Peacebuilding is an inherently political process, not a technocratic one. Although peace agreements and UN mandates often explicitly call for the UN peace mission and other external actors to oversee *political* reforms or transformations, there is an implicit assumption that these actors will not be getting their hands dirty by engaging in the kind of political horse trading, cajoling, threatening, and deal making that characterize political interaction in such settings; instead, international technocrats are to apply rules along with rewards and punishments for following or deviating from these rules.

This view overlooks the fact that domestic political actors are in fact actors who may or may not be disposed to follow the rules. In effective peace operations UN mission leaders and the representatives of major donors rely not on the willingness of domestic actors to recognize their authority and obey the rules but on their own ability to alter the costs to local actors of embracing the peace agreement, which includes not only laying down arms but also surrendering to the uncertainties of democratic politics. To alter these costs, external actors must have a credible capacity to impose costs and confer benefits in the eyes of domestic actors. We argue that UN peace operations on their own are unlikely to have such credibility.

This chapter proceeds as follows. The next section introduces the notion of adoption costs. Adoption costs refer to local elites' cost-benefit calculation about the risks and gains to be had from cooperating rather than defecting on the commitments required by the peace agreement. We then outline the expected characteristics of effective guarantors, based on a reading of the comparative literature on postconflict peacebuilding. Although bilateral donors can never replace UN peace missions, we argue that they complement these missions in indispensable ways. In the following section we explore the conditions under which bilateral actors are likely to serve as effective guarantors, highlighting the impact of relationships among domestic political elites. We use the cases of Mozambique, Liberia, and Rwanda to illustrate the contribution of bilateral donors toward securing sustainable peace under different conditions. In Mozambique and Liberia the role of bilateral donors was critical in spite of the common tendency to attribute success in each case primarily to the UN mission. In Rwanda, by contrast, strong domestic actors had little need of external support to overcome internal political challenges. Although they still relied on international aid, donors were often unable or unwilling to truly condition aid funds on performance or to influence policy.

We make two main claims. First, we find that the UN is most effective when the leading bilateral donor backs it up. A division of labor, in which the UN and bilateral actors assume responsibility for separate tasks, does not seem to be as effective as when both the UN and the major bilateral donor provide complementary forms of support for the same tasks. Second, both the relationship between the major bilateral donor and domestic elites *and* the relationships among competing domestic actors affect adoption costs in important ways. Although bilateral actors are often better placed than multilateral actors to establish effective relationships with domestic elites, in some cases the nature of domestic political relationships limits the influence of even the most credible external actors on peacebuilding outcomes.

One caveat is in order before proceeding further. This paper deals only with cases where there is an actual peace agreement, and we are concerned with what happens after that agreement is signed. We do not examine the role of external actors in the process of getting belligerents to the negotiating table in the first place. We examine the period after a UN peace operation has been deployed to the country in question, not how the decision about whether and how to intervene in a given country is made.

ADOPTION COSTS AND PEACEBUILDER LEVERAGE

Effective guarantors lower adoption costs for actors who will benefit from the terms of the settlement but lack confidence that the rules will be enforced. They can also allay the concerns of those who face risks to their physical, political, or economic security if they embrace the terms of the settlement. Effective guarantors lower the cost of moving from war to peace by ensuring the benefits of peace and minimizing its dangers for the weaker party.

In assessing adoption costs we look at the impact of the peace settlement on domestic actors' physical, political, and economic security, following the work of Hartzell and Hoddie.[3] We are interested not just in the end of conflict but in the set of institutional reforms required to fulfill the terms of the postwar political settlement that is part of the peace process. This often includes restructuring security forces, establishing or strengthening democratic institutions, anticorruption measures, and human rights protections. Including such measures as part of a peace settlement can alleviate political and security concerns among warring parties and enable the peace process to go forward.[4] But implementing these reforms implies potential costs for domestic political actors.

For rebels, laying down arms and moving into civilian life implies surrendering their security to the very government authorities they have been battling with lethal force. For their part, governments seek to create conditions to guarantee that rebel soldiers are effectively disarmed and demobilized or integrated into the state's security sector. Many if not most peace agreements contain provisions for disarmament, demobilization, and restructuring of security forces. Even with such assurances, domestic actors' assessment of risk will depend both on who is to oversee these processes as well as the balance of forces between rebels and government.

In addition to physical security, governments and rebels may be concerned with their access to political and economic power. As Eva Bertram points out, "peace building is nothing less than the reallocation of political power; it is not a neutral act."[5] Zartman, among others, highlights the importance of political inclusion as a foundation for peace: "Insurgents must be assured of getting a real role in a new political system, with guarantees of protecting that role, so that the agreement becomes not just the end of the war but the beginning of a new partnership that does not let the old neglect and discrimination happen again."[6] For incumbent factions, embracing more inclusive, democratic politics brings considerable risk that they might lose the means to maintain their political authority. Political actors may also face an economic price for adopting the postwar political settlement. For example, where rebels have used lootable natural resources to finance their war, the end of war will also mean an end to unfettered access to these resources. UNITA faced this dilemma in Angola in 1997 and found the adoption costs of peace too high. Similarly, where governments have used the war as cover for the diversion of resources away from development and into private bank accounts, peace comes with costs.

Hartzell and Hoddie argue that institutions for political and economic power sharing might effectively substitute for external guarantors by demonstrating warring parties' commitment to a peaceful settlement.[7] But brand-new institutions are unlikely to constrain the behavior of powerful actors once the agreement is signed, especially in the short term. Belligerents often seek to build provisions into the peace agreement that guarantee them some measure of access to political and economic power. Credible external guarantors, alongside provisions that make it hard for one side to exclude the other from access to political or economic participation, are more likely to lower adoption costs for domestic elites.

Adoption costs depend both on domestic political actors' assessments of how the terms of the peace settlement will affect them—if enforced—and on their assessment of external actors' ability to enforce those terms. For this reason the identity of the external interveners matters. But one size does not fit all. No category of external actor will be effective in all cases. There will be cases in which domestic political actors face such high adoption costs that external actors can do little or nothing to allay them. Nevertheless, we argue that under certain circumstances that we explore below, bilateral donors can be critical to the success of the peace settlement.

Effective Guarantors

What makes an effective guarantor? An effective guarantor is one with sufficient resources, capacity, and credibility to induce the cooperation by relevant domestic actors that is necessary to implement a peace agreement. In the post–Cold War period "implementing the peace agreement" usually includes establishing formally democratic political systems as well as physical security. Because some of these measures are costly for domestic actors to adopt, effective guarantors employ a range of negative and positive incentives to get the job done. These include, most important, reducing uncertainty regarding physical, political, or economic security of former belligerents and offering tangible benefits or costs, monetary or in-kind support, or threatening sanctions or the use of force. As Fortna points out, such interventions support peacekeeping by "raising the costs of war and the benefits of peace."[8] External actors play a similar role throughout the peacebuilding process as political actors weigh the costs of implementing the terms of a peace agreement and democratic reforms.

Merely providing resources and troops is not sufficient to guaranteeing the peace. Especially when adoption costs are high, external actors use their resources to "cajole" reluctant leaders and engage in a process of "continuous bargaining" over implementing the peace agreement.[9] The leverage of external actors depends not only on the amount of resources they provide but also on their ability to bargain effectively, promote a consistent agenda, monitor behavior on the ground, and use that information to respond flexibly to changing conditions.[10] Even where adoption costs are lower, domestic leaders' ability to fulfill the terms of the peace agreement may depend on receiving the external backing necessary to implement costly measures and guarantee their political survival. Domestic actors are interested in their prospects not only for the present and immediate future but for the more distant future as well. External actors' ability to credibly commit to future support—and withhold resources in case of noncompliance—may affect their calculations over whether to embrace the terms of the postwar democratic political settlement.

In the extensive literature seeking to explain effective peacebuilding efforts, there is broad agreement that in order to be effective in confronting these challenges, peacebuilders should:

1. be flexible and responsive to changing circumstances on the ground;
2. be able to identify spoilers and deal effectively with them;
3. understand the incentive structures facing key domestic actors (including understanding root and immediate causes of tension and conflict, capacity constraints, political challenges, and economic opportunities)[11]; and
4. be able to coordinate with other external actors in order to "speak with one voice."[12]

These "lessons learned" suggest that the UN is at a distinct disadvantage as an effective external guarantor in postconflict peacebuilding or at least that it could be helpfully supplemented by other external actors.

First, UN peace missions are recently created, ad hoc amalgamations. Domestic political actors have no basis on which to assess the UN mission's credibility in their country at the start of that mission; instead, domestic actors must take their cues from bilateral actors who are known to them. Major donors' behavior with an established presence in the country may be far more consequential to the success or failure of peace missions than has been acknowledged thus far. In other words, the behavior of established bilateral donors provides important signals to domestic political actors about the risks and benefits of implementing the peace agreement.

Bilateral donors are likely to have greater local knowledge, more flexibility, and the ability to impose conditionality on discrete components of the peace process that are not within reach of the UN mission, with its heavy bureaucracy and broad mandate. Bilateral donors interacting directly with domestic elites in the peace implementation process may also present higher audience costs to elites considering defection from the agreement. Walter points out that powerful states might dilute their influence in this respect when they participate in multilateral missions because choosing to act under a UN umbrella could signal weak rather than strong commitment to enforcing the peace agreement (because they are not willing to take direct bilateral action).[13] Conversely, bilateral actors working in complement to the UN mission can help compensate for the UN's inability to impose audience costs on its own.

There is an important temporal dimension as well. Credibility may come from long-standing relationships in which donors have demonstrated to domestic elites their ability to deliver the goods. Bilateral actors may play important roles in providing ancillary support to create the background conditions necessary to induce domestic elites' cooperation. This is often done behind the scenes, before and during peace talks themselves. Bilateral donors may have long-standing relationships with one or another of the belligerents, which enhances their ability to act at least as "partial" guarantors for one side. Other comparative advantages of bilateral actors may not come into play until the longer term—as guarantors of economic support, providers of technical and financial aid for necessary administrative reforms, and long-term monitors of the democratic process at election times as well as between elections. Domestic political actors might be willing to discount their immediate interests in order to win approval from international actors if they believe that support from these actors will be crucial and forthcoming in the future. Such reciprocity is not likely from a relatively short-lived UN mission but may well be expected from a bilateral donor with established roots and interests in the country.

Bilateral donors are not ultimately responsible for the overall outcome of the peace implementation mission. They may therefore be better able to apply pressure or supply positive incentives to improve compliance on specific aspects of the process that the UN may feel obliged to overlook because of pressure to achieve the overall goal on schedule, an unwillingness to ruffle the feathers of the government, or a lack of human or financial resources to attend to these nuances.

This perspective calls into question the assumption that impartial actors make the best guarantors. It also undermines the idea that ad hoc peace missions cobbled together from multilateral contributions or "coalitions of the willing" make effective guarantors of peace agreements. It suggests instead that bilateral donors play not just a supporting role but also a potentially determining role in shaping domestic elites' attitudes and behavior in postconflict settings. This suggests a need for a better understanding of the role bilateral actors have played in successful or unsuccessful peace operations. Importantly, money or financial leverage is not the only or even necessarily the most important issue. It is not simply the amount of aid provided by a donor during the process but the relationships and local knowledge of major donors or "development partners" that may play a pivotal role in the outcome of peace operations.

Second, peacebuilding is not a two-sided interaction with a unitary external actor—the UN mission—on one hand and "domestic actors" on the other. Post-conflict settings are very complex environments in which the multitude of external actors resembles Migdal's description of countries with strong societies and weak states. In Migdal's formulation weak states compete with myriad rival sources of social authority to make the authoritative rules that will dictate citizens' behavior. In the peacebuilding context the UN peace mission and various bilateral actors share a common broad goal (peace) but have divergent short-term objectives and offer different costs and benefits for domestic actors doing business with them. Various external actors may offer peace through development, or peace through democracy, or peace without strings. They may offer security guarantees or not, financial incentives or not, reputational enhancement or not. Domestic actors can choose to accept what each of these external actors is offering (or not). The offers are not always consistent with one another and may work at cross purposes. Virtually every study of postconflict peacebuilding, whether focused on bilateral donors or the UN, bemoans the lack of coordination and cooperation amongst external actors.

Thus, domestic political actors may know relatively little about the resources and capacities of most external actors seeking to contribute to postconflict peace-building, particularly UN missions. Each UN mission has a different mandate, different leadership, and participation from different countries with different capacities. Even if the contingents and mandate of a mission are known in advance, it is not safe to make sweeping assumptions about how fully and how effectively the mandate will be implemented.

In addition, the multiplicity of external actors may tempt domestic political elites to play these actors off one another in order to maximize gains for themselves. Domestic political elites can bid up the price of cooperation on a particular agenda item, take advantage of information asymmetry among external actors about what is happening in a particular geographic or issue area, or exploit preexisting relationships they may have with particular donors to achieve more favorable terms of participation.

This picture of external peacebuilders as a diverse array of "free agents," creating a buffet of opportunities for domestic political actors to modify the terms of their participation in the postwar settlement, is in stark contrast to much of the literature, which presents peacebuilding as a two-sided affair with the UN on one side of the table and domestic elites on the other.

Domestic Politics and External Influence

The arguments laid out so far suggest that external actors' ability to serve as effective guarantors of peacebuilding processes depends on their capabilities for achieving unified and coherent approaches. The domestic side of the equation also affects the potential for peacebuilder leverage. Domestic political actors, whose cooperation is critical to the successful implementation of reforms, are embedded in political and economic relationships that affect the risks and benefits of a given set of reforms. Even after a peace agreement is signed, political actors must often struggle to maintain authority and to survive politically vis-à-vis other factions vying for power. The relative strength and vulnerability of political factions and the relationships among them affect the adoption costs of implementing the terms of the peace agreement as well as the value of external resources and guarantees. Relationships among domestic factions also affect their ability to maneuver around external actors or to manipulate information asymmetries or multiple donors to achieve their desired results. The relationships within the postconflict country thus shape external actors' opportunities for leverage. The influence of external actors depends, in turn, on their ability to navigate and respond to these domestic relationships.

Under what conditions, then, can external actors serve as credible guarantors and affect the behavior of domestic political elites in ways that support peacebuilding? When and how do they lower adoption costs in practice? First, relationships between external actors and domestic political elites create or diminish leverage. A recent comparative study of nine cases of postconflict peacebuilding finds that aid per se has a limited impact on democratic outcomes.[14] Instead, aid relationships work on outcomes in more complex and nuanced ways, most important by creating the potential for donors to exercise conditionality and by facilitating trust between domestic elites and external actors that is necessary for peacebuilder leverage. These positive effects come most important through the relationships that donors who contribute to and participate in peacebuilding missions have established with domestic elites over long years of aid provision.

The relationships that exist between donors and domestic political actors and among donors themselves at the onset of the intervention are important because they affect mutual confidence between peacebuilders and domestic political actors and, hence, add to or subtract from the credibility of donors as external guarantors, the ability of donors to coordinate with one another, and the degree to which donors have local knowledge about political, social, cultural, and other conditions that could affect the peacebuilding process. A history of consistent support for the government from a given group of donors during the humanitarian crisis brought on by war, for example, can give that donor group credibility with domestic political actors. Trust in external peacebuilders lowers elite adoption costs by reducing perceived threats posed by the democratic political settlement and enhancing confidence among domestic leaders that external actors will follow through with their commitments.

Where donors have a history of working together in a country before or during the war, they can more easily overcome the coordination and cooperation challenges that plague many peace missions. Donor cooperation in a humanitarian emergency can provide a precedent and even an institutional template (such as donor working groups) for cooperation during the peace process. Coherence among donors reduces local actors' ability to "divide and conquer" external actors during the peacebuilding process in order to evade provisions they dislike. And it increases donor ability to implement conditionality, thereby increasing peacebuilder leverage.[15] Local knowledge and connections forged from long experience in a country also increase external actors' ability to implement conditionality effectively. In short, the degree to which peacebuilders leverage the resources available to them—and, indeed, their ability to mobilize resources from their own governments—depends to a considerable extent on preexisting relationships between donors and domestic elites and on relationships forged or modified throughout the peacebuilding process.

On the other side of the equation relationships between domestic elites also affect adoption costs and external actors' ability to serve as effective guarantors. In a study of the impact of external assistance on postconflict institution building, Berg finds that external resources are most influential when political elites are most vulnerable politically or when they face internal political challenges that leave them reliant on external support for their political survival.[16] Domestic political actors with fragmented political coalitions or who lack control over a reliable source of revenue are more likely to depend on external support to manage political challenges and consolidate their authority. Conversely, leaders with a more cohesive political base or control over a concentrated revenue source face higher adoption costs in the potential loss of control over resources or state institutions as well as lower benefits of external assistance relative to domestic sources of support. Relationships among domestic elites not only determine adoption costs but also affect the value of external assistance to domestic leaders and, thereby, shape the opportunities for influence available to external actors.

Within the context of domestic political struggles the credibility of external actors and the confidence of domestic leaders that they will fulfill their commitments affect the leaders' calculation of the benefits of external assistance. For leaders of factions that are relatively vulnerable politically, externally provided funds, legitimacy, informational advantages, and physical protection can compensate for the limitations on their authority that come with democratic reforms and help them neutralize challenges from rival factions. Peacebuilders with a history of providing assistance, deep relationships, and the ability to reliably commit to long-term support are more likely to inspire the necessary confidence and to help them respond to domestic political challenges. The flexibility of bilateral actors also enhances their credibility that they will withhold support if domestic leaders fail to uphold their commitments.

Even the most credible external actors may not always achieve the leverage necessary to influence local actors, however. Leaders of factions who are embedded in powerful and cohesive domestic networks or who dominate the political landscape may lose more from adopting reforms that undermine their source of authority and may gain less from external support. These leaders are less likely to develop effective relationships with external actors or to respond to external pressure for reforms that threaten their interests. External actors therefore find fewer opportunities for leverage where a cohesive political faction dominates the postconflict political context.

Over time, however, external actors may also disrupt local networks or shift the balance of power among competing factions. Where opportunities for external leverage are limited, such changes may open new opportunities by weakening powerful networks. Conversely, changes in domestic networks that reinforce a party's domestic power base or reduce their reliance on external support may reduce external influence. For external actors, achieving and maintaining leverage requires detailed knowledge of the changing local context and the ability to respond in ways that reinforce opportunities for influence.

Given the complexities of postconflict politics, serving as effective guarantors requires the ability to develop deep knowledge of local political and economic networks, respond credibly and flexibly to changing conditions, and maintain effective relationships with domestic elites that help them minimize domestic adoption costs. Bilateral actors are more likely than the UN to achieve these capabilities. Nonetheless, the reality of local politics often limits the potential for even the most credible and coherent external actors to influence core aspects of the peacebuilding process. The next three sections flesh out the argument made here by examining three important cases in sub-Saharan Africa: Mozambique, Liberia, and Rwanda.

BILATERAL DONORS AND PEACEBUILDING IN MOZAMBIQUE[17]

The Mozambican case provides examples in which bilateral actors played a critical role in assuring the peace by successfully deploying their extensive local knowledge and the political capital gained from long experience in the country as well as from the understanding of a longer-term commitment from aid donors in an aid-dependent country. Major donors provided domestic elites with demonstrations of their ability to enforce the peace by using a range of strategies that were beyond the reach of the UN mission alone.

In postwar Mozambique donors successfully used a variety of modalities for providing aid conditioned on and designed to give direct support to advances in the peace process. After the 1992 signing of the General Peace Agreement (GPA) between the government of Mozambique and the rebel group Renamo, the peace process was formally overseen by UNOMOZ (United Nations Observation Mission in Mozambique), and the UN operation has received much of the credit for the success of the peace process in Mozambique. Although UNOMOZ was crucial in overseeing the ceasefire and providing the overarching formal framework within which the peace process was carried out, the success of this process largely depended upon flexible and responsive interventions on the part of bilateral donors, who filled in critical gaps left by UNOMOZ. These donors had significant country experience, local standing with domestic actors, and resources independent of those allocated for the UN peace operation. They also had a stake in the outcome of the peace process that was tied to their longer-term interests as donors in Mozambique. These factors permitted donors to employ effective conditionality on discrete aspects of the peace process.

Peace conditionality, "the use of aid as a lever to persuade conflicting parties to make peace, to implement peace accords, and to consolidate peace," was employed in Mozambique on two levels.[18] First, the country's major donors committed to a large infusion of aid upon signing of the peace agreement in Rome in 1992. This commitment of aid was based on the expectation that the government of Mozambique and Renamo would move forward to implement the commitments each had made in Rome.

However, as the peace process unfolded, donors involved themselves in the details of the implementation process in ways that enabled them to exercise an implicit conditionality over specific measures. The broad quid pro quo of money for progress in the peace process developed into the use of more narrowly targeted peace conditionality to overcome specific obstacles over the course of the implementation process. UNOMOZ as an institution was limited both by its mandate and by resource constraints, and it strictly limited its involvement or the sharing of its equipment and other resources for other parts of the electoral process for which it was not specifically tasked (its priorities were electoral observation and administration).[19] Bilateral donors stepped in at many points during the implementation and electoral processes to offer support where UNOMOZ could not. These bilateral actors not only achieved an unaccustomed degree of coordination among themselves with respect to important goals and activities in support of the political transition they also succeeded in limiting the government's ability to "divide and conquer" the donor community by allowing donors to speak with one voice on the most important issues of implementation. The fact that Aldo Ajello, as special representative of the secretary-general (SRSG), so visibly supported these efforts by bilateral donors was crucial.

In addition, donors sometimes conditioned their own donations on the participation of a critical mass of other donors to ensure that their own contributions would not go toward a fatally underfunded project. In these ways donors selectively exerted leverage over not only leaders of the warring parties but also UNOMOZ and one another, shaping and reshaping key aspects of the process along the way.

Thus, the specific peace conditionalities that helped produce a successful transition from war to peace in Mozambique were not planned in advance of the peace operation but developed by donors in response to specific challenges that arose over the course of implementing the peace agreement. When problems arose in the implementation of the agreement, donors stepped in, singly or in groups, to provide good offices, inject additional resources, and remind both sides of their commitments.

Donors' history of engagement in Mozambique provided the necessary backdrop for the application of micro-level conditionality in support of the peace process. By the time of the peace process the major donors were known quantities to the government and Renamo. The so-called like-minded donors had been intimately involved with supporting the state since independence. The United States, Italy, the World Bank, and other donors provided significant support later on but were established actors well before the war ended. This is not to say that relations between these donors and the government or Renamo were uniformly warm. Nevertheless, major donors had established a track record with the government by the time of the peace agreement, and their priorities and proclivities were clear. This was a very different government-donor relationship from the conditional sets of relationships that often emerged elsewhere in the 1990s.

Extended experience in the country gave donors the local knowledge necessary to sense what kinds of positive and negative inducements were most likely to work. Conditionality could be fine-tuned through consideration of the context. Moreover, donors had significant experience working with one another in Mozambique in the context of the humanitarian emergency during the civil war. This experience; their shared understanding of the political, social, and economic contexts; and the absence of complicating factors like lucrative natural resources or strategic political or economic importance made donors more willing and able to cooperate with one another.

Mozambique's experience supports the arguments of scholars who find that peace conditionality is likely to work best where conditions imposed are specific, flexible, and well matched to the problem; where donors share common goals and are able to create coordination mechanisms; and where short-term conditions are part of a longer-term relationship and set of goals. Thus, although donors used aid to overcome specific sticking points, these punctual interventions were clearly part of a set of longer-term goals that donors would continue to support for many years after the formal transition. These included macroeconomic stabilization, not least to provide a favorable investment climate for foreign investors; strengthening the management of public finance and the overall capacity of the Mozambican state to provide basic services; and democratic governance. In the years after the transitional general elections in 1994 donors have continued to support Renamo financially, provide support for election implementation and monitoring, and play an active part in monitoring and conditioning their aid on the requirement that both the government and Renamo remain committed to maintaining peace and moving forward with democratization.

The Mozambican case reinforces many of the findings from the literature on the role of third-party guarantors in securing negotiated peace settlements. Specifically, it provides insight into the complex interactions that underpin effective leverage for outside actors during the peace implementation process. For example, a number of scholars find that belligerents in both interstate and civil wars are influenced by "audience costs."[20] Fortna argues that "the international community has a strong effect on belligerents' decisions about war and peace. States worry about international audience costs."[21] Audience costs are the opportunity costs of breaching the agreement and are higher when international actors are able to monitor implementation closely and respond with rewards or punishment as appropriate. The effectiveness of audience costs is often diminished in UN operations because UN peace operations tend to be multifaceted, with responsibility for overseeing the ceasefire, elections, human rights, and more. Fortna finds in her study of interstate war that "the effects of international audience costs are often limited, either by the UN's desire to maintain neutrality or by great powers turning a blind eye for strategic reasons."[22]

The same often holds true in post–civil war peacekeeping. Typically, leaders of peace operations are forced to prioritize between, say, timely elections or compliance on the ceasefire and accountability on human rights. Efforts to take a firm stand on one particular issue may face opposition by powerful members of the Security Council or compromise the mission's ability to carry out another dimension of its mandate. The literature suggests that although third parties *can* affect the behavior of belligerents in positive ways, the terms of their involvement tend to limit their effectiveness in this regard.

In Mozambique this problem was avoided because of the intensive, direct involvement of bilateral donors in areas that were technically covered by the UN mandate and because of the active cooperation of the SRSG with bilateral donors. Nevertheless, the structure and multifaceted nature of the mission gave UNOMOZ itself little effective leverage in some of these areas. The UN had formal authority to oversee demobilization and elections; bilateral donors had the resources, knowledge, and practical capacity to make it work. Bilateral donors supplemented UN funding for elections, party transformation, and disarmament, demobilization, and reintegration (DDR) and played a direct role in monitoring these aspects of the agreement. Even if the UN itself was forced to turn a blind eye to violations of agreements on one or more of these dimensions in exchange for success on another or to ignore government transgressions in order to continue to operate, bilateral donors, working with the blessing of the SRSG, had the ability to impose direct conditionality, and they did so.

When the parties engaged in excessive foot-dragging on key measures of electoral law during the Multiparty Conference, donors withdrew funding for the conference facilities. When Renamo pulled out of the elections on the eve of voting, donors promised to investigate Renamo's concerns. When donors feared demobilized soldiers would become a source of instability in the countryside after their severance pay ran out, they designed and funded a program to extend their benefits.[23] None of this would have been possible for the UN peace mission alone, whose multifaceted mandate made it incapable of taking calculated risks in one area out of fear that this might compromise its role in others. The direct involvement of bilateral actors allowed the international community as a whole to fine-tune its role as a credible guarantor of the peace agreement.

BILATERAL AND MULTILATERAL DONORS IN LIBERIA

The case of Liberia after 2003 provides further evidence for the role played by bilateral actors in supporting a peace process beyond what was possible by the United Nations and other multilateral actors. Although the United Nations was formally responsible for implementing certain elements of the peace agreement, it relied heavily on bilateral actors for financial support and political backing. At crucial times during the process bilateral actors used their long-standing reputation with local actors, local knowledge, and ability to make credible threats to enforce key terms of the peace agreement. Bilateral actors also helped reduce the adoption costs of democratic reforms by developing the confidence of Liberian leaders and helping them to overcome domestic political challenges.

The complementary roles of bilateral actors were recognized in the Comprehensive Peace Agreement (CPA), which ended the conflict in 2003. The CPA requested the assistance of the United Nations, the African Union (AU), and the Economic Community of West African States (ECOWAS) to implement key provisions such as maintaining security, demobilizing combatants, organizing elections, and strengthening state institutions. The agreement also recognized the role of bilateral actors and called specifically on Liberia's largest bilateral donor, the United States, to "play a lead role" in organizing the restructuring of the Armed Forces of Liberia.[24] Even where multilateral actors were designated to play the primary role, bilateral actors provided most of the funding, either by contributing to funds managed by the United Nations or through direct bilateral assistance programs. Bilateral actors also provided logistical and material support to enable multilateral actions. For example, the United States and Nigeria provided the logistics and the personnel needed to deploy the ECOWAS force that stabilized Monrovia at the end of the conflict and provided ongoing support to the United Nations Mission in Liberia (UNMIL) peacekeeping force. Bilateral actors played active roles in organizing many of the core peacebuilding processes and providing the political backing, coordination, or moral support when obstacles arose.

Bilateral actors helped to advance implementation of the peace agreement by helping to overcome opposition or disagreements at key moments. Many of the terms of the peace agreement were costly for Liberian political actors in threatening their political influence or access to resources. Bilateral actors' intervention with promises to provide or withhold funding or other forms of support enabled them to work through these challenges. Even when the UN was nominally in the lead, it often called upon bilateral actors to help. For example, the United Nations Civilian Police Mission (UNPOL) component of UNMIL was designated in the CPA to play the lead role in restructuring and training the Liberian National

Police. Early on in the process UN officials ran into opposition to their plan to vet and retrain every police officer, which they saw as essential to building a credible force. The leaders of the main warring factions preferred to reserve places for their fighters, whereas top police officials opposed being subjected to investigation and retraining. After difficult negotiations, the issue was resolved after the US ambassador conditioned the provision of bilateral resources on the acceptance of the UN's terms for the police restructuring process.[25] US officials also helped reassure individual leaders that they would provide them with political backing and financial assistance to carry out these difficult decisions.

Organizational and political constraints within UNMIL forced it repeatedly to rely on the United States and other bilateral actors to overcome roadblocks in the peacebuilding process. The Liberian case confirms the findings from the literature on the importance of coherent action for effective peacebuilding as well as the difficulty of the UN in this area. Achieving leverage through conditionality requires sufficient unity to achieve coherent goals and positions as well as the ability to gather information, share it internally, and use it to respond to specific issues. The UN mission in Liberia, which included the UNMIL peacekeeping force along with numerous UN agencies joined by loose coordination structures, had trouble achieving coherent positions and managing information internally. Within UNMIL short rotations of personnel from different countries, with different backgrounds, skill sets, and leadership styles, often inhibited the development of relationships with Liberian counterparts necessary for deeper local knowledge and responsiveness to changing conditions. Especially in areas like police development, which required both detailed knowledge and a coherent, long-term approach, the diversity of backgrounds and operational approaches impeded the development of unified doctrine or policies. When UNMIL did achieve clear positions, it often struggled to enforce them because it could not threaten to withhold assistance or impose audience costs without soliciting the support of its member states.

Instead, the UN often relied on bilateral actors who were involved in these processes on the ground. Bilateral actors were better positioned to develop the credibility, local knowledge, and flexibility necessary to apply conditions to address specific issues. The United States in particular had a long history of close ties with Liberia, starting from Liberia's establishment with US government support in the early 1800s and continuing with US financial and political backing through the 1980s.[26] The United States had played a central role in negotiating the CPA. The US ambassador had developed personal credibility by remaining in Monrovia during the worst episodes of fighting in 2003 after many other international officials departed and by sheltering thousands of Liberians in the US embassy compound. Liberian and US officials communicated frequently and developed close personal relationships. These close connections allowed US officials to develop a deeper understanding of local constraints and to respond to specific challenges as they arose. In the case of the police, for example, American UNPOL advisors would report obstacles to US Embassy officials, who could raise them during their frequent conversations with senior Liberian officials. As the largest bilateral donor, the United States could achieve significant impact by threatening to withhold its resources or backing to individual leaders or programs.

Other bilateral actors also played an important role. For instance, the United Kingdom had developed a reputation for credible intervention in neighboring Sierra Leone, other European countries provided expertise or funding for particular issues, and regional players like Nigeria and Ghana offered crucial pieces of assistance or reassurance to unblock stalled negotiations or help advance reforms. Coordination was most effective when the lead bilateral donor used its dominant role to set the policy agenda and bring other donors along.

The role of bilateral actors in Liberia extended beyond supporting specific reform efforts to serving as credible guarantors of the peacebuilding process. This role was rooted in the political context within Liberia. The leaders of the National Transitional Government of Liberia (NTGL) and the government of Ellen Johnson-Sirleaf, elected in 2005, relied heavily on external backing to manage the political challenges within the country. Within the NTGL, which was made up of representatives from the three main warring factions (the LURD, MODEL, and remnants of the Charles Taylor government), eighteen political parties, and numerous special interest groups, no faction or leader was powerful enough to consolidate its authority. Some, like the members of the former government, were under physical threat, and many relied heavily on external support. The Johnson-Sirleaf administration was also politically vulnerable. With a combined total of only twelve out of ninety-four seats in the two houses of the legislature and saddled with over $3.5 billion in national debt, the new president depended on the support of several powerful warlords and faction leaders to maintain a political coalition and bring revenue into the state coffers. Faced with this fragmented political environment, political leaders would depend heavily on external support to bolster their internal political legitimacy and to secure desperately needed funds.

External support helped these relatively weak leaders overcome the substantial costs of implementing the terms of the peace agreement and adopting reforms. For example, restructuring the police and military challenged the interests of rival politicians from the warring factions who hoped to retain influence over those forces, while governance and anticorruption measures undermined access to financial resources for members of the transitional government and legislature. Leaders confronting opposition to these reforms needed the active support of external actors both to finance the reforms and to provide political backing—and sometimes physical protection. Liberian leaders' willingness to adopt these difficult reforms depended in large part on their confidence that external actors would provide the necessary support. External actors' credibility in the eyes of local leaders was therefore crucial in shaping decisions.

Their relationships with Liberian leaders and their responsiveness to the rapidly changing political environment helped bilateral actors establish their credibility. The US government's role as the dominant funder and sponsor of the peace process—its funding amounted to over $1 billion in the first decade after the conflict—raised its visibility in the process and provided its officials with unlimited access. US Embassy officials met frequently with leaders of all of the main factions within the NTGL and used their ability to provide or withhold resources and political support to secure their cooperation on a wide range of issues, from disarmament and security sector reform to elections and governance. During her first term as president, Johnson-Sirleaf visited the White House five times and addressed a joint session of the US Congress. Frequent communication facilitated trust among Liberian and US officials and enabled US officials to respond to changing conditions and promise assistance or threaten to withhold it when obstacles arose. The UNMIL mission, meanwhile, was hampered by a short-term mandate, changing leadership, and constraints imposed by member states, which undermined its credibility as a long-term partner. In some cases the same constraints also undermined the effectiveness of bilateral support. In areas where the United States and bilateral actors were less involved in taking an active role or where bilateral support was perceived as insufficiently credible or consistent, Liberian leaders were less able to rely on their support, and the implementation of reforms suffered as a result.

The most sensitive areas of peacebuilding were handled through the active intervention of bilateral actors. For example, the United States took the lead on restructuring the military, committing over $250 million to the process in the first five years.[27] After a series of negotiations, US and Liberian officials signed a bilateral agreement that formalized a US commitment to fund and Liberian agreement to restructure the force. The commitment of US financial and political support enabled Liberian leaders to make politically controversial decisions, including disbanding the entire armed forces and starting a new recruitment from scratch.[28] The United States funded and managed a comprehensive vetting and recruitment process that involved teams of investigators deployed around the country to overcome informational constraints and enforced strict recruitment standards. US officials' involvement in recruitment decisions shielded Liberian officials from pressure by political factions to secure places for their supporters in the new force. Conversely, in the absence of meaningful involvement by multilateral actors, the dominant role of the United States has engendered criticism that it has undermined the legitimacy of the reforms among some segments of Liberian society and that the military remains overly dependent on external backing and financing.[29]

Similarly, US and European officials were instrumental in creating the Governance and Economic Management Assistance Programme (GEMAP). The program aimed to reduce rampant corruption by placing foreign financial experts within Liberian government agencies with the authority to approve or disapprove expenditures. Viewed as a threat to Liberia's sovereignty and opposed by factions that were benefiting from looting government resources, the plan was nonetheless adopted by NTGL chairman Gyude Bryant after concerted pressure by bilateral donors. The United States, the EU, and several bilateral donors threatened to withhold the considerable funds they had promised for reconstruction and security sector reform and to hold Bryant personally responsible for the loss of outside funding.[30] In this case multilateral support from ECOWAS and the UN along with technical oversight by the World Bank and the IMF provided broader legitimacy for the program.

The Liberian case thus reveals the complementary roles multilateral and bilateral actors play in the peacebuilding process. The presence of multilateral peacekeeping forces organized by the United Nations, ECOWAS, and the AU were essential to building confidence among previously warring factions, providing the legitimacy for external involvement, and mobilizing personnel and resources. Bilateral actors were better placed than the United Nations to help Liberian elites overcome the adoption costs of reform based on their long-standing relationship, local knowledge, flexibility, and responsiveness to changing conditions. In turn, the broad legitimacy of the UN and other multilateral actors enabled bilateral actors to act forcefully and unequivocally. Although peacebuilders were not successful in all areas of peacebuilding in Liberia, in the successful instances bilateral and multilateral actors acted in complementary roles.

RWANDA

Rwanda was a case with strong and cohesive incumbent domestic political leaders facing a weak and fragmented opposition. Our theory would predict that such leaders would be less likely to embrace reforms that might undermine their physical, economic, or political security. In addition, several factors weakened the potential for donor leverage. Rwanda revised its constitution to accommodate multiparty politics in 1991, and for some observers the democratization process and the outbreak of civil war are inextricably linked. Multiple attempts to reach a negotiated peace in 1992 and 1993 included the provision for the formation of a unity government, and democracy was enshrined in the August 1993 Arusha Accords. A UN observation mission, UNAMIR, was established in October 1993. However, after renewed fighting and the genocide that ensued between April and June 1994 UNAMIR was dramatically downsized. Although attempts were made to bolster the UN force with UNAMIR II in May 1994, the only real international muscle deployed after the onset of genocide came in the form of Operation Turquoise, a French-led mission authorized by the UN with a Chapter VII mandate, which began in June 1994. The fighting ended in military victory for the Rwanda Patriotic Front (RPF). There was no new ceasefire or peace agreement, although a broad-based national unity government was installed in July 1994.

Donors with the longest presence in Rwanda before the war, such as France, enjoyed little influence with the new regime. France's ties with the Habyarimana regime, which the RPF replaced, as well as the RPF's historic ties to Anglophone Africa undermined Francophone influence. The United States and the UK have since forged strong political and security ties with the Rwandan Patriotic Front government, but these ties have yielded comparatively little influence over the regime in the wake of the genocide. Compared to Mozambique, where leaders faced both a fear that resources would be withdrawn for noncooperation and an opposition with the potential to spoil the peace settlement, the case of Rwanda highlights the limits of external leverage, especially where domestic opposition to the regime is weak. In Rwanda the costs to domestic political actors of adopting democracy were relatively high, whereas the costs of failing to do so were low. Following the 1994 genocide the government faced few political opponents or other veto players within Rwanda; instead, it faced armed extremists and political opponents based outside the country. The former in particular helped the government to limit democratic and human rights reform without risking loss of external support.

Although Rwanda's leaders were heavily dependent on external aid and diplomatic support, they were able to resist external pressure for reform without losing support. Victory on the battlefield gave the Rwandan Patriotic Front little incentive to compromise, and the genocide gave credence to that government's claims that democratization could endanger the country's security. As a result, the ruling party faced no meaningful domestic political opposition once it had consolidated its authority. Moreover, the international community's failure to act effectively in the face of the genocide undermined the credibility of bilateral actors as well as that of the UN.[31] This included those with long-standing relationships in the country. The government effectively resisted donor pressures to democratize, publicly rebuking donors who pushed too hard for political reform.[32] This resistance did not significantly affect aid flows—in short, bilateral donors failed to apply conditionality, despite their experience with the country and its leaders that might have permitted them to do so effectively.

Bilateral donors had begun pressing for democratic reforms in Rwanda as early as 1990. According to Uvin, the United States played a leading role in this push, reducing aid in 1992 in the face of human rights violations. However, US humanitarian aid increased the next year. In 1993 the United States and several European donors threatened to cut aid in response to a negative UN human rights report but did not in fact reduce aid allocations. According to some observers, donors feared that exerting too much pressure would endanger the Arusha peace agreement.[33] After the genocide France, Belgium, Switzerland, and Germany sought to pressure the government on refugee return and transitional justice. Though the government paid lip service to these goals, progress was limited. As Hayman points out, "as far as the RPF was concerned, by its failure to prevent or stop the genocide and its provision of aid to camps where the guilty were fed alongside the innocent—in quantities which dwarfed aid to Rwanda itself—the international community had lost its 'right to criticize' the new regime."[34]

Conditionality was ineffective both because donors did not consistently apply it and because domestic political leaders had the necessary political and economic resources to resist external pressure related to both the timing and content of postconflict reforms. Hayman notes that "since 1994, external actors have been constrained by collective guilt over the genocide which limits their leverage over the regime, and by differences amongst them in terms of strategic and developmental objectives as well as their individual relations with the new regime."[35] Moreover, there is a history of division amongst donor countries in their attitude toward the government of Rwanda. During the first five years after the conflict donors were almost divided into two opposing camps: those who were positive about the new regime (often new donors who had a limited history of bilateral relations with the country, such as the Netherlands, Sweden, and the UK) and those who were negative about the new regime (those with longer histories in the country, including ties to the former regime, such as France and Belgium). Positions became less polarized as time passed, but donors' different stances affected aid in the early years after the conflict. The government was able to rely on certain friends and could afford to ignore demands made by other donors.[36]

For example, the run-up to Rwanda's first legislative and presidential elections since the genocide, held in 2003, saw the first real application of conditions to aid directly related to democracy. A clampdown on opposition parties and voices as well as human rights abuses led several donors to withhold or threaten to withhold aid, including the European Commission, the United Kingdom, and the Netherlands. The UK halted aid to the media sector when the government did not liberalize the airwaves, and the Netherlands did not disburse their aid to the elections; the European Commission released the money but only after the elections had taken place. These actions had limited effect in the absence of meaningful domestic political pressure to comply with donor stipulations. The action taken by the Netherlands was ultimately undermined by other donors releasing funds and coming out in support of the government. As Hayman points out, since 1994 "RPF has controlled political space and only allowed a gradual, and controlled, democratic process to develop on their terms and in such a way as to not threaten their power or national stability and security."[37]

CONCLUSION

Peacebuilding after civil war involves deeply political interactions among domestic and external actors. In deciding how to approach the terms of the postwar settlement, domestic leaders weigh the costs and benefits of specific provisions of the agreement while external actors seek to alter these costs and benefits to promote particular outcomes. The empirical evidence presented here suggests that the impact of external aid on peacebuilding outcomes is mediated by the relationships between donors and domestic elites, the extent to which leaders rely on external support to manage political challenges, and the degree to which donors are able to respond to political realities within the country to mitigate the costs of adopting reforms.

This chapter suggests two generalizable conclusions. First, leverage from aid depends on the relationships that aid provision creates over time among donors who fund and/or implement key aspects of peacebuilding and local actors whose support is crucial for their implementation. The relationships that exist between donors and domestic political actors at the onset of the intervention are important because they affect mutual confidence between peacebuilders and domestic political actors and, hence, add to or subtract from donors' credibility as external guarantors. These relationships evolve in response to the political conditions within the postconflict country, as changing political relationships affect domestic actors' receptiveness to external support.

Second, aid increases leverage where it is structured in such a way that it enables donors to respond flexibly to unforeseen challenges in the peace process, and it is most effective when individual donors are able to tie their own contributions to actions required of domestic political actors to move the peacebuilding process forward. Donors with resources and the organizational wherewithal to make timely interventions using those resources have more leverage than those who do not. Aid is *not* effective in increasing leverage or mitigating the adoption costs of democracy when donors are unable or unwilling to apply conditionality, when they lack a clear commitment to democracy over other concerns, when they lack the coherence necessary to act decisively and predictably, and when they lack the local knowledge and connections necessary to take advantage of opportunities to gain leverage.

We used these insights to argue that bilateral donors may enjoy structural advantages over UN missions in implementing postconflict political and other institutional reform. In addition, a comparison of these three cases allows us to refine the theory as initially advanced. First, we asserted that bilateral actors can serve as more credible guarantors of postconflict political settlements. The structural factors that enhance their coherence, flexibility, and responsiveness relative to multilateral actors enable them to more credibly lower the adoption costs of these settlements for domestic political actors. We found that the most effective instances of peacebuilding arise when bilateral actors complement multilateral assistance through credible and flexible commitments of support. Second, bilateral actors are not always effective in this role. Their ability to lower the relative cost of adopting particular aspects of the peace agreements depends not only on the resources and modalities of intervention but also on domestic political networks and the balance of power among these actors. We asserted at the outset of this chapter that domestic political networks were important because they affect adoption costs and the value of external assistance. Weaker leaders are more likely to accept outside help in order to bolster their domestic positions, whereas leaders who are already strong may have less to gain from external support and more to lose from the establishment of democratic political institutions, the implementation of comprehensive security sector reform, or anticorruption efforts. The leverage of even the most credible bilateral actors depends on the extent to which their assistance helps leaders overcome the domestic political challenges that raise the costs of accepting such reforms.

In Liberia politically vulnerable leaders accepted reforms because external support lowered their adoption costs by providing politically useful funding, legitimacy, and information that helped overcome domestic political challenges.

Although the UN was in the lead on many aspects of peacebuilding, it often turned to the United States and other bilateral actors to reinforce its stance with credible commitments of support or threats to withhold it. Conversely, bilateral actors benefited from the broader legitimacy provided by the UN and ECOWAS.

In Mozambique incumbents in power at the onset of peace were by far the stronger party in terms of their ability to make the transition to competitive politics, compared to Renamo. However, they were dependent on the international community for the resources necessary for postconflict economic rehabilitation, and they used their cooperation in the peace process to leverage more advantageous terms of support from bilateral donors and multilateral institutions like the World Bank. Despite the political advantages of the ruling party, the opposition Renamo was a potential spoiler who needed and received vital assurances and resources from major bilateral donors. The UN alone would have been unable to provide such guarantees for either party.

Finally, in Rwanda strong incumbents faced little domestic opposition after the war and genocide there. Instead, the government faced a credible security threat in the form of cross-border attacks by opposition forces who had gained refuge in eastern Democratic Republic of Congo. These leaders had little need of external support to overcome domestic challenges, and on sensitive issues bilateral donors were unwilling to press hard to overcome the incumbents' resistance.

Thus, in two of our three cases, Mozambique and Liberia, bilateral actors' ability to credibly commit to provide or withhold resources, develop trust with local actors, and respond flexibly to their specific needs as determined by the context was crucial in ensuring that their assistance overcame local adoption costs. Multilateral actors did not have the same abilities, although they provided broader legitimacy that bilateral actors often lack. In Rwanda even those abilities were not sufficient due to the domestic context.

The contribution of external actors to peacebuilding processes is far more complex—and far more political—than often described. Although external actors often help improve stability and support democratic reforms in fulfillment of peace agreements, their impact depends on political relationships both within and outside the recipient country. In this chapter we have explored several characteristics of external actors and domestic politics that shape these relationships. How donors succeed in understanding and managing these dynamics is crucial to their impact on the political dimensions of peacebuilding.

NOTES

1. Therese Pettersson and Peter Wallensteen, "Armed Conflicts 1946–2014," *Journal of Peace Research* 52, no. 4 (2015), p. 539.

2. United Nations, Peacekeeping Operations, www.un.org/en/peacekeeping/operations.

3. Caroline Hartzell and Matthew Hoddie, "Institutionalizing Peace: Power Sharing and Post–Civil War Conflict Management," *American Journal of Political Science* 47, no. 2 (2003), pp. 318–322.

4. Barbara F. Walter, *Committing to Peace: The Successful Settlement of Civil Wars* (Princeton, NJ: Princeton University Press, 2002).

5. Eva Bertram, "Reinventing Governments: The Promise and Perils of UN Peace Building," *Journal of Conflict Resolution* 39, no. 3 (1995).

6. I. William Zartman, *Elusive Peace: Negotiating an End to Civil Wars* (Washington, DC: Brookings Institution, 1995), p. 339.

7. Hartzell and Hoddie, "Institutionalizing Peace."

8. Virginia Page Fortna, *Does Peacekeeping Work? Shaping Belligerents' Choices After Civil War* (Princeton, NJ: Princeton University Press, 2008), 86.

9. Christoph Zuercher and Jens Narten, "Peacebuilding Is Interaction: Explaining the Outcomes of Postwar Democratic Transitions," paper presented at APSA Annual Meeting in Toronto, Canada, 2009; Michael Barnett and Christoph Zuercher, "The Peacebuilder's Contract: How External Statebuilding Reinforces Weak Statehood," in *The Dilemmas of Statebuilding: Confronting the Contradictions of Postwar Peace Operations*, ed. Roland Paris and Timothy D. Sisk (London: Routledge, 2008).

10. Lise Morjé Howard, *UN Peacekeeping in Civil Wars* (Cambridge: Cambridge University Press, 2007),

11. Diana Cammack, Dinah McLeod, Alina Rocah Menocal, with Karin Christiansen, "Donors and the 'Fragile States' Agenda: A Survey of Current Thinking and Practice," report submitted to the Japan International Cooperation Agency, March 2006.

12. Tetsuro Ijo, "Cooperation, Coordination and Complementarity in International Peacemaking: The Tajikistan Experience," *International Peacekeeping* 12, no. 2 (Summer 2005), pp. 189–204.

13. Barbara Walter, "The Critical Barrier to Civil War Settlements," *International Organization* 51, no. 3 (Summer 1997), pp. 335–364.

14. Christoph Zuercher, Carrie Manning, Kristie D. Evenson, Rachel Hayman, Sarah Riese, and Nora Roehner, *Costly Democracy: Peacebuilding and Democratization After War* (Stanford, CA: Stanford University Press, 2012).

15. For a full discussion of these effects in the Mozambique case see Carrie Manning and Monica Malbrough, "Bilateral Donors and Aid Conditionality in Post-Conflict Peacebuilding: The Case of Mozambique," *Journal of Modern African Studies* no. 1 (2010), pp. 143–169.

16. Louis-Alexandre Berg, "Fragmented State Building: Elite Consolidation, Party Fractionalization and Intervention After Civil War," paper presented at the 2016 Annual Meeting of the International Studies Association. See also Louis-Alexandre Berg, "From Weakness to Strength: The Political Roots of Security Sector Reform in Bosnia and Herzegovina," *International Peacekeeping* 21, no. 2 (2014), pp. 149–164.

17. This section draws on Manning and Malbrough, "Bilateral Donors and Aid Conditionality."

18. Georg Frerks, *The Use of Peace Conditionality in Conflict and Post-Conflict Settings: A Conceptual Framework and a Checklist* (The Hague: Netherlands Institute of International Relations, 2006), p. 1.

19. Nicole Ball and Sam Barnes, "Mozambique," in *Good Intentions: Pledges of Aid for Postconflict Recovery*, ed. Shepard Foreman and Stewart Patrick (Boulder, CO: Lynne Rienner Press, 2000).

20. Michael Doyle and Nicholas Sambanis, eds. *Making War and Building Peace: United Nations Peace Operations* (Princeton, NJ: Princeton University Press, 2006); Virginia Page Fortna, *Peace Time: Cease-Fire Agreements and the Durability of Peace* (Princeton, NJ: Princeton University Press, 2004); Walter, "The Critical Barrier."

21. Fortna, *Peace Time*, p. 213.

22. Ibid., p. 205.

23. Carrie L. Manning, *The Politics of Peace in Mozambique: Post-Conflict Democratization, 1999–2000* (Westport, CT: Praeger, 2002).

24. Comprehensive Peace Agreement Between the Government of Liberia, The Liberians United for Reconciliation and Democracy, The Movement for Democracy in Liberia and the Political Parties, Accra, Ghana, August 18, 2003, Article VII.

25. Berg, "Fragmented State Building."

26. See Jeremy I. Levitt, *The Evolution of Deadly Conflict in Liberia* (Durham, NC: Carolina Academic Press, 2005); and Amos Sawyer, *Beyond Plunder: Toward Democratic Governance in Liberia* (Boulder, CO: Lynne Rienner, 2005).

27. For an overview of the Security Sector Reform program see Mark Malan, *Security Sector Reform in Liberia: Mixed Results from Humble Beginnings* (Carlisle Barracks, PA: Strategic Studies Institute, U.S. Army War College, March 2008).

28. Arrangement Between the Government of the United States of America and the National Transitional Government of Liberia Concerning Security Sector Reform in the Republic of Liberia, May 17, 2005.

29. Thomas Jaye, "Liberia: Parliamentary Oversight and Lessons from Internationalized Security Sector Reform," 2008, www.agora-parl.org/node/867.

30. Renata Dawn and Laura Bailey, "Liberia's Governance and Economic Management Assistance Program: A Joint Review by the Department of Peacekeeping Operations' Peacekeeping Best Practices Section and the World Bank's Fragile States Group," May 2006, http://siteresources.worldbank.org/INTLICUS/Resources/DPKOWBGEMAPFINAL.pdf.

31. Rachel Hayman, "External Democracy Promotion in Post-Conflict Zones: Evidence from Cases: Rwanda," Free University Berlin, 2009, http://aix1.uottawa.ca/~czurcher /czurcher/Transitions_files/Final%20Report%20Rwanda.pdf.

32. Ibid.

33. See, for example, Peter Uvin, *Aiding Violence: The Development Enterprise in Rwanda* (West Hartford, CT: Kumarian Press, 1998).

34. Hayman, "External Democracy Promotion," p. 39.

35. Ibid., p. 41.

36. Ibid.

37. Ibid., p. 43.

The African Union's Peace and Security Architecture—from Aspiration to Operationalization

Ulf Engel

INTRODUCTION

In recent years the African continent has (re)gained agency in international relations.[1] This is mainly due to the African Union (AU), which, after a political and institutional transition from the Organization of African Unity (OAU) in the years 1999–2002, is increasingly representing African interests in the emerging post–Cold War multipolar world order. Both in global and in intra-African relations the Union and, in particular, the AU Commission (AUC) in core policy fields has become the distinguishable voice of its member states.[2] Given the experience of the 1990s but also more with recent trends in violent conflict, the Union's most important policy field is peace and security. In 2015/2016 it was facing ongoing violent conflicts in Burundi, the Central African Republic (CAR), Egypt, Guinea-Bissau, Libya, Mali, Somalia, Sudan (Darfur), Sudan/South Sudan (including Abyei), and the Democratic Republic of the Congo (DRC). In addition it dealt with postconflict constellations—inter alia, in Burundi, CAR, Comoros, DRC, Eritrea/Ethiopia, Guinea, Liberia, and Sierra Leone.[3] And increasingly it is struggling with forms of terrorism and violent extremism that involve, amongst others, the Lord's Resistance Army (LRA); al-Qaeda and its affiliates, including al-Qaeda in the Islamic Maghreb (AQIM), al Shabaab, al-Mourabitoun, and Ansar Dine; as well as the so-called Islamic State (IS) and its affiliates, including Boko Haram and Majlis Shura Shabab al-Islam.[4]

It is against this background that the African Union has embarked on establishing an ambitious and complex African Peace and Security Architecture (APSA). In the following chapter the progress of implementing the APSA will be reviewed with a view to the five pillars of this architecture, as described in the 2002 Protocol Relating to the Establishment of the Peace and Security Council (PSC), which entered into force on December 26, 2003: the PSC, the Panel of the Wise, the African Standby Force (ASF), the Continental Early Warning System (CEWS), and the Peace Fund.[5] In addition, key strategic partnerships with the United Nations (UN) and the European Union (EU) will be briefly reviewed. By way of conclusion, remaining challenges in fully operationalizing the APSA will be highlighted.

FROM "NONINTERVENTION" TO "NONINDIFFERENCE": NEW NORMS AND INSTITUTIONS

As part of the transformation from the OAU (which was established on May 25, 1963) to the African Union, member states confirmed the principles that already had guided intra-OAU relations: national sovereignty, noninterference in internal affairs, territorial integrity, and equality of member states.[6] Yet important for the normative foundations of inter-African relations and clearly reflecting the experience of the genocide in Rwanda in 1994, they also added the right of the Union "to intervene in any Member State pursuant by a decision of the Assembly in respect of grave circumstances."[7] After an amendment to the original Constitutive Act, adopted by the second ordinary session of the AU Assembly held July 10–12, 2003, in Maputo, Mozambique, grave circumstances include "war crimes, genocide and crimes against humanity as well as a serious threat to legitimate order to restore peace and security to the Member States of the Union, upon the recommendation of the Peace and Security Council."[8] In the academic debate this change from the principle of noninterference to at least nonindifference usually is attributed to a shift in interests among AU member states from what is labeled as regime security to human security and the related rise of the international norm of a responsibility to protect (R2P) that treats sovereignty not just as a right of states but as a responsibility (including the right of other states to interfere whenever this responsibility is not exercised).[9]

The transition to the African Union represents a political compromise that reflected different interests and visions of Pan-African unity.[10] In the end, a pragmatic approach was favored over more ambitious dreams about establishing the Union Government and creating the "United States of Africa" (as proposed by the late Libyan leader Muammar Gaddafi).[11] At the center of the new continental body is the African Union Commission (AUC), which has replaced the rather weak OAU general secretariat (with currently some fourteen hundred staff).[12]

Inter alia, the Commission's mandate is to represent the Union; initiate proposals for consideration by other organs; implement the decisions taken by other organs; organize and manage the meetings of the Union; act as the custodian of the "Constitutive Act" and its protocols, the treaties, legal instruments, and decisions adopted by the Union; coordinate and monitor the implementation of AU decisions; work out draft common AU positions; and coordinate the actions of member states in international negotiations. It is also tasked with ensuring the promotion of peace, democracy, security, and stability; providing operational support to the PSC; and coordinating and harmonizing the programs and policies of the Union with those of the regional economic communities (RECs).[13] The latter are seen as integral parts of the Union. The officially recognized eight partner RECs of the Union are the Community of Sahel-Saharan States (CEN-SAD), the Common Market for Eastern and Southern Africa (COMESA), the East African Community (EAC), the Economic Community of Central African States (ECCAS), the Economic Community of West African States (ECOWAS), the Intergovernmental Authority on Development (IGAD) based at the Horn of Africa, the Southern African Development Community (SADC), and the Arab Maghreb Union (UMA).

Under its three chairpersons—former Malian president Alpha Oumar Konaré (2003–2008), former Gabonese foreign minister Jean Ping (2008–2012), and former South African foreign minister Nkosazana Dlamini-Zuma (2012–2016)—the Commission has become a player in its own right, with an increasingly distinctive policy agenda and interests of its own. Partly the rise of the Commission has been attributed to the impact of "Africrats," the continental body's bureaucrats, in the process of the institutionalization of the African Union.[14] So far the three commissioners for Peace and Security have been the crucial personalities in driving this agenda, all three being Algerian career diplomats: Amb. Saïd Djinnit (2004–2008), Amb. Ramtane Lamamra (2008–2013), and Amb. Smaïl Chergui (since 2013), for many years assisted by the Director of Peace and Security El-Ghassim Wane (who was appointed UN assistant secretary-general for Peacekeeping Operations in December 2015). The Department for Peace and Security (PSD) administers all APSA-relevant support. It is made up of five divisions and one secretariat: conflict prevention and early warning, crisis management and postconflict reconstruction and development, defense and security, peace support operations (PSOs), and peace and security finance, as well as the PSC secretariat.

Still far from a substantial communitarization (*Vergemeinschaftung*) of policies or a noticeable delegation of sovereignty to the Commission by member states but close to a policy coordination and harmonization role, the Commission increasingly has become the locus of managing the Union's peace and security activities. Thus, the Commission organizes and sets the agenda of PSC meetings, and up to now it has also drafted all major PSC communiqués and decisions as well as related summit documents.

In relation to external actors the Commission has tried to develop further the principle of "African solutions for African problems" but had to concede a major setback with the developments unfolding in Libya in 2011 when a NATO-led alliance intervened on the basis of a UN mandate to enforce a no-fly zone. While the African Union as a whole struggled hard to make up its mind about the nature of the conflict in Libya and adequate responses (existing policy scripts simply did not foresee popular uprisings and revolutions), it lost precious time and was soon outmaneuvered by NATO, which obviously harbored plans toward regime change.[15] The Union's plan for conflict resolution was neglected, and its mediation efforts, spearheaded by an Ad Hoc High-Level Committee chaired by South African president Jacob Zuma, were sidelined. In a report presented to an extraordinary summit of the AU Assembly, held April 25–26, 2011, in Addis Ababa, an obviously highly frustrated AUC chairperson therefore deplored "the reluctance of members of the international community to fully acknowledge the AU role in the promotion of peace in the continent and their selective application of the principle of ownership." He claimed that any partnership on conflict resolution should be "fully based on Africa's leadership" because "without such leadership, there will be no ownership and sustainability; because we understand the problems far better than even the closest partners; because we know which solutions will work, and how we can get there; and because, fundamentally, these problems are ours, and our peoples will live with their consequences."[16]

OPERATIONALIZING THE FIVE APSA PILLARS

Initially the full operationalization of the APSA was expected for 2010. However, the first APSA assessment that was conducted in 2010 identified specific gaps, needs, and priorities, with a particular focus on the key components of the APSA, and discussed varying degrees of progress. Specifically it drew attention to challenges of "vertical coordination" and noted that the level of coordination between the AU and the RECs/RMs (Regional Mechanisms for Conflict Prevention, Management, and Resolution) had made some progress, especially relating to the operationalization of two key components of the APSA: the ASF and the CEWS. According to Fisher and colleagues, "This is partly explained by the fact that the ASF and the CEWS have clearly articulated roadmaps, thereby providing more structured basis for their operationalization."[17]

Yet in other areas far less progress was observed. Moreover, the report ascertains that "the various APSA components are developing at different paces, [and that] the level of horizontal coordination has been limited."[18] This refers to a lack of interlocking the APSA components between the Union and the RECs/RMs as well as between RECs and RECs. Furthermore, the report raised issues of sustainability and subsidiarity. On the basis of the 2010 APSA Assessment, the Peace and Security Department's Programme Management Team developed an

"APSA Roadmap 2011–2013."[19] In 2014 a team led by South African scholar Laurie Nathan conducted a second APSA Assessment, leading to the "APSA Roadmap 2016–2020."[20] According to this assessment, major progress has been made since 2010, though there were still a number of outstanding issues, and the APSA was not yet fully operational.

The Peace and Security Council

The PSC met for the first time on March 16, 2004, and has held almost six hundred meetings since, usually at the level of Permanent Representatives (at least once a year it also meets at the level of Heads of State and Government). The Council's main tasks are "[a] promotion of peace, security and stability in Africa; [b] early warning and preventive diplomacy; [c] peace-making, including the use of good offices, mediation, conciliation and enquiry; [d] peace support operations and intervention, pursuant to article 4 (h) and (j) of the Constitutive Act; [e] peace-building and post-conflict reconstruction; [f] humanitarian action and disaster management; [and g] any other function as may be decided by the Assembly."[21] The PSC is composed of fifteen members, elected by the five African regions (North, West, Central, East, and South) on the basis of equal rights; ten members are elected for a term of two years, and five members are elected for a term of three years. Retiring members are immediately eligible for reelection.[22] Usually meetings are closed (and there are no verbatim reports), but increasingly open meetings are conducted (e.g., on the role of women and children in conflict). In contrast to the UN Security Council, there are no veto rights. Decisions are made on the principle of consensus and, if necessary, by simple majority (on procedural matters) or by a two-thirds majority (on all other matters).[23] Since its inception the PSC has addressed almost all major conflicts in Africa (save, e.g., Zimbabwe), including the 2010 postelection crisis in Côte d'Ivoire and the 2011 popular uprisings in Northern Africa, the so-called Arab Spring,[24] but also numerous postconflict situations.[25]

Rightfully the APSA 2014 Assessment noted that the "PSC has become the center of major decision making on peace and security in Africa and is viewed as such by the international community. It provides a common platform for Member States to deliberate and take decisions for action."[26] The PSC has contributed to the resolution of conflicts "in, *inter alia*, Somalia, Burundi, Mali, the DRC, Comoros, Madagascar and Côte d'Ivoire; the PSC has strengthened its partnerships with its counterparts at the UN, the EU and the Arab League; and the PSC has taken a consistent stand in condemning coups, leading to suspension, sanctions and demands for the return to constitutional order."[27] But the report also stresses that coordination and cooperation between the PSC and the RECs/RMs had not been strengthened and that the PSC "does not consult adequately the RECs/RMs on PSC deliberations that affect them."[28] On the relation between the Council and the Panel of the Wise (see below), the study notices that despite the sound working relations, "there is a lack of operational clarity on what kind of advice the PSC expects from the Panel, which is an advisory organ, and there exists no procedure for the [Panel] to routinely provide input to the PSC on conflicts or potential conflicts."[29] Finally, the provisions of the PSC Protocol on engagement with civil society organizations "have not been adequately implemented."[30]

According to the APSA Roadmap 2016–2020, a number of critical issues have not yet been resolved, including the establishment of enforcement and compliance mechanisms with regard to the implementation of PSC decisions; "the low level of interaction between the PSC and similar structures at the REC level; interaction between the PSC, the Panel of the Wise and the Chairperson's Special Envoys, Representatives and Mediators needs to be structured; and the increasing work load of the PSC Secretariat needs to be addressed."[31]

The Panel of the Wise, Mediation, and Preventive Diplomacy

The Panel of the Wise is meant to support the PSC's efforts and those of the AUC chairperson, particularly in the area of conflict prevention.[32] It is composed of five highly respected African personalities that are selected by the AUC chairperson in consultation with member states and on the basis of regional representation. The role of the Panel mainly is to advise the PSC and the AUC chairperson. In this function the Panel enjoys considerable freedom of action; it can pronounce itself on any issue relating to promoting and maintaining peace, security, and stability in Africa.[33] The Panel also fulfills an important horizon-scanning function with regard to new conflict trends. The panelists serve for three years. For the period 2014–2017 the Panel's members are Albina Faria de Assis Pereira Africano (a former Angolan government minister and special advisor to the president, for Central Africa), former Ugandan vice president Speciosa Wandira Kazibwe (East), former foreign minister of Algeria and former Arab League and UN special envoy for Syria Lakhdar Brahimi (Northern), former Mozambican prime minister Luisa Diogo, and former Togolese prime minister and OAU secretary-general Edem Kodjo (West).[34]

The Panel of the Wise was only launched on December 18, 2007, and initially strived hard to find its role and develop a visible agenda. Major topics the Panel did address in the following years concerned election-related violence; transitional justice and nonimpunity; mitigating the vulnerabilities of women and children in conflict; strengthening governance for peace, security, and stability; and mediation and preventive diplomacy.[35] According to the APSA 2014 Assessment, the importance of the Panel "resides in its engagement in preventive diplomacy and, to a lesser degree, in mediation throughout the continent"; in early warning collaboration with CEWS (see below); and in its engagement with similar institutions at the level of the RECs/RMs.[36] The latter includes the SADC Panel of Elders and a Mediation Reference Group, the ECOWAS Council of the Wise, the EAC Panel of Eminent Persons, the COMESA Committee of Elders, and the CEN-SAD

Permanent High-Level Mediator for Peace and Security. Many RECs are in the process of creating mediation units (IGAD has already done so), and likewise, the Panel is aiming at strengthening the Union's mediation capacities through a Knowledge Management Framework, among other strategies. On April 12, 2013, the AU and the RECs established the Pan-African Network of the Wise (PanWise) that aims to bring together relevant mediation actors of the Union, the RECs, and African civil societies in order to enhance collaboration between the structures and harmonize the approaches of the AU and RECs through workshops and joint missions research.[37]

Meanwhile the Panel of the Wise has developed a practice of visiting countries several months before elections to assess the political and security-related environment. Usually these missions are carried out in collaboration with the AU Department of Political Affairs (DPA) and CEWS.[38] However, the APSA 2014 Assessment offers the critique that although the Panel's interaction with the PSC has intensified in recent years, "there remains a lack of clarity on what kind of advice the PSC expects" from the Panel. Furthermore, there was "no institutionalized procedure" for the Panel "to provide input to PSC reports and participate in debates on conflicts or potential conflicts."[39] In addition there was an "inadequate follow-up" on the implementation of the Panel's recommendations and no mechanism to monitor its activities.[40]

With regard to preventive diplomacy and mediation, the APSA 2014 Assessment identifies "the absence of sustained professional support to mediators and special representatives and envoys in the field"—that is, the lack of a mediation support unit—as a major deficit.[41] Against this background the Commission's chairperson has frequently appointed special envoys and special representatives to act as the Union's mediators.[42] Currently there are thirteen high-level representatives, special envoys, and special representatives deployed across the continent, many of whom act as mediators—for instance, on Sudan (former South African president Thabo Mbeki), Darfur (former ECOWAS secretary-general Mohamed Ibn Chamba), and Mali and the Sahel (former Burundian president Pierre Buyoya).[43]

So far the Union has undertaken its most sustained effort at mediation in Burundi, where it acts in close collaboration with both the UN and the EAC. Following the decision of President Pierre Nkurunziza to run for an unconstitutional third five-year term and the subsequent elections held in July 2015—which were boycotted by the opposition and led to widespread protests, a failed coup d'état, mass killings, and hundreds of thousands of people fleeing the country—the AU PSC for the first time built up a scenario of intimidation under Article 4(h) of the Constitutive Act, threatening to send a peace-keeping force of five thousand to the country.[44] Although there was no consensus at the following AU Assembly in January 2016 to support this course of action, the AU at least decided to send two hundred human rights observers and one hundred military experts to back up the AU and EAC mediation on the ground.[45]

The African Standby Force and Contemporary Peacekeeping in Africa

The African Standby Force is being established under the auspices of the African Union by the various RECs in order to enable the PSC to perform its responsibilities with respect to the deployment of peace support missions and intervention pursuant to article 4(h) and (j) of the Constitutive Act. It is composed of five regional multidisciplinary contingents, with civilian and military components ready for rapid deployment under different scenarios (between fourteen and ninety days).[46] In this respect a Military Staff Committee (MSC) supports the PSC.

The APSA Roadmap 2016–2020 lists a number of achievements with regard to the ASF's operationalization, including the development of "a suite of common policy documents, an annual continental training implementation and coordination meeting, harmonized training standards and annual training directives that guide Member States and RECs/RMs."[47] Good progress is also reported on the development of the rapid deployment capability (RDC) concept.[48] "Considerable progress" has equally been observed on the development of the civilian and police components of the ASF, yet the civilian "has continued to lag behind the military and police components." Overall the capacity of African PSOs is said to have "increased in numbers and quality." The ASF was tested in two major training exercises, the AMANI AFRICA command postexercise, conducted in October 2010 in Addis Ababa, and the Amani II field training exercise that was concluded in November 2015 in South Africa. By the end of 2015 the African Union declared full operational capability of the ASF—despite the fact that the regional standby forces have not developed structures uniformly and some regions lag behind (e.g., North and Central).[49]

Hence, the APSA 2014 Assessment is concerned with the Union's "inability to mobilize adequate political will of the AU Member States to commit to proactive measures and, second, the unavailability of critical force enablers and multipliers in the form of intelligence, protected mobility, airlift, helicopters, field hospitals and field support capabilities among most Member States."[50] The Union and RECs/RMs' experiences in Somalia, CAR, and Mali, where AU-led interventions lacked efficiency, supported this perception. In addition, the Assessment concludes that the "ASF mandates are grossly mismatched with available resources."[51] In fact, conceptually the African Union has maintained some level of confusion, and institutionally there are some disconnects. In particular this holds true for the question of how some elements of the APSA relate to the 2004 Common African Defense and Security Policy (CADSP) or the Union's policy on postconflict and reconstruction (PCRD).[52]

In light of the fact that the ASF was not fully operational until very recently, the Union had to rely on alternative mechanisms in peacekeeping and peace-support operations. Basically there were three different kinds: (1) AU peacekeeping missions, (2) hybrid AU/UN missions, and (3) coalitions of the willing-and-able. The African Union maintains one major stand-alone mission, the AU Mission in Somalia (AMISOM), which supports the Transitional Federal Government against the al-Shabaab militia. Troop-contributing countries include Burundi, Ethiopia, Djibouti, Kenya, and Uganda. The PSC created AMISOM on January 19, 2007, with an initial six-month mandate. In addition there is the AU/UN Hybrid Operation in Darfur (UNAMID) that started operating in 2004 as the African Union Mission in Sudan (AMIS) and was transformed into the hybrid mission in 2007.[53] Some missions were transferred from AU to UN, such as the transition in 2013 from the African-led International Support Mission in Mali (AFISMA) to the UN Multidimensional Integrated Stabilization Mission in Mali (MINUSMA) or, in 2014, from the African-led International Support Mission in the CAR (MISCA) to the UN Multidimensional Integrated Stabilization Mission in the CAR (MI-NUSCA). However, in Somalia the original vision of the Union of transitioning AMISOM to a UN peacekeeping operation has not yet taken place.[54] And finally, there are foreign and continental coalitions, such as the US-backed African Crisis Response Initiative of the early 2000s, the more recent five-thousand-men-strong African Capacity for Immediate Response to Crises (ACIRC) for rapid deployment within thirty days, or the South African–led intervention force in North Kivu/DRC that fought in 2013 against the so-called March 23 Movement (mandated as the UN Force Intervention Brigade, FIB).[55] In addition, the African Union is relying on regional coalitions such as the Lake Chad Basin Commission (LCBC) and Benin, who operationalize the Multinational Joint Task Force (MNJTF) established to combat Boko Haram, or the Regional Cooperation Initiative for the Elimination of the Lord's Resistance Army (RCI-LRA) in Eastern Africa.

The Continental Early Warning System: Developing Direct and Structural Conflict Prevention

In order to facilitate the anticipation and prevention of conflicts the African Union has established a Continental Early Warning System (CEWS).[56] It comprises a Situation Room as well as desk and conflict analysts, and it is linked to the observation and monitoring units of the RMs. CEWS collects and monitors open-source data, engages in strategic conflict and peace analysis, and provides policy response options for decision makers. In particular the AUC chairperson "shall use the information gathered through the Early Warning System timeously to advise the Peace and Security Council on potential conflicts and threats to peace and security in Africa and recommend the best course of action."[57]

According to the APSA 2014 Assessment, considerable progress has been made in addressing the following recommendations in the 2010 APSA Assessment: "recruit additional analysts for CEWS and the early warning units of the RECs; provide joint training and skills development; ensure connectivity between the AUC and RECs; engage with decision makers; and increase and strengthen collaboration with other stakeholders."[58] In addition, early warning systems (EWS) have been established on regional levels; in the "PSC Protocol" the RECs are actually described as "part of the overall security architecture of the Union, which has the primary responsibility for promoting peace, security and stability in Africa."[59] These EWS include CEWARN at IGAD, ECOWARN at ECOWAS, EACWARN at the EAC, COMWARN at COMESA, and MARAC at ECCAS. SADC's EWS is intelligence based. CEWS, CEWARN, and ECOWARN have been rather functional for some time. The CEWS and the RECs have made considerable progress in terms of putting the necessary infrastructure, methodology, and systems in place. The data-gathering and monitoring function of CEWS is well established, with various reports, including early warning reports, situation updates, flash reports, and weekly updates. A task force has been set up for interdepartmental coordination.[60]

However, the APSA 2014 Assessment also acknowledges that there is only "limited interaction and feedback from primary users to the CEWS management"—that is, a weak linkage between early warning and early response by decision makers.[61] Consequently the CEWS management does not always know to what extent the AU decision makers find its early warning products useful. In addition, there are capacity and human resources constraints. Other challenges include the low connectivity between the CEWS and the EWS of the RECs, the lack of connectivity between national EWS and REC EWS, and the variation of levels of operationalization of various EWS at the level of the RECs.[62]

The Committee of Intelligence and Security Services (CISSA), based in Addis Ababa, also provides additional early warning information for the AUC chairperson and the PSC.[63] Information coming from CEWS and CISSA is reconciled at the Intelligence and Security Committee in the Bureau of the AUC Chairperson. It was only in February 2016 that the PSC decided that the AU Commission, working with the RECs/RMs and CISSA, should provide quarterly briefings on early warning to the Council.[64]

Conceptually CEWS has always put more of an emphasis on direct, immediate conflict prevention; only recently has it systematically addressed the dimension of structural, long-term conflict prevention. In 2013–2015 the AU Commission developed a Continental Structural Conflict Prevention Framework (CSCPF): through an instrument that is based on the principles of the voluntary African Peer-Review Mechanism (APRM) of the New Partnership for Africa's Development (NEPAD), the Commission is planning to develop country structural vulnerability assessments and, on this basis, country vulnerability mitigation strategies that address the root causes of state fragility and vulnerability.[65]

The Peace Fund: Ownership vs. Financial Dependence

In principle, finance for peace support missions and other operational activities related to peace and security should be provided by a special fund, the Peace Fund, which is made up of financial appropriations from the regular budget of the Union.[66] However, in reality AU member states do not provide sufficient funds for maintaining their continental body; instead, the Union has developed extremely high levels of dependency on external donors, or "international partners." The level of external funding of the AU's core budget has increased from 27.3 percent in 2007 to 71.8 percent in 2014, and when it comes to, for instance, peacekeeping in Africa, the United Nations pays up to 96 percent of the expenses (see below).[67]

The APSA 2014 Assessment therefore warns that the "AUC as a whole, and APSA in particular, are heavily dependent on external partners" and concludes that the "inadequacy of Member State funding constrains the AU's ability to act as a major security actor."[68] Clearly the high level of dependence on external funding "gives donors undue involvement in and influence over African peace and security activities. It compromises the AU's independence and constrains the AU's scope and freedom of action in the sphere of peace and security. It also raises the question of what activities and components would be sustainable if the priorities of some key donors were to change and/or their levels of financing were reduced."[69]

In order to improve the situation, the AU member states decided in 2009 to increase their contributions to the Peace Fund from 6 percent to 12 percent of the AU regular budget. However, the APSA 2014 Assessment noted that in 2014 member states' contributions stood at only 7 percent.[70] Currently the bulk of the funding comes from just four member states: Algeria, Egypt, Nigeria, and South Africa are providing 48 percent of the Union's budget (for FY2016 the budget estimate was US$416.9 million).[71] It is only fairly recently that the AU has shown more commitment to readdressing its financial dependence. The 25th AU Assembly held in Johannesburg, South Africa, on June 15–16, 2015, decided that the Union should aim at covering, from its own resources, 100 percent of the organization's operational budget, 75 percent of the program budget (covering economic development), and 25 percent of the peace and security budget.[72] To boost the Union's finances, a High-Level Panel on Alternative Sources of Financing the African Union, led by former Nigerian president Olusegun Obasanjo, suggested raising a $10 levy on flight tickets to and from African destinations and a $2 levy on each night spent in a hotel in Africa.[73] These measures would translate into an estimated additional revenue of US$730 million a year. According to AU sources, an additional half-a-cent tax on SMS messages, which had been included in the financing proposal, would raise an annual revenue of US$1.6 billion.[74] However, the proposal was not adopted in 2015. Instead, in July 2016 the AU Assembly decided to introduce a 0.2 levy "on all eligible imported goods into the Continent to finance the African Union Operational Program and Peace Support Operations Budgets starting from the year 2017."[75]

Strategic Peace and Security Issues

To expedite the full operationalization of the APSA, the AU Commission has developed the "APSA Roadmap 2016–2020." It provides "a shared understanding of the results to be achieved by all APSA stakeholders, it articulates a shared understanding of the roles and functions each need to increase collaboration and coordination among all stakeholders involved in APSA."[76] With regard to the division of labor between the Union and the RECs, the Roadmap ties on to the 2008 "Memorandum of Understanding on Cooperation in the Area of Peace and Security signed between the AU and the RECs/RMs."[77] The Roadmap reiterates the "Solemn Declaration" adopted by the Assembly of AU Heads of State and Government on the 50th Anniversary of the Organization of African Unity/African Union, held in Addis Ababa, Ethiopia on May 25, 2013. It furthers the Union's initiative on "Silencing the Guns: Pre-Requisites for Realising a Conflict-Free Africa by the Year 2020."[78] Finally, it details the joint aims of the AUC and the RECs/RMs in five strategic priority areas: conflict prevention, including early warning and preventive diplomacy; crisis/conflict management, including ASF and mediation; postconflict reconstruction and peace building; strategic security issues, such as illegal flows of small arms and light weapons, improvised explosive devices, weapons of mass destruction, disarmament, counterterrorism, illicit financial flows, transnational organized crime, and cyber-crime; and coordination and partnerships. Other policy issues that are cross-cutting but not detailed include the promotion and defense of human rights, the mitigation of the impact of climate change with inclusive and sustainable natural resource governance, sustainable youth empowerment, and migration and refugee dynamics.

Though not part of the APSA, two policy fields have strongly developed in recent years: counterterrorism and maritime security. Originally initiated by the US war on terrorism, combating "terrorism and violent extremism" is at the center of the policies of various regional alliances (e.g., in the contexts of the so-called Nouakchott and Djibouti processes), RECs, and international partnerships.[79] The African Union is trying to coordinate and harmonize related policies; although it has not developed a holistic framework, it has developed an AU Model Law on antiterrorism.[80] The Algiers-based African Centre for the Study and Research on Terrorism (ACSRT) plays an important role in advising member states on relevant AU and international counterterrorism decisions and instruments. Addressing the nexus between terrorism and transnational organized crime, the APSA 2016–2020 Roadmap foresees the establishment of an African Mechanism for Police Cooperation (AFRIPOL) to provide a strategic, operational, and tactical basis for intelligence sharing in combating transnational crimes.[81]

Despite the fact that piracy off the Somali coast has declined in intensity since 2012, maritime security is another APSA-related policy field. It is located between traditional security politics (with regard to piracy, maritime terrorism, and unregulated fishing), developmental and environmentalist concerns, and efforts to regain economic sovereignty over African territorial and offshore waters (the so-called blue economy). But despite the adoption of the "2050 African Integrated Maritime (AIM) Strategy" in January 2014, its security-relevant dimensions were poorly integrated into APSA, both politically and institutionally: it only played an APSA-relevant role from 2010 to 2014.[82]

INTERNATIONAL PARTNERSHIPS

As a sovereignty-boosting strategy the African Union relies heavily on the development of two strategic global partnerships, one with the United Nations, the other with the European Union.[83] The UN General Assembly (UNGA) already stressed on September 17, 2007, the need for closer cooperation and coordination between the UN and the African Union. This position was further elaborated in a 2008 report by the UN secretary-general (UNSG) and in a UN Security Council (UNSC) resolution. The Union detailed its vision of the AU/UN partnership in May 2010. In 2014 a "Joint United Nations–African Union Framework for an Enhanced Partnership in Peace and Security" was established, and a "UN-AU Framework for an Enhanced Partnership in Peace and Security" has already been drafted (November 17, 2015).

The APSA 2014 Assessment holds that the UN/AU cooperation "has made a vital contribution to peace and security on the continent,"[84] despite the fact that sometimes political differences remain and the AU feels it is being played by the P3. Since 2006 there are annual PSC/UNSC consultations. In addition, regular meetings are held between the UN Special Representative for the AU and the AU Commissioner for Peace and Security. Within this framework an Ad-hoc Working Group on Conflict Prevention and Resolution in Africa was set up, and in September 2010 a Joint Task Force on Peace and Security (JTF) was launched. In addition there are biannual desk-to-desk meetings. Since 2009 the AU maintains a Permanent Observer Mission to the United Nations, and in July 2010 the UN established an Office to the African Union (UNOAU).

EU/AU cooperation is based on the 2007 Joint Africa-Europe Strategy (JAES) and Plan of Action that was adopted at the second EU-Africa Summit held on December 8–9, 2007, in Lisbon, Portugal. The partnership involves all twenty-eight EU members and all fifty-four African states (that includes Morocco, which is not a Union member). The current Roadmap 2014–2017 sets out concrete targets within five priority areas: peace and security; democracy, good governance, and human rights; human development; sustainable and inclusive development and growth and continental integration; and global and emerging issues. Within this framework regular meetings are held at the level of ministerial summits between the two Commissions and the Political and Security Committee/PSC, EU Military Committee (EUMC)/AU MSC, and crisis management teams on both sides (the Joint Africa–EU Expert Groups) as well as through regular consultations between African and EU Heads of Delegation in Addis Ababa, Brussels, and New York.

Both partnerships have played a major role in peacekeeping in African conflicts. The UN has been involved since 1960, starting with a mission in the Congo.[85] The UN is putting up the bulk of financial resources for nine current peacekeeping missions in Africa, which amounted in FY2015/2016 to a record $6.840 billion, or 82.65 percent of all its expenditure on peacekeeping (in the previous five FYs the budget for Africa averaged $5.541 billion). Current missions include MINURSO for Western Sahara, MINUSCA in the CAR, MINUSMA in Mali, MONUSCO in the DRC, UNAMID in Darfur/Sudan, UNMIL in Liberia, UNMISS in the Sudan, UNISFA in Abyei, UNOCI in the Côte d'Ivoire, and UNSOA as support for AMISOM in Somalia. In addition, since 2006 the UN also builds capacity in the area of peace and security.[86]

The EU has also increasingly intervened in African conflicts.[87] Completed military, police, and civilian missions include EUFOR in the CAR (2014–2015), EUFOR in Chad (2008–2009), Artemis, EUPOL Kinshasa, EUFOR DRC and EUPOL in the DRC (2003, 2005–2007, 2006 and 2007–2014, respectively), EU SSR in Guinea-Bissau (2008–2010), and EUAVSEC in South Sudan (2012–2014). The ongoing missions include EUMAM in the CAR (since 2015), EUCAP Nestor in Djibouti, Somalia, Seychelles and Tanzania (since 2012), EUSEC in the DRC (since 2005), EUBAM in Libya (since 2013), EUTM and EUCAP in Mali (since 2013 and 2014 respectively), EUCAP in Niger (since 2012), as well as EUNAVFOR in Atalanta and EUTM in Somalia (since 2008 and 2010, respectively).[88]

Financially the EU has assisted the Union and the RECs through the Africa Peace Facility (APF). Between December 2003 and December 2014 a total amount of €1.454 billion has been contracted and more than €1.320 billion has been disbursed (or US$1,478 billion at current exchange rates, which, obviously, have been far higher in the past thirteen years).[89] Through the Union the EU also supports the peace and security activities of the RECs/RMs, which provides the former with an effective coordination and harmonization instrument. Primarily the APF supports African-led PSOs, the operationalization of the APSA, and initiatives under the Early Response Mechanism (ERM). Thus, the EU cofinances AMISOM and—before they transformed into UN missions—the PSOs in the CAR (MISCA) and Mali (AFISMA).

CONCLUSIONS

The African Union, the RECs, and APSA are clearly the centerpiece of Africa's "new regionalisms."[90] The Union has quickly developed thorough "actorness," both vis-à-vis member states and the international community. Although "full operationalization" of the APSA still lags behind and will not be completed before 2018–2020, compared to the OAU's forty-year history, the Union has made huge progress in many fields within a rather short span of time. For the coming five years the Union has defined six strategic priorities for further developing the APSA: strengthening the PSC's coordinating function, improving inter- and intradepartmental collaboration/coordination, fully implementing the MoU between the AU and the RECs/RMs, strengthening the role of the AU Liaison Offices at the RECs, continuing the policy and strategic dialogue with APSA partnerships, and improving financial ownership of APSA.[91]

The history of the operationalization of the APSA suggests that there are at least four additional challenges. First, APSA still needs to be coordinated and harmonized more systematically within the AUC, between the AUC and the RECs/RMs, as well as between the RECs. Second, at the level of policies and practices the APSA has to be integrated far more closely with the complementary African Governance Architecture (AGA) that is based on the Charter on Democracy, Elections and Governance, which was adopted in July 2007 and became effective in January 2012.[92] In this context existing compliance mechanisms vis-à-vis member states need to be strengthened, political contradictions between RECs and the Union need to be overcome, and a clear definition and shared understanding of the principle of subsidiarity needs to be developed.[93] Third, the AUC as the driver of these processes periodically will have to renew the political buy-in of member states, many of which are not in line with the liberal AUC agenda. Fourth, so far the African Union has been a government and elite project that hasn't reached out to African citizens, parliaments, private sectors, and civil societies.[94] Truly becoming a people's union still requires a huge effort.

NOTES

1. See William Brown, "A Question of Agency: Africa in International Politics," *Third World Quarterly* 10, no. 1 (2012), pp. 1889–1908; Sophie Harman and William Brown, "In from the Margins? The Changing Place of Africa in International Relations," *International Affairs* 89, no. 1 (2013), pp. 69–87; Lesley Blauuw, "African Agency in International Relations: Challenging Great Powers Politics," in *Africa in Global International Relations. Emerging Approaches to Theory and Practice*, ed. Paul-Henri Bischoff, Kwesi Aning, and Amitav Acharya (London, New York: Routledge, 2016), pp. 85–107; and Jo-Ansie van Wyk, "Africa in International Relations: Agent, Bystander or Victim?" in Bischoff, Aning, and Acharya, *Africa in Global International Relations*, pp. 108–120.

2. See Ulf Engel, "The Changing Role of the AU Commission in Inter-African Relations: The Case of APSA and AGA," in *Africa in World Politics. Engaging a Changing Global Order*, ed. John W. Harbeson and Donald Rothchild (Boulder, CO: Westview Press, 2013), pp. 186–206.

3. See AU Assembly of Heads of State and Government, *Report of the Peace and Security Council on Its Activities and the State of Peace and Security in Africa* [Assembly/AU/2 (XXVI)] (Addis Ababa: African Union, 2016). Recent data on conflict trends is provided by the Armed Conflict Location and Event Data Project, Conflict Trends, www.acleddata.com/research-and-publications/conflict-trends-reports. For a general overview see also William Reno, *Warfare in Independent Africa* (New York: Cambridge University Press, 2011); and Paul D. Williams, *War and Conflict in Africa* (Cambridge: Polity Press, 2011).

4. AU PSC, *Communiqué Issued After the 571st PSC Meeting Held at the Level of Heads of State and Government in Addis Ababa, Ethiopia, on January 29, 2016* [PSC/AHG/COMM.1 (DLXXI)] (Addis Ababa: African Union, 2016), para. 5.

5. See also African Union, *Protocol Relating to the Establishment of the Peace and Security Council* (Durban: African Union, 2002).

6. On the history of the OAU see Klaas van Walraven, *Dreams of Power: The Role of the Organization of African Unity in the Politics of Africa, 1963–1993* (Aldershot, UK: Ashgate, 1996).

7. African Union, *Constitutive Act of the African Union* (Lomé: African Union, 2000), para. 4(h).

8. AU Assembly, *Decision on the Amendments to the Constitutive Act* [Assembly/AU/ Dec.26 (II)] (Addis Ababa: African Union, 2003). For a discussion see Evarist Baimu and Kathryn Sturman, "Amendment to the African Union's Right to Intervene: A Shift from Human Security to Regime Security?" *African Security Review* 12, no. 2 (2003), pp. 37–45.

9. See also Ben Kioko, "The Right of Intervention Under the African Union's Constitutive Act: From Non-Interference to Non-Intervention," *International Review of the Red Cross* 85, no. 852 (2003), pp. 807–824; Paul D. Williams, "From Non-Intervention to Non-Indifference: The Origins and Development of the African Union's Security Culture," *African Affairs* 106, no. 423 (2007), pp. 253–279; and Musifiky Mwanasali, "From Non-Interference to Non-Indifference: The Emerging Doctrine of Conflict Prevention in Africa," in *The African Union and Its Institutions*, ed. John Akokpari, Angela Muvumba Sellström, and Timothy Murithi (Cape Town and Auckland Park: Centre for Conflict Resolution and Fanele, 2008). See also Eboe Hutchful, "From Military Security to Human Security," in Akokpari, Sellström, and Murithi, *African Union and Its Institutions*; and Ademola Abass, "African Peace and Security and Protection of Human Security," in *Protecting Human Security in Africa*, ed. Ademola Abass (New York: Oxford University Press, 2010). For the international policy debate on R2P see International Commission on Intervention and State Sovereignty, *The Responsibility to Protect: Report by the International Commission on Intervention and State Sovereignty* (Ottawa: International Development Research Centre, 2001); and United Nations, *A More Secure World: Our Shared Responsibility. Report of the Secretary-General's High-Level Panel on Threats, Challenges and Change* (New York: United Nations, 2004). On Africa see Tim Murithi, "The Responsibility to Protect as Enshrined in Article 4 of the Constitutive Act of the African Union," *African Security Review* 16, no. 3 (2007), pp. 14–24.

10. See also Thomas Kwesi Tieku, "Explaining the Clash and Accommodation of Interests of Major Actors in the creation of the African Union," *African Affairs* 103, no. 411 (2004), pp. 249–267; and Antonia Witt, "The African Union and Contested Political Order(s)," in *Towards an African Peace and Security Regime*, ed. Ulf Engel and João Gomes Porto (Farnham, UK, Burlington, VT: Ashgate, 2013).

11. See also Engel, *The Changing Role of the AU Commission*, pp. 188–194.

12. African Union, *Constitutive Act*, para. 20.

13. African Union, *Statutes of the Commission of the African Union* [ASS/AU/2(I)–d] (Durban: African Union, 2002); as amended by AU Assembly, *Decision on the Proposed Amendments to the Rules of Procedure of the Assembly of the Union, the Executive Council and the Permanent Representatives' Committee, and the Statutes of the Commission* [Assembly/AU/Dec.146 (VIII)] (Addis Ababa: African Union, 2007).

14. Thomas K. Tieku, "The Evolution of the African Union Commission and Africrats," in *The Ashgate Research Companion to Regionalisms*, ed. Timothy M. Shaw, J. Andrew Grant, and Scarlett Cornelissen (Farnham, UK: Ashgate, 2011).

15. See AU PSC, *Declaration of the Ministerial Meeting of the Peace and Security Council on the State of Peace and Security in Africa* [PSC/PR/BR.1 (CCLXXV)] (Addis Ababa: African Union, 2011); AUC Chairperson, *Report of the Chairperson of the Commission on the Activities of the AU High–Level Ad Hoc Committee on the Situation in Libya* [PSC/PR/2 (CCLXXV)] (Addis Ababa: African Union, 2011); and *Report of the Chairperson of the Commission on the Situation in Libya and on the Efforts of the African Union for a Political Solution to the Libyan Crisis* [PSC/AHG/3 (CCXCI)] (Addis Ababa: African Union, 2011). See also Gerrie Swart, "A Right to Intervene . . . A Reluctance to Protect? Probing the African

Union's Response to and Failed Intervention in the Libyan Crisis," in *New Mediation Practices in African Conflicts*, ed. Ulf Engel (Leipzig: Leipziger Universitätsverlag, 2012).

16. AUC Chairperson, *Report of the Chairperson of the Commission on Current Challenges to Peace and Security on the Continent and AU's Efforts. Enhancing Africa's Leadership, Promoting African Solutions* [EXT/ASSEMBLY/AU/2. (01.2011)] (Addis Ababa: African Union, 2011), para. 48.

17. See also Louis M. Fisher et al., *Moving Africa Forward: African Peace and Security Architecture (APSA). 2010 Assessment* (Addis Ababa: African Union, 2010), para. 3.

18. Ibid., para. 5.

19. African Union, *African Peace and Security Architecture (APSA) Roadmap, 2011–2013* (Addis Ababa: African Union, 2011).

20. Laurie Nathan et al., *African Peace and Security Architecture (APSA). 2014 Assessment Study. Final Report* (African Union: Addis Ababa, 2015); and African Union, *APSA Roadmap 2016–2020* (Addis Ababa: African Union, 2016).

21. African Union, *PSC Protocol*, para. 6.

22. Ibid., paras. 8 (1, 5). On January 30–31, 2016, the AU Assembly held in Addis Ababa endorsed the following PSC members elected by the AU Council of Ministers: Ethiopia, Uganda, Tanzania, and Burundi (East African region), Algeria, and Libya (North), Nigeria, Gambia, Niger, and Guinea (West), Chad, and Equatorial Guinea (Central) as well as South Africa, Namibia, and Mozambique, www.peaceau.org/en/page/88-composition-of-the-psc.

23. African Union, *PSC Protocol*, para. 8(12–13).

24. See also AUC Chairperson, *Report of the Chairperson of the Commission on the Situation in Cote d'Ivoire* [PSC/PR/2 (CCLXXIII)] (Addis Ababa: African Union, 2011); and *Report of the Chairperson of the Commission on the Situation in Tunisia* [PSC/PR/Comm.2 (CCLVII)] (Addis Ababa: African Union, 2011). See also AU PSC, *Report of the Peace and Security Council on Its Activities and the State of Peace and Security in Africa* [Assembly/AU/6 (XIX)] (Addis Ababa: African Union, 2012), para. 2.

25. See also Paul D. Williams, "The Peace and Security Council of the African Union: Evaluating an Embryonic International Institution," *Journal of Modern African Studies* 47, no. 4 (2009), pp. 603–626; Kathryn Sturman and Aïssatou Hayatou, "The Peace and Security Council of the African Union: From Design to Reality," in *The New Peace and Security Architecture of the African Union*, ed. Ulf Engel and João Gomes Porto (Farnham, UK, Burlington VT: Ashgate, 2010); and Tim Murithi and Hallelujah Lulie, eds., *The African Union Peace and Security Council. A Five-Year Appraisal* (Pretoria: Institute for Strategic Studies, 2015).

26. Nathan et al., *APSA 2014 Assessment Study*, para. 4.

27. Ibid., para. 5.

28. Ibid., para. 6.

29. Ibid., para. 7.

30. Ibid., para. 8.

31. African Union, *APSA Roadmap 2016–2020*, p. 15.

32. African Union, *PSC Protocol*, para. 11(1). See also African Union, "Modalities for the Functioning of the Panel of the Wise as Adopted by the Peace and Security Council at Its 100th PSC Meeting on 12 November 2007" (mimeo).

33. See also Tim Murithi and Charles Mwaura, "The Panel of the Wise," in Engel and Gomes Porto, *The New Peace and Security Architecture*; and João Gomes Porto and Kapinga Yvette Ngandu, *The African Union's Panel of the Wise: A Concise History* (Durban: The African Centre for the Constructive Resolution of Disputes, African Union, 2016), www.un.org/en/africa/osaa/pdf/pubs/2016aupanelofwise.pdf.

34. Panel of the Wise, African Union Peace and Security, www.peaceau.org/en/page /29-panel-of-the-wise-pow.

35. See AU Panel of the Wise, *Election-Related Disputes and Political Violence: Strengthening the Role of the African Union in Preventing, Managing, and Resolving Conflict* (New York: International Peace Institute, 2010); Panel of the Wise, *Peace, Justice and Reconciliation: Opportunities and Challenges in the Fight Against Impunity* (New York: International Peace Institute, African Union, 2013).

36. Nathan et al., *APSA 2014 Assessment Study*, para. 15.

37. African Union, *APSA Roadmap 2016–2020*, pp. 16–17.

38. Nathan et al., *APSA 2014 Assessment Study*, paras. 16 and 19.

39. Ibid., para. 18. See also African Union, *APSA Roadmap 2016–2020*, p. 17.

40. Nathan et al., *APSA 2014 Assessment Study*, para. 21.

41. Ibid., para. 92.

42. African Union, *Communiqué Issued After the 360th PSC Meeting Held in Addis Ababa, Ethiopia, on March 22, 2013* [PSC/PR/COMM.(CCCLX)].

43. African Union, "List of Special Envoys of the Chairperson of the Commission," www.au.int/en/cpauc/envoys.

44. AU PSC, *Communiqué Issued After the 565th PSC Meeting Held in Addis Ababa, Ethiopia, December 17, 2015* [PSC/PR/COMM.(DLVX)] (Addis Ababa: African Union, 2015).

45. AU PSC, *Communiqué Issued After the 581st PSC Meeting Held in Addis Ababa, Ethiopia, on March 9, 2016* [PSC/PR/COMM.(DLXXXI)] (Addis Ababa: African Union, 2016).

46. African Union, *PSC Protocol*, para. 13(1). See Jakkie Cilliers and Johann Potgieter, "The African Standby Force," in Engel and Gomes Porto, *The New Peace and Security Architecture*.

47. Here and in the following see African Union, *APSA Roadmap 2016–2020*, p. 17.

48. See also Jonathon Rees, "Africa's Army Guns for Peace," *African Independent*, November 27, 2015.

49. On the state of operationalization in the five regions see the reports commissioned by the Swedish Ministry of Defense in 2015 and 2016, www.foi.se/en/Our-Knowledge /Security-policy-studies/Africa/Africa1/Publications.

50. Nathan et al., *APSA 2014 Assessment Study*, para. 37.

51. Ibid., para. 39.

52. AU Assembly, *Solemn Declaration on a Common Defence and Security Policy Adopted by the 2nd Extraordinary Session of the AU Assembly in Sirte, Libya, on February 24, 2004*, www.peaceau.org/uploads/declaration-cadsp-en.pdf. See also Omar Touray, "The Common African Defence and Security Policy," *African Affairs* 104, no. 417 (2005), pp. 635–656. See AU Commission, *African Union Policy on Post-Conflict Reconstruction and Development* (Addis Ababa: African Union, 2006); and African Union, *First Progress Report of the Chairperson of the Commission on AU's Efforts on Post-Conflict Reconstruction and Development in Africa*, Presented at the 352nd PSC meeting held in Addis Ababa, Ethiopia, on January 16, 2013 [PSC/PR/2 (CCCLII)] (Addis Ababa: African Union, 2013).

53. See also Tim Murithi, "The African Union's Evolving Role in Peace Operations: The African Union Mission in Burundi, the African Union Mission in Sudan and the African Union Mission in Somalia," *African Security Review* 17, no. 1 (2008), pp. 70–82; and Paul D. Williams, "The African Union's Peace Operations: A Comparative Analysis," *African Security* 2, no. 2–3 (2009), pp. 97–118.

54. African Union, *Report of the African Union Commission on the Strategic Review of the African Union Mission in Somalia (AMISOM), Presented at the 365th PSC Meeting Held*

in Addis Ababa, Ethiopia, on February 27, 2013 [PSC/PR/2 (CCCLVI)] (Addis Ababa: African Union, 2013).

55. Paul Omach, "The African Crisis Response Initiative: Domestic Politics and the Convergence of National Interests," *African Affairs* 99, no. 394 (2000), pp. 73–95; and Romain Esmenjaud, "The African Capacity for Immediate Response to Crisis: Conceptual Breakthrough or Anti-Imperialist Phantom?" *African Security Review* 23, no. 2 (2014), pp. 172–177. See African Union, *Report of the Chairperson of the Commission on the Operationalisation of the Rapid Deployment Capacity of the African Standby Force and the Establishment of an "African Capacity for Immediate Response to Crisis,"* 6th Ordinary Meeting of the Specialised Technical Committee on Defence, Safety and Security, Preparatory Meeting of Chiefs of Staff, Addis Ababa, Ethiopia, April 29–30, 2013 [RPT/exp/VI/STCDSS/(i-a)2013] (Addis Ababa: African Union, 2013); and UN Security Council, *Resolution 2098 Concerning the Democratic Republic of the Congo (DRC)*, adopted at the 6943rd UNSC meeting, New York, March 29, 2013 [S/RES/2098 (2013)].

56. African Union, *PSC Protocol*, para. 12(1). See El-Ghassim Wane et al., "The Continental Early Warning System: Methodology and Approach," in Engel and Gomes Porto, *The New Peace and Security Architecture*; and AU Commission, *Meeting the Challenge of Conflict Prevention in Africa: Towards the Operationalization of the Continental Early Warning System*, 2nd rev. ed. (Leipzig: Leipziger Universitätsverlag).

57. African Union, *PSC Protocol*, para. 12(5).

58. Nathan et al., *APSA 2014 Assessment Study*, para. 51.

59. African Union, *PSC Protocol*, para. 16(1).

60. African Union, *APSA Roadmap 2016–2020*, p. 15.

61. Nathan et al., *APSA 2014 Assessment Study*, para. 52.

62. African Union, *APSA Roadmap 2016–2020*, p. 16.

63. See also Lauren Hutton, "Regional Security and Intelligence Cooperation in Africa: The Potential Contribution of the Committee on Intelligence and Security Services of Africa," in Engel and Gomes Porto, *Towards an African Peace and Security Regime*.

64. AU PSC, *Press Statement Issued After the 577th PSC Meeting Held in Addis Ababa, Ethiopia, February 23, 2016* [PSC/PR/COMM.2 (DII)] (Addis Ababa: African Union, 2016).

65. AU PSC, *Communiqué Issued After the 476th PSC Meeting Held in Addis Ababa, Ethiopia, on December 16, 2014* [PSC/PR/BR (DLXXVII)] (Addis Ababa: African Union, 2014); and AU PSC, *Communiqué Issued After the 502nd PSC Meeting Held in Addis Ababa, Ethiopia, on April 29, 2015* [PSC/PR/COMM.2 (DII)] (Addis Ababa: African Union, 2015). Conceptually see African Development Bank, *Ending Conflict and Building Peace in Africa: A Call to Action: High Level Panel on Fragile States* (Addis Ababa: African Development Bank and African Union, 2014); and AU PSC, *Communiqué Issued After the 463rd PSC Meeting Held in Addis Ababa, Ethiopia, on October 27, 2014* [PSC/PR/COMM (CDLXIII)] (Addis Ababa: African Union, 2014).

66. African Union, *PSC Protocol*, para. 21.

67. Ulf Engel, *The African Union Finances—How Does It Work?* (Leipzig: Centre for Area Studies, 2015), pp. 17 and 20–21.

68. Nathan et al., *APSA 2014 Assessment Study*, paras. 79 and 80, respectively.

69. Ibid., para. 80.

70. Ibid., para. 76.

71. AU Assembly, Decision on the Scale of Assessment and Implementation of Alternative Sources of Financing the African Union, 26th Ordinary Session of the AU Assembly Held in Addis Ababa, Ethiopia on January 30–31, 2016 [Assembly/AU/Dec.602 (XXVI)] (Addis Ababa, African Union, 2016), p. 4.

72. AU Assembly, *Decision on the Budget of the African Union for the 2016 Financial Year, 25th Ordinary Session of the AU Assembly Held in Johannesburg, South Africa on June 14–15, 2015* [Assembly/AU/Dec.577 (XXV)] (Johannesburg: African Union, 2015), para. 8.

73. AU Assembly, *Decision on the Scale of Assessment and Alternative Sources of Financing the African Union, 25th Ordinary Session of the AU Assembly Held in Johannesburg, South Africa on June 14–15, 2015* [Assembly/AU/Dec.578 (XXV)] (Johannesburg: African Union, 2015), para. 5; in combination with AU Assembly, *Decision on the Report of Alternative Sources of Financing the African Union, 24th Ordinary Session of the AU Assembly Held in Addis Ababa, Ethiopia, on January 30–31, 2015* [Assembly/AU/Dec.559 (XXIV)] (Addis Ababa: African Union, 2015).

74. Engel, *The AU Finances*, p. 23.

75. AU Assembly, *Decision on the Outcome of the Retreat of the Heads of States and Government, Ministers of Foreign Affairs and Ministers of Finance on the Financing of the African Union, 27th Ordinary Session of the AU Assembly held in Kigali, Rwanda, 17–18 July 2016* [Assembly/AU/Dec.605 (XXVII)] (Addis Ababa: African Union, 2016), para. 5(1)1.

76. African Union, *APSA Roadmap 2016–2020*, p. 7.

77. African Union, *Memorandum of Understanding on Cooperation in the Area of Peace and Security Between the African Union, the Regional Economic Communities and the Coordinating Mechanisms of the Regional Standby Brigades of Eastern Africa and Northern Africa* (Addis Ababa: African Union, 2008).

78. African Union, *50th Anniversary Solemn Declaration*. Adopted at the Golden Jubilee OAU/AU Summit, Held in Addis Ababa, Ethiopia on May 25, 2013 (Addis Ababa: African Union, 2013); and African Union, *Agenda 2063. The Africa We Want* ["Silencing the Guns"], 2nd ed. (Addis Ababa: African Union, 2014). See also Gilbert M. Khadiagala, *Silencing the Guns: Strengthening Governance to Prevent, Manage, and Resolve Conflicts in Africa* (New York: International Peace Institute, 2015).

79. See OAU, *OAU Convention on Prevention and Combating of Terrorism, Adopted by the 35th Ordinary Session of the OAU Summit Held in Algiers, Algeria, on July 14, 1999* (Algiers: OAU, 1999); and African Union, *Protocol to the OAU Convention on Prevention and Combating of Terrorism, Adopted at the 3rd Ordinary Session of the AU Assembly Held in Addis Ababa, Ethiopia, on July 8, 2004* (Addis Ababa: African Union, 2004). See also the fourth and so far latest AUC chairperson report on terrorism: AUC Chairperson, *Report of the Chairperson of the Commission on Terrorism and Violent Extremism in Africa, Presented at the 455th PSC Meeting Held at the Level of Heads of State and Government in Nairobi, Kenya, on September 2, 2014* [PSC/AHG/2 (CDLV)] (Addis Ababa: African Union, 2014). On the notion of "terrorism" and its socially constructed nature see Nicholas Onuf, "Making Terror/ism," *International Relations* 23, no. 1 (2009), pp. 53–60.

80. Nathan et al., *APSA 2014 Assessment Study*, para. 190.

81. African Union, *APSA Roadmap 2016–2020*, p. 52f.

82. African Union, *2050 Africa's Integrated Maritime (AIM) Strategy*, draft (Addis Ababa: African Union, 2012); and AU Assembly, *Decision on the Adoption and Implementation of the Integrated African Strategy for the Seas and Oceans 2050 Adopted at the 22nd Ordinary Session of the AU Assembly Held in Addis Ababa, Ethiopia, on January 30–31, 2014* [Assembly/AU/16 (XXII)] (Addis Ababa: African Union, 2014). See also Ulf Engel, "The African Union, the African Peace and Security Architecture, and Maritime Security," *African Security* 7, no. 3 (2014), pp. 207–227.

83. If not stated otherwise, this section is based on Ulf Engel, "The African Union, the United Nations, and the European Union: Crafting International Partnerships in the Field of Peace and Security," in *The African Union: Regional and Global Challenges*, ed. Adekeye

Adebajo (forthcoming, 2016). See also AUC Chairperson, *Report of the Chairperson of the Commission on the African Union–United Nations Partnership: The Need for Greater Coherence, Presented at the 397th PSC Meeting Held at the Level of Heads of State and Government in New York on September 23, 2014* [PSC/AHG/3. (CCCXCVII)] (New York: African Union, 2014).

84. Nathan et al., *APSA 2014 Assessment Study*, para. 125.

85. See also Norrie Macqueen, *United Nations Peacekeeping in Africa Since 1960* (Harlow, London: Pearson Education, 2002); Adekeye Adebajo, *UN Peacekeeping in Africa: From the Suez Crisis to the Sudan Conflicts* (Boulder, CO: Lynne Rienner Publishers, 2011); and Joachim Koops, Norrie MacQueen and Thierry Tardy, eds., *The Oxford Handbook of United Nations Peacekeeping Operations* (Oxford: Oxford University Press, 2015).

86. See also Arthur Boutellis and Paul D. Williams, *Peace Operations, the African Union, and the United Nations: Toward More Effective Partnerships* (New York: International Peace Institute, 2015).

87. See also Katarina Engberg, *The EU and Military Operations. A Comparative Analysis* (London: Routledge, 2013); and Maurzio Carbone, ed., *The European Union in Africa. Incoherent Policies, Asymmetrical Partnership, Declining Relevance?* (Manchester, New York: Manchester University Press, 2013).

88. What Is the Partnership?, The Africa-EU Partnership, www.africa-eu-partnership .org/en/about-us/what-partnership. See also Alex Vines, "Rhetoric from Brussels and Reality on the Ground: The EU and Security in Africa," *International Affairs* 86, no. 5 (2010), pp. 1091–1108.

89. Here and in the following see European Commission, *African Peace Facility: Annual Report 2014* (Luxembourg: Publication Office of the European Union, 2015).

90. As to the concept see Timothy M. Shaw, J. Andrew Grant, and Scarlett Cornelissen, eds., *The Ashgate Research Companion to Regionalisms* (Farnham, UK: Ashgate, 2011); Fredrik Söderbaum, *Rethinking Regionalism* (London: Palgrave Macmillan, 2016); and Ulf Engel et al., eds., *Regional Reconfigurations of the Global Order* (London: Routledge, 2016).

91. African Union, *APSA Roadmap 2016–2020*, pp. 54–59.

92. African Union, *African Charter on Democracy, Elections and Governance* (Addis Ababa: African Union, 2007).

93. See also Nathan et al., *APSA 2014 Assessment Study*, paras. 108–109.

94. See also ibid., para. 254.

Reconciling Sovereignty with Responsibility: A Basis for International Humanitarian Action

Francis M. Deng

INTRODUCTION

The end of the Cold War was greeted with relief throughout the world. It was assumed that the era of global tension and insecurity was over and that humanity had ushered in a new world order that would guarantee peace, security, and respect for the universal principles of human rights and democratic freedoms. The reverse has been the case.

With the disappearance of the bipolar alliance system and control mechanisms of the Cold War, a process of violent disintegration became the plight of many states, especially under formerly oppressive regimes. As the situations in the former Yugoslavia, in the former Soviet Union, and on the African continent have testified since the end of the Cold War, conflicts around the world have resulted in unprecedented humanitarian tragedies and, in some cases, have led to partial and even total collapse of states.

A new development that has complicated the situation further has been the emergence of international terrorism, dramatized by the horrific assault on the twin towers of the World Trade Center in New York on September 11, 2001. That event triggered a global war on terror that, although unifying the international community against terror, appears to have polarized the world in a way somewhat reminiscent of the Cold War ideological divide. Although sporadic terrorist assaults have been widespread, prime examples of organized terrorist movements have included al-Qaeda (global), Taliban (Afghanistan), al-Shabaab (Somalia), Boko Haram (Nigeria), and most recently, the Islamic State of Iraq and Syria (ISIS, Middle East). As was the case in the Cold War, states have been inclined to compromise human rights protection in the name of security from a real or perceived threat of terror.

These developments have stimulated a multifaceted trend toward international involvement in weak, impoverished, and conflict-prone countries, both on humanitarian grounds and to prevent them from providing a fertile ground for international terrorism. The result has been a complex situation involving sometimes conflicting motivations. On the one hand, there have been mounting pressures for global humanitarian action, sometimes involving forced intervention, with an urgent quest for peacemaking and peacekeeping. On the other hand, there has been the ideologically driven war on terror that has polarized the international community into those accused or suspected of supporting terror and those fighting it. The end result of both forces has been an inevitable erosion of traditional concepts of sovereignty in order to ensure international humanitarian access to protect and assist needy populations and punish actual terrorists.

The targeted states have had divergent reactions: cooperation on the part of those governments that have stood to benefit from an alliance with the United States and other major allies in the war on terror and defensive militancy on the part of those perceived as perpetrators or supporters of international terrorism. In both cases states have become fearful of international intervention and have reasserted with defensive vigor the traditional principles of sovereignty and territorial integrity. The resulting tug-of-war has acquired a cross-cultural dimension confronting the international community with severe dilemmas, as both positions represent legitimate concerns.

Much has been said and written about the processes of economic, political, and cultural globalization in the post–Cold War world. There has been, however, a process of fragmentation and localization concurrently underway that has not received commensurate attention. In Africa and, indeed, in many parts of the world the state has been undergoing a formidable national identity crisis in which forces in internal confrontation and their external supporters are contesting sovereignty. This crisis has been rooted primarily in the problems of racial, ethnic, cultural, and religious diversities, rendered conflictual by gross disparities in the shaping and sharing of power, national resources, and opportunities for social, cultural, and economic development.

Indeed, the state confronts a dualistic fate in the post–Cold War international system. During the Cold War there was a tendency to relate all the problems around the world to the ideological confrontation of the superpowers. But in the post–Cold

War era problems have now been better understood as occurring in the national and regional context, where internal conflicts, violations of human rights, denial of democracy, and mismanagement of the economy have become the pressing problem areas. In confronting these problems, states have been pulled in opposite directions by the demands of various local groups and by the pressures of globalization of the market economy and universalizing political and cultural trends. The assignment of responsibility for addressing these challenges must take into account a fundamental shift that has taken place in the post–Cold War era. In place of dependency, increasingly there have been demands that states assume national responsibility and accountability for their circumstances. This new scenario implies recasting sovereignty as a concept of responsibility for the security and general welfare of the citizens, with accountability at the regional and international levels.

The guiding principle for reconciling these conflicting positions on sovereignty has been to assume that under normal circumstances governments that enjoy internal legitimacy are concerned about the welfare of their people, will provide them with adequate protection and assistance, and, if unable to do so, will invite or welcome foreign assistance and international cooperation to supplement their own efforts. Conflict arises only in those exceptional instances where a state has collapsed, the government lacks the requisite capacity, and/or it is unwilling to invite or permit international involvement, notwithstanding a high level of human suffering. This is often the case in civil conflicts characterized by racial, ethnic, cultural, or religious crises of national identity in which the conflicting parties perceive the affected population as part of "the enemy." The essential need is to fill the vacuum of moral responsibility created by such circumstances that makes international intervention such a moral imperative.

The paradox of the compelling circumstances that necessitate such intervention is that the crisis has gone beyond prevention and has become an emergency situation in which masses of people have fallen victim to humanitarian tragedy. Now it has become more costly to provide the needed humanitarian relief than it would have been at an earlier stage. The obvious policy implication is that the international community must develop normative and operational principles for a doctrine of preventive intervention. Such an approach would require addressing the root causes of conflict, formulating normative guidelines, establishing the mechanisms for an appropriate institutional response, and developing strategies for timely intervention.

This is indeed a tall order. The humanitarian crisis resulting from the genocidal war in the western Sudanese region of Darfur, for example, the inability or unwillingness of the Sudanese government to stop the carnage, and the impotence of the international community to intervene effectively to protect the civilian population have indicated that often the stakes are too high for potential international interveners. There are, however, no easy alternatives but to reaffirm the state's primary responsibility to protect and assist its citizens and, if it lacks the capacity, to call on the international community to assist in a positive spirit of cooperation.

Should it lack the capacity and/or the will to do so, the responsibility to protect must inevitably fall on the international community in its multilevel structures: subregional, regional, global, and alliances of willing and capable states, preferably acting collectively but unilaterally if need be, to stop genocide, war crimes, ethnic cleansing, and crimes against humanity. These are the pillars of what is now known as the Responsibility to Protect (R2P). The question is how to make this phased sharing of responsibility effective.

THE MAGNITUDE OF THE CRISIS

It is fair to say that crises of genocide, war crimes, ethnic cleansing, and crimes against humanity affect some regions more than others. Internal conflicts and their catastrophic consequences has perhaps devastated Africa the most. During my term as representative of the secretary-general on this issue (2007–2012), of an estimated 20 million to 25 million internally displaced persons worldwide, over 10 million were African, as were many refugees throughout the world. It was in Africa—specifically Rwanda—that the world witnessed genocide comparable to the horrors of Nazi Germany. In the conflict in the southern region of Sudan, nearly 2 million people were estimated to have died since the civil war resumed in 1983, about a quarter having perished as a result of war-induced famine and related humanitarian tragedies.

The conflict in Darfur resulted in the death of between two and four hundred thousand people, displaced over 2 million people, and forced 1 million people to seek refuge in Chad. The Democratic Republic of Congo has also been a theater of massive carnage. In Liberia and Sierra Leone untold atrocities were perpetrated by all sides. And the collapse of Somalia has stood out as the prime example of a failed state on the continent.

African leaders, diplomats, scholars, and intellectuals have recognized the plight of their countries and their peoples and have demonstrated a responsiveness commensurate to the challenge. The OAU Mechanism for Conflict Prevention, Management and Resolution proposed by its secretary general, Salim Ahmed Salim, at the 1992 Dakar summit and adopted at the June 1993 Cairo summit represented this shift in attitude. In introducing his proposal to the Council of Ministers in 1992, the secretary general said,

> Conflicts have cast a dark shadow over the prospects for a united, secure and prosperous Africa which we seek to create. . . . Conflicts have caused immense suffering to our people and, in the worst case, death. Men, women and children have been uprooted, dispossessed, deprived of their means of livelihood and thrown into exile as refugees as a result of conflicts. This de-humanization of a large segment of our population is unacceptable and cannot be allowed to continue. Conflicts have engendered hate and division among our people and undermined the prospects of the long-term stability and unity of our countries

and Africa as a whole. Since much energy, time and resources have been devoted to meeting the exigencies of conflicts, our countries have been unable to harness the energies of our people and target them to development.[1]

The change of the Organization of African Unity (OAU) to the African Union (AU) was more than a change of names. It signified a substantive and procedural shift from the old sacrosanct commitment to the narrow concept of state responsibility and from noninterference in the internal affairs of states to a more responsible and responsive oversight and constructive involvement to promote peace, security, and stability within state borders. Article 4(h) of the Constitutive Act of the AU provided for "the right of the Union to intervene in a member State pursuant to a decision of the Assembly in respect of grave circumstances, namely war crimes, genocide and crimes against humanity." In promotion and protection of a democratic system of governance, Article 4(p) also provided for the "condemnation and rejection of unconstitutional changes of government," implicitly by military coups. To meet the challenge, however, Africa must address sovereignty.

THE ISSUE OF SOVEREIGNTY

Protecting and assisting the masses of people affected by internecine internal conflicts has entailed reconciling the possibility of international intervention with traditional concepts of national sovereignty. The post–Cold War international community has reapportioned responsibility for addressing these problems to the affected states themselves, with a graduated sharing of responsibility and accountability at the subregional and regional levels and, residually, throughout the international community, both multilaterally and bilaterally. In this emerging policy framework national sovereignty has acquired a new meaning. Instead of being perceived as a means of insulating the state against external scrutiny or involvement, it has increasingly been postulated as a normative conception of responsibility, implying potentially increased external observation.

The concept of national sovereignty has come increasingly to require a system of governance that is based on democratic popular citizen participation, constructive management of diversities, respect for fundamental rights, and equitable distribution of national wealth and opportunities for development. For a government or a state to claim sovereignty, it must establish legitimacy by meeting minimal standards of good governance or responsibility for the security and general welfare of its citizens and all those under its jurisdiction. Fulfillment of these standards, in turn, requires the formulation of a normative framework stipulating standards for the responsibilities of sovereignty and a system of accountability at the various interactive levels, from national to subregional and regional to international. The consensus now is that the problems are primarily internal and that, however external their sources or continued linkages, the responsibility for solutions, especially in the post–Cold War era, falls first on Africans themselves.

Africans have recognized that the time has long since come to stop blaming colonialism for Africa's persistent problems. The irony, however, is that the principal modern agent of Africa's political and economic development and the interlocutor in the international arena, the state, is itself a creature of foreign intervention. Although Africans have, for the most part, accepted the state with its colonially defined borders, African states have lacked the indigenous roots for internal legitimacy. And although democracy has been expanding since the end of the Cold War, it has tended to be rather narrowly associated with elections that often have not been entirely free and fair; indeed, the state is often not representative or responsive to the demands and expectations of its domestic constituencies. It is important in this context to distinguish between recognizing the unity and territorial integrity of the state and questioning its policy framework, which might be attributable to a regime or might be structural in nature. A structural problem would require a fundamental refashioning of the state itself to meet both the internal standards of good governance and the international requirements of responsible sovereignty.

Failure on the one level usually implies failure on the other. When a state fails to meet the standards prescribed for membership in the international community, thereby exposing itself to external scrutiny and possible sanctions, it is likely to assert sovereignty and cultural relativism in an attempt to barricade itself against the threat of foreign interference. Sovereignty has evolved enough not only to prescribe democratic representation but also to justify outside intervention. As one scholar of international law observed, "In the process, the two notions have merged. Increasingly, governments recognize that their legitimacy depends on meeting a normative expectation of the community of states. This recognition has led to the emergence of a community expectation: that those who seek the validation of their empowerment patently govern with the consent of the governed. Democracy, thus, is on the way to becoming a global entitlement, one that increasingly will be promoted and protected by collective international processes."[2] Another has argued that "there is a clear trend away from the idea of unconditional sovereignty and toward a concept of responsible sovereignty. Governmental legitimacy that validates the exercise of sovereignty involves adherence to minimum humanitarian norms and a capacity to act effectively to protect citizens from acute threats to their security and well-being that derive from adverse conditions within a country."[3]

During the extensive consultations I conducted in connection with my UN mandate as representative of the secretary-general on internally displaced persons (1992–2004), representatives of several governments commented that national sovereignty carries with it responsibilities that, if not met, put a government at risk of forfeiting its legitimacy. One spokesperson for a major power even went as far as saying, "To put it bluntly," if governments do not live up to those responsibilities (among which he specified the protection of minority rights), "the international community should intervene by force."[4] Representatives of African countries who have voiced global humanitarian concerns have expressed similar views.

Such pronouncements have almost become truisms that are rapidly making narrow concepts of legality obsolete. When the international community does decide to act—as it did when Iraq invaded Kuwait, when Somalia descended into chaos and starvation, and (albeit less decisively) when the former Yugoslavia disintegrated, especially in Kosovo—controversy over issues of legality have become futile or of limited value as a brake to guard against precipitous change. One observer summarized the new sense of urgency regarding the need for an international response, the ambivalence of the pressures for the needed change, and the pull of traditional legal doctrines as follows:

> In the post–Cold War world . . . a new standard of intolerance for human misery and human atrocities has taken hold. Something quite significant has occurred to raise the consciousness of nations to the plight of peoples within sovereign borders. There is a new commitment—expressed in both moral and legal terms—to alleviate the suffering of oppressed or devastated people. To argue today that norms of sovereignty, non-use of force, and the sanctity of internal affairs are paramount to the collective human rights of people, whose lives and well-being are at risk, is to avoid the hard questions of international law and to ignore the march of history.[5]

To intervene is, however, not an easy choice. In 1991 former UN secretary-general Javier Perez de Cuellar highlighted this dilemma when he said, "We are clearly witnessing what is probably an irresistible shift in public attitudes towards the belief that the defense of the oppressed in the name of morality should prevail over frontiers and legal documents." But he also asked, "Does [intervention] not call into question one of the cardinal principles of international law, one diametrically opposed to it, namely, the obligation of non-interference in the internal affairs of states?"[6] In his 1991 annual report he wrote of the new balance that must be struck between sovereignty and the protection of human rights:

> It is now increasingly felt that the principle of non-interference with the essential domestic jurisdiction of States cannot be regarded as a protective barrier behind which human rights could be massively or systematically violated with impunity. . . . The case for not impinging on the sovereignty, territorial integrity and political independence of States is by itself indubitably strong. But it would only be weakened if it were to carry the implication that sovereignty, even in this day and age, includes the right of mass slaughter or of launching systematic campaigns of decimation or forced exodus of civilian populations in the name of controlling civil strife or insurrection. With the heightened international interest in universalizing a regime of human rights, there is a marked and most welcome shift in public attitudes.
>
> To try to resist it would be politically as unwise as it is morally indefensible. It should be perceived as not so much a new departure as a more focused awareness of one of the requirements of peace.[7]

Preferring to avoid confronting the issue of sovereignty, de Cuellar called for a "higher degree of cooperation and a combination of common sense and compassion," arguing that "we need not impale ourselves on the horns of a dilemma between respect for sovereignty and the protection of human rights. . . . What is involved is not the right of intervention but the collective obligation of States to bring relief and redress in human rights emergencies."[8]

In *An Agenda for Peace* de Cuellar's successor, Boutros Boutros-Ghali, wrote that respect for sovereignty and integrity is "crucial to any common international progress," but he went on to say that "the time of absolute and exclusive sovereignty . . . has passed," that "its theory was never matched by reality," and that it is necessary for leaders of states "to find a balance between the needs of good internal governance and the requirements of an ever more interdependent world."[9] As one commentator noted, "The clear meaning was that governments could best avoid intervention by meeting their obligations not only to other states, but also to their own citizens. If they failed, they might invite intervention."[10]

But although negative interpretations of sovereignty prevail as "a prerogative to resist claims and encroachments coming from outside national boundaries—the right to say no," the question can be and has been posed as to whether erasing the doctrine of sovereignty from political leaders' minds would reduce those forms of human suffering associated with extreme governmental failure. Falk asks, "Would such an erasure strengthen sentiments of human solidarity on which an ethos of corrective responsibility and individual accountability depends?"[11] The withdrawal of the international community from Somalia once the humanitarian intervention proved costly in American lives, the astonishing disengagement from Rwanda in the face of genocide in 1994, and the indifference to the atrocities and gross human rights violations in Liberia, Sierra Leone, and Sudan, to mention just a few examples—as contrasted to the dramatic, high-tech intervention on behalf of the Kurds in Iraq and the Albanians in Kosovo—prompt a resounding "no" in answer to the question. Selectivity in the manner and scale of response is the fundamental reality.

Boutros-Ghali's successor as secretary-general was even more vocal than his predecessors on the need to curtail the constraints of sovereignty. In an address to the Commission on Human Rights on April 7, 1999, Kofi Annan said, "When civilians are attacked and massacred because of their ethnicity, as in Kosovo, the world looks to the United Nations to speak up for them. When men, women and children are assaulted and their limbs hacked off, as in Sierra Leone, here again the world looks to the United Nations. When women and girls are denied their right to equality, as in Afghanistan, the world looks to the United Nations to take a stand." Emphasizing the expectation of "our global constituency" that the UN will intervene to protect "the tortured, the oppressed, the silenced, the victims of 'ethnic cleansing' and injustice," Annan posed a rhetorical, but pertinent question: "If, in the face of such abuses, we do not speak up and speak out, if we do not act in defense of human rights and advocate their lasting universality, how can we answer that global constituency?"[12]

Although sovereignty as such is no longer a barrier to intervention on human rights and humanitarian grounds, the determining factor is the political will of other states based on national interest, combined with a compelling level of humanitarian concern. However, assertions of sovereignty can also be invoked by powers lacking the will to become involved. Because intervention is often costly in terms of lives and material, it is convenient to avoid it unless imperative national interest dictates otherwise. Sovereignty then elicits benign conformity to the principle of noninterference or provides a convenient excuse for inaction. If the constraints of sovereignty against justifiable intervention are to be circumvented and, more important, if governments and other controlling authorities such as insurgent movements are to be inspired or at least motivated to discharge their obligations, it is necessary to prescribe "normative sovereignty," or "sovereignty as responsibility."[13]

The international community's ambivalence about intervention arises not only from reluctance to become involved but also from motives for external intervention, which are by no means always altruistic. Self-interest therefore dictates an appropriate and timely action in terms of self-protection. This was the point made by the then secretary-general of the Organization of African Unity, Salim Ahmed Salim, in his bold proposals for an OAU mechanism for conflict prevention and resolution. "If the OAU, first through the Secretary-General and then the Bureau of the Summit, is to play the lead role in any African conflict," he said, "it should be enabled to intervene swiftly, otherwise it cannot be ensured that whoever (apart from African regional organizations) acts will do so in accordance with African interests."[14] Criticizing the tendency to respond only to worst-case scenarios, Salim also emphasized the need for preemptive intervention: "The basis for 'intervention' may be clearer when there is a total breakdown of law and order . . . and where, with the attendant human suffering, a spill-over effect is experienced within the neighboring countries. . . . However, pre-emptive involvement should also be permitted even in situations where tensions evolve to such a pitch that it becomes apparent that a conflict is in the making."[15]

The secretary-general went so far as to suggest that the OAU should take the lead in transcending the traditional view of sovereignty, building on the African values of kinship, solidarity, and the notion that "every African is his brother's keeper."[16] Considering that "our borders are at best artificial," Salim argued, "we in Africa need to use our own cultural and social relationships to interpret the principle of non-interference in such a way that we are enabled to apply it to our advantage in conflict prevention and resolution."[17]

In traditional Africa one such cultural resource has been third-party intervention for mediation and conciliation, which is always expected, regardless of the will of the parties directly involved in a conflict. Even in domestic disputes relatives and elders intercede without being invited. Indeed, "saving face," which is critical to conflict resolution in Africa, requires that such intervention be unsolicited. But, of course, African concepts and practices under the modern conditions of the nation-state must still balance consideration for state sovereignty against the compelling humanitarian need to protect and assist the dispossessed.

Even in the modern context, however, state sovereignty notwithstanding, as former secretary-general Kofi Annan put it, there is a need for a third party to speak out and say, "Stop, this is enough. This cannot be allowed to happen." Elaborating on the role of a third party, Annan said, "the third party has a very important role we should never underestimate, not only in speaking out trying to get help, but it also gives inspiration and strength to those who are caught in the situation."[18] Annan was even more emphatic when he said, "Governments must not be allowed to use sovereignty as a shield to systematically deny their people of human rights and undertake gross systematic abuses of human rights. If that were to happen, shouldn't the international community have some responsibility of going to assist these people?"[19]

The normative frameworks proposed by the OAU secretary-general and the UN secretary-general's *Agenda for Peace* were predicated on respect for the sovereignty and integrity of the state as crucial to the existing international system. However, the logic of the transcendent importance of human rights as a legitimate area of concern for the international community—especially where order has broken down or where the state is incapable of acting or unwilling to act responsibly to protect the masses of citizens—would tend to make international inaction quite indefensible. Even in less extreme cases of acute internal conflicts, the pivotal actors' perspectives on such issues as the national or public interest are bound to be sharply divided both internally and in terms of their relationship to the outside world. After all, internal conflicts often entail a contest of the national arena of power and, hence, sovereignty. Every political intervention from outside has its internal recipients, hosts, and beneficiaries. Under those circumstances there can hardly be said to be indivisible national sovereignty behind which the nation stands united.

It is not always easy to determine the degree to which a government of a country devastated by civil war is truly in control when, as often happens, rebel or opposing forces control sizable portions of the territory. Frequently, though a government may remain in effective control of the capital and the main garrisons, even when much of the countryside in the war zone will have practically collapsed. How would a partial but significant collapse such as this be factored into determining the degree to which civil order in the country has broken down?

A government cannot present a clear face to the outside world when it keeps others from stepping in to offer protection and assistance in the name of sovereignty after allowing hundreds of thousands (and maybe millions) to starve to death when food can be made available to them; to be exposed to deadly elements when they could be provided with shelter; to be indiscriminately tortured, brutalized, and murdered by opposing forces, contesting the very sovereignty that is supposed to ensure their security; or to otherwise allow them to suffer in a vacuum of moral leadership and responsibility. Under such circumstances the international community is called upon to step in and fill the vacuum created by such neglect. If the lack of protection and assistance is the result of the country's incapacity, the government would, in all likelihood, invite or welcome such international intervention. But where the neglect is a willful part of a policy emanating from internal conflict, preventive and corrective interventions become necessary.

As former secretary-general Kofi Annan argued that the issue is more than the culpability of governments but the limits to their capacity in the face of the globalizing challenges facing them: "I can understand a nation's right . . . to protect its sovereignty. On the other hand, . . . the traditional concept of sovereignty is being changed by the developments in the world today, from globalization—there are lots of areas governments do not control. They do not control the external factors that affect their economy. They do not control financial flows. They do not control some of the environmental issues. Why should abuse of human rights be the only area that they should insist they should be allowed to control without any interference?"[20]

It is most significant that the Security Council, in its continued examination of the secretary-general's *Agenda for Peace*, welcomed the observations contained in the report concerning the question of humanitarian assistance and its relationship to peacemaking, peacekeeping, and peacebuilding.[21] In particular, the Council established that, under certain circumstances "there may be a close relationship between acute needs for humanitarian assistance and threats to international peace and security"[22]; indeed, it "[noted] with concern the incidents of humanitarian crises, including mass displacements of population becoming or aggravating threats to international peace and security."[23] The Council further expressed the belief "that humanitarian assistance should help establish the basis for enhanced stability through rehabilitation and development" and "noted the importance of adequate planning in the provision of humanitarian assistance in order to improve prospects for rapid improvement of the humanitarian situation."[24]

Absolute sovereignty is clearly no longer defensible; it never was, but it has now been significantly curtailed. The critical question now is under what circumstances the international community is justified in overriding sovereignty to protect the dispossessed populations within state borders. The common assumption in international law is that such action is justified when there is a threat to international peace. The position the Security Council now supports is that massive violations of human rights and displacement within a country's borders may constitute such a threat.[25] Others contend that a direct threat to international peace as the basis for intervention under Chapter Seven of the UN Charter has become more a legal fiction than the principle justifying international action, nearly always under conditions of extreme humanitarian tragedies.

To avoid costly emergency relief operations, the international community must develop a response to conflict situations before they deteriorate into humanitarian tragedies. Such a response calls for placing an emphasis on peacemaking through preventive diplomacy, which in turn requires an understanding of the sources of conflicts and a willingness to address them at their roots.

RECASTING SOVEREIGNTY AS RESPONSIBILITY: RECENT DEVELOPMENTS

Recasting sovereignty as responsibility was the fundamental norm that guided my work and dialogue with governments for twelve years as representative of the UN secretary-general on internally displaced persons (IDPs) from 1992 to 2004. Two initiatives helped shape my perspective on the emerging challenge. One was the development of an African Studies Project in the Foreign Policy Studies Program at the Brookings Institution. The other was participating in the initiative of then former head of state of Nigeria and subsequently twice-elected president Olusegun Obasanjo toward a Helsinki-like Conference on Security, Stability, Development, and Cooperation in Africa (CSSDCA).

In the Brookings Africa Project we made an initial assessment of conflicts in Africa and the challenges they posed in the post–Cold War era.[26] Next we undertook national and regional case studies to deepen our understanding of the issues involved.[27] A synthesis of these case studies led to the main conclusion that as conflicts were now being properly perceived as internal, they also primarily became the responsibility of governments to prevent, manage, and resolve. Governance became perceived primarily as conflict management.

Within the framework of regional and international cooperation, state sovereignty has been postulated as entailing the responsibility for effective conflict management. The envisaged responsibility involved managing diversity; ensuring equitable distribution of wealth, services, and development opportunities; and participating effectively in regional and international arrangements for peace, security, and stability. In subsequent work we tried to put more flesh on the skeleton of the responsibilities of sovereignty, building largely on human rights and humanitarian norms and international accountability.

Because internal conflicts often spill across international borders, their consequences also spill across borders, threatening regional security and stability. In the "apportionment" of responsibilities in the post–Cold War era, therefore, regional organizations provide the second layer of the needed response. Still, the international community remains the residual guarantor of universal human rights and humanitarian standards in the quest for global peace and security—hence, the stipulation of sovereignty as responsibility with implicit accountability to the regional and international layers of cooperation.

The development of the Helsinki process for Africa was motivated by the concern that the post–Cold War global order was likely to result in the withdrawal of the major powers and the marginalization of Africa. It was, therefore, imperative for Africa to take charge of its destiny and observe principles that would appeal to the West and thereby provide a sound foundation for a mutually agreeable partnership. This was found in the Helsinki framework of the Economic and Security Cooperation in Europe, which became the Organization for Security and Cooperation in Europe (OSCE).

In Africa a series of meetings culminated in the 1991 Kampala Conference, attended by some five hundred people, including several heads of state and representatives from all walks of life. The conference produced the Kampala Document, which elaborated the four "calabashes," so termed to distinguish them from the Organization for Security and Cooperation in Europe's "baskets," to give them an African orientation. The calabashes are security, stability, development, and cooperation. The CSSDCA by the OAU was initially blocked by a few governments that felt threatened by its normative principles. Obasanjo's imprisonment by the Nigerian dictator Sani Abacha also removed the leverage needed to exert pressure on the OAU. With the return to power of Obasanjo as the elected president of Nigeria, he was able to push successfully for incorporating CSSDCA into the OAU mechanism for conflict prevention, management, and resolution.[28]

In connection with these initiatives I began to focus attention on promoting the need to balance conventional notions of sovereignty with the responsibility of the state to provide protection and general welfare to citizens and all those under state jurisdiction.[29] Given the sensitivity and controversy surrounding my mandate as representative of the UN secretary-general on internally displaced persons (IDPs), responsible for the protection and assistance of internally displaced populations worldwide, the only way to bridge the need for international protection and assistance for this population and the barricades of the negative approach to sovereignty was to build on the evolving norm of sovereignty as a positive concept of state responsibility toward its citizens and those under its jurisdiction. Most states discharged this responsibility under normal circumstances and, if they lacked the capacity to do so, called on the international community to assist them in discharging their responsibility. But in the exceptional cases where states failed to do so, the international community needed to assume that responsibility, if necessary, by overriding state sovereignty.

In making that argument in my dialogues with governments, I would end by noting that the best way for a state to protect and preserve its sovereignty is to discharge—and be seen to discharge—its responsibility to protect and assist its needy citizens or call for international assistance to complement its efforts. Otherwise, the world will not watch innocent civilians die or suffer without intervening. As Secretary-General Kofi Annan explained, "If citizens' rights are respected, there will be no need for anyone to want to intervene either through diplomatic means or coercive means. . . . The governments should see it not as a license for people to come in and intervene. We are talking about those situations where there are serious and gross and systematic violations of human rights. I think that governments who protect their citizens and their rights and do not create that kind of situation have no reason to worry that anyone would intervene."[30] The main point, however, was to persuade the governments to accept the positive recasting of sovereignty and the responsibility it entails. This approach was quite effective in the dialogue with governments.

The principle of sovereignty as responsibility recast as the responsibility to protect was strengthened and mainstreamed by the Canadian-sponsored Commission on Intervention and State Sovereignty, which has continued to gain wide support within the international community.[31] In 2004 the Secretary-General's High Level Panel on Threats, Challenges, and Changes also endorsed the principle. This was followed by the secretary-general's creation of the office of the special advisor on the prevention of genocide, also in 2004. In 2005 the secretary-general released his report "In Larger Freedom: Toward Security Development and Human Rights for All." As the UN prepared for its sixtieth-anniversary celebration, the secretary-general pleaded that "we must embrace the responsibility to protect."[32] The World Summit of Heads of State and Government, which convened in New York in September 2005, "stressed the need for the General Assembly to continue consideration of the responsibility to protect populations from genocide, war crimes, ethnic cleansing, and crimes against humanity."[33]

Kofi Annan, who at the beginning of his first term as secretary-general had provoked considerable controversy by calling for the international community's right of humanitarian intervention, reflected on the progress made in stipulating the responsibility to protect: "The Canadian Commission . . . took the concept further, and in fact gave it a better diplomatic name than I had done. I had referred to humanitarian intervention, and then took up the "responsibility to protect"—that the governments have the responsibility to protect their people, and where they fail or show unwillingness to do that or are incapable of doing it, that responsibility may fall on the international community and the membership at large, the world community, to do something about it."[34]

The challenge that postulating sovereignty as responsibility has posed for the international community is that it implies accountability. Obviously, the internally displaced themselves and other victims of internal conflicts trapped within international borders, marginalized, excluded, often persecuted, have little capacity to hold their national authorities accountable. Only the international community, including subregional, regional, and international organizations, has the leverage and clout to persuade governments and other concerned actors to discharge their responsibility or otherwise fill the vacuum of irresponsible or irresponsive sovereignty. A soft but credible threat of consequences in case of failure to discharge the responsibility of sovereignty, combined with the promise of the benefits of international legitimacy and cooperation, offers an effective inducement.

However, the fact is that often governments of some affected countries, even if willing to discharge the responsibility of assisting and protecting their needy populations, lack resources and the capacity to do so. Offering them support in a way that links humanitarian assistance with protection in a holistic, integrated approach to human rights should make the case more compelling and persuasive. No government deserving any legitimacy can request material assistance from the outside world and reject concern with the human rights of the people on whose behalf it requests assistance. Doing so would be like asking the international community to feed them without ensuring their safety and dignity—an implausible logic. Now that the standard of sovereignty as responsibility or the responsibility to protect has been set, the international community's focus should shift to the need for implementation and persuading states to honor it as an essential ingredient of their legitimacy, both domestically and internationally.

ADDRESSING THE CAUSES OF CONFLICT

In most countries torn apart by war the sources and causes of conflict are generally recognized as inherent in the traumatic experience of state formation and nation building, complicated by colonial intervention and repressive postcolonial policies. The starting point, as far as Africa is concerned, is the colonial nation-state, which brought together diverse groups who were, paradoxically, kept separate and unintegrated. Regional ethnic groups were broken up and affiliated with others within the artificial borders of the new state, and colonial masters imposed a superstructure of law and order to maintain relative peace and tranquility.

The independence movement was a collective struggle for self-determination that reinforced the notion of unity within the artificial framework of the newly established nation-state. Initially, independence came as a collective gain that did not delineate who was to get what from the legacy of centralized power and wealth. But because colonial institutions had divested the local communities and ethnic groups of much of their indigenous autonomy and sustainable livelihood, replacing them with a degree of centralized authority and dependency on the welfare state system, the struggle for control became unavoidable once control of these institutions passed on to the nationalists at independence. The outcome was often conflict—over power, wealth, and development—that led to gross violations of human rights, denial of civil liberties, disruption of economic and social life, and the consequential frustration of efforts for development. As the Cold War raged, however, these conflicts were seen not as domestic struggles for power and resources but as extensions of the superpower ideological confrontation. Rather than helping to resolve them peacefully, the superpowers often worsened the conflicts by providing military and economic assistance to their own allies.

Although the end of the Cold War removed this aggravating external factor, it also removed the moderating role of the superpowers, both as third parties and as mutually neutralizing allies. The results have been unmitigated brutalities and devastation from identity conflicts. It can credibly be argued that the gist of these internal conflicts is that the ethnic pieces that were put together by the colonial glue and reinforced by the old world order are now pulling apart and that ethnic groups are reasserting their autonomy or independence. Old identities, undermined and rendered dormant by the structures and values of the nation-state system, are reemerging and demanding participation, distribution, and legitimacy. In fact, it may be even more accurate to say that the process has been going on in a variety of ways within the context of the constraints imposed by the nation-state system.

The larger the gap in the participation and distribution patterns based on racial, ethnic, or religious identity, the more likely the breakdown of civil order and the conversion of political confrontation into violent conflict. When the conflict turns violent, the issues at stake become transformed into a fundamental contest for state power. The objectives may vary in degree from a demand for autonomy to a major restructuring of the national framework, either to be captured by the demand-making group or to be more equitably reshaped. When the conflict escalates into a contest for the "soul" of the nation, it turns into an intractable zero-sum confrontation. The critical issue then is whether the underlying sense of injustice, real or perceived, can be remedied in a timely manner, avoiding the zero-sum level of violence.

Viewing the crisis from the global perspective, it is also pertinent to recall the words of UN secretary-general Boutros-Ghali, who observed in *An Agenda for Peace*, "One requirement for solutions to these problems lies in commitment to human rights with a special sensitivity to those of minorities, whether ethnic, religious, social or linguistic."[35] On the need to strike a balance between the unity of larger entities and respect for the sovereignty, autonomy, and diversity of various identities, the secretary-general further noted, "The healthy globalization of contemporary life requires in the first instance solid identities and fundamental freedoms. The sovereignty, territorial integrity and independence of states within the established international system, and the principle of self-determination for peoples, both of great value and importance, must not be permitted to work against each other in the period ahead. Respect for democratic principles at all levels of social existence is crucial: in communities, within states and within the community of states. Our constant duty should be to maintain the integrity of each while finding a balanced design for all."[36]

Where discrimination or disparity is based on race, ethnicity, region, or religion, it is easy to see how appropriate constitutional provisions and laws protecting basic human rights and fundamental freedoms can combat it. But where discrimination or disparity arises from conflicting perspectives on national identity, especially ones based on religion, the cleavages become more difficult to bridge. In some instances religion, ethnicity, and culture become so intertwined that they are not easy to disentangle. Such is the case in the Sudan, where Islam has gained momentum and is aspiring to offer region-wide and, indeed, global ideological leadership. Islam in the Sudan has been closely associated with Arabism, which also gives the movement a composite ethnic, cultural, and religious identity, even though the Islamists themselves espouse the nonracial ideals of the faith. The composite identity of Islam and Arabism poses the threat of subordination to non-Muslims, who also perceive themselves as non-Arabs. It is consequently resisted, especially in the non-Arab, non-Muslim South that, after half a century of armed struggle, became independent on July 9, 2011.

What makes the role of religion particularly formidable is that there are legitimate arguments on both sides of the religiously based conflict. On the one hand, the Islamists, representing the Arabized Muslim majority, want to fashion the nation on the basis of their faith, which they believe does not allow the separation of religion and the state. The non-Muslims and the more liberally minded or secular Muslims, on the other hand, reject this, seeing it as a means of inevitably relegating them to a lower status as citizens; they insist on secularism as a more mutually accommodating basis for a pluralistic process of nation building. The dilemma is whether an Islamic framework should be used to encompass a religiously mixed society, imposing a minority status on the non-Muslims, or whether secularism should be the national framework, thereby imposing on the Muslim majority the wishes of the non-Muslim minority. The crisis in national identity that this dualism has posed is that there is not yet a consensus on a framework that unquestionably establishes the unity of the country. During the colonial period the country was governed as two separate entities in one; after independence it intermittently became embroiled in war with itself over the composite factors of religion, ethnicity, race, and culture.

If responsibility for Africa's problems is now being assigned to the Africans as represented by their states, the logic should extend down to embrace citizen participation, a process that might be termed the challenge of localization. This process would broaden the basis of participation to include not only the wide array of organizations within the now-popular notion of civil society but also and primarily Africa's indigenous, territorially defined, local communities, with their organizational structures, value systems, institutional arrangements, and ways of using their human and material resources.

Given its centrality and pervasiveness, ethnicity is a reality no country can afford to completely ignore. Thus, African governments have ambivalently tried to dismiss it, marginalize it, manipulate it, corrupt it, or combat it in a variety of ways. But no strategic formula for its constructive use has been developed, despite the fact that an overwhelming majority of Africans, however urbanized or modernized, belong to known "tribal" or ethnic origins and remain in one way or another connected to their groups.[37] Indeed, as one African scholar noted, "Urban populations straddle the two geographical spaces—urban and rural—with the result [that] the politics of one easily spills into the politics of the other."[38] The other side of this spectrum is flexibility or adaptability that allows considerable room for molding identity to suit changing conditions or serve alternating objectives, some destructive.

Ethnic identities in themselves are not conflictual, just as individuals are not inherently in conflict merely because of their different identities and characteristics; rather, it is unmanaged or mismanaged competition for power, wealth, or status broadly defined that provides the basis for conflict. Today virtually every

African conflict has some ethno-regional dimension to it.[39] Even those conflicts that may appear to be free of ethnic concerns involve factions and alliances built around ethnic loyalties. Analysts tend to hold one of two views regarding the role of ethnicity in these conflicts. Some see ethnicity as a source of conflict; others see it as a tool used by political entrepreneurs to promote their ambitions.[40] In reality it is both. Ethnicity, especially when combined with territorial identity, is a reality that exists independently of political maneuvers. To argue that ethnic groups are unwitting tools of political manipulation is to underestimate a fundamental social reality and to assume that members of the group lack value judgment on the issues involved. Conversely, given the emotional fervor and the group dynamics of the identity issues it evokes, ethnicity is clearly a resource for political manipulation and entrepreneurship, which African states are loath to manage constructively.

Ethiopia, after Eritrea's breakaway, can claim credit for being the only African country that is trying to confront the problem head-on by recognizing territorially based ethnic groups, granting them not only a large measure of autonomy but also the constitutional right of self-determination, even to the extent of secession.[41] Ethiopia's leaders assert emphatically that they are committed to the right of self-determination, wherever it leads. But it can also be argued that giving the people the right to determine their destiny leads them to believe that their interests will be safeguarded, which should give them a reason to opt for unity. In fact, the Ethiopian constitution stipulates that the right to independence can be exercised only after following an elaborate process to establish the necessity and appropriateness of that ultimate step, and indeed, no ethnic community has so far exercised or demanded the right to independence constitutionally.

In contrast to the case of Ethiopia, the 2005 Comprehensive Peace Agreement (CPA) that ended the decades of war in southern Sudan granted the people of the South the right of self-determination through a referendum to be held after a six-year interim period to decide whether to remain in a united Sudan under the interim arrangements of the CPA or to become an independent state. The agreement, however, stipulated that during the interim period efforts would be made to make unity an attractive option for the South. In the end the South voted overwhelmingly for independence, which was declared on July 9, 2011, indicating that unity had not been made attractive.

Unfortunately, although Sudan initially received the independence of the South positively and became the first to recognize the new state, relations subsequently deteriorated, generating clashes that threatened a return to war. Whereas a number of unresolved issues, such as the sharing of oil revenues, border demarcation, citizenships, and the status of the contested border area of Abyei, account for the tensions, the major source of tensions is the ongoing conflict between Khartoum and the liberation movements in the marginalized regions of the North, some of whom had allied with the South in the war that raged for decades. The vision of a new Sudan freed from any discrimination due to race, ethnicity, religion, culture, or gender—which the southern-based Sudan People's Liberation Movement and

Army (SPLM/A) had postulated as the objective of the struggle, not secession—had also inspired these northern groups to join the struggle.

Southern independence left these groups still under the discriminating domination of the old Sudan system. They have therefore reconstituted themselves as SPLM/A-North and have continued the struggle for the new Sudan, hoping for support from the independent South. Sudan has, however, used allegations of support for them from the South not only to justify military incursions into the South but actively to instigate and support tribal militias to undermine and destabilize the state of South Sudan. Although the international community has been calling on both countries to stop support for armed opposition groups within each other's territory, what is needed is for Khartoum to negotiate with these groups in good faith, address their legitimate concerns, and request South Sudan, as its former ally, to use its good offices to mediate a just resolution to the conflict.

As the initial hope for a unity vote in the stipulated referendum in southern Sudan indicated, self-determination does not necessarily mean secession. After all, one of the options of self-determination is to remain within the state. But perhaps even more significant is the reconceptualization of self-determination as a principle that allows people to choose their own administrative status and machinery within the country.[42] It has been noted that internal self-administration "might be more effectively used in a way that would help avoid suffering of the kind that so regrettably becomes commonplace when communities feel that their only option is to fight for independence."[43] In that sense self-determination becomes closely associated with democracy and protection of minorities and not conterminous with independence. As Sir Arthur Watts, one of the principal proponents of internal self-determination, has observed, independence is a complicated process that can be traumatic. For many communities it is not necessarily the best option. Often, no advantage is gained by insisting on independence, excluding other kinds of arrangements, especially if leaders would grant a community all it wants without the additional burdens of a wholly independent existence.[44]

Shortly after its independence from Sudan on July 9, 2011, South Sudan exploded in violence—initially within the presidential guard—that soon escalated into a civil war that increasingly assumed an ethnic dimension. As I argued in my book *Bound by Conflict: Dilemmas of the Two Sudans*, despite the sharp differences between the grievances that inspired the struggle of the South against the North and those that inspired the internal southern conflict, there is a common thread between the situations: the desire of ethnic and regional groups to be self-determining and self-governing in opposition to control by the perceived dominant ethnic groups that wield central national power and resources.[45]

Ultimately the only sustainable unity is one based on mutual understanding and agreement. Unfortunately, however, the normative framework for national unity in modern Africa is not the result of consensus. Except for a very few cases, as in postapartheid South Africa, Africans won their independence without negotiating an internal social contract that would forge and sustain national consensus.

Of course, the leaders of various factions, ethnic or political, negotiated a framework that gave them the legitimacy to speak for the country in their demand for independence.

Political elites certainly negotiated a common ground for independence in Zimbabwe, Namibia, and, with less satisfactory results, Angola. And independent leaders debated over federalism in Nigeria and ethnic representation in Kenya, Uganda, and the Ivory Coast (Côte d'Ivoire). Indeed, in virtually every African country, parallel to negotiations with the colonial powers, intense dialogue and negotiation between various groups preceded independence. But these were tactical agreements to rid the country of its colonial yoke and, in any case, were elitist negotiations that did not involve the grassroots, as the South African negotiations did through a broad-based network of political organizations and elements of civil society.

Typically the constitutions that African countries adopted at independence were drafted for them by the colonial masters and, contrary to the authoritarian modes of government adopted by the colonial powers, laden with idealistic principles of liberal democracy to which Africa had not previously been introduced and with which it had no experience. The regimes built on these constitutions were in essence grafted foreign conceptualizations that had no indigenous roots and therefore lacked legitimacy. In most cases they were soon overthrown with no remorse or regrets from the public. But these upheavals involved only a rotation of like-minded elites or, worse, military dictators, intent on occupying the seat of power vacated by the colonial masters. They soon became their colonial masters' images.

In the overwhelming majority of countries the quest for unity underscored the intensity of disunity, sometimes resulting in violent conflicts, many of which have intensified in the post–Cold War era—as evidenced by Burundi, Congo, Liberia, Sierra Leone, Somalia, Rwanda, and Zaire, now the Democratic Republic of Congo. African states must respond to the demands of justice, equity, and dignity by their component elements or risk disintegration and collapse. As Michael Chege has noted in a different context, "It is time to bring this highly variegated menu to African statesmen and citizens and to convince them that self-determination of groups need not always lead to the feared disintegration of the present states into a myriad of small ethnic units."[46]

There are four policy options for managing pluralistic identities. One is to create a national framework with which all can identify without any distinction based on race, ethnicity, tribe, or religion. This is clearly the most desirable option. The second option is to create a pluralistic framework to accommodate diversity in nations that are racially, ethnically, culturally, or religiously divided. Under this option, probably a federal arrangement, groups would accommodate each other's differences with a uniting commitment to the common purpose of national identification and nondiscrimination. For more seriously divided countries the third option may be some form of power sharing, combined with decentralization that may expand federalism into confederalism. Finally, where even this degree of accommodation is not workable and where territorial configurations permit, partition ought to be accepted.

This is the normative framework in which the crisis in the Sudanese region of Darfur should be addressed. Although Sudan has made appreciable progress in ending the half-century-long war in the South, including the acceptance of self-determination that led to southern secession, Sudan remains challenged by chronic crises of identity that are deeply rooted in its history. It urgently needs to reconcile the injustices of its past with the promise of a national framework that will define a country in which all of its citizens can feel the dignity of belonging and enjoy the rights of citizenship on equal footing. The country continues to be challenged by the tragedy in the Darfur region, the tensions that threaten eruption in the eastern Beja region, and the even more violent conflicts in South Kordofan and Blue Nile states, where SPLM/A-North is actively engaged with the center.

In this respect it is worth noting that the international response to Darfur has tended to see the crisis in terms of isolation rather than as an aspect of a national quest for justice and equality that began in the South in the 1950s, extended to the adjacent regions of the North in the mid-1980s, then to the Beja region in the late 1980s, and finally to Darfur. The response of the dominant Arab center has been to fight ruthlessly to preserve its power against the threats posed by proliferating rebellions in the marginalized and discriminated-against non-Arab regions of the country.

The appropriate response from the international community should be three-fold: provide humanitarian assistance to the needy, protect the civilian population, and press for a political solution to achieve peace with justice. As long as war rages on, the government will continue to use Arab tribal militias, of which the infamous Janjaweed are the most notorious but are only illustrative of a more widespread tool the state uses as a weapon against the rebels. Whatever the government may say in response to the pressure from the international community, it will never rein in the Janjaweed and other militias as criminals to be punished. They are allies in the genocidal war for survival. If, however, emphasis is placed on the search for peace, there is a good chance that all parties may be induced to adopt a more positive and constructive attitude toward international support for the peace process.

Punitive measures, such as sanctions and indictment of those responsible for war or obstructing progress toward peace, are often used as threats to induce cooperation. But they generate their own paradoxical responses. Although the Rome Statute that was signed on July 17, 1998, which established the International Criminal Court (ICC), is seen as a positive development in international criminal justice, its implementation has raised serious dilemmas. Indicting leaders who may be critical to promoting peace may be self-defeating. Indicting mid-level authorities with limited roles in making peace may be an exercise in futility. Besides, states' cooperation in apprehending those indicted is often lacking. Although the threat of indictment may have some deterrent effect, a threat is only effective if it is credible. Lack of credibility may indeed undermine the ICC's efficacy.

Sudan is a good example of this paradox. Even though the ICC has indicted President Omer-al Bashir and several leaders of his ruling party, yet they continue to operate and travel around the world undeterred. President al-Bashir continues to be popularly elected and remains a strong figure in the country. His cooperation in accepting the independence of South Sudan was widely acclaimed in the international community, so much so that I once remarked in a meeting of the UN Senior Management that an indicted leader may well receive the Nobel Peace Prize.

Although the ICC will probably continue to grow into an effective court, at least for now it confronts serious challenges. In Africa, which has experienced the most indictments for perhaps the understandable reason that it is the continent most affected by violence and violations of human rights, the general reaction has been that Africans are targeted. There has even been a call for African states to withdraw from the Rome Statute and create an African Criminal Court. Until the international criminal justice system is firmly established and effective, the best way to pursue peace is to engage leaders constructively to cooperate in peacemaking and to address the root causes of conflicts to achieve durable solutions.

THE IMPACT OF THE WAR ON TERROR

In the aftermath of September 11, 2001, the war on terror has created a world order that, to a certain degree, has recalled the Cold War ideological polarization into Western democratic and Eastern communist blocs, with the United States and the Soviet Union heading these blocs. The difference is that these former superpowers are no longer consistently on opposite sides but indeed are on the same side in the global war on terror. What is still in common with the Cold War ideological divide is that, from a human rights perspective, what was crucial in evaluating the performance of a given country was what bloc it fell into. The tendency was to support any government that was ideologically allied with the superpower concerned, whatever its domestic record on human rights, democracy, or good governance in general. Conversely, the evils of a government on the opposite side were considered legitimate targets for exposure and condemnation.

In a way a similar polarization appears to have emerged with the global war on terror. This is reflected in a number of ways, including military confrontations in which many innocent civilians fall victim to the crossfire. Although the obvious cases are Afghanistan and Iraq, the war on terror is also fueling the hostilities and atrocities of the chronic conflicts in the Middle East. Ethiopia's invasion of Somalia, which aimed at ousting the Islamists deemed as posing a terrorist threat in the region, paradoxically aggravated a situation that seemed to have improved under the dominant Islamic courts. The war on terror has also induced responses in the United States and other Western democracies that restrict human rights and civil liberties in the name of security, as the controversy over the treatment of prisoners in Guantánamo attests. In the polarization generated by the war on terror, the tendency has seemed to be that as long as a government is an ally in the war, its own human rights record at home can be overlooked or criticized rhetorically without punitive action. Furthermore, governments opportunistically declare rebel movements to be terrorists, however justified their struggle, and expect political and even military support from their allies in the war against terror.

The global war on terror has reversed the post–Cold War withdrawal of superpower strategic interests in Africa and turned the continent into a theater of confrontation with Islamic terrorists. As Lieutenant Commander Pat Paterson of the US Navy Special Operations Command in Europe explained in an article titled "Into Africa: A New Frontier in the War on Terror," for the United States, in its war with a growing movement of Islamic fundamentalism, the biggest political and military concern in Africa is terrorism.[47] The dire conditions of border disputes, ethnic conflicts, corruption and mismanagement, famine, and HIV make Africa a fertile breeding ground for Muslim extremism and terrorist recruitment. "On a continent where 50% of the population is under 15 years old and where the population is expected to grow from 800 million to 2 billion by 2050, this vast pool of angry, unskilled youth is a population vulnerable to jihadist sentiment and creates a critical problem demanding immediate attention."[48]

Paterson goes on to substantiate the presence and activities of Islamic terrorists on the continent: "The history of al Qaeda in Africa goes back to 1991, when Osama bin Laden used Sudan as his operating base until US and international pressure forced the Sudanese government to withdraw the welcome mat for him in 1996. In August 1998 al Qaeda exploded two massive car bombs outside the U.S. embassies in Dar es Salaam, Tanzania, and Nairobi, Kenya, killing 224 people (including 12 Americans) and injuring 5,000. In response, US Navy warships fired cruise missiles into suspected terror sites near Khartoum later that month during Operation Infinite Reach."[49] Evidence of terrorist activities continues in Paterson's account: "In 2002, al Qaeda operatives killed 15 people in an Israeli-owned hotel in Mombasa, Kenya, and simultaneously fired surface-to-air missiles at an Israeli passenger jet departing Mombasa's airport. In 2003, four suicide bombers attacked Jewish, Spanish, and Belgian sites in Casablanca, Morocco, killing 33 people. The 11 March 2004 train bombings in Madrid were carried out by African jihadists and killed 191 people and wounded 1,400 others. The 7 July 2005 London bombers who killed 51 people and injured more than 700 were assisted by collaborators from Africa."

In September 2005 the US Department of State listed the African organization Salafist Group for Preaching and Combat (GSPC) as a foreign terrorist organization, putting it on par with al-Qaeda. The GSPC gained notoriety with its June 2003 kidnapping of thirty-two Western tourists in Algeria. Terrorist groups such as GSPC use the vast ungoverned expanses of the Sahara Desert to their advantage, ferrying arms, cash, and contraband along established smuggling routes.[50]

Africans were reported to be fighting the United States in Afghanistan and Iraq: "Pentagon officials estimate that 25% of the foreign fighters in Iraq—estimated to be 5,000–8,000—are Africans. The officials also have indicated that a stream of veteran jihadists from the conflicts in Iraq and Afghanistan are returning to Africa to train new soldiers and use insurgent tactics against their native countries."[51]

With Africa emerging as a significant scene, if not actor, in the global war on terror, the US government has quietly opened up a front in East Africa: "Military spending in the four years following 9/11 doubled the amount expended in the preceding four years. The total spent or allocated for arms, training, and regional peacekeeping operations that focus primarily on training and arming sub-Saharan militaries in the four-year period from 2002 until the end of 2005 amounted to $597 million, whereas for 1998–2001 it was $296 million. At that rate it was estimated that it would take a comparatively few years to equal the $1.5 billion that some believed was spent during the three decades of the Cold War on arms for African allies."[52]

The US Africa Command, AFRICOM, which was announced in February 2007 and became operational in the fall of 2008, aimed at working in concert with African partners to create a stable security environment in which political and economic growth could take place. This meant combining humanitarian development assistance with helping Africans pursue the war against terrorism more effectively. As Ryan Henry, principal Defense Department undersecretary for policy, told reporters in June 2007, "AFRICOM will emphasize humanitarian assistance, civic action, military professionalism, border and maritime security assistance, and responses to natural disasters." He added that terrorism was a problem in Africa, and it was something African nations were very concerned about, but "it is clearly not the primary focus" of AFRICOM, which has no intention of committing troops to the continent to pursue terrorists.[53]

Generally speaking the war on terror poses a threat to human rights and democratic freedoms, as Jennifer Cooke and Steve Morrison pertinently cautioned: "As Africa has become conspicuously important in the intensified global war on terror and in U.S. efforts to win support within multilateral forums for military action against Iraq, policymakers confront the risk that geopolitical goals may trump locally specific human rights, democracy, and developmental interests. If this risk is not managed effectively, the United States easily could make mistakes reminiscent of the Cold War, in which the United States based strategic partnerships overwhelmingly on African leaders' anticommunist credentials, with enduring negative consequences for African governance and U.S. credibility on the continent."[54]

Even in the Sudan, where the war on terror appeared to have produced positive results in pressuring the parties to end the war in the South, lest they be accused of terror with severe consequences, contradictory developments have taken place. Although the government in Khartoum remained on the State Department's list of states that support terrorism and Congress continued to be vocally antagonistic to the National Islamic Front, renamed the National Congress Party (NCP) and in control of the government in Khartoum, the Bush administration adopted an ambivalent attitude toward Khartoum, and the NCP shrewdly responded opportunistically to gain Washington's favor. As an observer noted, President Omar al-Bashir's regime, "having hosted Osama bin Laden in Khartoum in the 1990s, has played its hand carefully in the U.S. war on terror. Under pressure from Washington, Khartoum sent its intelligence chief, Salah Abdallah Gosh, to brief Western intelligence officials about al-Qaeda networks in Sudan and beyond."[55]

As Greg Miller and Josh Meyer have reported, "Sudan has moved beyond sharing historical information on al-Qaeda into taking part in on-going counter-terrorism operations, focusing on areas where its assistance is likely to be most appreciated."[56] They go on to write,

> Sudan has secretly worked with the CIA to spy on the insurgency in Iraq, an example of how the U.S. has continued to cooperate with the Sudanese regime even while condemning its suspected role in the killing of thousands of civilians in Darfur.
>
> President Bush has denounced the killings in Sudan's western region as genocide and has imposed sanctions on the government in Khartoum. But some critics say the administration has soft-pedaled the sanctions to preserve its extensive intelligence collaboration with Sudan.
>
> The relationship underscores the complex realities of the post–Sept. 11 world, in which the United States has relied heavily on intelligence and military cooperation from countries, including Sudan and Uzbekistan, that are considered pariah states for their records on human rights.[57]

Sudan's cooperation with the United States is said to go beyond Iraq. "Sudan has helped the United States track turmoil in Somalia, working to cultivate contacts with the Islamic Courts Union and other militias in an effort to locate al-Qaeda suspects hiding there" and "has provided extensive cooperation in counter-terrorism operations, acting on U.S. requests to detain suspects as they pass through Khartoum." The paradox is that "at a time when Sudan is being condemned in the international community, its counter-terrorism work has won precious praise. The U.S. State Department at one point issued a report calling Sudan a 'strong partner in the war on terror.'"[58] This ambivalent attitude toward Khartoum may be a factor in the contradictory hard-talk, soft-action attitude that the United States has adopted on the international response to the genocidal conflict in Darfur. Indeed, the sanctions announced by the Bush administration in late May 2007 were described as "window dressing," designed to appear tough while putting little real pressure on the Sudan or the Arab militias, which the country is believed to be using against rebels and civilians alike in Darfur.[59]

Another paradoxical development as a result of the war on terror was initially improved relations between the United States and Libya, despite Muammar

Gadhafi's controversial human rights record. The United States restored full diplomatic relations with Libya in June 2006 and removed it from the State Department's list of terrorism sponsors, ending long-standing tensions in bilateral relations and US-imposed sanctions. Objectively, it is noteworthy that in later years Gadhafi made significant constructive changes. He began to be viewed as having played a positive role in Africa, his most striking achievement being his initiative and strong support for the African Union. He also took steps to align himself with the United States in an effort to gain Western trust. His government apologized for its past violence, accepted responsibility for the 1988 terrorist attack on an airplane over Lockerbie, Scotland, dismantled its weapons of mass destruction program in 2003, and cooperated with the United States in the war on terror.

It is, however, widely contended that Libya's track record of human rights abuses was still among the worst in the world, calling into question whether Gadhafi's administration was worthy of US support. Freedom House gave Libya the lowest possible rating in all categories—political rights, civil liberties, and freedom—citing poor prison conditions, arbitrary arrest and detention, torture, domestic violence against women, the prohibition of independent human rights organizations, and the ban on independent press. Any form of political opposition was brutally and unsubtly quelled.[60]

Critics of the US and European shift in policy toward Libya argued that it would entrench Libya's poor human rights record:

> The United States and the European Union face the risk that their new diplomatic partnerships with Libya will help legitimize the regime and perpetuate the country's poor conditions. Libyan dissidents claim that Qaddafi will most likely use this new relationship to consolidate his political base and continue stamping out any possibility for political reform. There are also repercussions in the international arena. The United States has portrayed the war on terror as not only a military conflict but also an ideological struggle; current nation-building processes in Iraq and Afghanistan are inextricably linked with the words and values of "freedom," "liberty," and "democracy." In Libya, Qaddafi's eager suppression of the opposition Libyan Islamic Fighting Group (LIFG), recognized as a terrorist organization, has only reinforced beliefs that U.S. and EU motives are not those of building democracy but of self-interested security. Critics of a Western alliance with the Qaddafi regime claim that this "Western hypocrisy" further alienates the Muslim world and gives radical Islamists even more ammunition to attack the West.[61]

Of course, this was unsustainable, as demonstrated by Gadhafi's eventual demise in the face of UN-sanctioned NATO intervention in support of an internal uprising, part of the "Arab Spring."

Thus, the global war on terror, although justified by the horrific events of September 11, 2001, triggered a chain of policies and actions that threaten to reverse the progress made in the international promotion and protection of human rights. Although hindsight on whether a more targeted pursuit of the individual criminals involved in that incident that might have produced different results would be superfluous and futile, there is reason to think carefully about how to pursue the war on terror without compromising the human rights standards that have been painstakingly developed since the end of World War II and the creation of the United Nations. Considering that African states are already prone to the abuse of power and egregious violations of human rights, this development poses a particular danger to be guarded against in the continent.

OPERATIONAL STRATEGIES OF INTERVENTION

Although addressing the issue of sovereignty and the root causes of conflict are critical prerequisites to intervention, formulating credible operation principles is the most pivotal factor in the equation. These principles relate to institutional mechanisms and strategies for action, both preventive and corrective. Ideally, from an institutional or organizational perspective, problems should be addressed and solved within the immediate framework, with wider involvement necessitated only by the failure of the internal efforts. Hence, conflict prevention, management, or resolution progressively move from the domestic domain to the regional and, ultimately, to the global levels of concern and action.

As already noted, those conflicts in which the state is an effective arbiter do not present particular difficulties because they are manageable within the national framework. The problem arises when the state itself is a party to the conflict. Under those conditions external involvement becomes necessary. In the African context it is generally agreed that the next-best level of involvement should be the AU, but there are obvious constraints on its role, as its ineffectiveness in Darfur demonstrated. One such constraint has to do with limited resources, both material and human. But perhaps even more debilitating is the question of political will, as in the intimate context of the region, governments feel they are subject to conflicts arising from the problematic conditions of state formation and nation building and are therefore prone to resist any form of external scrutiny. And because the judge of today may well be the accused of tomorrow, there is a temptation to avoid confronting such problems. The result is evasiveness and malign neglect. Beyond the AU, the United Nations is the next logical organization, for it represents the international community in its global context. But the UN suffers from the same constraints affecting the AU, though to a lesser degree. It, too, must deal with the problem of resources and the reciprocal protectiveness of vulnerable governments.

As recent events have demonstrated, the role of the major Western powers acting unilaterally, multilaterally, or within the framework of the United Nations— though often susceptible to accusations of selectivity and self-interested strategic motivation—has become increasingly pivotal. The problem in this regard is their unwillingness to become involved or their lack of adequate preparedness for such involvement. Perhaps the most important aspect of the involvement of Western industrial democracies in foreign conflicts is the fact that the gravity of the humanitarian tragedies involved often moves these nations to act. Thus, their involvement is both an asset in terms of arresting the tragedy and a limitation in terms of preventing the tragedy at an earlier stage. Even with respect to humanitarian intervention, lack of preparedness for an appropriate and timely response is generally acknowledged as a major limitation.[62]

Nevertheless, some argue that there is a strong presumption that these countries' interests are powerfully engaged and that they will eventually be driven to uphold and promote such interests through humanitarian intervention in crisis situations. Industrial democracies, they further argue, cannot operate without defending standards of human rights and political procedures that are being egregiously violated. Indeed, they themselves cannot prosper in an irreversibly international economy if large, contiguous populations descend into endemic violence and economic depression. Given these compelling reasons and the lack of preparedness for any well-planned response, the United States and Western European countries are particularly prone to crisis-induced reactions that are relatively easy to execute and, indeed, more symbolic than effective in addressing the substantive issues involved.

There will always be elements in a country who welcome intervention, especially among the disadvantaged groups to whom it promises tangible benefits. But because intervention is, of course, a major intrusion from the outside, resistance on the grounds of national sovereignty or pride is also a predictable certainty. For that reason the justification for intervention must be reliably persuasive, if not beyond reproach, as John Steinbruner has argued, "The difference between an intervention that succeeds and one that is destroyed by immune reaction would depend on the degree of spontaneous acceptance or rejection by the local population."[63]

To avoid or minimize this "immune reaction," such an intervention would have to be broadly international in character. The principles used and the objectives toward which the intervention is targeted must transcend political and cultural boundaries or traditions and concomitant nationalist sentiments. In other words, it must enjoy an effective degree of global legitimacy. Steinbruner states, "The rationale that could conceivably carry such a burden presumably involves human rights so fundamental that they are not derived from any particular political or economic ideology."[64]

The strategy for preventive or corrective involvement in conflict should constitute gathering and analyzing information and otherwise monitoring situations with a view toward establishing an early-warning system through which the international community could be alerted to act. The quest for a system of response to conflict and attendant humanitarian tragedies was outlined by the then–UN secretary-general Boutros Boutros-Ghali when, referring to the surging demands on the Security Council as a central instrument for the prevention and resolution of conflicts, he wrote that the aims of the United Nations must be:

> To seek to identify at the earliest possible stage situations that could produce conflict, and to try through diplomacy to remove the sources of danger before violence results;
>
> Where conflict erupts, to engage in peacemaking aimed at resolving the issues that have led to conflict;
>
> Through peace-keeping, to work to preserve peace, however fragile, where fighting has been halted and to assist in implementing agreements achieved by the peacemakers;
>
> To stand ready to assist in peace-building in its differing contexts: rebuilding the institutions and infrastructures of nations torn by civil war and strife; and building bonds of peaceful mutual benefit among nations formerly at war;
>
> And in the largest sense, to address the deepest causes of conflict: economic despair, social injustice and political oppression. It is possible to discern an increasingly common moral perception that spans the world's nations and peoples, and which is finding expression in international laws, many owing their genesis to the work of this Organization.[65]

The action envisaged to address conflict situations and their humanitarian consequences is a four-phase strategy that would involve monitoring developments to draw early attention to impending crises, interceding in time to avert the crisis through diplomatic initiatives, mobilizing international action when necessary, and addressing the root causes to restore peace, security, and stability.[66] The first step would be to detect and identify the problem through various early-warning mechanisms for collecting, evaluating, and reporting information. If a sufficient basis for concern were established, the appropriate mechanism would be invoked to take preventive diplomatic measures and avert the crisis. At first, such initiatives might be taken within the framework of regional arrangements—for example, the Conference on Security and Cooperation in Europe, the Organization of American States, or the African Union. In the United Nations such preventive initiatives would naturally fall on the secretary-general, acting personally or through special representatives, to bring the situation to the attention of the Security Council for appropriate action. If diplomatic initiatives did not succeed, and depending on the level of human suffering involved, the secretary-general and the Security Council might decide to mobilize an international response, ranging from further diplomatic measures to forced humanitarian intervention not only to provide emergency relief but also to facilitate the search for an enduring solution to the causes of the conflict. A strategy aimed at this broader objective would require a close understanding of the causal link between the conditions and developments leading to the outbreak of the crisis and finding solutions that address the root causes to ensure sustainable peace and stability.

CONCLUSION

Africa's turbulent transformation, initiated by the colonial scramble for the continent in the nineteenth century, contained by external domination for much of the first half of the twentieth century, reactivated by the independence movement in the second half of the century, and subdued by the Cold War bipolar control mechanism, is now engaging in a renewed quest of self-liberation from within. Although this initially meant more self-reliance with minimum external interference, motivated by the strategic interests of the Cold War era, the global war against international terrorism in the early twenty-first century has reactivated international concern and propensity for varying forms of intervention. The context in which this is taking place is poised delicately between globalization and isolation, initially bordering on the marginalization of Africa, but in the context of the global war on terror, putting Africa back at the center as a potential breeding ground for international terrorism.

Paradoxically, pressures for humanitarian intervention counterbalance the major powers' ideological withdrawal, whereas the war on terror threatens to relegate human rights to a lower level of concern. This situation calls for a more cost-effective sharing of responsibility, with the Africans assuming the primary role and their international partners lending a complementary affirmative helping hand. Whether this equation is sustainable or the war on terror will take the upper hand and lead Africa back to intensifying dependency remains a question.

Whatever the answer to that question, the policy framework that apportions responsibilities in accordance with the emerging scale must place the first tier of responsibility on the state. At the next level up the international ladder regional actors are increasingly being challenged and motivated by the realization that their own national security is closely connected with the security of their neighbors. This realization has propelled a range of initiatives in which neighbors offer their good offices for third-party mediation in internal conflicts but, if their counsel is not heeded, intervene unilaterally or collectively to achieve their objectives. But as the case of Darfur has shown, regional capacities may be inadequate for the task, and the supportive role of the international community will continue to be a necessity for effective action. The best remedy is internal peace, security, and stability.

A number of African leaders have embraced programs of political and economic reforms that would enhance regional security and stability. Some of their peers remain doggedly committed to authoritarian methods of governance. The international community, weary of shouldering responsibility for Africa's problems, is striving to win the leaders intent on reform, give them the support they need to carry out their programs, and thereby provide them with the incentive to do so in earnest. These measures imply the stipulation of national sovereignty as responsibility with regional and international accountability. The way to guard against unwelcome international intervention is to discharge the responsibilities of sovereignty and be seen to be doing so.

An important dimension of such accountability is therefore the reform of state structures, institutions, and processes to be more equitable in their management of diversities. This reform will require pushing the process of reversing Africa's international dependency to enhance the autonomy of internal actors, ethnic groups, and members of civil society in order to mobilize and engage them in self-reliant processes of governance and sustainable development. The state has been the intermediary and often the bottleneck in the chain of Africa's dependent relationship with the outside world. The required reform must broaden the scope of decision making through extensive and genuine decentralization. It must make a more constructive use of indigenous structures, values, and institutions for self-governance and self-sustaining development from within. Governments genuinely committed to reform should have no difficulty supporting this approach, whereas those that insist on centralization of authority wittingly or unwittingly expose their authoritarian disposition and risk regional and international scrutiny or admonition and, possibly, condemnation and reprisals.

The time is certainly opportune for reconciling sovereignty with the responsibilities of good governance. In balancing national sovereignty and the need for international action to provide protection and assistance to victims of internal conflicts and humanitarian tragedies, certain principles are becoming increasingly obvious as policy guidelines.

First, sovereignty carries with it responsibilities for the well-being of the population. It is from this precept that the legitimacy of a government derives, whatever the political system or prevailing ideology. The relationship between the controlling authority and the populace should ideally ensure the highest standards of human dignity, but at a minimum it should guarantee food, shelter, physical security, basic health services, and other essentials.

Second, in the many countries where armed conflicts and communal violence have caused massive internal displacement, the countries are so divided on fundamental issues that legitimacy and, indeed, sovereignty are sharply contested. This is why there is always a strong faction inviting or at least welcoming external intervention. Under those circumstances the validity of sovereignty must be judged, using reasonable standards to assess how much of the population is represented, marginalized, or excluded.

Third, living up to the responsibilities of sovereignty implies that there is a transcendent authority capable of holding the supposed sovereign accountable. Some form of an international system has always existed to ensure that states conform to accepted norms or face the consequences in the form of unilateral, multilateral, or collective action. Equality among sovereign entities has always been a convenient fiction; it has never been backed by realities because some powers have always been more dominant than others and therefore have been explicitly or implicitly charged with responsibility for enforcing the agreed-upon norms of behavior. Considering that hardly any African country has the requisite capacity, "hegemonic stability" has not been a pattern, although Nigeria and South Africa have exercised considerable influence in their subregions.

Fourth, such a role imposes on the dominant authority or power certain leadership responsibilities that transcend parochialism or exclusive national interests and serve the broader interests of the community or the human family, an area where African countries, with their politics of identity, have suffered a deficit.

When these principles are translated into practical action in countries torn apart by internal conflicts, a number of implications emerge. For example, sovereignty cannot be an amoral function of authority and control; respect for fundamental human rights and humanitarian principles must be among its most basic values. Similarly, the enjoyment of human rights must encompass equitable and effective participation in the political, economic, social, and cultural life of the country, at least as a widely accepted national aspiration. This system of sharing must guarantee that all individuals and groups belong to the nation on an equal footing with the rest of the people, however identified; they must also be sufficiently represented and not discriminated against on the basis of the prevailing views of identity.

To ensure that these normative goals are met or at least genuinely pursued, the international community as represented by the United Nations is the ideal authority. The imperatives of the existing power structures and processes may, however, require that other powers capable of acting on behalf of the international community exercise that authority. Multilateral action may therefore be justified under certain circumstances. Any type of less collective action should be closely circumscribed to guard against selectivity and exploitation for less lofty objectives of a more exclusively national character—objectives that may erode the transcendent moral authority of global leadership for the good of all humankind.

As a polarity emerges between those African governments committed to participatory democracy, respect for human rights, and responsible international partnership and those bent on repression and resistance to reform, the international community should adopt a dual strategy that effectively supports reform with positive incentives and discourages resistance with punitive sanctions. Living up to the responsibilities of sovereignty implies a transcendent authority capable of holding the supposed sovereign accountable. Although the international community has made appreciable progress in responding to humanitarian tragedies, much more needs to be done to ensure that governments adhere to the responsibilities of sovereignty by ensuring the security, fundamental rights, civil liberties, and general welfare of their citizens and all those under their domestic jurisdiction.

Although the world is far from a universal government, the foundations, pillars, and perhaps even structures of global governance are taking shape with the emergence of a post–Cold War international order in which the internally dispossessed are bound to benefit. Unmasking sovereignty to reveal gross violations of human rights is no longer an aspiration; it is a process that has already started.

Governments and other human rights violators are being increasingly scrutinized for such violations. What is now required is to make them fully accountable and to provide international protection and assistance for the victims of human rights violations and unremediated humanitarian tragedies within their domestic jurisdiction. In other words, what is called for is not something entirely new but rather an intensification and improvement of what has already been unfolding.

The global war on terror is obviously a complication insofar as it creates a Cold War–type polarization between allies and enemies. However, in the end, just as internal conflicts require internal solutions to ensure just peace, security, and stability, a global alliance against terrorism must also address the internal conditions that breed international terrorism. Addressing the symptoms without going to the root causes in the crisis of national identity—acute economic disparities, poverty, deprivation, and all forms of indignities in an otherwise flourishing world—experienced not only externally but also internally for the few, will continue to generate internal conflicts in Africa with external ramifications. True security must be comprehensive and inclusive or else those left out will remain a source of instability, both internally and globally.

NOTES

1. Boutros Boutros-Ghali, in a statement of his proposals to the Council of Ministers in Dakar, Senegal, in 1992. The main documents in these three areas of African initiative are as follows: The Kampala Document Toward a Conference on Security, Stability, Development and Cooperation in Africa (Kampala, Uganda: Africa Leadership Forum and Secretariat of the Organization of African Unity and the United Nations Economic Commission for Africa, 1991); Dent Ocaya-Lakidi, Africa's Internal Conflicts: The Search for a Response, Report of an Arusha, Tanzania, High-Level Consultation, March 23–25, 1992, prepared for the International Peace Academy; OAU, Council of Ministers, Fifty-Sixth Ordinary Session, Report of the Secretary-General on Conflicts in Africa: Proposals for an OAU Mechanism for Conflict Prevention and Resolution, CM/1710 (L.VI) (Addis Ababa: Organization of African Unity, June 22–27, 1992); OAU, Council of Ministers, Fifty-Seventh Ordinary Session, Interim Report of the Secretary-General on the Mechanism for Conflict Prevention, Management and Resolution, CM/1747 (L.VI) (Addis Ababa: Organization of African Unity, February 15–19, 1993); and OAU, Council of Ministers, Fifty-Seventh Ordinary Session, Report of the Secretary-General, CM/Plen/Rpt (L.VII) (Addis Ababa: Organization of African Unity, February 15–19, 1993). Also pertinent to the issues involved is UN Secretary-General Boutros Boutros-Ghali's report, An Agenda for Peace, originally published as document A/47/277 S/24111, June 17, 1992.

2. Thomas M. Franck, "The Emerging Right to Democratic Governance," *American Journal of International Law* 86, no. 1 (January 1992), p. 46.

3. Richard Falk, "Sovereignty and Human Dignity: The Search for Reconciliation," in *African Reckoning: A Quest for Good Governance*, ed. Francis M. Deng and Terrence Lyons (Washington, DC: Brookings Institution, 1998), p. 13.

4. Francis M. Deng, *Protecting the Dispossessed: A Challenge for the International Community* (Washington, DC: Brookings Institution, 1993), p. 14.

5. David J. Scheffer, "Toward a Modern Doctrine of Humanitarian Intervention," *University of Toledo Law Review* 23 (Winter 1992), p. 2.

6. UN press release SG/SM/4560, April 24, 1991, cited in Gene M. Lyons and Michael Mastanduno, *Beyond Westphalia: International Intervention, State Sovereignty and the Future of International Society* (Hanover, NH: Dartmouth College, 1992), p. 2. Portions of this statement are also cited in Scheffer, "Toward a Modern Doctrine of Humanitarian Intervention," p. 262.

7. Javier Perez de Cuellar, *Report of the Secretary-General on the Work of the Organization* (New York: United Nations, 1991).

8. Ibid., p. 13.

9. Boutros-Ghali, An Agenda for Peace, p. 5.

10. Scheffer, "Toward a Modern Doctrine of Humanitarian Intervention," pp. 262–263.

11. Falk, "Sovereignty and Human Dignity," p. 12.

12. Global Policy Forum, Statement by Secretary-General Kofi Annan, April 7, 1999, at www.globalpolicy.org/nations/kofi2.htm.

13. Francis M. Deng, Sadikiel Kimaro, Terrence Lyons, Donald Rothchild, and I. William Zartman, eds., *Sovereignty as Responsibility: Conflict Management in Africa* (Washington, DC: Brookings Institution, 1996).

14. OAU, Council of Ministers, Report of the Secretary-General on Conflicts in Africa.

15. Ibid.

16. Ibid.

17. Ibid.

18. Kofi Annan, interview, "Frontline: Ghosts of Rwanda," PBS, February 17, 2004, at www.pbs.org/wgbh/pages/frontline/shows/ghosts/interviews/annan.html.

19. Ibid.

20. Kofi Annan, interview, *Online News Hour*, PBS, October 18, 1999, at www.pbs.org/newshour/bb/international/july-dec99/annan_10-18.html.

21. Note by the president of the Security Council, S/25344, February 26, 1993.

22. Ibid., p. 1.

23. Ibid., p. 2.

24. Ibid.

25. Ibid.

26. Francis M. Deng and I. William Zartman, eds., *Conflict Resolution in Africa* (Washington, DC: Brookings Institution, 1991).

27. Deng et al., *Sovereignty as Responsibility*.

28. Francis M. Deng and Terrence Lyons, eds., *African Reckoning: A Quest for Good Governance* (Washington, DC: Brookings Institution, 1998).

29. Francis M. Deng and I. William Zartman, *A Strategic Vision for Africa: The Kampala Movement* (Washington, DC: Brookings Institution Press, 2002).

30. Kofi Annan, interview, *Online News Hour*, PBS, October 19, 1999.

31. For my various contributions to the normative theme of the responsibility of sovereignty see the following books, chapters, and articles; Deng and Lyons, *African Reckoning*; Francis M. Deng, "Sovereignty and Humanitarian Responsibility: A Challenge for NGOs in Africa and the Sudan," in *Vigilance and Vengeance: NGOs Preventing Ethnic Conflict in Divided Societies*, ed. Robert I. Rotberg (Washington, DC: Brookings Institution and the World Peace Foundation, 1996); Deng, Kimaro, Lyons, Rothchild, and Zartman, *Sovereignty as Responsibility*; Francis M. Deng, "Reconciling Sovereignty with Responsibility: A Basis for International Humanitarian Action," in *Africa in World Politics: Reforming Political Order*, ed. John W. Harbeson and Donald Rothchild (Boulder, CO: Westview Press, 1995); F. M. Deng, "Frontiers of Sovereignty: A Framework of Protection, Assistance and

Development for the Internally Displaced," *Leiden Journal of International Law* 8, no. 2 (1995).

32. UN Report of the High Level Panel on Threats, Challenges, and Changes, A More Secure World: Our Shared Responsibility (New York: United Nations, 2004), paras. 199–203; and Kofi Annan, In Larger Freedoms: Toward Development, Security and Human Rights for All, UN Doc. A/59/2005, March 21, 2005, para. 135.

33. General Assembly 2005, World Summit Outcome, UN Doc. A/60/L1, September 15, 2005, para. 139.

34. Kofi Annan, interview, "Frontline: Ghosts of Rwanda."

35. Boutros-Ghali, An Agenda for Peace, p. 9.

36. Ibid., pp. 9–10.

37. Donald Rothchild, *Managing Ethnic Conflict in Africa* (Washington, DC: Brookings Institution, 1997), pp. 20–21.

38. Thandika Mkandawire, "Shifting Commitments and National Cohesion in African Countries," in *Common Security and Civil Society in Africa*, ed. Lennart Wohlgemuth, Samantha Gibson, Stephan Klasan, and Emma Rothschild (Uppsala, Sweden: Nordiska Afrikainstitutet, 1999), p. 15.

39. Roberta Cohen and Francis Deng, eds., *The Forsaken People: Case Studies of the Internally Displaced* (Washington, DC: Brookings Institution, 1998).

40. According to one source, ethnicity is important in African politics because it serves as an "organizing principle of sound action," which makes it "basically a political . . . phenomenon." See Naomi Chazan et al., *Politics and Society in Contemporary Africa* (Boulder, CO: Lynne Rienner Publishers, 1988), pp. 110, 120. And as UN secretary-general Kofi Annan observed in a paper presented to an international conference on "The Therapeutics of Conflict," when he was still undersecretary-general for Peacekeeping Operations: "Many [of the civil wars] have also been perceived as showing strong symptoms of ethnic conflict. Ethnic conflict as a symptom is, at best, extremely difficult to assess. . . . Ethnic differences are not in and of themselves either symptoms or causes of conflict; in societies where they are accepted and respected, people of vastly different backgrounds live peacefully and productively together. Ethnic differences become charged—conflictual—when they are used for political ends, when ethnic groups are intentionally placed in opposition to each other." See Kofi Annan, "The Peacekeeping Prescription," in *Preventive Diplomacy*, ed. Kevin M. Cahill, MD (New York: Basic Books, 1996), p. 176.

41. The Constitution of the Federal Democratic Republic of Ethiopia (Addis Ababa, December 8, 1994) provides in Article 39, Number 1, that "every nation, nationality and people in Ethiopia has an unconditional right to self-determination, including the right to secession." It also states in Article 39, Number 3, that "every nation, nationality and people in Ethiopia has the right to a full measure of self-government which includes the right to establish institutions of government in the territory that it inhabits and to equitable representation in regional and national governments."

42. This is the essence of the proposal that the state of Liechtenstein presented to the General Assembly of the United Nations in 1991, a proposal that aimed at establishing a new international legal framework in which self-determination, defined primarily as self-administration, might be pursued within the existing state framework. See Wolfgang Danspeckgruber and Sir Arthur Watts, eds., *Self-Determination and Self-Administration: A Sourcebook* (Boulder, CO: Lynne Rienner Publishers, 1997).

43. Ibid., p. 1.

44. Sir Arthur Watts, "The Liechtenstein Draft Convention on Self-Determination Through Self-Administration," in Danspeckgruber and Watts, *Self-Determination and Self-Administration*, p. 23.

45. Francis M. Deng, *Bound by Conflict: Dilemmas of the Two Sudans* (New York: Fordham University Press 2016), p. 1.

46. Cited in a review of Francis M. Deng, "Africa and the New World Disorder," *Brookings Review* (Spring 1993), p. 3. For a more comprehensive discussion of ethnic diversity in the context of democratization, see Chege's article, "Remembering Africa," in *Foreign Affairs* 71, no. 1 (1992), pp. 146–163.

47. Pat Paterson, "Into Africa: A New Frontier in the War on Terror," *United States Naval Institute Proceedings* 132, no. 5 (May 2006), p. 32.

48. Ibid.

49. Ibid.

50. Ibid.

51. Ibid.

52. Sandra T. Barnes, "Global Flows: Terror, Oil, and Strategic Philanthropy," *Africa Studies Review* 48, no. 1 (2005), pp. 1–22, at 1, 6. See also Thomas P. M. Barnett, "The Americans Have Landed," *Esquire*, June 11, 2007.

53. Jim Fisher-Thompson, "New Africa Command to Have Unique Structure, Mission," *USINFO*, June 22, 2007, at http://iipdigital.usembassy.gov/st/english/article /2007/06/200706221700271ejrehsifo.4897272.html#axzz27afokJBw. See also "U.S. Africa Command at Initial Operation Capacity," U.S. Africa Command, Stuttgart, Germany, Press Release 08–001, October 1, 2007, at http://iipdigital.usembassy.gov/st/english /text trans/2007/10/20071003140010xjsnommiso.3377954.html#axzz27afokJBw.

54. Jennifer G. Cook and J. Stephen Morrison, "Building an Ethic of Public Policy Discourse: An Appeal to African Studies Community," *African Issues* 30, no. 2 (2002), p. 63.

55. "Africa's Year of Terror Tactics," *New York Beacon*, January 11–17, 2007, p. 10.

56. Greg Miller and Josh Meyer, "Sudan Aids CIA's Efforts in Iraq," *Los Angeles Times*, June 11, 2007.

57. Ibid. See also Hans Pienaar, "Spooks, Hacks, Party in Secretive Sudan," *Tribune*, June 10, 2007, p. 14.

58. Miller and Meyer, "Sudan Aids CIA's Efforts in Iraq."

59. Ibid.

60. Samantha Fang, "A Worthy Ally? Reconsidering U.S.-Libyan Relations," *Harvard International Review* 29, no. 3 (Spring 2007), p. 7.

61. Ibid.

62. John Steinbruner, "Civil Violence as an International Security Problem," memorandum, November 23, 1992, addressed to the Brookings Institution Foreign Policy Studies Program staff. See also Chester A. Crocker, "The Global Law and Order Deficit: Is the West Ready to Police the World's Bad Neighbors?" *Washington Post*, December 20, 1992, p. C1.

63. Steinbruner, "Civil Violence as an International Security Problem."

64. Ibid.

65. Boutros-Ghali, An Agenda for Peace, pp. 7–8.

66. For a more elaborate discussion of these phases as applied to the crisis of the internally displaced, see the UN study in document E/CH.4/1993/35 and the revised version of that study in Deng, *Protecting the Dispossessed*. This study was considered by the Commission on Human Rights at its forty-ninth session, during which its findings and recommendations were endorsed and the mandate of the special representative of the secretary-general was extended for two years to continue to work on the various aspects of the problem presented in the study.

About the Contributors

LOUIS-ALEXANDRE BERG

Louis-Alexandre Berg is assistant professor of Global Studies and Political Science in the Global Studies Institute at Georgia State University. He was previously a research fellow at the Belfer Center for Science and International Affairs at the Harvard Kennedy School and a Jennings-Randolph Peace Scholar at the US Institute of Peace. He also has served as an advisor to the World Bank, the US Agency for International Development (USAID), the US State Department, and the UN Development Program on programs related to justice and security-sector development, governance, and conflict mitigation. His research examines the impact of foreign aid and intervention on state formation in countries affected by civil war and the causes and consequences of violent conflict and crime. Dr. Berg holds a PhD in Government from Georgetown University, a masters from the Woodrow Wilson School at Princeton University, and a BA from Brown University.

JOHN CAMPBELL

John Campbell is the Ralph Bunche senior fellow for Africa policy studies at the Council on Foreign Relations in New York. Rowman & Littlefield published his book *Morning in South Africa* in May 2016 and the second edition of *Nigeria: Dancing on the Brink* in June 2013. He writes the blog *Africa in Transition* and edits both the Nigeria Security Tracker and the Sub-Saharan Security Tracker. From 1975 to 2007 Campbell served as a US Department of State Foreign Service officer. He served twice in Nigeria, as political counselor from 1988 to 1990 and as ambassador from 2004 to 2007. He also served as deputy assistant secretary for human resources, dean of the Foreign Service Institute's School of Language Studies, and director of the Office of UN Political Affairs. From 2007 to 2008 he was a visiting professor of international relations at the University of Wisconsin–Madison. He was also a Department of State mid-career fellow at Princeton University's Woodrow Wilson School of Public and International Affairs. Campbell received a BA and MA from the University of Virginia and a PhD in seventeenth-century English history from the University of Wisconsin–Madison.

FRANCIS M. DENG

Francis M. Deng was the first permanent representative of South Sudan to the United Nations from 2012 to 2016. He was appointed in 2007 by Secretary-General Ban Ki-Moon as special advisor on the Prevention of Genocide at the level of undersecretary, a position he held until 2016. Deng served as representative of the UN secretary-general on internally displaced persons from 1992 to 2004, as human rights officer in the UN Secretariat from 1967 to 1972, and as ambassador of the Sudan to Canada, Denmark, Finland, Norway, Sweden, and the United States. He also served as Sudan's minister of state for foreign affairs. After leaving his country's service he joined a succession of think tanks, universities, and research institutions. Deng holds a bachelor of laws with honors from Khartoum University and a master of laws and a doctor of the science of law from Yale University. He has authored and edited over thirty books in the fields of law, conflict resolution, internal displacement, human rights, anthropology, folklore, history, and politics and has also written two novels on the theme of the crisis of national identity in the Sudan. Among his numerous awards in his country and abroad, Deng is corecipient with Roberta Cohen of the 2005 Grawemeyer Award for Ideas Improving World Order and the 2007 Merage Foundation American Dream Leadership Award. In 2000 Deng also received the Rome Prize for Peace and Humanitarian Action.

ULF ENGEL

Ulf Engel is professor of African politics at University of Leipzig. He is the coeditor of *The New Politics of Regionalism: Perspectives from Africa, Latin America and Asia-Pacific* (2016) and "Imagining, Implementing, and Integrating the African Peace and Security Architecture: The African Union's Challenges," special issue of *African Security* 7 (3) (with J. Gomes Porto); editor of *New Mediation Practices on African Conflicts* (2012); and coauthor of *Africa's New Peace and Security Architecture* (2010), among other books. Since 2011 he has been a member of the AEGIS (Africa-Europe Group for Interdisciplinary Studies, Leiden) Advisory Council. He is also professor extraordinary of political science in the Department of Political Science of Stellenbosch University, a fellow at the Stellenbosch Institute for Advanced Study, and a visiting professor at the Institute for Peace and Security Studies at Addis Ababa University. His research interests include the African Union's policies on peace and security as well as governance, changing stateness in Africa, and new spatialities of power in Africa.

JOHN W. HARBESON

John W. Harbeson is professor emeritus of political science in the Graduate Center and at City College in the City University of New York and professorial lecturer in the Johns Hopkins University School of Advanced International Studies. He is the author, editor, or coeditor of *Land Reform and National Building in Kenya*; *The Ethiopian Transformation*; *Civil Society and the State in Africa*; *Responsible Government: The Global Challenge*; *The Military in African Politics*; five editions of *Africa in World Politics*; and more than eighty articles and book chapters. He has been a Jennings Randolph Senior Fellow at the US Institute of Peace and a visiting fellow at Princeton's Center of International Studies, and he has served as the US Agency for International Development's regional democracy and governance advisor for eastern and southern Africa. He was elected to the American Political Science Association's (APSA) governing council and cofounded its comparative democratization section. He founded its African Politics Conference Group, now an organized section of the American Political Science Association and a coordinate group of the African Studies Association and the International Studies Association. He serves on the Woodrow Wilson Center's Africa Program Advisory Council.

PRINCETON N. LYMAN

Ambassador (retired) Princeton N. Lyman was US special envoy for Sudan and South Sudan from March 2011 to March 2013. He is currently senior advisor to the president of the US Institute of Peace. From 2003 to 2006 he held the Ralph Bunche Chair for Africa Policy Studies at the Council on Foreign Relations and continued as an adjunct senior fellow at the Council from 2006 to 2010. Ambassador Lyman's career in government included assignments as deputy assistant secretary of state for Africa, ambassador to Nigeria, director of refugee programs, ambassador to South Africa, and assistant secretary of state for international organization affairs. Earlier in the US Agency for International Development he was director of USAID in Addis Ababa, Ethiopia. He has taught at Georgetown University and at the Johns Hopkins School of International Affairs. He has published books and articles on foreign policy, African affairs, economic development, HIV/AIDS, UN reform, terrorism, and peacekeeping.

CARRIE MANNING

Carrie Manning is professor of political science at Georgia State University. She is the coauthor of *Costly Democracy* (2012) and author of *The Making of Democrats: Elections and Party Development in Postwar Bosnia, El Salvador, and Mozambique*

(2008) and *The Politics of Peace in Mozambique: Post-Conflict Democratization, 1992–2000* (2002). Her research interests include political party development and party system formation in postconflict democracies, local governance and the challenges for postconflict peacebuilding, role of relief and development NGOs in state-building, and rule of law promotion.

TODD MOSS

Todd Moss is chief operating officer and senior fellow at the Center for Global Development (CGD). He is also an adjunct professor at Georgetown University and a former deputy assistant secretary of state for African Affairs. Moss is the author of *African Development: Making Sense of the Issues and Actors* (2011) and *Oil to Cash: Fighting the Resource Curse Through Cash Transfers* (2015). At CGD his work focuses on US-Africa relations, energy, and financial issues facing sub-Saharan Africa. Previously he led the center's work on Nigerian debt, Zimbabwe's economic recovery, and the African Development Bank. Moss is also the author of the Ryker thriller series about diplomats in Africa, including *The Golden Hour* and *Minute Zero*.

M. ANNE PITCHER

Anne Pitcher is a professor of African Studies and Political Science and a faculty associate at the Center for Political Studies in the Institute for Social Research at the University of Michigan. Her current research examines the political economy of urban residential development and the role of bureaucratic agencies in Africa. Her publications include *Politics in the Portuguese Empire* (Oxford University Press, 1993), *Transforming Mozambique: The Politics of Privatization, 1975–2000* (Cambridge University Press, 2002), and many articles. Her most recent book, *Party Politics and Economic Reform in Africa's Democracies* (Cambridge, 2012) won an Honorable Mention for best book award from the African Politics Conference Group, an organized section of the American Political Science Association and the African Studies Association (ASA). She currently coedits with Kelly Askew a series for the University of Michigan Press called *African Perspectives*. She is also vice president of the ASA and will serve as its president beginning in 2017.

WILLIAM RENO

William Reno is professor of political science and director of the Program of African Studies at Northwestern University. He is the author of *Corruption and State Politics in Sierra Leone* (1995), *Warlord Politics and African States* (1998), and *Warfare in Independent Africa* (2011). His research interests include investigations to explain variations in the organization and behavior of armed groups in complex conflicts and the role of patronage networks and other nonformal relationships in influencing the decisions of leaders of armed groups. He also is interested in the relationships between states and armed groups in sub-Saharan Africa and how these relationships shape the nature of counterinsurgency efforts on the part of bureaucratically weak states with disorganized militaries.

FILIP REYNTJENS

Filip Reyntjens is professor of African law and politics at the Institute of Development Policy and Management (IOB), University of Antwerp. His recent books include *The Great African War: Congo and Regional Geopolitics, 1996–2006* (2009) and *Political Governance in Post-Genocide Rwanda* (2013). He is a full member of the Belgian Royal Academy of Overseas Sciences and has chaired the IOB for many years. In addition to his work on legal pluralism, dispute settlement, and the quality of democracy, his studies focus on the law and politics of sub-Saharan Africa, especially the Great Lakes region.

DONALD ROTHCHILD

The late Donald Rothchild was professor of political science at the University of California at Davis from 1965 until his death in January 2007. His university awarded him a distinguished professorship in 2003. He was the author or editor of more than two dozen books and over seventy articles over a career spanning almost fifty years. He wrote extensively and authoritatively on a wide range of topics including conflict mediation, international political economy, US foreign policy toward Africa, ethnic politics, international regimes, international security, and Africa's place in contemporary world politics. He also wrote important work on Ghana, civil society, Afro-Marxist regimes, and state-society relations. He was elected twice to the presidency of the International Political Science Association's Research Committee on Ethnicity and Politics.

IAN TAYLOR

Ian Taylor is professor in International Relations at the University of St. Andrews and also chair professor in the School of International Studies, Renmin University of China. He is also professor extraordinary in Political Science at the University of Stellenbosch, South Africa; visiting professor at the University of Addis Ababa; and a visiting scholar at Mbarara University of Science and Technology, Uganda. He is interested in sub-Saharan Africa's political economy and its international relations, the history of Afro-Asian diplomacy, the notion of "rising powers," and the implications for global governance and development (and for Africa specifically). He has authored ten academic books and edited another twelve, as well as over

150 peer-reviewed articles and book chapters. Prior to working at St. Andrews he taught African politics for four years at the University of Botswana. He is a commissioner of the fourteen-person Commonwealth Scholarship Commission and has conducted research in and/or visited forty African countries. His most recent books are *Global Governance and Transnational Capitalist Hegemony: The Myth of the "Emerging Powers"* (2016); *Africa Rising? BRICS—Diversifying Dependency* (2014); *The Forum on China-Africa Cooperation* (2011); and *The International Relations of Sub-Saharan Africa* (2010).

AILI MARI TRIPP

Aili Mari Tripp is professor of Political Science and Gender and Women's Studies at the University of Wisconsin–Madison. She also holds the Evjue Bascom Professorship in Gender and Women's Studies. Tripp's research has focused on women and politics in Africa, women's rights legal reform in North Africa, women and peacebuilding in Africa, women's movements in Africa, transnational feminism, African politics (with particular reference to Uganda and Tanzania), and the informal economy in Africa. Her most recent book is *Women and Power in Post-Conflict Africa* (2015). She is author of several award-winning books, including *Museveni's Uganda: Paradoxes of Power in a Hybrid Regime* (2010); *African Women's Movements: Transforming Political Landscapes* (2009) with Isabel Casimiro, Joy Kwesiga, and Alice Mungwa; and *Women and Politics in Uganda* (2000). Her first book was *Changing the Rules: The Politics of Liberalization and the Urban Informal Economy in Tanzania* (1997). Born in the UK, Tripp has lived fifteen years in Tanzania and has dual citizenship in the United States and Finland. Her writing is based on extensive fieldwork in Tanzania, Uganda, Kenya, Liberia, Angola, and Morocco. Tripp recently served as president of the African Studies Association.

CRAWFORD YOUNG

Crawford Young is Rupert Emerson and H. Edwin Young Professor Emeritus of Political Science at the University of Wisconsin–Madison, where he taught from 1963 to 2001. He also served as visiting professor in Congo-Kinshasa, Uganda, and Senegal. His major works include *Politics in the Congo* (1965), *The Politics of Cultural Pluralism* (1976), *Cooperatives and Development: Agricultural Politics in Ghana and Uganda* (with Neal Sherman and Tim Rose, 1981), *Ideology and Development in Africa* (1982), *The Rise and Decline of the Zairian State* (with Thomas Turner, 1985), *The African Colonial State in Comparative Perspective* (1994), and most recently *The Postcolonial State in Africa* (2012). *The Politics of Cultural Pluralism* won the Herskovits Prize of the African Studies Association and was co-winner of the Ralph Bunche Award of the American Political Science Association; *The African Colonial State in Comparative Perspective* won the Gregory Luebbert

Prize of the Comparative Politics Section of the APSA. He is a fellow of the American Academy of Arts and Sciences.

I. WILLIAM ZARTMAN

I. William Zartman is the Jacob Blaustein Professor Emeritus of International Organization and former director of the Conflict Management Program at the Paul Nitze School of Advanced International Studies of Johns Hopkins University (SAIS). For twenty years he was director of the SAIS African Studies Program. Previously he taught at the University of South Carolina, American University in Cairo, and New York University. He has been Olin Professor at the US Naval Academy and Halevy Professor at the Institute of Political Studies in Paris. He is a past president of the Middle East Studies Association and of the American Institute of Maghrib Studies and is past president of the Tangier American Legation Institute for Moroccan Studies. He is the author, coauthor, or editor of more than twenty books, the most recent of which include *The Global Power of Talk*; *Negotiation and Conflict Management: Essays on Theory and Practice*; *Engaging Extremists*; *The Slippery Slope to Genocide*; *Getting In: Mediators' Entry into the Settlement of African Conflicts*; *Cowardly Lions: Missed Opportunities to Prevent Deadly Conflict and State Collapse*; and *Rethinking the Economics of War: The Intersection of Need, Creed and Greed*. He has a PhD from Yale and an honorary doctorate from the Louvain.

Index